Exam 70-462: Administering Microsoft SQL Server 2012 Databases

OBJECTIVE		
INSTALL AND CONFIGURE (19 PERCENT)		
Plan installation.	1	1
Install SQL Server and related services.	1	2
Implement a migration strategy.	4	1
Configure additional SQL Server components.	3	1
Manage SQL Server Agent.	11	1
MAINTAIN INSTANCES AND DATABASES (17 PERCENT)		
Manage and configure databases.	3	2
Configure SQL Server instances.	2	1
Implement a SQL Server clustered instance.	8	1
Manage SQL Server instances.	2	2
OPTIMIZE AND TROUBLESHOOT (14 PERCENT)		
Identify and resolve concurrency problems.	10	2
Collect and analyze troubleshooting data.	9	1–6
Audit SQL Server instances.	6	3
MANAGE DATA (20 PERCENT)		
Configure and maintain a back up strategy.	11	2
Restore databases.	11	3
Implement and maintain indexes.	10	1
Import and export data.	4	2
IMPLEMENT SECURITY (18 PERCENT)		
Manage logins and server roles.	5	1
Manage database permissions.	6	1
Manage users and database roles.	5	2
Troubleshoot security.	6	2
IMPLEMENT HIGH AVAILABILITY (12 PERCENT)		
Implement AlwaysOn.	8	2
Implement database mirroring.	7	1
Implement replication.	7	2

Exam Objectives   The exam objectives listed here are current as of this book's publication date. Exam objectives are subject to change at any time without prior notice and at Microsoft's sole discretion. Please visit the Microsoft Learning website for the most current listing of exam objectives: *http://www.microsoft.com/learning/en/us/exams/70-462.mspx.*

Training Kit (Exam 70-462): Administering Microsoft® SQL Server® 2012 Databases

Orin Thomas
Peter Ward
boB Taylor

PUBLISHED BY
Microsoft Press
A Division of Microsoft Corporation
One Microsoft Way
Redmond, Washington 98052-6399

Library of Congress Control Number: 2012938612
ISBN: 978-0-7356-6607-8

Printed and bound in the United States of America.

Eighth Printing: August 2015

Microsoft Press books are available through booksellers and distributors worldwide. If you need support related to this book, email Microsoft Press Book Support at mspinput@microsoft.com. Please tell us what you think of this book at http://www.microsoft.com/learning/booksurvey.

Acquisitions Editor: Anne Hamilton
Developmental Editor: Karen Szall
Project Editor: Karen Szall
Editorial Production: nSight, Inc.
Technical Reviewer: boB Taylor; Technical Review services provided by Content Master, a member of CM Group, Ltd.
Copyeditor: Kerin Forsyth
Indexer: Lucie Haskins
Cover: Twist Creative • Seattle

Contents

Contents

What do you think of this book? We want to hear from you!

Microsoft is interested in hearing your feedback so we can continually improve our
books and learning resources for you. To participate in a brief online survey, please visit:

microsoft.com/learning/booksurvey

Chapter 10   Indexes and Concurrency   417

What do you think of this book? We want to hear from you!

Microsoft is interested in hearing your feedback so we can continually improve our
books and learning resources for you. To participate in a brief online survey, please visit:

microsoft.com/learning/booksurvey

Introduction

This training kit is designed for information technology (IT) professionals who support or plan to support Microsoft SQL Server 2012 databases and who also plan to take Exam 70-462, "Administering Microsoft SQL Server 2012 Databases." It is assumed that before you begin using this kit, you have a solid, foundation-level understanding of SQL Server 2012 and have used the product extensively either in one of the release candidate versions or with the release to manufacturing (RTM) version. Although this book helps prepare you for the 70-462 exam, you should consider it one part of your exam preparation plan. You require meaningful, real-world experience with SQL Server 2012 to pass this exam.

The material covered in this training kit and on exam 70-462 relates to the technologies in SQL Server 2012. The topics in this training kit cover what you need to know for the exam as described on the Skills Measured tab for the exam, which is available at *http://www.microsoft .com/learning/en/us/exam.aspx?ID=70-462&locale=en-us#tab2*.

By using this training kit, you will learn how to do the following:

- Install and configure SQL Server 2012
- Manage SQL Server instances and databases
- Optimize and troubleshoot SQL Server 2012
- Manage SQL Server 2012 data
- Implement instance and database security
- Implement high availability

Refer to the objective mapping page in the front of this book to see where in the book each exam objective is covered.

System Requirements

The following are the minimum system requirements your computer needs to meet to complete the practice exercises in this book and to run the companion CD. To minimize the time and expense of configuring physical computers for this training kit, it's recommended that you use Hyper-V, which is a feature of Windows Server 2008, Windows Server 2008 R2, Windows Server 2012, and certain editions of Windows 8. You can use other virtualization software instead, but the instructions are written assuming that you are using a solution that supports 64-bit operating systems hosted as virtual machines.

Hardware Requirements

This section presents the hardware requirements for Hyper-V, the hardware requirements if you are not using virtualization software, and the software requirements.

Virtualization Hardware Requirements

If you choose to use virtualization software, you need only one physical computer to perform the exercises in this book. That physical host computer must meet the following minimum hardware requirements:

- x64-based processor that includes both hardware-assisted virtualization (AMD-V or Intel VT) and hardware data execution protection. (On AMD systems, the data execution protection feature is called the No Execute or NX bit. On Intel systems, this feature is called the Execute Disable or XD bit.) These features must also be enabled in the BIOS. (Note: You can run Windows Virtual PC without Intel-VT or AMD-V.)
- 8.0 GB of RAM.
- 80 GB of available hard disk space if you are using differencing virtual hard disks.
- DVD-ROM drive.
- Internet connectivity.

Physical Hardware Requirements

If you choose to use physical computers instead of virtualization software, use the following list to meet the minimum hardware requirements of the practice exercises in this book:

- Six personal computers, each with a 1.4-GHz, 64-bit processor, minimum 2 GB of RAM, 50 GB hard disk drive, network card, video card, and DVD-ROM drive.
- All six computers must be connected to the same network.

Software Requirements

The following software is required to complete the practice exercises:

- **Windows Server 2008 R2**   You can download an evaluation edition of Windows Server 2008 R2 at the Microsoft Download Center at *http://www.microsoft.com /downloads*.
- **SQL Server 2012**   You can download an evaluation edition of SQL Server 2012 at the Microsoft Download Center at *http://www.microsoft.com/downloads*.
- **AdventureWorks2012 and AdventureWorksDW2012 databases**   These can be obtained through this book's companion content page at *http://go.microsoft.com /FWLink/?Linkid=251256*.

Practice Setup Instructions

This section contains abbreviated instructions for setting up the domain controller (DC), SQL-A, SQL-B, SQL-C, SQL-D, and SQL-Core computers used in the practice exercises in all chapters of this training kit. To perform these exercises, first install Windows Server 2008 R2 Enterprise edition with Service Pack 1 using the default configuration, setting the administrator password to **Pa$$w0rd**. For server SQL-Core, install Windows Server 2008 R2 Enterprise Edition with Service Pack 1 in the default server core configuration, setting the administrator password to **Pa$$w0rd**.

> **IMPORTANT**   **DOWNLOAD REQUIRED SOFTWARE**
>
> Before you begin preparing the practice computers, you must have a copy of Windows Server 2008 R2 Enterprise edition with Service Pack 1 (either as an .iso file or as a DVD).

Prepare a Computer to Function as a Windows Server 2008 R2 Domain Controller

1. Log on to the first computer on which you have installed Windows Server 2008 R2 with Service Pack 1, using the Administrator account and the password **Pa$$w0rd**.

2. Open an elevated command prompt and issue the following commands:

   ```
   Netsh interface ipv4 set address "Local Area Connection" static 10.10.10.10
   ```

3. Enter the following command:

   ```
   netdom renamecomputer %computername% /newname:DC
   ```

4. Restart the computer and log on again, using the Administrator account.

5. Click Start. In the Search Programs And Files text box, type the following:

   ```
   Dcpromo.
   ```

6. When the Active Directory Domain Services Installation Wizard starts, click Next twice.

7. On the Choose A Deployment Configuration page, choose Create A New Domain In A New Forest and then click Next.

8. On the Name The Forest Root Domain page, enter Contoso.com, and then click Next.

9. On the Forest Functional Level page, set the forest functional level to Windows Server 2008 R2 and then click Next.

10. On the Set Domain Functional Level page, ensure that Windows Server 2008 R2 is set and then click Next.

11. On the Additional Domain Controller Options page, ensure that the DNS Server option is selected and then click Next. When presented with the warning that the delegation for the DNS server cannot be created, click Yes when asked whether you want to continue.

12. Accept the default settings for the Database, Log Files, and SYSVOL locations and click Next.

13. In the Directory Services Restore Mode Administrator Password dialog box, enter the password **Pa$$w0rd** twice, and then click Next.

14. On the Summary page, click Next to begin the installation of Active Directory Domain Services (AD DS) on computer DC. When the wizard completes, click Finish. When prompted, click Restart Now to reboot computer DC.

Prepare AD DS

1. Log on to server DC, using the Administrator account.

2. Using Active Directory Users And Computers, create a user account named Kim_Akers in the Users container and assign the account the password **Pa$$w0rd**. Configure the password to never expire. Add this user account to the Enterprise Admins, Domain Admins, and Schema Admins groups.

3. Open the DNS console and create a primary reverse lookup zone for the subnet 10.10.10.x. Ensure that the zone is stored within AD DS and is replicated to all DNS servers running on domain controllers in the forest.

Prepare a Member Server and Join It to the Domain

1. Ensure that computer DC is turned on and connected to the network or virtual network to which the second computer is connected.

2. Log on to the second computer on which you have installed Windows Server 2008 R2 with Service Pack 1, using the Administrator account and the password **Pa$$w0rd**.

3. Open an elevated command prompt and issue the following commands:

```
Netsh interface ipv4 set address "Local Area Connection" static 10.10.10.20

Netsh interface ipv4 set dnsservers "Local Area Connection" static 10.10.10.10
primary
```

4. Enter the following command:

```
netdom renamecomputer %computername% /newname:SQL-A
```

5. Restart the computer and then log on again, using the Administrator account.

6. From an elevated command prompt, issue the following command:

```
netdom join SQL-A /domain:contoso.com
```

7. Restart the computer. When the computer restarts, log on as contoso\Administrator and then turn off the computer.

Prepare a Second Member Server and Join It to the Domain

1. Ensure that computer DC is turned on and connected to the network or virtual network to which the second computer is connected.

2. Log on to the third computer on which you have installed Windows Server 2008 R2 with Service Pack 1, using the Administrator account and the password **Pa$$w0rd**.

3. Open an elevated command prompt and issue the following commands:

```
Netsh interface ipv4 set address "Local Area Connection" static 10.10.10.30

Netsh interface ipv4 set dnsservers "Local Area Connection" static 10.10.10.10 primary
```

4. Enter the following command:

```
netdom renamecomputer %computername% /newname:SQL-B
```

5. Restart the computer and then log on again, using the Administrator account.

6. From an elevated command prompt, issue the following command:

```
netdom join SQL-B /domain:contoso.com
```

7. Restart the computer. When the computer restarts, log on as contoso\Administrator. Turn off the computer.

Prepare a Third Member Server and Join It to the Domain

1. Ensure that computer DC is turned on and connected to the network or virtual network to which the second computer is connected.

2. Log on to the third computer that you have installed Windows Server 2008 R2 with Service Pack 1 on using the Administrator account and the password **Pa$$w0rd**.

3. Open an elevated command prompt and issue the following commands:

```
Netsh interface ipv4 set address "Local Area Connection" static 10.10.10.40

Netsh interface ipv4 set dnsservers "Local Area Connection" static 10.10.10.10 primary
```

4. Enter the following command:

```
netdom renamecomputer %computername% /newname:SQL-C
```

5. Restart the computer and then log on again using the Administrator account.

6. From an elevated command prompt, issue the following command:

```
netdom join SQL-C /domain:contoso.com
```

7. Restart the computer. When the computer restarts, log on as contoso\Administrator. Turn off the computer.

Prepare a Fourth Member Server and Join It to the Domain

1. Ensure that computer DC is turned on and connected to the network or virtual network to which the second computer is connected.

2. Log on to the fourth computer on which you have installed Windows Server 2008 R2 with Service Pack 1, using the Administrator account and the password **Pa$$w0rd**.

3. Open an elevated command prompt and issue the following commands:

```
Netsh interface ipv4 set address "Local Area Connection" static 10.10.10.50

Netsh interface ipv4 set dnsservers "Local Area Connection" static 10.10.10.10 primary
```

4. Enter the following command:

```
netdom renamecomputer %computername% /newname:SQL-D
```

5. Restart the computer and then log on again, using the Administrator account.

6. From an elevated command prompt, issue the following command:

```
netdom join SQL-D /domain:contoso.com
```

7. Restart the computer. When the computer restarts, log on as contoso\Administrator. Turn off the computer.

Prepare a Computer Running the Server Core Installation Option and Join It to the Domain

1. Ensure that computer DC is turned on and connected to the network or virtual network to which the second computer is connected.

2. Using the Administrator account and the password **Pa$$w0rd,** log on to the computer on which you have installed Windows Server 2008 R2 with Service Pack 1 in the Server Core configuration.

3. From the Administrator command prompt, enter the following commands:

```
Netsh interface ipv4 set address "Local Area Connection" static 10.10.10.60

Netsh interface ipv4 set dnsservers "Local Area Connection" static 10.10.10.10
primary
```

4. Enter the following command to configure the computer's name:

```
netdom renamecomputer %computername% /newname:SQL-CORE
```

5. Enter the following command to restart the computer:

```
Shutdown /r /t 5
```

6. Restart the computer and log back on, using the Administrator account.

7. Enter the following command to join the computer to the domain:

```
netdom join SQL-CORE /domain:contoso.com
```

8. Enter the following command to restart the computer:

```
Shutdown /r /t 5
```

9. Restart the computer. When the computer restarts, log on as contoso\Administrator.
   Turn off the computer, using the following command:

```
Shutdown /s /t 5
```

Using the Companion CD

A companion CD is included with this training kit. The companion CD contains the following:

- **Practice tests**   You can reinforce your understanding of the topics covered in this training kit by using electronic practice tests that you customize to meet your needs. You can practice for the 70-462 certification exam by using tests created from a pool of 200 practice exam questions, which give you many practice exams to help you prepare for the certification exam. These questions are not from the exam; they are for practice and preparation.

- **An eBook**   An electronic version (eBook) of this book is included for when you do not want to carry the printed book with you.

> **NOTE**   **SAMPLE SQL SERVER 2012 DATABASES**
>
> The practices in this book rely on two sample databases: AdventureWorks2012 and AdventureWorksDW2012. You can download these databases for your use from the book's companion content page at *http://go.microsoft.com/FWLink/?Linkid=251256.*

How to Install the Practice Tests

To install the practice test software from the companion CD to your hard disk, perform the following steps:

1. Insert the companion CD into your CD drive and accept the license agreement. A CD menu appears.

> **NOTE IF THE CD MENU DOES NOT APPEAR**
>
> If the CD menu or the license agreement does not appear, AutoRun might be disabled on your computer. Refer to the Readme.txt file on the CD for alternate installation instructions.

2. Click Practice Tests and follow the instructions on the screen.

How to Use the Practice Tests

To start the practice test software, follow these steps:

1. Click Start, All Programs, and then select Microsoft Press Training Kit Exam Prep.

   A window appears that shows all the Microsoft Press training kit exam prep suites installed on your computer.

2. Double-click the practice test you want to use.

When you start a practice test, you choose whether to take the test in Certification Mode, Study Mode, or Custom Mode:

- **Certification Mode**   Closely resembles the experience of taking a certification exam. The test has a set number of questions. It is timed, and you cannot pause and restart the timer.

- **Study Mode**   Creates an untimed test during which you can review the correct answers and the explanations after you answer each question.

- **Custom Mode**   Gives you full control over the test options so that you can customize them as you like.

In all modes, the user interface when you are taking the test is basically the same but with different options enabled or disabled, depending on the mode.

When you review your answer to an individual practice test question, a "References" section is provided that lists where in the training kit you can find the information that relates to that question and provides links to other sources of information. After you click Test Results to score your entire practice test, you can click the Learning Plan tab to see a list of references for every objective.

How to Uninstall the Practice Tests

To uninstall the practice test software for a training kit, use the Program And Features option in Windows Control Panel.

Acknowledgments

A book is put together by many more people than the authors whose names are listed on the cover page. We'd like to express our gratitude to the following people for all the work they have done in getting this book into your hands: Karen Szall, boB Taylor, Carol Whitney, Kerin Forsyth, and Lucie Haskins.

Errata & Book Support

We've made every effort to ensure the accuracy of this book and its companion content. Any errors that have been reported since this book was published are listed on our Microsoft Press site:

http://go.microsoft.com/FWLink/?Linkid=251255

If you find an error that is not already listed, you can report it to us through the same page.

If you need additional support, email Microsoft Press Book Support at *mspinput@microsoft.com*.

Please note that product support for Microsoft software is not offered through the addresses above.

We Want to Hear from You

At Microsoft Press, your satisfaction is our top priority, and your feedback our most valuable asset. Please tell us what you think of this book at:

http://www.microsoft.com/learning/booksurvey

The survey is short, and we read every one of your comments and ideas. Thanks in advance for your input!

Stay in Touch

Let's keep the conversation going! We're on Twitter: *http://twitter.com/MicrosoftPress*.

Preparing for the Exam

Microsoft certification exams are a great way to build your resume and let the world know about your level of expertise. Certification exams validate your on-the-job experience and product knowledge. While there is no substitution for on-the-job experience, preparation through study and hands-on practice can help you prepare for the exam. We recommend that you round out your exam preparation plan by using a combination of available study materials and courses. For example, you might use the Training Kit and another study guide for your "at home" preparation, and take a Microsoft Official Curriculum course for the classroom experience. Choose the combination that you think works best for you.

> *NOTE* **PASSING THE EXAM**
>
> Take a minute (well, one minute and two seconds) to look at the "Passing a Microsoft Exam" video at *http://www.youtube.com/watch?v=Jp5qg2NhgZ0&feature=youtu.be.* It's true. Really!

CHAPTER 1

Planning and Installing SQL Server 2012

Exam objectives in this chapter:

- Plan installation.
- Install SQL Server and related services.

Getting the deployment of Microsoft SQL Server 2012 right can help you avoid a lot of pain later in the deployment's life cycle. At some point, most organizations have felt constrained by a decision that seemed quite innocuous at the time it was made, but which, in the long run, restricted the capacity of the SQL Server deployment to continue to meet organizational needs. In this chapter, you'll learn about planning your SQL Server 2012 deployment and preparing servers and infrastructure to host SQL Server 2012. You'll also learn how to deploy SQL Server 2012 on computers running both the traditional and Server Core operating system options, including how to deploy specific features such as SQL Server Integration Services (SSIS).

> **IMPORTANT**
>
> ***Have you read page xxvi?***
>
> It contains valuable information regarding the skills you need to pass the exam.

Lessons in this chapter:

Before You Begin

To complete the lessons in this chapter, make sure that you have completed the setup tasks for installing computers DC, SQL-A, SQL-B, and SQL-CORE as outlined in the introduction to this book.

No additional configuration is required for this chapter.

Lesson 1: Planning Your Installation

In this lesson, you'll learn how to evaluate a given set of installation requirements, determine an appropriate deployment plan, and determine appropriate hardware on which to run SQL Server 2012. You'll learn how to plan the installation of SQL Server 2012 on the Server Core version of Windows Server 2008 R2 SP1 and find out how you can perform an initial performance benchmark.

After this lesson, you will be able to:

- Evaluate the installation requirements.
- Design the installation of SQL Server and its components.
- Plan for capacity.
- Determine hardware requirements.
- Design storage for new databases.
- Configure a standby database for reporting purposes.
- Plan Server Core–mode installation.
- Perform an initial performance benchmark.

Estimated lesson time: 60 minutes

Evaluating Installation Requirements

When evaluating installation requirements, you must determine which SQL Server 2012 features are necessary, given your organization's installation needs and the operating system and hardware configuration required to support that deployment. For example, if you must support only eight processor cores, database mirroring, and the SQL Server Import and Export Wizard, SQL Server 2012 Standard edition might be appropriate. If your organization needs more than 16 processor cores, you must deploy SQL Server 2012 Enterprise edition.

> **MORE INFO** **COMPREHENSIVE FEATURES BY EDITION**
>
> When each feature is discussed throughout this book, the editions that support that feature are listed. Rather than reproduce many pages of feature tables, a comprehensive list of available features of each edition of SQL Server 2012 is available in the following document: *http://msdn.microsoft.com/en-us/library/cc645993(v=SQL.110).aspx*.

Operating System Requirements

Which operating system you use for the deployment of SQL Server 2012 will depend on the edition of SQL Server 2012 you choose to install. Windows Server 2008 R2 SP1 is an x64-bit operating system that supports all editions of SQL Server 2012. Windows Vista SP2 x86 is a 32-bit operating system that supports only the x86 versions of SQL Server 2012 Developer and SQL Server 2012 Express editions. The different versions of SQL Server 2012 and the operating systems on which they can run are listed in Table 1-1.

TABLE 1-1 Operating System Requirements

SQL Server 2012 edition	Operating system
SQL Server 2012 x64 Enterprise, Business Intelligence, and Web	■ Windows Server 2008 R2 SP1 Datacenter, Enterprise, Standard, and Web ■ Windows Server 2008 SP2 Datacenter, Enterprise, Standard, and Web
SQL Server 2012 x86 Enterprise, Business Intelligence, and Web	■ Windows Server 2008 R2 SP1 Datacenter, Enterprise, Standard, and Web ■ Windows Server 2008 (x64 and x86) SP2 Datacenter, Enterprise, Standard, and Web
SQL Server 2012 x64 Standard	■ Windows Server 2008 R2 SP1 Datacenter, Enterprise, Standard, Foundation, and Web ■ Windows Server 2008 SP2 Datacenter, Enterprise, Standard, and Web ■ Windows 7 SP1 x64 Ultimate, Enterprise, and Professional ■ Windows Vista SP2 x64 Ultimate, Enterprise, and Business
SQL Server 2012 x86 Standard	■ Windows Server 2008 R2 SP1 Datacenter, Enterprise, Standard, Foundation, and Web ■ Windows Server 2008 (x64 and x86) SP2 Datacenter, Enterprise, Standard, and Web ■ Windows 7 SP1 (x64 and x86) Ultimate, Enterprise, and Professional ■ Windows Vista SP2 (x64 and x86) Ultimate, Enterprise, and Business
SQL Server 2012 x64 Developer, Express, Express with Tools, and Express with Advanced Services	■ Windows Server 2008 R2 SP1 Datacenter, Enterprise, Standard, Foundation, and Web ■ Windows Server 2008 (x64) SP2 Datacenter, Enterprise, Standard, and Web ■ Windows 7 SP1 (x64) Ultimate, Enterprise, Professional, Home Premium, and Home Basic ■ Windows Vista SP2 (x64) Ultimate, Enterprise, Business, Home Premium, and Home Basic
SQL Server 2012 x86 Developer, Express, Express with Tools, and Express with Advanced Services	■ Windows Server 2008 R2 SP1 Datacenter, Enterprise, Standard, Foundation, and Web ■ Windows Server 2008 (x64 and x86) SP2 Datacenter, Enterprise, Standard, and Web ■ Windows 7 SP1 (x64 and x86) Ultimate, Enterprise, Professional, Home Premium, and Home Basic ■ Windows Vista SP2 (x64 and x86) Ultimate, Enterprise, Business, Home Premium, and Home Basic

Processor and RAM Requirements

Knowing processor and RAM requirements is helpful when provisioning hardware for SQL Server. It is also useful when provisioning virtual machines with the appropriate level of resources. Although you can deploy SQL Server 2012 with the minimum processor and RAM, doing so will most likely lead to performance problems. The main difference between the 64-bit and 32-bit versions of SQL Server 2012 in terms of minimum requirements is which processors the versions support. The 64-bit versions of SQL Server 2012 Enterprise, SQL Server 2012 Business Intelligence, SQL Server 2012 Standard, SQL Server 2012 Developer, and SQL Server 2012 Web (64-bit) all have the following hardware requirements:

- **Processor**   AMD Opteron, AMD Athlon 64, Intel Xeon with Intel EM64T support, or Intel Pentium IV with EM64T support is required.
- **Minimum Processor Speed**   The minimum is 1.4 GHz; the recommended processor speed is 2.0 GHz or faster.
- **Minimum RAM**   The minimum is 1 GB; the recommended RAM is 4 GB or more.

Sixty-four-bit SQL Server 2012 Express, Express with Tools, and Express with Advanced Services editions have the same processor requirements as the other 64-bit editions but require a minimum of 512 MB of RAM and a recommended RAM of 1 GB or more.

Thirty-two-bit SQL Server 2012 Enterprise, SQL Server 2012 Business Intelligence, SQL Server 2012 Standard, SQL Server 2012 Developer, and SQL Server 2012 Web editions have the following hardware requirements:

- **Processor**   Pentium III-compatible processor or newer is required.
- **Minimum Processor Speed**   The minimum is 1.0 GHz; the recommended processor speed is 2.0 GHz or faster.
- **Minimum RAM**   The minimum is 1 GB; the recommended RAM is 4 GB or more. On 32-bit systems with more than 3GB of memory, you should use the /3GB or /PAE startup switches.

Thirty-two-bit SQL Server 2012 Express, Express with Tools, and Express with Advanced Services editions have the same processor requirements as the other 32-bit editions but require a minimum of 512 MB of RAM and a recommended RAM of 1 GB or more.

Hard Disk Requirements

The amount of storage space required for the SQL Server 2012 program files depends on the features you install. If fully installed, features consume the amount of disk space listed in Table 1-2.

TABLE 1-2 Feature Hard Disk Requirements

Feature	Disk space used
Analysis Services and data files	345 MB
Client Components	1823 MB
Database Engine and data files, Replication, Full-Text Search, and Data Quality Services	811 MB
Integration Services	591 MB
Master Data Services	243 MB
Reporting Services and Report Manager	304 MB

Windows Installer uses temporary files on the system drive during installation. The installation process consumes at least 4 GB of space on the system drive during setup, even when SQL Server features are installed on a different volume. SQL Server Books Online (BOL) is not included with the SQL Server 2012 setup media and can be downloaded from the Microsoft website. When downloaded, BOL consumes approximately 200 MB of disk space.

You can configure the location where features are stored during setup. Figure 1-1 shows the dialog box in which you can configure the location of directories and files used by Database Engine.

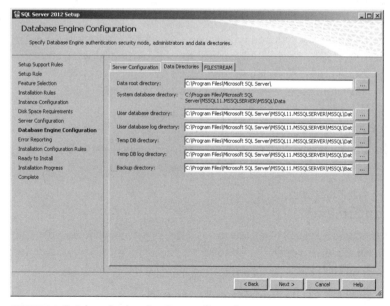

FIGURE 1-1 Database Engine directory configuration

Installing SQL Server 2012 on a Domain Controller

Although Microsoft does not recommend that you install SQL Server 2012 on a computer that functions as a domain controller, it is possible to deploy SQL 2012, given the following restrictions:

- SQL Service accounts on a domain controller cannot run under a local service account.
- You cannot promote a member server that has SQL Server 2012 installed to become a domain controller.
- You cannot demote a domain controller that has SQL Server 2012 installed to become a member server.
- SQL Server Setup is unable to create security groups or provision SQL Server service accounts on a read-only domain controller (RODC). Setup fails in this situation.

Software Requirements

SQL Server Setup installs some prerequisite software features. You must obtain and install other features for deploying SQL Server 2012. SQL Server 2012 has the following software requirements:

- **.NET 3.5 SP1**   Required for the Database Engine, Reporting Services, Replication, Master Data Services, Data Quality Services, and SQL Server Management Studio. It is not installed by SQL Server Setup.
- **.NET 4.0**   Required for SQL Server 2012. It is installed by SQL Server Setup for all editions except SQL Server Express, which will attempt to download the installation files from the Microsoft website.
- **Windows PowerShell 2.0**   Required for SQL Server 2012. It is not installed or enabled by SQL Server Setup.
- **Internet Explorer 7 or later**   Required for Microsoft Management Console (MMC), SQL Server Data Tools (SSDT), Report Designer feature of Reporting Services, and HTML help. It is included with the Windows Server 2008, Windows Server 2008 R2, Windows Vista, and Windows 7 operating systems.

> *MORE INFO*   **HARDWARE AND SOFTWARE REQUIREMENTS**
>
> You can learn more about SQL Server 2012 hardware and software requirements at
> *http://msdn.microsoft.com/library/ms143506(v=SQL.110).aspx.*

Virtualization Requirements

Microsoft fully supports SQL Server 2012 when it is run as a virtual machine under Hyper-V when Hyper-V is run on the following operating systems:

- Windows Server 2008 SP2 (Standard, Enterprise, Datacenter)
- Windows Server 2008 R2 SP1 (Standard, Enterprise, Datacenter)

The primary difference between running SQL Server 2012 on a traditional deployment and running it within a virtual machine is that Microsoft recommends shutting down SQL 2012 instances that are running within virtual machines before shutting down the virtual machines.

> **MORE INFO** **VIRTUALIZATION BEST PRACTICES**
>
> You can learn more about SQL Server virtualization best practices at *http://sqlcat.com* */sqlcat/b/whitepapers/archive/2008/10/03/running-sql-server-2008-in-a-hyper-v* *-environment-best-practices-and-performance-recommendations.aspx.*

Designing the Installation

Prior to installing SQL Server 2012, you need to know which *components*, known as *features*, to install to accomplish your objectives. Two types of features are available when installing SQL Server 2012: instance features and shared features. *Instance features* can operate side by side and are separate for each instance of SQL Server 2012. The following instance features are available in SQL Server 2012 Enterprise edition:

- **Database Engine Services**   Provides the core service for storing, processing, and securing data; provides controlled access, rapid transaction processing, and high availability

- **SQL Server Replication**   Allows for copying and distributing data and database objects from one database to another; supports synchronization of databases for consistency

- **Full-Text and Semantic Extractions For Search**   Supports Full-Text Extraction for fast text search; supports Semantic Extraction for key phrases and similarity search

- **Data Quality Services**   Facilitates both computer-assisted and interactive methods of managing data source quality and integrity

- **Analysis Services**   Supports online analytical processing (OLAP) and data mining

- **Reporting Services – Native**   Facilitates the creation, management, and delivery of reports through email and interactive web-based formats

Shared features need to be installed only once and can be used, where appropriate, by all instances on a single server. Shared features are as follows:

- **Reporting Services – SharePoint**   Integrates report viewing and management through SharePoint.

- **Reporting Services Add-in for SharePoint Products**   Provides management and user interfaces that allow integration between SharePoint and SQL Server Reporting Services (SSRS).

- **Data Quality Client**   Interacts with data source quality and integrity services.

- **SQL Server Data Tools** SQL Server Development Environment, formerly known as the Business Intelligence Development Studio, is a Visual Studio 2010 shell that enables you to create Analysis Services, Integration Services, and Report Server projects.

- **Client Tools Connectivity** Includes additional components for communication between servers and clients.

- **Integration Services** Facilitates the movement, integration, and transformation of data between data stores.

- **Client Tools Backward Compatibility** Includes SQL Distributed Management Objects, Decision Support Objects, and Data Transformation Services, all of which are discontinued or deprecated features that might be needed for backward compatibility.

- **Client Tools Software Development Kit (SDK)** Includes resources that developers can use.

- **Documentation Components** Installs the Help viewer, which can connect to the online library. You can also configure the Help viewer to download BOL from the Microsoft website, but BOL is not included as part of the SQL Server 2012 installation media.

- **Management Tools – Basic** Includes SQL Server Management Studio support for Database Engine, SQLCMD, SQL Server PowerShell, and Distributed Replay Administration Tool.

- **Management Tools – Complete** Includes SQL Server Management Studio support for Reporting Services, Analysis Services, Integration Services, SQL Server Profiler, Database Tuning Adviser, and SQL Server Utility Manager.

- **Distributed Replay Controller** Manages the actions of distributed replay clients.

- **Distributed Replay Client** Enables Multiple Distributed Replay clients to function in concert to simulate workloads against SQL Server instances.

- **SQL Client Connectivity SDK** Includes the SQL Server Native Client (ODBC/OLE DB) software development kit (SDK) for developing database applications.

- **Master Data Services** Provides the platform for integrating data from separate systems across an organization.

> **MORE INFO** **SQL SERVER 2012 FEATURES**
>
> You can find more about the features supported by each edition at *http://msdn.microsoft .com/en-us/library/cc645993(v=SQL.110).aspx*.

Planning Scale Up versus Scale Out Basics

Scalability determines how well an application uses increased resources to increase *capacity*. For example, an application that comfortably handles the workload of 10 concurrent users on a dual-processor system might be able to handle the workload of more than 100 concurrent users comfortably on a 20-processor system if it scales well. Some applications do not scale well, and running those applications on increasingly powerful platforms might lead to only minor improvements in performance. Whether an application scales well is often a result of how it has been created, and in some cases, database administrators are unable to increase capacity by increasing hardware resources. There are two basic methods of increasing capacity of applications running on SQL Server 2012—*scaling up* and *scaling out*:

- **Scaling Up**   Involves increasing the system resources on the current server. For example, you might add additional and faster processors and more RAM as a method of improving capacity. As an alternative, you might migrate the existing database to a newer, more powerful server.

- **Scaling Out**   Enables you to increase capacity by using multiple SQL servers. There are several ways in which you can scale out, including configuring peer-to-peer replication and AlwaysOn with readable secondaries.

There are many factors to consider when determining whether you should plan to scale up or scale out to increase capacity. In some situations, a single very powerful server might be more expensive than several less powerful servers. If the argument is purely financial, it might be better to scale out than to upgrade to very expensive, high-performance components. The drawbacks to scaling out include increased operating system and SQL Server licensing costs. Using multiple, less powerful, and less expensive servers is also likely to cost you more in electricity costs and costs associated with hosting an increased number of servers.

> **MORE INFO**   **SCALING OUT SQL SERVER**
>
> You can learn more about scaling out SQL Server at *http://msdn.microsoft.com/en-us /library/ms345392.aspx*.

 Quick Check

- What is the main difference between scaling up and scaling out?

Quick Check Answer

- Scaling up involves increasing capacity by upgrading the current hardware to more powerful hardware. Scaling out involves increasing capacity by deploying additional servers.

Shrinking and Growing Databases

When configuring database size, you can choose to create a small database that grows as necessary or to create a fixed database size. The advantage of using a fixed database size is that you minimize file fragmentation. The disadvantage of using a fixed database size is that you might run into problems if the database grows in size over time and the space allocated to the database is filled.

You can view the size of the database and the space available for the database on the General page of the Database Properties dialog box, shown in Figure 1-2. You can use the sp_spaceused stored procedure to determine the database size and free space available on a database and to display the number of rows, disk space reserved, and disk space used by table, indexed view, or Service Broker queue.

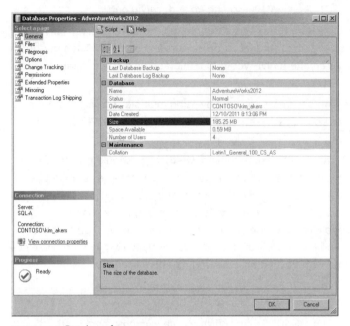

FIGURE 1-2 Database free space

Increasing Database Size

By default, database files automatically grow as they approach capacity. You can change this setting by editing the properties of a database and configuring the *autogrowth* settings, shown in Figure 1-3. The drawback of allowing databases to grow automatically is that growth can lead to file fragmentation. File *fragmentation* can lead to degraded performance. A better technique when configuring a database is allocating more space to the database files because this will minimize fragmentation.

You can increase the size of database files manually on the Files page of Database Properties and use this properties page to increase the database's initial size. You can also use ALTER DATABASE to increase the size of a database manually. For example, to increase the size of the AdventureWorks2012 database, use the following code:

```
USE [master]
GO
ALTER DATABASE [AdventureWorks2012] MODIFY FILE
   ( NAME= N'AdventureWorks2012_Data', SIZE = 256000KB )
GO
```

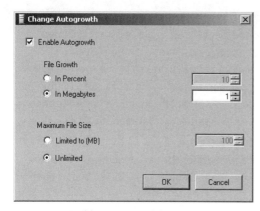

FIGURE 1-3 Enable Autogrowth

Decreasing Database Size

When a database is configured to *autoshrink*, Database Engine automatically shrinks databases that have free space. You configure the AUTO_SHRINK database option either by using the ALTER DATABASE statement or by configuring the database options, as shown in Figure 1-4. Autoshrink will cause indexes to become fragmented. If you remove a lot of data from a database and want to reclaim space, it is often better from a performance perspective to shrink the database manually and then rebuild the indexes than it is to leave autoshrink on.

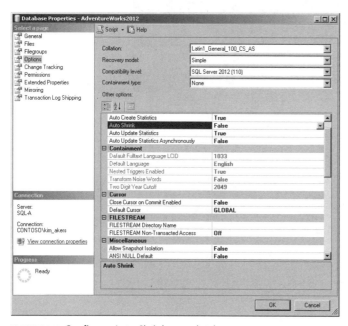

FIGURE 1-4 Configure Auto Shrink on a database

Shrinking data files enables you to recover space by moving data pages from the end of the file to unused space closer to the front of the file. When the process has reclaimed enough free space at the file's end, the unallocated pages at the end of the file can be returned to the file system. You cannot make a database smaller than the size specified when it was originally created or smaller than the last specified size set using a file-size-changing operation such as DBCC SHRINKFILE. For example, if you originally created a database that was 500 MB in size and it grew to 1000 MB, you cannot shrink the database to smaller than 500 MB even if you delete all data in the database.

To shrink a database, you must have membership in either the sysadmin fixed server role or the db_owner fixed database role. To shrink a database by using SQL Server Management Studio, perform the following steps:

1. Expand the Databases node and right-click the database you want to shrink.

2. Click Tasks, Shrink, and then Database. This opens the Shrink Database dialog box shown in Figure 1-5. This dialog box displays the available free space and the currently allocated space.

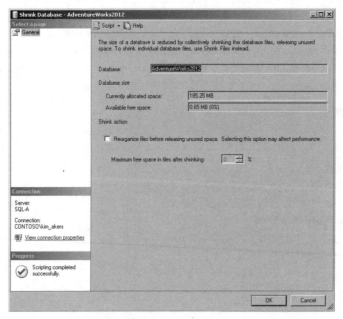

FIGURE 1-5 Shrink Database dialog box

You can use DBCC SHRINKDATABASE to shrink a database. For example, to shrink the AdventureWorks2012 database, you would use the following code:

```
Use [AdventureWorks2012]
GO
DBCC SHRINKDATABASE(N'AdventureWorks2012')
GO
```

MORE INFO   DATABASE SHRINKING

You can learn more about database shrinking at *http://msdn.microsoft.com/en-us/library /ms189080(v=sql.110).aspx.*

Designing the Storage for New Databases

Designing storage for new databases involves making decisions about hardware and the placement of database files. When providing storage hardware for databases on traditionally deployed computers or on computers hosted as virtual machines, you should look toward redundant array of inexpensive disks (RAID) technologies to ensure that you get a good mix of fault tolerance and performance enhancement. Many enterprise-level SQL deployments use RAID 1+0 (a stripe of mirrors) or RAID 0+1 (a mirror of stripes). If your SQL Server 2012 deployment is virtualized, it is likely that the storage fabric that hosts the virtual machines will use one of these redundant, high-performance disk technologies. The Windows Server 2008 and Windows Server 2008 R2 operating systems support software RAID 0, RAID 1, and RAID 5, of which only RAID 1 and RAID 5 offer any fault tolerance. Only small deployments tend to use the software RAID options built into the Windows operating system.

After you've decided which storage technology will host database files, you must decide how you will design the database files. SQL Server 2012 databases use three types of files:

- **Primary**   Primary data files use the .mdf extension. These files contain startup information for the database and pointers to other files the database uses; data and objects can be stored in these files. Every database has a primary data file, and many smaller databases use only a primary data file and a transaction log file. The AdventureWorks sample database with which you will be interacting throughout this book uses this configuration.

- **Secondary**   Optional, or secondary, files store user data and spread data across multiple disks where each file is hosted on a separate disk drive. Using technologies such as RAID 1+0 reduces the need for secondary data files from a performance perspective. In enterprise database deployments, spreading database files across multiple drives— such as smaller, high-performance, solid-state disks—might be necessary due to size constraints. You can increase the size of a database by adding additional secondary files. You can have more than one secondary file. Secondary files typically use the .ndf extension.

- **Transaction Log**   This log, which each database requires, stores information that can be used to recover the database. Transaction log files use the .ldf extension.

You can add secondary files by using ALTER DATABASE with the ADD FILE argument. For example, to add a file named ExtraFile to the AdventureWorks2012 database, use the following:

```
ALTER DATABASE [AdventureWorks2012] ADD FILE ( NAME = N'ExtraFile',
FILENAME = N'C:\AdventureWorks2012\ExtraFile.ndf' , SIZE = 4096KB,
FILEGROWTH = 1024KB ) TO FILEGROUP [PRIMARY]
```

Recognize circumstances in which you need to use secondary files.

Each SQL Server 2012 database has a primary *filegroup*, which contains the primary data files and any secondary data files that have not been allocated to other filegroups. You can use filegroups to increase performance when you use partitioning. Multiple filegroups also assist in reducing backup times when performing partial backups. You'll learn more about partitioning in Chapter 3, "Configuring SQL Server 2012 Components." You can add filegroups on the Filegroups page in the Database Properties dialog box, shown in Figure 1-6, or add them by using ALTER DATABASE with ADD FILEGROUP. For example, to add the filegroup Additional to database AdventureWorks2012, use the following:

```
ALTER DATABASE [AdventureWorks2012] ADD FILEGROUP [Additional]
```

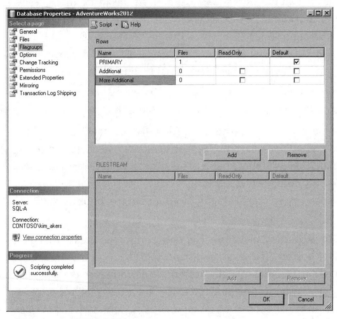

FIGURE 1-6 Additional filegroups

MORE INFO   FILES AND FILEGROUPS

You can learn more about files and filegroups at *http://msdn.microsoft.com/en-us/library /ms189563(v=SQL.110).aspx*.

Remembering Capacity Constraints

When planning your SQL Server 2012 deployment, you should keep in mind the capacity constraints of the SQL Server Database engine. For example, a database cannot exceed 524,272 terabytes, no single data file can exceed 16 terabytes, and you can host a maximum of 32,767 databases on a single instance of SQL Server. Capacity constraints can also influence database development, with a limit of 16 columns per primary key, a maximum of 253 foreign key references per table, and a maximum of 32,767 user connections.

> **MORE INFO CAPACITY**
>
> This chapter does not list every possible capacity statistic of SQL Server 2012 because most of them will not be relevant to the 70-462 exam. You can learn more about SQL Server 2012 capacity at *http://msdn.microsoft.com/en-us/library/ms143432(v=SQL.110).aspx*.

Identifying a Standby Database for Reporting

SQL Server 2012 supports several types of standby database. You can use database mirroring to maintain a single standby database for a corresponding production database. This type of standby database is known as a *mirror database*. You can also use log shipping to maintain one or more warm standby databases. This type of standby database is known as a *secondary database*. A readable secondary database that can service reporting queries requires the use of AlwaysOn availability groups. You will learn more about standby databases in Chapter 7, "Mirroring and Replication" and more about AlwaysOn availability groups in Chapter 8, "Clustering and AlwaysOn."

> **MORE INFO STANDBY DATABASES**
>
> You can learn more about using high-availability technologies for standby databases at *http://msdn.microsoft.com/en-us/library/ms190202(v=sql.110).aspx*.

Identifying Windows-Level Security and Service-Level Security

During the installation of SQL Server 2012, the user is prompted to provide service account credentials. The default service accounts suggested vary depending on whether SQL Server 2012 is installed on a computer running Windows Vista or Windows Server 2008 or on a computer running Windows 7 or Windows Server 2008 R2. On computers running Windows Vista or Windows Server 2008 operating systems, the following default service accounts are used:

- **NETWORK SERVICE**   Database Engine, SQL Server Agent, Analysis Services, Integration Services, Reporting Services, SQL Server Distributed Replay Controller, SQL Server Distributed Replay Client

- **LOCAL SERVICE**   SQL Server Browser, FD Launcher (Full-Text Search)
- **LOCAL SYSTEM**   SQL Server VSS Writer

On computers running Windows 7 or Windows Server 2008 R2 operating systems, the following default accounts are used:

- **Virtual Account or Managed Service Account**   Database Engine, SQL Server Agent, Analysis Services, Integration Services, Replication Services, SQL Server Distributed Replay Controller, SQL Server Distributed Replay Client, FD Launcher (Full-Text Search)
- **LOCAL SERVICE**   SQL Server Browser
- **LOCAL SYSTEM**   SQL Server VSS Writer

For Windows 7 and Windows Server 2008 R2, you can use a *Managed Service Account* (MSA) or a Managed Local Account. The differences between these account types are as follows:

- **Managed Service Account (MSA)**   This special kind of domain account managed by a domain controller is assigned to a single member computer and used for running services. The MSA password is managed by the domain controller. MSAs can register a Service Principal Name (SPN) with Active Directory. MSAs use a $ name suffix; for example, CONTOSO\SQL-A-MSA$. You must create the MSA prior to running SQL Server Setup if you want to use an MSA with SQL Server services.
- **Virtual Accounts or Managed Local Accounts**   These virtual accounts can access the network in a domain environment and are used by default for service accounts during SQL Server 2012 setup when run on Windows 7 or Windows Server 2008 R2. Such accounts use the NT SERVICE\<SERVICENAME>format. You don't need to specify a password when using virtual accounts with SQL Server 2012 because this is handled automatically by the operating system.

EXAM TIP

Remember that you need to create the MSA prior to deploying SQL Server.

You should run SQL Server services, using the minimum possible user rights, and use an MSA or virtual account when possible. If you are manually configuring service accounts, use separate accounts for different SQL Server services. If it is necessary to change the properties of service accounts used for SQL Server 2012, use SQL Server tools such as SQL Server Configuration Manager, shown in Figure 1-7. This ensures that all necessary dependencies are updated, which does not happen if you use only the Services console.

Although you can configure domain accounts as service accounts, this strategy requires more effort because you must ensure that service account passwords are changed regularly. You must also manage SPNs, which are required for Kerberos authentication.

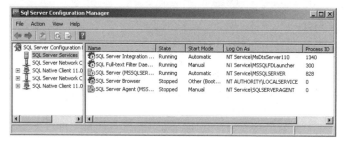

FIGURE 1-7 SQL Server Configuration Manager

> ***MORE INFO***   **SERVICE ACCOUNTS AND PERMISSIONS**
>
> You can learn more about Windows Service Accounts and permissions at *http://msdn*
> *.microsoft.com/en-us/library/ms143504(v=sql.110).aspx.*

Performing a Core Mode Installation

Unlike previous versions of SQL Server, SQL Server 2012 can be installed on computers running the Server Core version of Windows Server 2008 R2 as long as the host server is running Service Pack 1 or later. You can install all editions of SQL Server 2012 on Windows Server Datacenter, Standard, Enterprise, and Web operating systems in Server Core configuration.

SQL Server 2012 on Server Core has the following prerequisites, all of which are either included with Windows Server 2008 R2 with Service Pack 1 on Server Core or available through the SQL Server 2012 installation files:

- **.NET Framework 2.0 SP1**   Included with Windows Server 2008 R2 Server Core SP1: Setup enables this software if it is not already present.
- **.NET Framework 3.5 SP1**   Included with Windows Server 2008 R2 Server Core SP1: Setup enables this software if it is not already present.
- **.NET Framework 4 Server Core Profile**   Included with SQL Server 2012 installation files for all versions except SQL Server Express: In all editions except Express, setup installs this software as a prerequisite.
- **Windows Installer 4.5**   Present in Windows Server 2008 R2 Server Core SP1.
- **Windows PowerShell 2.0**   Present in Windows Server 2008 R2 Server Core SP1.

Windows Server 2008 R2 Server Core with SP1 supports the following SQL Server 2012 features:

- Database Engine Services
- SQL Server Replication
- Full-Text Search

- Analysis Services
- Client Tools Connectivity
- Integration Services Server

Microsoft Sync Framework is not included in the SQL Server 2012 installation files but can be downloaded from the Microsoft website and installed on Windows Server 2008 R2 Server Core with SP1. You can use the following tools to connect remotely to the Database Engine installed on Server Core:

- Management Tools – Basic
- Management Tools – Complete
- Distributed Replay Client

The following features are not supported on SQL Server 2012 on Windows Server 2008 R2 Server Core with SP1:

- Reporting Services
- SQL Server Data Tools (SSDT)
- Client Tools Backward Compatibility
- Client Tools SDK
- SQL Server Books Online
- Distributed Replay Controller
- Master Data Services
- Data Quality Services

To install SQL Server 2012 on a computer running Windows Server 2008 R2 Server Core with SP1, log on to the computer with an account that has local administrator privileges and use the Setup.exe command with the following options:

```
Setup.exe /qs /ACTION=Install /FEATURES=SQLEngine /INSTANCENAME=MSSQLSERVER
/SQLSVCACCOUNT="<DomainName\UserName>" /SQLSVCPASSWORD="<StrongPassword>"
/SQLSYSADMINACCOUNTS="<DomainName\UserName>" /AGTSVCACCOUNT="NT AUTHORITY\Network
Service" /IACCEPTSQLSERVERLICENSETERMS
```

You can use the following options to specify which features you want to install:

- **SQLENGINE**   Database Engine
- **REPLICATION**   Replication feature
- **FULLTEXT**   Full-Text feature
- **AS**   Analysis Services feature
- **IS**   Integration Services feature
- **CONN**   Connectivity features

For example, to install the Database Engine, Replication, Integration Services, and Connectivity features while designating the Kim Akers Contoso domain account for the MSSQLServer instance, use the following command:

```
Setup.exe /qs /Action=install /Features=SQLEngine,Replication,IS,Conn
/InstanceName=MSSQLServer /SQLSYSADMINACCOUNTS="Contoso\kim_akers"
/IAcceptSQLServerLicenseTerms
```

> **MORE INFO**   **INSTALLING ON SERVER CORE**
>
> You can learn more about installing SQL Server 2012 on a computer running the Server Core version of Windows Server 2008 R2 at *http://msdn.microsoft.com/en-us/library /hh231669(v=sql.110).aspx*.

Benchmarking a Server

Prior to deploying SQL Server 2012, you should determine the capacity of the I/O subsystem. *SQLIO* is a tool that you can use to determine this capacity. A benefit of SQLIO is that it allows you to identify hardware or I/O configuration issues before you deploy SQL Server 2012. SQLIO allows you to measure I/O against one or more test files to measure I/Os per second (IOPs), throughput (MB/s), and latency. SQLIO does this by reading and writing files of different sizes. You can increase the file size to simulate the projected size of your database. You determine the saturation point of an I/O subsystem by gradually increasing the load. The saturation point is the limit of your I/O subsystem's capacity.

> **MORE INFO**   **SQLIO INSTRUCTION VIDEO**
>
> SQLIO is a complicated utility that requires complex configuration. You can learn more about SQLIO in the instructional video found at *http://sqlserverpedia.com/blog/sql-server -performance-tuning/sqlio-tutorial/*.

If you are running SQLIO on Windows 7 or Windows Server 2008 R2, you should create an exception for SQLIO in Data Execution Prevention (DEP). To do this, go to System Properties in Control Panel, click Advanced, Performance Options, and select the Data Execution Protection tab. Click Add and specify the path to SQLIO.EXE, as shown in Figure 1-8.

> **MORE INFO**   **TROUBLESHOOTING SQLIO**
>
> To learn more about troubleshooting SQLIO, go to the TechNet article at *http://social .technet.microsoft.com/wiki/contents/articles/1263.aspx*.

FIGURE 1-8 Creating an exception in DEP for SQLIO

The *SQLIOSim* utility is included with the SQL Server 2012 product installation, and you can find it in the BINN directory of your SQL Server 2012 deployment. SQLIOSim performs similar tasks and replaces the SQLIOStress utility available for earlier versions of SQL Server. You can use SQLIOSim to perform readability and integrity tests on disk subsystems. It enables you to simulate read, write, checkpoint, backup, sort, and read-ahead activities for SQL Server 2012 deployments. If you only want to perform benchmark tests and determine I/O capacity of the storage system, use SQLIO. The SQLIOSim interface is shown in Figure 1-9.

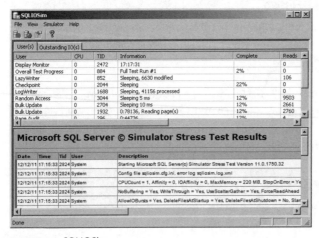

FIGURE 1-9 SQLIOSim

Test files that are similar to the size of the database that you intend to deploy. It is important to ensure that the total size of test files exceeds the amount of cache in the storage array, and using small test files can result in inaccurate data because the entirety of the small file might be cached in the array. You should also run tests for a long enough period to ensure that they are valid. You are more likely to detect configuration problems when running a long test than you are running a test over short periods. Many enterprise storage systems use self-tuning caches. Running longer tests facilitates optimal cache performance, which gives you a better idea of capacity.

PRACTICE: **Prepare for the Installation of SQL Server 2012**

In this practice, you run the System Configuration Checker and prepare Group Policy to support firewall rules that will enable remote management of the Database Engine.

EXERCISE 1   **System Configuration Checker**

In this exercise, run the System Configuration Checker from the SQL Server 2012 installation media. To complete this exercise, perform the following steps:

1. Log on to server SQL-A with the Kim Akers domain account.

2. Use Windows Explorer to navigate to the folder that hosts the SQL Server 2012 installation files and open Setup.exe, consenting to the UAC prompt.

3. On the Planning page, open System Configuration Checker.

4. After the setup support rules have installed, click Show Details to verify that no failures or warnings have occurred, as shown in Figure 1-10.

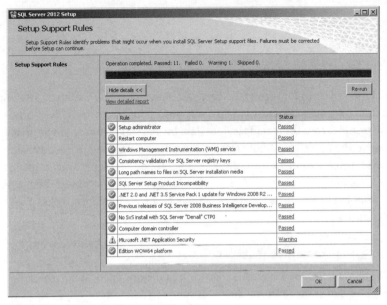

FIGURE 1-10 System Configuration Checker

EXERCISE 2 Configure Firewall Rules

In this exercise, configure a firewall rule and a connection security rule to enable remote management of the SQL servers you will be using throughout the exercises in this Training Kit. To complete this exercise, perform the following steps:

1. Log on to server DC with the Kim Akers domain account.

2. Use Active Directory Users And Computers to create a new organizational unit (OU) named **SQL-Servers**.

3. Move the computer accounts SQL-A, SQL-B, and SQL-CORE to the OU, as shown in Figure 1-11.

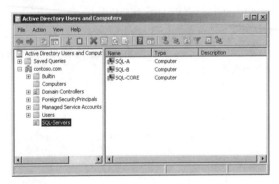

FIGURE 1-11 OU configuration

4. Use Group Policy Management Console to create a Group Policy Object (GPO) named **SQL-POLICY** in the domain and link it to the SQL-Servers OU.

5. Edit the SQL-POLICY GPO. Create an inbound rule in Windows Firewall with an Advanced Security node in the Computer Configuration\Policies\Windows Settings \Security Settings node. This inbound rule should have the following properties:

   - Program Rule
   - Program Path: C:\Program Files\Microsoft SQL Server\MSSQL11.MSSQLSERVER \MSSQL\Binn\sqlservr.exe
   - Allow the connection
   - Domain, Private, and Public profiles
   - Name: SQL-RemoteManagement-Inbound

6. Right-click the SQL-RemoteManagement-Inbound rule and select Properties. On the Scope tab, in the Remote IP Address section, select These IP Addresses and enter the **10.10.10.0/24** subnet. Verify that the dialog box matches Figure 1-12.

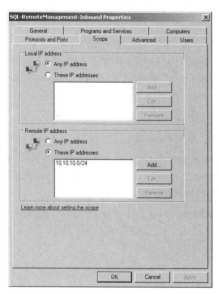

FIGURE 1-12 Firewall scope configuration

Lesson Summary

- All editions of SQL Server 2012 have a minimum RAM requirement of 1 GB except the Express editions, which have a minimum RAM requirement of 512 MB.
- SQL Server 2012 Enterprise, Business Intelligence, and Web editions can be run on the Windows Server 2008 R2 SP1 and Windows Server 2008 SP2 operating systems.

You can run the x86 version of these SQL Server 2012 editions on the x86 version of Windows Server 2008 SP2, but not on the x64 versions.

- The x64 versions of SQL Server 2012 require an AMD Opteron, AMD Athlon 64, Intel Xeon with Intel EM64T support, or Intel Pentium IV with EMT64 support with a minimum processor speed of 1.4 GHz and a recommended speed of 2.0 GHz or faster. The x86 versions of SQL Server 2012 require a Pentium III–compatible processor or newer that has a minimum speed of 1.0 GHz and a recommended speed of 2.0 GHz or faster.
- Scaling up involves adding better hardware; scaling out involves adding more SQL instances.
- Databases are configured to autogrow by default. You can configure a database to shrink automatically, but this is likely to lead to index fragmentation.
- Databases use primary files (.mdf), secondary files (.ndf), and transaction log files (.ldf).
- When SQL Server 2012 is deployed on Windows Server 2008 R2, it uses a virtual account, which is a locally managed account, by default. You can configure SQL Server 2012 to use an existing managed service account.
- SQL Server 2012 can be installed on Windows Server 2008 R2 SP1 in the Server Core configuration, although not all features are supported.
- You can use SQLIO to benchmark the I/O subsystem prior to SQL Server 2012 deployment, and you can use SQLIOSim to simulate read, write, checkpoint, backup, sort, and read-ahead activities.

Lesson Review

Answer the following questions to test your knowledge of the information in this lesson. You can find the answers to these questions and explanations of why each answer choice is correct or incorrect in the "Answers" section at the end of this chapter.

1. What is the minimum required amount of RAM for SQL Server 2012 Enterprise?

   A. 512 MB

   B. 1 GB

   C. 2 GB

   D. 4 GB

   E. 8 GB

2. Which of the following editions of SQL Server 2012 can you run on a computer that is running the Windows 7 Professional (x64) operating system? (Choose all that apply.)

   A. SQL Server 2012 (x64) Developer edition

   B. SQL Server 2012 (x64) Web edition

   C. SQL Server 2012 (x64) Enterprise edition

   D. SQL Server 2012 (x64) Standard edition

3. Which of the following features can you install if you are installing SQL Server 2012 Enterprise edition on a computer running Windows Server 2008 R2 SP1 Enterprise edition in the Server Core configuration? (Choose all that apply.)

   A. Database Engine Services

   B. SQL Server Replication

   C. Analysis Services

   D. Reporting Services

4. On which of the following operating systems can you deploy the 64-bit version of SQL Server 2012 Enterprise edition? (Choose all that apply.)

   A. Windows 7 Ultimate (x64) edition

   B. Windows Server 2008 R2 SP1 (x64) Standard edition

   C. Windows Server 2008 SP2 (x64) Enterprise edition

   D. Windows Server 2003 R2 (x64) Enterprise edition

5. You want to simulate read, write, checkpoint, backup, sort, and read-ahead activities for your organization's SQL Server 2012 deployment. Which of the following tools would you use to accomplish this goal?

   A. SQLIO

   B. SQLIOSim

   C. SQLIOStress

   D. chkdsk

Lesson 2: Installing SQL Server and Related Services

This lesson covers the steps to consider when preparing an operating system disk for the deployment of SQL Server 2012. You'll also learn how to install the SQL Server Database Engine and SQL Server Integration Services and how to add and remove SQL Server features. You'll learn what steps you take to ensure that connectivity can be established from other computers to the SQL Server deployment.

After this lesson, you be able to:

- Configure an operating system disk.
- Install SQL Server Database Engine.
- Install SQL Server Integration Services.
- Enable and disable SQL Server features.
- Verify connectivity to a SQL Server deployment.

Estimated lesson time: 60 minutes

Configuring an Operating System Disk

Prior to installing SQL Server 2012, ensure that you properly configure the volume that hosts your operating system. When configuring the disk that hosts the operating system, consider the following factors:

- Even if you are not installing the SQL Server 2012 program files on the volume that hosts the operating system, you must ensure that at least 4 GB is free for the temporary files used during SQL Server 2012 setup.
- Mirror (RAID 1) the disk that hosts the operating system. This will protect the operating system in case the disk fails.
- You should ensure that the operating system is up to date with all necessary service packs and updates prior to installing SQL Server 2012.

All editions of SQL Server 2012 require .NET Framework 3.5.1 to be present prior to installation. To install .NET Framework 3.5.1, you can either use the Features node of the Server Manager console on Windows Server 2008 and Windows Server 2008 R2 or run the following command from an elevated Windows PowerShell session when the ServerManager module is loaded:

```
Add-WindowsFeature NET-Framework-Core
```

To install .NET Framework 3.5.1 on a computer running a client operating system such as Windows 7, you must use Programs And Features in Control Panel and select Turn Features On And Off.

You should use NTFS as the file system for the computer that will host SQL Server 2012. NTFS enables you to use directory access control lists (ACLs) and Encrypting File System (EFS). If you use EFS, database files are encrypted under the account identity of the SQL Server service account (NT Service\MSSQLSERVER on Windows Server 2008 R2). If you need to alter the account associated with the SQL Server Service, you must decrypt any encrypted files and then re-encrypt them to the new service account.

Although SQL Server 2012 does support encryption, for additional security you can configure BitLocker full-disk encryption to encrypt the volumes that host the operating system, database program, and data files. If the physical security of the computer running SQL Server 2012 is ever compromised, BitLocker ensures that unauthorized users will find it difficult to recover data.

Installing the SQL Server Database Engine

The SQL Server Database Engine is the heart of SQL Server 2012 deployment. The Database Engine stores, processes, and secures data. SQL Server 2012 supports up to 50 instances of Database Engine on a single computer. You must run setup from a user account that is directly or indirectly a member of the local Administrators group. If you are running Setup.exe from a network share, ensure that the account you are using has Read and Execute permissions on that share.

EXAM TIP

Remember permissions required to install SQL Server.

As Figure 1-13 shows, when you choose to install the SQL Server Database Engine feature, you don't need to install other features on the server. Depending on your needs, you might only need to install SQL Server Database Engine on a server. For example, it is likely that you'll actually manage the server remotely from your desktop computer by using SQL Server Management Studio.

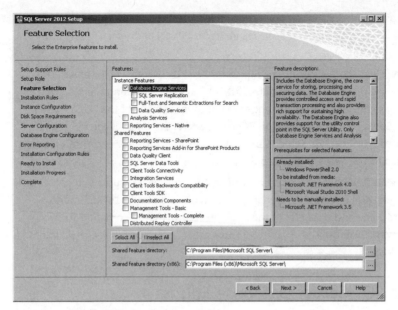

FIGURE 1-13 Database Engine install

To install SQL Server Database Engine on a computer, perform the following steps:

1. Ensure that the .NET Framework 3.5.1 feature is installed on the computer on which you will install SQL Server 2012.

2. Navigate to the volume that hosts the SQL Server installation files. Double-click Setup.exe. Provide consent at the UAC prompt.

3. On the SQL Server Installation Center page, click Installation.

4. On the Installation page of SQL Server Installation Center, shown in Figure 1-14, click New SQL Server Stand-Alone Installation Or Add Features To An Existing Installation.

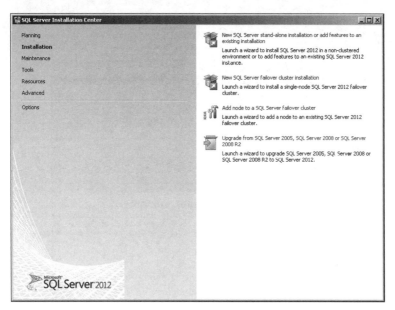

FIGURE 1-14 New SQL Server installation

5. The setup support rules run. These rules identify possible problems; for example, if the server needs to perform a restart operation due to the installation of other software, such as a security update. You can click Show Details to see the status of the rules.

6. Setup checks to see the availability of any updates to SQL Server 2012 through the Windows Update service. If setup is unable to contact a Windows Update server, it provides a warning message. You can click Next to bypass this screen.

7. Setup next installs the installation files and runs the Setup Support. Results are shown in Figure 1-15. Windows Firewall displays a warning, reminding you that you will need to configure Windows Firewall rules after the installation if you want to connect remotely to the Database Engine and other installed SQL Server 2012 features.

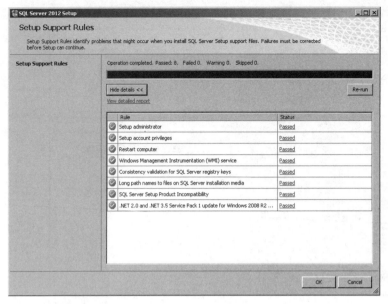

FIGURE 1-15 Setup Support Rules

8. On the Product Key page, you can enter a product key.

> **NOTE EVALUATION EDITION**
>
> If you do not provide a product key at this stage, SQL Server 2012 will be installed as an evaluation edition.

9. On the License Terms page, you must select I Accept The License Terms to proceed with setup.

10. On the Setup Role page, choose SQL Server Feature Installation.

11. On the Feature Selection page, select Database Engine Services and click Next. You can use this page to select an alternate location to install SQL Server shared features.

12. On the Installation Rules page, you see that the installation rules run and determine whether there are any blocking issues. If there are none, click Next.

13. On the Instance Configuration Rules page, choose Instance ID and Instance Root Directory, as shown in Figure 1-16. This page also lists existing instances on the computer.

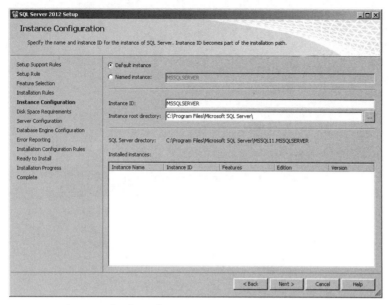

FIGURE 1-16 Instance Configuration

14. Review the Disk Space Requirements page and click Next.

15. On the Server Configuration page, you can accept the default service accounts or configure alternate service accounts. You can also configure collation settings. The default collation on computers with the United States regional setting is SQL_Latin1_General_CP1_CI_AS. You can use this dialog box to customize collation settings.

16. On the Database Engine Configuration page, shown in Figure 1-17, click Add Current User or Add and specify which User or Group accounts should be delegated the SQL Server Administrators right. You can use this page to choose between Windows Authentication Mode and Mixed Mode; you can also select the other tabs on this page to specify the Data Directories and whether FILESTREAM support is enabled for Transact-SQL access.

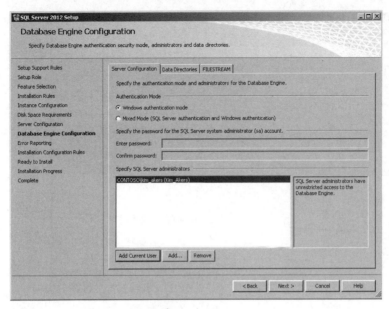

FIGURE 1-17 Database Engine Configuration page

17. On the Error Reporting page, you can choose whether to send Windows and SQL Server error reports to both Microsoft and your organization's corporate reporting server.

18. The Installation Configuration Rules configuration runs and determines whether any blocking issues might halt the installation of your configuration.

19. On the Ready To Install page, you can view a summary of your installation choices. A text file, named ConfigurationFile.ini, is saved. You can use this file to replicate the chosen configuration when installing other Database Engine instances. Click Install to install the Database Engine. You might need to restart the server when the installation completes.

> *MORE INFO*   **INSTALL THE SQL SERVER DATABASE ENGINE**
>
> You can find more information about installing the SQL Server Database Engine at *http://msdn.microsoft.com/en-us/library/ms144296(v=SQL.110).aspx.*

Installing SQL Server 2012 from the Command Prompt

As you learned in Lesson 1, you can also install SQL Server 2012 from the command prompt by executing Setup.exe from an elevated command prompt. You specify which features to install and other configuration settings through the command-line options. You can use command prompt installation in the following situations:

- Installing, upgrading, or removing an instance and shared feature of SQL Server 2012 on a local computer.

- Installing, upgrading, or removing a failover cluster instance.

- Upgrading from one SQL Server 2012 edition to another.

- Installing an instance of SQL Server 2012 on a computer by using parameters in a configuration file. This enables you to deploy the same configuration to multiple computers. It is also useful when installing SQL Server 2012 on multiple nodes of a failover cluster.

You can use the parameters listed in Table 1-3 with Setup.exe when installing SQL Server 2012.

TABLE 1-3   A Selection of Setup.exe Parameters

Parameter	function
/ACTION	Values: INSTALL, UNINSTALL
/IACCEPTSQLSERVERLICENSETERMS	Required to accept SQL licensing conditions
/CONFIGURATIONFILE	You can specify the configuration file to use.
/FEATURES	You can specify which features are installed. Available features include: ■ SQL Installs SQL Server Database Engine, Replication, Full-Text, and Data Quality Server ■ IS Integration Services features ■ AS Analysis Services features ■ RS Reporting Services features ■ DQC Data Quality client
/ROLE	You can choose a specific setup role. Available roles include: ■ AllFeatures_WithDefaults Will install all features that ship with the current edition ■ SPI_AS_ExistingFarm Installs Analysis Services as a PowerPivot named instance on existing SharePoint Server 2010 farm ■ SPI_AS_NewFarm Installs Analysis Services and Database Engine as a PowerPivot named instance on a new SharePoint Server 2010 farm
/INSTANCENAME	You can specify an instance name.
/PID	You can specify a product key. If no product key is specified, SQL Server 2012 is installed as an evaluation edition.
/QS	Installation runs in quiet mode without a user interface; used when installing on Server Core operating systems.

/AGTSVCSTARTUPTYPE	SQL Server Agent Startup mode
	■ Automatic
	■ Disabled
	■ Manual
/SQLSYSADMINACCOUNTS	Provision logons to be members of the sysadmin role
/SQLSVCACCOUNT	SQL Server service account
/SQLSVCPASSWORD	SQL Server service account password
/ISSVCACCOUNT	Integration Services service account
/ISSVCPASSWORD	Integration Services service account password
/ASSVCACCOUNT	Analysis Services service account
/ASSVCPASSWORD	Analysis Services service account password
/ASSYSADMINACCOUNTS	Administrator credentials for Analysis Services
/RSSVCACCOUNT	Reporting Services service account
/RSSVCPASSWORD	Reporting Services service account password

For example, to install the SQL Server Database Engine, Replication, Data Quality Server, and Full-Text Search features, use the following syntax:

```
Setup.exe /q /ACTION=Install /FEATURES=SQL /INSTANCENAME=MSSQLSERVER
/SQLSVCACCOUNT="<DomainName\UserName>" /SQLSVCPASSWORD="<StrongPassword>"
/SQLSYSADMINACCOUNTS="<DomainName\UserName>" /AGTSVCACCOUNT="NT AUTHORITY\Network
Service" /IACCEPTSQLSERVERLICENSETERMS
```

> **MORE INFO** **INSTALL SQL SERVER 2012 FROM THE COMMAND PROMPT**
>
> You can learn more about command-line installations at *http://msdn.microsoft.com/en-us /library/ms144259(v=SQL.110).aspx#Install.*

Installing SQL Server Integration Services

You use SQL Server setup to install SQL Server Integration Services (SSIS) as part of the normal installation process, but you can install only one instance of SSIS on a computer. You make remote connections to SSIS by specifying the target computer name, as shown in Figure 1-18.

FIGURE 1-18 Remote connection to SSIS

You can also install SSIS in the following situations:

- You can add SSIS to a computer that has no existing SQL Server 2012 installation as long as it meets the necessary hardware and software requirements.

- You can install SSIS for SQL Server 2012 on computers that host an existing deployment of SSIS for SQL Server 2005 or SQL Server 2008. This is the only exception to the rule about having a single instance of SSIS on a computer.

- You can upgrade SSIS for SQL Server 2005 or SQL Server 2008 to SSIS for SQL Server 2012. You will learn more about upgrading from previous versions of SQL Server in Chapter 4, "Migrating, Importing, and Exporting."

A complete installation of SSIS involves adding the following shared features:

- **SQL Server Data Tools**   Installs the tools you use to design packages

- **Management Tools – Complete**   Installs SQL Server Management Studio, which you use to manage packages

- **Client Tools SDK**   Enables you to install managed assemblies for Integration Services programming

When you install SSIS on computers running a 64-bit operating system, such as Windows Server 2008 R2, it will install only the 64-bit run time and tools, so if you need to run packages in 32-bit mode, you must choose to install the 32-bit run time and tools. You can accomplish this by installing the SQL Server Data Tools shared feature on 64-bit deployments.

You can use the Setup.exe command-line utility to add SSIS to an existing installation on both traditional and Server Core deployments of SQL Server 2012. For example, to add the SSIS feature to the default MSSQLSERVER instance, run the following command:

```
Setup.exe /qs /Action=Install /Features=IS /InstanceName=MSSQLServer
/IAcceptSQLServerLicenseTerms
```

If your deployment plans involve having a server dedicated for *ETL* (Extraction, Transformation, and Loading) processes, you should also deploy a local instance of the Database Engine because Integration Services stores packages in the msdb database and uses SQL Server Agent for scheduling those packages. If you choose not to install a local instance of Database Engine, SSIS packages will run on the server from which they were started rather than on the dedicated ETL server.

> **MORE INFO   INSTALLING INTEGRATION SERVICES**
>
> You can find more about installing SQL Server Integration Services at *http://msdn .microsoft.com/en-us/library/ms143731(v=SQL.110).aspx.*

Enabling and Disabling Features

You can add features to an existing SQL Server 2012 deployment by running SQL Server Installation Center, located in the Configuration Tools folder of the Microsoft SQL Server 2012 folder. You select the Installation section and then choose New SQL Server Stand-Alone Installation Or Add Features To An Existing Installation. After you specify the location of the SQL Server 2012 installation media, you go through a process that is similar to that which you use to install a new instance.

When running setup to enable new features, be sure that you choose Add Features To An Existing Instance Of SQL Server 2012, as shown in Figure 1-19, rather than the default Perform A New Installation Of SQL Server 2012.

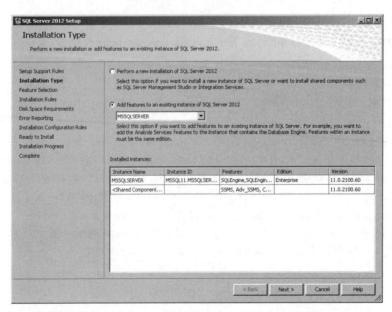

FIGURE 1-19 Add features to an existing instance of SQL Server 2012

You can use the Setup.exe command-line utility to add features to an existing installation on both traditional and Server Core deployments of SQL Server 2012. For example, to add the Integration Services feature to the default MSSQLSERVER instance, run the following command:

```
Setup.exe /qs /Action=Install /Features=IS /InstanceName=MSSQLServer
/IAcceptSQLServerLicenseTerms
```

Removing features from SQL Server 2012 is different from adding them. Instead of using the SQL Server Installation Center, you use Programs And Features within the operating system's control panel. To remove features from an existing SQL Server 2012 installation, perform the following steps:

1. Open Programs And Features from Control Panel.

2. Right-click Microsoft SQL Server 2012 and click Uninstall/Change.

3. In the SQL Server 2012 dialog box, choose Remove.

4. Click OK when the setup support files are installed.

5. In the Select Instance page, select the instance from which you want to remove features.

6. The Select Features page displays all features currently installed on the computer. Select the features you want to remove. Figure 1-20 shows the Integration Services and SQL Server Data Tools features selected for removal.

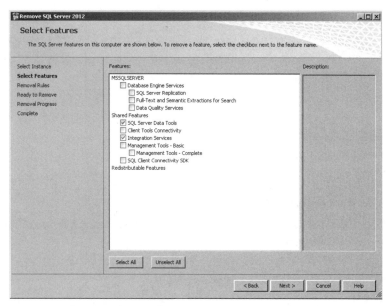

FIGURE 1-20 Removing features from an SQL Server 2012 installation

7. The removal rules run and determine whether any blocking issues are present. If there are no blocking issues, you can continue and remove the features.

You can use the Setup.exe command-line utility with the /Action=Uninstall option to remove a feature from SQL Server 2012. This works with both a traditional installation and with installations running Server Core. For example, to remove the Integration Services feature from the default MSSQLSERVER instance on a computer running either the traditional or Server Core version of Windows Server 2008 R2, use the command:

```
Setup.exe /qs /Action=Uninstall /Features=IS /InstanceName=MSSQLServer
```

You can determine which features are installed on SQL Server 2012 by running the Installed SQL Features Discovery Report. You can access this report through the Tools Menu of the SQL Server Installation Center. Output is an HTML file written to the \Microsoft SQL Server\110\Setup Bootstrap\Log\<last setup session> folder. The SQL Features Discovery Report is shown in Figure 1-21.

Microsoft SQL Server 2012 Setup Discovery Report

Product	Instance	Instance ID	Feature	Language	Edition	Version	Cluster
Microsoft SQL Server 2012	MSSQLSERVER	MSSQL11.MSSQLSERVER	Database Engine Services	1033	Enterprise Edition	11.0.2100.60	No
Microsoft SQL Server 2012	MSSQLSERVER	MSSQL11.MSSQLSERVER	SQL Server Replication	1033	Enterprise Edition	11.0.2100.60	No
Microsoft SQL Server 2012	MSSQLSERVER	MSSQL11.MSSQLSERVER	Full-Text and Semantic Extractions for Search	1033	Enterprise Edition	11.0.2100.60	No
Microsoft SQL Server 2012	MSSQLSERVER	MSSQL11.MSSQLSERVER	Data Quality Services	1033	Enterprise Edition	11.0.2100.60	No
Microsoft SQL Server 2012			Management Tools - Basic	1033	Enterprise Edition	11.0.2100.60	No
Microsoft SQL Server 2012			Management Tools - Complete	1033	Enterprise Edition	11.0.2100.60	No

FIGURE 1-21 Features discovery report

> **MORE INFO** **ADDING FEATURES TO AN INSTANCE OF SQL SERVER 2012**
>
> You can find more about adding features to an instance of SQL Server 2012 at *http://msdn.microsoft.com/en-us/library/cc281940(v=SQL.110).aspx*.

 Quick Check

- Which command do you use to remove a feature from SQL Server 2012 when it is installed on a Server Core version of Windows Server 2008 R2?

Installing SQL Server 2012 by Using a Configuration File

By installing SQL Server 2012 from a configuration file, you can standardize deployment and create a batch file that launches Setup.exe. Configurationfile.ini is a text file. You can use configuration files when Setup.exe is executed from the command line or by clicking Install Based On Configuration File in the Advanced section of SQL Server Installation Center, as shown in Figure 1-22.

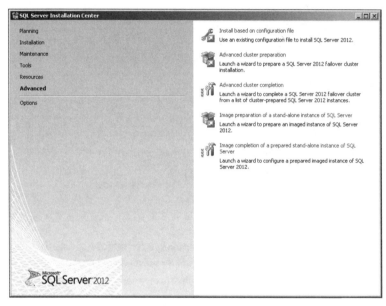

FIGURE 1-22 Install Based On Configuration File

You can generate a configuration file by performing the following steps:

1. Start Setup.exe.

2. Use the Installation Wizard to choose all appropriate feature and configuration options. These settings are written to the Configuration.ini file, the path of which will be shown on the Ready To Install page of SQL Server Setup, as shown in Figure 1-23. You can click Cancel at this time and then copy the Configuration.ini file to other locations without having to perform the actual installation.

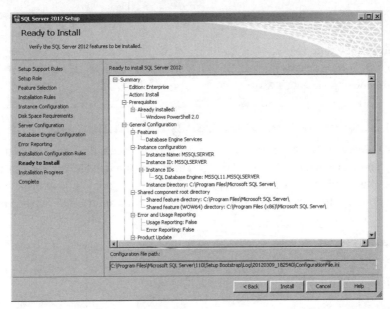

FIGURE 1-23 Create ConfigurationFile.ini

MORE INFO CONFIGURATION FILES

You can learn more about installing SQL Server 2012 by using a configuration file at *http://msdn.microsoft.com/en-us/library/dd239405(v=SQL.110).aspx.*

Testing Connectivity

After SQL Server 2012 is installed, you must verify that it is possible for remote clients to interact with the server. The simplest way of doing this is to attempt a connection by using the SQL Server 2012 client tools. For example, Figure 1-24 illustrates making a connection to a remote instance running on server SQL-CORE.

Installing SQL Server 2012 does not automatically configure firewall rules for the appropriate services installed; you must configure firewall rules manually on each server or configure them through the application of Group Policy. You can create firewall rules on each server by using the Netsh.exe command-line utility in the advfirewall firewall context. You can choose one of two approaches when configuring firewall rules for SQL Server 2012. The first approach is to configure program rules. The second is to configure port rules.

FIGURE 1-24 Remote connection using SQL client tools

When you configure program rules, you specify the program to which you want to allow access. For example, Figure 1-25 shows a firewall rule for the Database Engine that includes the path to the Sqlservr.exe binary.

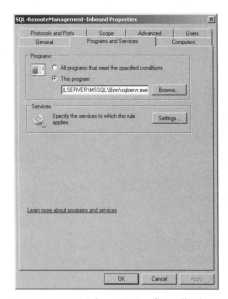

FIGURE 1-25 Database Engine firewall rule

To configure program rules for Database Engine, Analysis Services, Reporting Services, and Integration Services when installed in their default location in the default instance:

- Database Engine: C:\Program Files\Microsoft SQL Server\MSSQL11.MSSQLSERVER \MSSQL\Binn\sqlservr.exe
- Analysis Services: C:\Program Files\Microsoft SQL Server\MSAS11.MSSQLSERVER \OLAP\bin\msmdsrv.exe

- Integration Services: C:\Program Files\Microsoft SQL Server\110\DTS\Binn\MsDtsSrvr.exe

- Reporting Services: C:\Program Files\Microsoft SQL Server\MSRS11.MSSQLSERVER\Reporting Services\ReportServer\bin\ReportingServicesService.exe

By default, SQL Server 2012 named instances use dynamic ports. Because the port used by a named instance can change each time the Database Engine is started, configuring port-based rules can be challenging. To resolve this situation, you can create a program rule, or you can configure the Database Engine for an instance to use a fixed port.

To configure the Database Engine to use a fixed port, perform the following steps:

1. Open SQL Server Configuration Manager. Expand SQL Server Network Configuration. Expand Protocols for the Database Engine instance you want to configure. Double-click TCP/IP.

2. On the IP Addresses tab, shown in Figure 1-26, locate the IP address for which you will configure a port. Remove any area in the TCP Dynamic Ports text box for that IP address. Specify the TCP port to be used in the TCP Port text box. Restart the SQL Server instance to apply the changes.

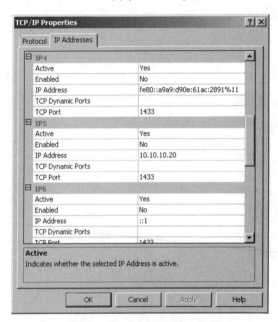

FIGURE 1-26 Configure Database Engine ports

MORE INFO **CONFIGURING THE DATABASE ENGINE TO USE A SPECIFIC PORT**

You can learn more about using Database Engine on a specific port at *http://msdn.microsoft.com/en-us/library/ms177440(v=SQL.110).aspx*.

SQL Database Engine uses the ports listed in Table 1-4.

TABLE 1-4 Database Engine Ports

Item	Port
Default Instance	TCP port 1433.
Named instances in default configuration	Dynamic port. You can configure named instances to use fixed TCP ports.
Dedicated Admin Connection	TCP Port 1434.
SQL Server Browser service	UDP port 1434.
SQL Server instance running over an HTTP end-point	TCP port 80 for CLEAR_PORT traffic. TCP port 443 for SSL_PORT traffic.
Service Broker	TCP Port 4022.
Database Mirroring	Chosen by the administrator. To determine the port, execute the following query: SELECT name, protocol_desc, port, state_desc FROM sys. tcp_endpoints WHERE type_desc = 'DATABASE_ MIRRORING'
Replication	TCP port 1433 for default instance.
Transact-SQL Debugger	TCP port 135.

EXAM TIP

Remember what TCP ports 1433 and 1434 are used for.

The ports that Reporting Services, Analysis Services, Integration Services, and other SQL features use are listed in Table 1-5.

TABLE 1-5 Additional Ports that SQL Server 2012 Features Use

Item	Port
Analysis Services	TCP port 2383 for default instance
SQL Server Browser Service	TCP port 2382: used only for an Analysis Services named instance
Reporting Services Web Services	TCP port 80
Reporting Services configured for use through HTTPS	TCP port 443
Integration Services: Microsoft remote procedure calls	TCP port 135
Integration services run time	TCP port 135
Microsoft Distributed Transaction Coordinator (MS DTC)	TCP port 135
SQL Server Management Studio browse connection to browser service	UDP port 1434

When configuring firewall rules, ensure that you limit the firewall rule scope so that the feature you are providing to the network can be accessed only by hosts on a specific network segment. For example, you might configure firewall rules so that inbound traffic will be accepted only from your organization's internal network or only from specific hosts on your organization's internal network. You can configure firewall rule scope on the Scope page of a rule's properties in Windows Firewall With Advanced Security or by using the Netsh.exe command in the advfirewall firewall context.

> **MORE INFO** **CONFIGURE FIREWALL TO ALLOW SQL SERVER ACCESS**
>
> You can learn more about configuring Windows Firewall to support SQL Server 2012 at *http://msdn.microsoft.com/en-us/library/cc646023(v=SQL.110).aspx.*

Connectivity problems can be more basic than traffic being blocked by Windows Firewall With Advanced Security. Sometimes connectivity problems are caused by your organization's network infrastructure suffering a failure such as a DNS server, router, or switch going offline. If you suspect that the connectivity problem isn't with the remote SQL server but is, instead, with the network infrastructure, perform the following tests to determine where the problem lies:

- Use the Ipconfig.exe command-line utility to verify IP address configuration. Your client or the target SQL server might be incorrectly configured with an incorrect address, subnet mask, default gateway, or DNS server assigned.

- Use the Nslookup.exe command to query DNS resolution for the name of the target SQL server. Prior to attempting this diagnostic step, flush the DNS cache by running the ipconfig /flushdns command to ensure that the query is run against the current DNS zone data.

- Use the Ping.exe command to verify network connectivity between your local host and the IP address of the server. Ping the server by using both IP address and fully qualified domain name (FQDN).

- Attempt to establish a connection by using the telnet utility to connect to port 1433.

- Use Sqlcmd.exe to connect to the server. For example, to connect to server SQL-B, issue the command:

```
Sqlcmd.exe -S SQL-B
```

> **MORE INFO** **CHECKING REMOTE SERVER CONNECTION OPTIONS**
>
> You can learn more about checking remote server connection options at *http://msdn .microsoft.com/en-us/library/ms179383(v=SQL.110).aspx.*

In this practice, you prepare computers for the installation of SQL Server 2012, install the SQL Server Database Engine, install SQL Server 2012 on a computer running the Server Core installation option, add features to an existing SQL Server 2012 deployment, and verify client connectivity.

EXERCISE 1   Prepare Computers for the Installation of SQL Server 2012

In this exercise, install the roles and features required to support SQL Server 2012 Database Engine. To complete this exercise, perform the following steps:

1. Log on to computer SQL-A with the Kim Akers domain account.
2. Use the Server Manager console to install the .NET Framework 3.5.1 feature.
3. Log on to computer SQL-B with the Kim Akers domain account.
4. From an elevated Windows PowerShell session, install the .NET Framework 3.5.1 feature.

EXERCISE 2   Install the SQL Server Database Engine

In this exercise, install the SQL Server Database Engine feature on servers SQL-A and SQL-B. To complete this exercise, perform the following steps:

1. While logged on to computer SQL-A with the Kim Akers domain account, use Windows Explorer to navigate to the location that hosts the SQL Server 2012 installation files and execute Setup.exe. Provide consent when prompted by UAC.
2. In SQL Server Installation Center, choose Installation. Choose New SQL Server Stand-Alone Installation Or Add Features To An Existing Installation.
3. After the Setup Support Files have installed, on the Product Key page, choose Evaluation as the Specify A Free Edition option.
4. Accept the license terms. Click Next when warned that SQL Server Setup could not search for updates.
5. Click Next on the Setup Support Rules page. Choose SQL Server Feature Installation, as shown in Figure 1-27.

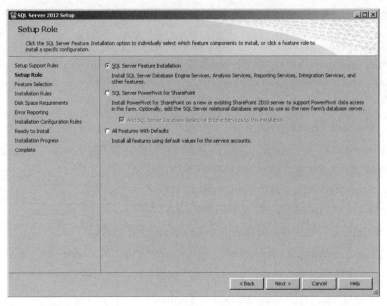

FIGURE 1-27 Setup Role

6. On the Feature Selection page shown in Figure 1-28, choose to install the following features and shared features:

- Database Engine Services
- SQL Server Replication
- Full-Text and Semantic Extractions For Search
- Data Quality Services
- SQL Server Data Tools
- Client Tools Connectivity
- Integration Services
- Management Tools – Basic
- Management Tools – Complete

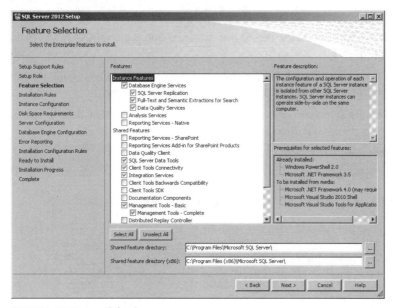

FIGURE 1-28 Feature Selection

7. On the Instance Configuration page, choose Default Instance.

8. On the Server Configuration page shown in Figure 1-29, accept the default Service Accounts settings.

9. On the Database Engine Configuration page, click Add Current User and ensure that Windows Authentication Mode is selected.

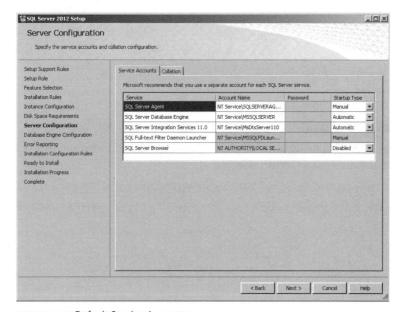

FIGURE 1-29 Default Service Accounts

10. Continue through the SQL Server 2012 Setup Wizard and install SQL Server 2012.

11. When installation completes, restart the computer and log on with the Kim Akers domain account.

12. While logged on to computer SQL-B with the Kim Akers domain account, repeat steps 1 through 5 of this exercise and then move on to the next step.

13. On the Feature Selection page shown in Figure 1-30, choose to install the following features and shared features:

    - Database Engine Services
    - Client Tools Connectivity

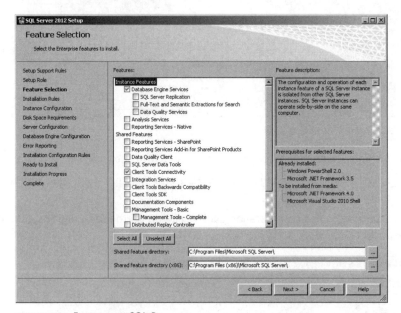

FIGURE 1-30 Features on SQL-B

14. On the Instance Configuration page, choose Default Instance.

15. On the Server Configuration page, accept the default Service Accounts settings.

16. On the Database Engine Configuration page, click Add Current User and ensure that Windows Authentication Mode is selected.

17. Continue through the SQL Server 2012 Setup Wizard and install SQL Server 2012.

18. When installation completes, restart the computer and log on with the Kim Akers domain account.

EXERCISE 3   Install SQL Server 2012 on a Computer Running Server Core

In this exercise, install the SQL Server 2012 Database Engine, integration services, and connectivity features on a computer running the Server Core installation option of Windows Server 2008 R2 Server Core with SP1. To complete this exercise, perform the following steps:

1. Log on to computer SQL-CORE with the Kim Akers domain account.

2. Ensure that the SQL Server 2012 installation media are accessible.

3. In the command prompt window, change to the volume hosting the SQL Server 2012 installation media.

4. In the command prompt window, type the following command:

    ```
    Setup.exe /qs /Action=install /Features=SQLEngine,IS,Conn
    /InstanceName=MSSQLServer /SQLSYSADMINACCOUNTS="Contoso\kim_akers"
    /IAcceptSQLServerLicenseTerms
    ```

5. When the installation completes, log off computer SQL-CORE.

EXERCISE 4   Add Features to SQL-B

In this exercise, you add features to the existing SQL Server 2012 instances on server SQL-B. To complete this exercise, perform the following steps:

1. Log on to computer SQL-B with the Kim Akers domain account.

2. Open the SQL Server Installation Center from the Microsoft SQL Server 2012 \Configuration Tools folder of the Start menu.

3. Choose New SQL Server Stand-Alone Installation Or Add Features To An Existing Installation from the Installation page.

4. Specify the location of the SQL Server 2012 installation media.

5. After the Setup Support rules have run, click Next on the Product Updates page.

6. On the Installation Type page as shown in Figure 1-31, select the Add Features To An Existing Instance Of SQL Server 2012 and choose the MSSQLSERVER instance.

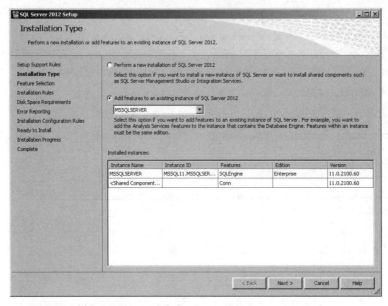

FIGURE 1-31 Add Features to an Existing Instance

7. On the Feature Selection page, add the Integration Services feature.

8. Review the Disk Space requirements and accept the default settings for the SQL Server Integration Services service account. Perform the installation and then log off server SQL-B.

EXERCISE 5 Verify Connectivity and Install AdventureWorks

In this exercise, verify remote connectivity by remotely connecting from server SQL-A to the SQL Server 2012 instances on servers SQL-B and SQL-CORE and also install the AdventureWorks sample database. To complete this exercise, perform the following steps:

1. Log on to computer SQL-A with the Kim Akers domain account.

2. Open SQL Server Management Studio and connect to the Database Engine on server SQL-A by using Windows Authentication.

3. Click the Connect button in Object Explorer. Select Database Engine and then connect to the Database Engine on server SQL-B.

4. Click the Connect button in Object Explorer. Select Database Engine and then connect to the Database Engine on server SQL-CORE.

5. Verify that Object Explorer has connections to the Database Engines on all three servers, as shown in Figure 1-32.

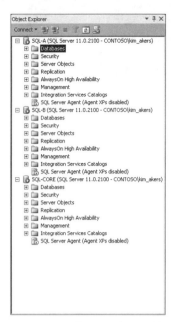

FIGURE 1-32 Object Explorer with connections to three servers

6. Download the AdventureWorks sample database file to server SQL-A from the following location: *http://go.microsoft.com/FWLink/?Linkid=251256*.

7. Copy the AdventureWorks2012_Data.mdf file to the C:\adventureworks2012 directory.

8. In Object Explorer, right-click the Databases node. Click Attach and specify the location of AdventureWorks2012_Data.mdf.

9. On the Attach Databases page, click the location of the log file and click Remove. Verify that the Attach Databases dialog box matches Figure 1-33 and then click OK.

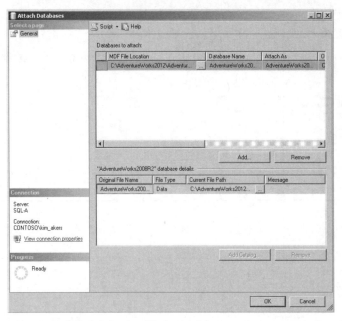

FIGURE 1-33 Attach AdventureWorks database

Lesson Summary

- The volume that hosts the operating system needs a minimum of 4 GB of available space to host the temporary SQL Server 2012 installation files.

- If you do not enter a product key, SQL Server 2012 will be installed as an evaluation edition.

- You can install up to 50 instances of the Database Engine on a single server.

- You can install only one instance of SSIS on a server.

- You can add features to an existing installation by using Setup.exe from the command line or by invoking SQL Server Setup through SQL Server Installation Center.

- You can remove features from an existing installation by using Setup.exe from the command line or by using Programs And Features in Control Panel.

- You must create firewall rules to enable remote connections to SQL Server 2012 features.

- You can verify connectivity to a remote instance of SQL Server 2012 features by using SQL Server Management Studio or SQLCMD.

Lesson Review

Answer the following questions to test your knowledge of the information in this lesson. You can find the answers to these questions and explanations of why each answer choice is correct or incorrect in the "Answers" section at the end of this chapter.

1. You are planning on deploying a server that will be dedicated for ETL (Extraction, Transformation, and Loading) processes. You want to ensure that SSIS (SQL Server Integration Services) packages will run on this dedicated ETL server and not on any other server on which they were started. Which of the following features must you install on the ETL server in addition to SSIS to accomplish this goal?

   A. Database Engine

   B. SQL Server Reporting Services

   C. SQL Server Analysis Services

   D. Client Tools SDK

2. You have installed the SQL Server Integration Services (SSIS) feature on a server running Windows Server 2008 R2 SP1. Which of the following features must you install if you want to ensure that you can run packages in 32-bit mode?

   A. Client Tools SDK

   B. Data Quality Client

   C. SQL Server Data Tools

   D. Client Tools Backwards Compatibility

3. You want to allow access to SQL Server Analysis Services on a server running Windows Server 2008 R2 for a client running SQL Server Management Studio on Windows 7. You have installed SQL Server Analysis Services in the default location. Which of the following paths should you use when creating the firewall rule by using Windows Firewall With Advanced Security?

   A. C:\Program Files\Microsoft SQL Server\MSSQL11.MSSQLSERVER\MSSQL\Binn \sqlservr.exe

   B. C:\Program Files\Microsoft SQL Server\MSAS11.MSSQLSERVER\OLAP\bin \msmdsrv.exe

   C. C:\Program Files\Microsoft SQL Server\110\DTS\Binn\MsDtsSrvr.exe

   D. C:\Program Files\Microsoft SQL Server\MSRS11.MSSQLSERVER\Reporting Services \ReportServer\bin\ReportingServicesService.exe

4. You want to remove SQL Server Integration Services from a server running the Windows Server 2008 R2 operating system that also has the Database Engine and SQL Server Analysis Services installed. Which of the following tools can you use to accomplish this goal?

   A. SQL Server Management Studio

   B. SQL Server Configuration Manager

        C. Add/Remove Programs in Control Panel

        D. SQL Server Installation Center

    5. You want to reproduce the same SQL Server 2012 installation configuration across five servers. Which of the following files will you generate by using SQL Server Setup to accomplish this goal?

        A. Configuration.xml

        B. Setup.ini

        C. Setup.xml

        D. ConfigurationFile.ini

Case Scenarios

In the following case scenarios, you apply what you have learned about planning server installs and upgrades. You can find answers to these questions in the "Answers" section at the end of this chapter.

Case Scenario 1: Planning Deployment of SQL Server 2012

Your organization is planning to deploy SQL Server 2012 Enterprise (x64) on several servers as a production database solution. Sam works in your organization as a database developer. As part of his role, Sam needs to test all the features that will be available on the production SQL Server 2012 instance. Sam has a laptop computer with Windows 7 Enterprise (x64) installed.

1. On which operating systems can you install the production database?

2. Which edition of SQL Server 2012 should you deploy on Sam's computer?

Case Scenario 2: SQL Server Deployment

You work for Contoso's Australian subsidiary. You need to deploy six SQL Server 2012 servers, two each in the cities of Sydney, Perth, and Adelaide, and you must ensure that these servers are configured in the same way.

1. How much free space should you ensure is available on each server's operating system disk before you attempt to install SQL Server 2012?

2. If you were using only the SQL Server installation media, what steps could you take to ensure that the SQL servers in Sydney, Perth, and Adelaide are configured in the same way?

Suggested Practices

To help you successfully master the exam objectives presented in this chapter, complete the following tasks.

Configure Additional Firewall Rules and Generate a Features Discovery Report

Prior to attempting to complete each task in the following practices, list the steps you would take to accomplish the task. After completing the task, assess how accurately you predicted the necessary steps.

- **Practice 1**   Configure and test program-based firewall rules for SQL Server Integration Services so that you can manage the SSIS instance on server SQL-CORE from server SQL-A.
- **Practice 2**   Verify the features installed on server SQL-A by generating a report in HTML format.

Adding and Removing Features and Adding Databases to SQL Server 2012 on a Computer Running a Server Core Operating System

Prior to attempting to complete each task in the following practices, list the steps you would take to accomplish the task. After completing the task, assess how accurately you predicted the necessary steps.

- **Practice 1**   Remove and then reinstall the SQL Server Integration Services feature from server SQL-CORE.
- **Practice 2**   Install the AdventureWorks database on server SQL-CORE.

Answers

This section contains the answers to the lesson review questions and solutions to the case scenarios in this chapter.

Lesson 1

1. **Correct Answer: B**
   - **A.** **Incorrect:** 512 MB of RAM is the minimum required for SQL Server 2012 Express edition. The Enterprise edition requires a minimum of 1 GB of RAM.
   - **B.** **Correct:** The Enterprise edition requires a minimum of 1 GB of RAM.
   - **C.** **Incorrect:** The Enterprise edition requires a minimum of 1 GB of RAM.
   - **D.** **Incorrect:** The Enterprise edition requires a minimum of 1 GB of RAM.
   - **E.** **Incorrect:** The Enterprise edition requires a minimum of 1 GB of RAM.

2. **Correct Answers: A and D**
   - **A.** **Correct:** You can install SQL Server 2012 (x64) Developer on a computer running the Windows 7 Professional (x64) operating system.
   - **B.** **Incorrect:** You cannot install SQL Server 2012 (x64) Web on a computer running the Windows 7 Professional (x64) operating system.
   - **C.** **Incorrect:** You cannot install SQL Server 2012 (x64) Enterprise on a computer running the Windows 7 Professional (x64) operating system.
   - **D.** **Correct:** You can install SQL Server 2012 (x64) Standard on a computer running the Windows 7 Professional (x64) operating system.

3. **Correct Answers: A, B, and C**
   - **A.** **Correct:** You can install Database Engine Services on a computer running Windows Server 2008 R2 SP1 Enterprise edition in the Server Core configuration.
   - **B.** **Correct:** You can install SQL Server Replication on a computer running Windows Server 2008 R2 SP1 Enterprise edition in the Server Core configuration.
   - **C.** **Correct:** You can install Analysis Services on a computer running Windows Server 2008 R2 SP1 Enterprise edition in the Server Core configuration.
   - **D.** **Incorrect:** You cannot install Reporting Services on a computer running Windows Server 2008 R2 SP1 Enterprise edition in the Server Core configuration.

4. **Correct Answers: B and C**
   - **A.** **Incorrect:** You cannot deploy the 64-bit version of SQL Server 2012 Enterprise edition on Windows 7 Ultimate (x64) edition. You can install this edition of SQL Server 2012 on Windows Server 2008 and Windows Server 2008 R2 only.
   - **B.** **Correct:** You can deploy the 64-bit version of SQL Server 2012 Enterprise edition on Windows Server 2008 R2 SP1 (x64) Standard edition.

C. **Correct:** You can deploy the 64-bit version of SQL Server 2012 Enterprise edition on Windows Server 2008 SP2 (x64) Enterprise edition.

D. **Incorrect:** You cannot deploy the 64-bit version of SQL Server 2012 Enterprise edition on Windows Server 2003 R2 (x64) Enterprise edition.

5. **Correct Answer: B**

A. **Incorrect:** SQLIO is used to perform benchmark tests to determine the I/O capacity of the storage subsystem.

B. **Correct:** You can use SQLIOSim to simulate read, write, checkpoint, backup, sort, and read-ahead activities.

C. **Incorrect:** SQLIOStress is the version of SQLIOSim that was available for SQL Server 2000. You can't use SQLIOStress with SQL Server 2012.

D. **Incorrect:** Chkdsk is a utility that you can use to check for disk errors. You can't use Chkdsk to simulate SQL activities as a form of benchmarking.

Lesson 2

1. **Correct Answer: A**

A. **Correct:** Integration Services stores packages in an instance of the Database Engine and uses SQL Server Agent for scheduling those packages. If you do not have a local instance of the Database Engine, SSIS packages will run on the server on which they were started.

B. **Incorrect:** SSRS is not required to run SSIS packages locally on an ETL server that has SSIS installed. You must install a local instance of the Database Engine to run SSIS packages locally.

C. **Incorrect:** SSAS is not required to run SSIS packages locally on an ETL server that has SSIS installed. You must install a local instance of the Database Engine to run SSIS packages locally.

D. **Incorrect:** The Client Tools SDK is not required to run SSIS packages locally on an ETL server that has SSIS installed. You must install a local instance of the Database Engine to run SSIS packages locally.

2. **Correct Answer: C**

A. **Incorrect:** The Client Tools SDK includes the software development kit that has resources for programmers. It does not allow you to run SSIS packages in 32-bit mode on a computer running a 64-bit operating system.

B. **Incorrect:** The Data Quality Client allows you to perform data quality operations against Data Quality Server. You can't use this feature to run SSIS packages in 32-bit mode on a computer running a 64-bit operating system.

C. **Correct:** Installing the SQL Server Data Tools shared feature allows you to run SSIS packages in 32-bit mode on a computer running a 64-bit operating system.

D. Incorrect: Client Tools Backwards Compatibility enables backward compatibility for packages created in previous versions of the product but does not enable you to run SSIS packages in 32-bit mode on a computer running a 64-bit operating system.

3. **Correct Answer: B**

   A. Incorrect: This path is used by the Database Engine, not by Analysis Services.

   B. Correct: Use this path when configuring a program-based firewall rule for Analysis Services.

   C. Incorrect: This path is used by Integration Services, not by Analysis Services.

   D. Incorrect: This path is used by Reporting Services, not by Analysis Services.

4. **Correct Answer: C**

   A. Incorrect: You cannot use SQL Server Management Studio to remove installed features from an SQL Server 2012 deployment.

   B. Incorrect: You cannot use SQL Server Configuration Manager to remove installed features from an SQL Server 2012 deployment.

   C. Correct: You use either Add/Remove Programs in Control Panel or the Setup.exe command-line utility to remove an installed feature.

   D. Incorrect: You cannot use SQL Server Installation Center to remove installed features from an SQL Server 2012 deployment. You can use SQL Server Installation Center to add new features to an existing deployment.

5. **Correct Answer: D**

   A. Incorrect: SQL Server Setup generates a file named ConfigurationFile.ini to store installation settings. Setup does not generate a file named Configuration.xml.

   B. Incorrect: SQL Server Setup generates a file named ConfigurationFile.ini to store installation settings. Setup does not generate a file named Setup.ini.

   C. Incorrect: SQL Server Setup generates a file named ConfigurationFile.ini to store installation settings. Setup does not generate a file named Setup.xml.

   D. Correct: SQL Server Setup generates a file named ConfigurationFile.ini to store installation settings.

Case Scenario 1

1. You can install SQL Server 2012 Enterprise (x64) edition on computers running Windows Server 2008 R2 SP1 and Windows Server 2008 SP2 (x64).

2. You should deploy SQL Server 2012 Developer (x64) edition because this has the same features as SQL Server Enterprise (x64) edition, the main difference being licensing and use in production environments.

Case Scenario 2

1. You should ensure that there is at least 4 GB of available space on the operating system disk prior to attempting to install SQL Server 2012.

2. You could ensure that the SQL servers in Sydney, Perth, and Adelaide are configured in the same way by generating a configuration file when installing the first server and then using that configuration file to deploy the additional servers.

CHAPTER 2

Configuring and Managing SQL Server Instances

Exam objectives in this chapter:

- Configure SQL Server instances.
- Manage SQL Server instances.

SQL Server instances are separate deployments of Database Engine, Analysis Services, and Reporting Services hosted on the same computer. Each instance may have one Database Engine, one Analysis Services, and one Reporting Services service installed. Each instance has its own program files, directory, and security configuration. A user who can create and drop databases in one instance might not have rights to change databases hosted on another instance, even though both instances are installed on the same host. Multiple instances on the same host enable you to deploy SQL Server multiple times without requiring extra operating system deployments. There are also licensing benefits to deploying multiple instances of SQL Server on the same host. SQL Server 2012 enables you to deploy up to 50 Database Engine instances on a single host server.

Lessons in this chapter:

Before You Begin

To complete the lessons in this chapter, make sure that you have:

- Completed the setup tasks for installing computers DC, SQL-A, SQL-B, and SQL-CORE as outlined in the introduction of this book.
- Completed the setup tasks outlined in the end-of-lesson practice exercises in Chapter 1, "Planning and Installing SQL Server 2012."

No additional configuration is required for this chapter.

Lesson 1: Configuring SQL Server Instances

Instance-level options are sometimes described as SQL Server options. This lesson covers configuring SQL Server instance-level options such as memory use, fill factor, processor, and I/O affinity. You also learn about the model database and Database Mail.

> **After this lesson, you will be able to:**
> - Configure a SQL instance to use only certain CPUs.
> - Configure server-level settings such as memory allocation.
> - Configure Database Mail.
> - Configure clustered instances including Microsoft Distributed Transaction Coordinator (MSDTC).
> - Configure and standardize databases by using the model database.
>
> **Estimated lesson time: 60 minutes**

Instance-Level Settings

You can use Database Engine settings, instance settings, and server settings interchangeably. When talking about SQL Server server settings, you are talking about settings for an instance, not settings that apply to every instance of SQL Server on a host computer. When you configure settings in the Server Properties dialog box, those settings apply only to the instance you are configuring, not to other instances of the Database Engine installed on the same host computer. You will learn more about installing additional instances in Lesson 2, "Managing SQL Server Instances."

You can configure instance-level settings, such as fill factor and minimum and maximum memory use, through the Server Properties dialog box. You can access this dialog box by right-clicking a specific instance within SQL Server Management Studio and then choosing Properties. The Server Properties dialog box, shown in Figure 2-1, contains the following pages:

- **General**   View general information about the instance, including the host operating system, root directory, and server collation. You can't modify settings on this page.
- **Memory**   Configure instance memory options, including minimum, maximum, index creation memory, and minimum memory per query.
- **Processors**   Configure processor affinity and I/O affinity, limit worker threads, boost SQL Server priority, and use Windows fibers (lightweight pooling).
- **Security**   Configure server authentication, logon auditing, server proxy account, Common Criteria compliance, C2 audit tracing, and cross-database ownership chaining.

- **Connections**   Configure maximum connections; query governor and default connection options, whether to allow remote connections, and whether to require distributed transactions for server-to-server communication.

- **Database Settings**   Configure default index fill factor, default backup media retention, recovery filter, and database default locations.

- **Advanced**   Configure FILESTREAM options; enable contained databases; and trigger firing, two-digit year cutoff, network packet size, remote logon timeout, and parallelism options.

- **Permissions**   Configure instance-level permissions.

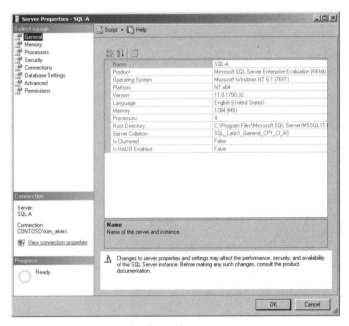

FIGURE 2-1 Server Properties General page

Configuring Memory Allocation

By default, a SQL Server 2012 instance uses memory dynamically, querying the host operating system on a periodic basis to determine how much free memory is available and releasing memory back to the host as needed to avoid paging. If the instance needs more memory and memory is available, a SQL Server 2012 instance will request memory from the host operating system.

You can use the Min Server Memory and Max Server Memory instance-level settings to configure the amount of memory (in megabytes) an instance of SQL Server 2012 uses. The *min server memory* value ensures that the instance has a minimum memory allocation. An instance does not use this amount of memory at startup, but when client load reaches this amount, SQL Server 2012 will not release memory back to the operating system if it means going below this value. If an instance never uses the minimum amount specified, that amount will not be reserved by the instance, and memory will be released back to the operating system.

EXAM TIP

Remember that the minimum reserve will not apply if the minimum reserved memory is not used.

When SQL Server 2012 is run on a 32-bit operating system, the lowest maximum memory value you can allocate is 64 MB. If SQL Server 2012 is run on a 64-bit operating system, the lowest maximum memory value you can allocate is 128 MB. The default setting for minimum server memory is 0, and the default maximum server memory is 2,147,483,647 MB. A setting of 0 means that the minimum server memory value is not set. You can configure these values on the Memory page of an instance's properties, as shown in Figure 2-2.

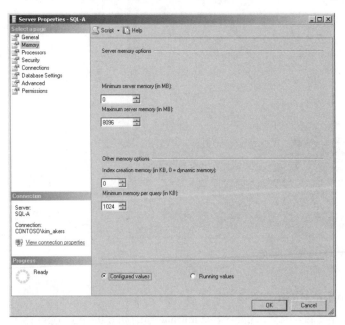

FIGURE 2-2 Server Properties Memory page

You can use sp_configure when advanced options are enabled to configure maximum and minimum server memory. For example, to configure an instance to use a minimum of 1024 MB of memory and a maximum of 8,096 MB of memory, use the following query:

```
EXEC sys.sp_configure 'show advanced options', 1;
GO
RECONFIGURE;
```

```
GO
EXEC sys.sp_configure 'min server memory', 1024;
GO
EXEC sys.sp_configure 'max server memory', 8096;
GO
RECONFIGURE;
GO
```

If you have deployed more than one instance of the Database Engine on a single host server, you can manage memory by using the following strategies:

- Use maximum server memory to limit the amount of memory each instance uses. Allocate memory based on expected instance usage. Ensure that the total allocated memory does not exceed the total physical memory of the host system. This strategy has the drawback of limiting an instance to an upper boundary when other instances might not fully use their allocation.

- Use minimum server memory to establish minimum memory settings for each instance. Ensure that the total minimum memory sum is 1 or 2 GB less than the total physical memory of the host system. This strategy has the advantage of allowing instances to use more than a fixed allocation when possible.

- If you do nothing, the host operating system allocates memory on a first-come, first-served basis. SQL Server 2012 does not attempt to balance memory usage across instances, meaning that memory might be disproportionately allocated when in contention. To avoid this, Microsoft recommends that you use either the maximum server memory or minimum server memory allocation strategy on computers that host multiple SQL Server 2012 instances.

> **MORE INFO** **MEMORY ALLOCATION**
>
> You can learn more about memory allocation at *http://msdn.microsoft.com/en-us/library /ms178067(v=SQL.110).aspx.*

Configuring Processor and I/O Affinity

Processor affinity assigns specific server processors to specific threads. This eliminates processor reloads and reduces thread migration across processors. *I/O affinity* binds an instance's disk I/O to a specific set of CPUs. You configure processor and I/O affinity on the Processors page of an instance's Server Properties dialog box, as shown in Figure 2-3. The default setting for each instance is to configure processor affinity mask and I/O affinity mask automatically for all processors on the host server.

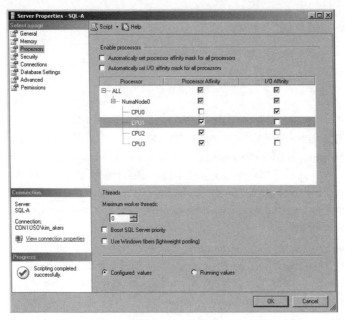

FIGURE 2-3 Server Properties Processors page

When configuring affinity through SQL Server Management Studio, you cannot configure both processor affinity and I/O affinity for the same processor. It is possible to configure processor affinity and I/O affinity for the same processor by using Transact-SQL, although this is not recommended and will decrease performance.

To distribute SQL worker threads across CPUs 2 and 3 based on server workload, use the following Transact-SQL statement:

```
ALTER SERVER CONFIGURATION SET PROCESS AFFINITY CPU = 2,3
```

To distribute SQL worker threads across all CPUs based on server workload, use the following command:

```
ALTER SERVER CONFIGURATION SET PROCESS AFFINITY CPU = AUTO
```

> **MORE INFO** **AFFINITY**
>
> You can learn more about processor affinity at *http://technet.microsoft.com/en-us/library /ms186255(SQL.110).aspx*.

You can also use sp_configure with the affinity mask option in Transact-SQL to configure processor affinity. The affinity mask option and the affinity64 mask option that is used when there are more than 32 processors will be removed in future versions of SQL Server and should be avoided when possible because they can be used only on servers that have up to 64 processors.

You can't configure I/O affinity by using the ALTER SERVER CONFIGURATION statement and must instead use sp_configure with the affinity I/O mask option. Microsoft recommends that you do not modify affinity I/O mask from the default setting.

> **MORE INFO AFFINITY I/O MASK OPTION**
>
> You can learn more about the affinity I/O mask option at *http://msdn.microsoft.com/en-us /library/ms189629(v=SQL.110).aspx.*

EXAM TIP

Understand the difference between processor affinity and I/O affinity.

Configuring Fill Factor

Fill factor determines the percentage of space on each leaf-level page that is filled with data when an index is created or rebuilt. The remaining space is used for future growth. Fill factor is configured as a percentage value between 1 and 100. The server-wide default is 0. Fill factor can be configured at the individual index level and at the server level. You will learn more about configuring indexes in Chapter 10, "Indexes and Concurrency."

> **NOTE FILL FACTOR**
>
> Fill factor values of 100 and 0 are functionally the same.

You can configure the default index fill factor on the Database Settings page of Server Properties, as shown in Figure 2-4. This configures the fill factor for that instance but not for other instances installed on the same computer.

You can set the instance-wide fill factor value by using the sp_configure stored procedure. You can change the fill factor only on an instance-wide basis when the advanced options value is set to 1. For example, to set the instance-wide fill factor configuration option to 90, use the following code:

```
sp_configure 'show advanced options', 1;
GO
RECONFIGURE;
GO
sp_configure 'fill factor', 90;
GO
RECONFIGURE;
GO
```

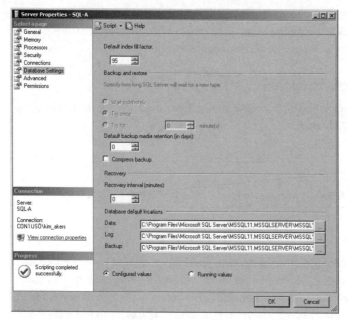

FIGURE 2-4 Default index fill factor

Database Configuration and Standardization

The *model* database serves as the template for all new databases that you create on an instance of SQL Server 2012. This includes the *tempdb* database, which the instance creates each time it starts. Creating a new database involves making a complete copy of the contents of the model database, including all database options such as recovery model, *Auto Close*, and *Auto Shrink*. Any modifications you make to the model database will apply to databases you create in the future.

> **EXAM TIP**
>
> **Remember the purpose of each of the system databases.**

The model database has the default options listed in Table 2-1.

TABLE 2-1 Model Database Default Settings

Database Option	Default Value
ALLOW_SNAPSHOT_ISOLATION	OFF
ANSI_NULL_DEFAULT	OFF
ANSI_NULLS	OFF
ANSI_PADDING	OFF

ANSI_WARNINGS	OFF
ARITHABORT	OFF
AUTO_CLOSE	OFF
AUTO_CREATE_STATISTICS	ON
AUTO_SHRINK	OFF
AUTO_UPDATE_STATISTICS	ON
AUTO_UPDATE_STATISTICS_ASYNC	OFF
CHANGE_TRACKING	OFF
CONCAT_NULL_YIELDS_NULL	OFF
CURSOR_CLOSE_ON_COMMIT	OFF
CURSOR_DEFAULT	GLOBAL
Database Availability Options	ONLINE MULTI_USER READ_WRITE
DATE_CORRELATION_OPTIMIZATION	OFF
DB_CHAINING	OFF
ENCRYPTION	OFF
NUMERIC_ROUNDABORT	OFF
PAGE_VERIFY	CHECKSUM
PARAMETERIZATION	SIMPLE
QUOTED_IDENTIFIER	OFF
READ_COMMITTED_SNAPSHOT	OFF
RECOVERY	FULL
RECURSIVE_TRIGGERS	OFF
Service Broker Options	DISABLE_BROKER
TRUSTWORTHY	OFF

You cannot alter the properties of the model database by:

- Adding files or filegroups or removing a primary filegroup, data file, or log file.
- Modifying the collation. The model database uses the server collation.
- Modifying the database owner. The model database is owned by dbo.
- Dropping the database.
- Dropping the guest user.
- Enabling change capture.
- Creating a database mirror.
- Renaming the model database or primary file group.

- Setting the model database to OFFLINE.
- Setting the database or primary filegroup to READ_ONLY.
- Creating procedures, view, or triggers by using the WITH ENCRYPTION option.

You can configure the Recovery Model, Auto Close, Auto Shrink, and other options for all future databases that you create on an instance on the Options page of the model database in SQL Server Management Studio, as shown in Figure 2-5.

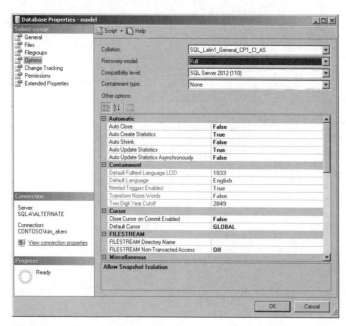

FIGURE 2-5 Model database properties

You can use the ALTER DATABASE statement with the SET RECOVERY option to configure the recovery option for the model database. For example, use the following Transact-SQL statement to modify the recovery model of the model database to FULL:

```
USE [master]
GO
ALTER DATABASE [model] SET RECOVERY FULL WITH NO_WAIT
GO
```

You can also configure the database recovery option to SIMPLE or BULK_LOGGED. You'll learn more about database recovery options in Chapter 3, "Configuring SQL Server 2012 Components."

Auto Close determines whether a database is automatically closed and its resources freed when there are no connections to the database. You can use the ALTER DATABASE statement with the SET AUTO_CLOSE option to configure Auto Close for the model database by using

Transact-SQL. For example, use the following Transact-SQL statement to enable Auto Close on the model database:

```
USE [master]
GO
ALTER DATABASE [model] SET AUTO_CLOSE ON WITH NO_WAIT
GO
```

When you enable Auto Shrink, the Database Engine automatically shrinks databases that have free space. You can use the ALTER DATABASE statement with the SET AUTO_SHRINK option to configure Auto Shrink settings on the model database by using Transact-SQL. For example, use the following Transact-SQL statement to enable Auto Shrink on the model database:

```
USE [master]
GO
ALTER DATABASE [model] SET AUTO_SHRINK ON WITH NO_WAIT
GO
```

> **MORE INFO** **MODEL DATABASE**
>
> You can learn more about the model database at *http://technet.microsoft.com/en-us /library/ms186388(SQL.110).aspx.*

Distributed Transaction Coordinator

Prior to deploying SQL Server 2012 on a failover cluster, you need to determine whether to create the *Microsoft Distributed Transaction Coordinator* (MSDTC) cluster resource. The MSDTC cluster resource is not required when you are installing only the Database Engine component, although it might be necessary if you are installing the Database Engine additional components, such as Integration Services, or if you intend to use distributed transactions. A distributed transaction is a transaction that runs across multiple servers. MSDTC is not required if transactions run across multiple instances hosted on the same server. You do not need MSDTC for instances that host only Analysis Services.

You configure MSDTC to function in a cluster by using Failover Cluster Manager, as shown in Figure 2-6. Failing to configure MSDTC by using the High Availability Wizard will not block you from installing SQL Server 2012 on a cluster, but application functionality might be impaired. You'll learn more about configuring clusters in Chapter 8, "Clustering and AlwaysOn."

> **MORE INFO** **INSTALL MICROSOFT DISTRIBUTED TRANSACTION COORDINATOR**
>
> You can learn more about installing Microsoft Distributed Transaction Coordinator at *http://msdn.microsoft.com/en-us/library/ms189910(v=sql.110).aspx.*

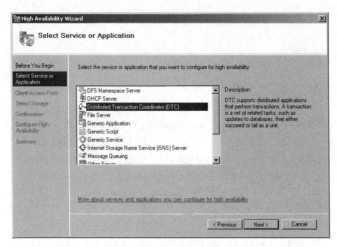

FIGURE 2-6 Configuring MSDTC by using Failover Cluster Manager

 Quick Check

■ Which system database must you modify if you want all future databases to use the Full recovery model?

Quick Check Answer

■ You must modify the model database because all new databases created on an instance inherit settings from the model database.

Configuring Database Mail

Database Mail enables the SQL Server Database Engine to send email messages. Developers can use Database Mail to create database applications that can send email. Database Mail uses the SMTP protocol, so any compatible SMTP server can receive messages. Database Mail on SQL Server 2012 has the following properties:

■ The Database Mail process is isolated from the SQL Server Database Engine. If the Database Mail process fails, SQL Server queues messages until it becomes available.

■ Database Mail can use more than one target SMTP server. If one SMTP server is unavailable, Database Mail routes mail through another server.

■ Database Mail is cluster aware and can be installed on failover clusters.

■ You can configure multiple mail profiles within a SQL Server instance. SQL application developers choose an appropriate profile when sending messages.

Database Mail stored procedures are disabled by default. It is only possible to transmit messages using Database Mail; it is necessary to be a member of the DatabaseMailUserRole database role in the msdb database.

You configure Database Mail by performing the following steps:

1. Open SQL Server Management Studio.

2. Right-click Database Mail under the Management node and then click Configure Database Mail. This launches the Database Mail Configuration Wizard. Click Next.

3. On the Select Configuration Task page shown in Figure 2-7, choose Set Up Database Mail By Performing The Following Tasks and then click Next.

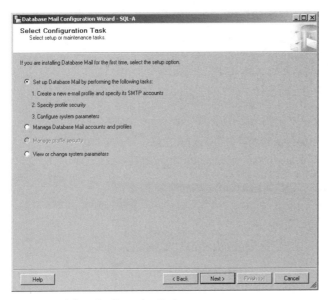

FIGURE 2-7 Select Configuration Task

4. In the Microsoft SQL Server Management Studio dialog box informing you that the Database Mail feature is not available, click Yes.

5. On the New Profile page, provide a profile name and a description and then click Add.

6. In the New Database Mail Account dialog box, as shown in Figure 2-8, provide email account details and click OK. On the New Profile page, click Next.

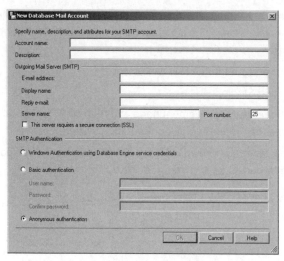

FIGURE 2-8 New Database Mail Account dialog box

7. On the Manage Profile Security page, click Next.

8. On the Configure System Parameters page, as shown in Figure 2-9, choose values for Account Retry Attempts and other settings and then click Next.

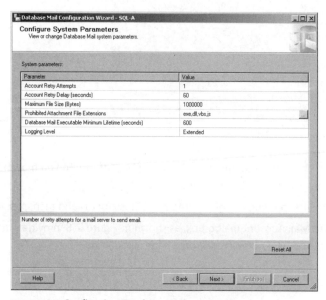

FIGURE 2-9 Configuring Database Mail system parameters

9. On the Complete The Wizard page, click Finish.

You have the option of enabling Database Mail when you run the Configure Database Mail Wizard. You can also enable Database Mail by using the sp_configure stored procedure with the Database Mail XPs option. To enable Database Mail by using sp_configure, use the following code:

```
sp_configure 'show advanced options', 1;
GO
RECONFIGURE;
GO
sp_configure 'Database Mail XPs', 1;
GO
RECONFIGURE;
GO
```

You can disable Database Mail by changing the Database Mail XPs value to 0.

EXAM TIP

Remember which stored procedure you use to enable Database Mail.

You can create Database Mail accounts by using the sysmail_add_account_sp stored procedure. For example, to create a Database Mail account named Example that uses the address example@contoso.com and the SMTP server smtp.contoso.com, use the following code:

```
EXECUTE msdb.dbo.sysmail_add_account_sp
@account_name = 'Example',
@email_address = 'example@contoso.com',
@mailserver_name = 'smtp.contoso.com';
```

> **MORE INFO** **SYSMAIL_ADD_ACCOUNT_SP**
>
> You can learn more about sysmail_add_account_sp at *http://msdn.microsoft.com/en-us /library/ms182804(v=sql.110).aspx.*

You can configure Database Mail system parameters by using the sysmail_configure_sp stored procedure. By using this stored procedure, you can configure account retry attempts, account retry delay, how long the external mail process remains active, attachment encoding, maximum attachment size, prohibited attachment extensions, and logging level. For example, to configure Database Mail to retry 15 times before considering the account unreachable, use the following code:

```
EXECUTE msdb.dbo.sysmail_configure_sp
'AccountRetryAttempts', '15';
```

> **MORE INFO** **SYSMAIL_CONFIGURE_SP**
>
> You can learn more about sysmail_configure_sp at *http://msdn.microsoft.com/en-us /library/ms186321(v=sql.110).aspx.*

Database Mail profiles determine which users are able to send messages by using Database Mail:

- *Public profiles* can be accessed by all users of any mail-host database.
- *Private profiles* can be accessed by a specific user of a mail-host database only. To configure a private profile, this user must be an msdb database user.

You configure public profile and private profile settings on the Manage Profile Security page, which is accessible through the Database Mail Configuration Wizard, shown in Figure 2-10.

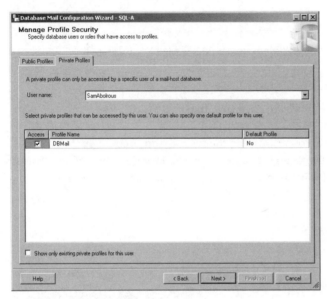

FIGURE 2-10 Manage Profile Security page

> **MORE INFO** **DATABASE MAIL CONFIGURATION**
>
> You can learn more about Database Mail configuration at *http://technet.microsoft.com /en-us/library/ms189635(SQL.110).aspx.*

PRACTICE **Configure SQL Server 2012 Instance-Level Settings**

In this practice, apply what you learned in the lesson to perform SQL Server configuration tasks, including configuring memory and fill factor settings for an instance, configuring Database Mail, and configuring the properties of the model database.

EXERCISE 1   Configure Minimum Memory and Fill Factor

In this exercise, you configure the minimum memory and default fill factor settings for a SQL Server 2012 instance. To complete this exercise, perform the following steps:

1. Log on to server SQL-A with the Kim_Akers user account.
2. Open SQL Server Management Studio and connect to the default instance on SQL-A.
3. Use sp_configure to set the minimum amount of server memory used by instance SQL-A as 512 MB.
4. Use sp_configure to set the default fill factor on the SQL-A instance to 90%.

EXERCISE 2   Configure Database Mail on SQL-A

In this exercise, you configure Database Mail on server SQL-A. To complete this exercise, perform the following steps:

1. Log on to server SQL-A with the Kim_Akers user account.
2. Open SQL Server Management Studio.
3. Use sp_configure to enable Database Mail.
4. Start the Database Mail Configuration Wizard and create a new profile named DBMail.
5. Create a new Database Mail account with the following settings:
   - Account Name: sql-a
   - E-Mail Address: sql-a@contoso.com
   - Server Name: smtp.contoso.com
   - SMTP Authentication: Anonymous authentication
6. Configure DBMail as the default public profile.
7. Configure the following Database Mail system parameters:
   - Account Retry Attempts: 5
   - Account Retry Delay (Seconds): 120
   - Database Mail Executable Minimum Lifetime (Seconds): 800
8. Use sysmail_configure_sp to change the Account Retry Attempts value to 10.

EXERCISE 3   Configure New Database Standardization

In this exercise, you configure the model database to ensure that all future databases you create on instance SQL-A will use the simple recovery model and have Auto Shrink and Auto Close enabled. To complete this exercise, perform the following steps:

1. Using SQL Server Management Studio, edit the properties of the model database and configure the database to use the simple recovery model.
2. Use Transact-SQL to enable Auto Shrink and Auto Close on the model database.
3. Create a new database named **Exemplar**. Verify that the database uses the simple recovery model and is configured to Auto Shrink and Auto Close.

Lesson Summary

- You can configure instance-level settings such as fill factor, minimum memory use, maximum memory use, processor, and I/O affinity through the Server Properties dialog box.

- You can use the sp_configure stored procedure to configure minimum server memory, maximum server memory, fill factor, and I/O affinity. You can configure processor affinity by using sp_configure, although ALTER SERVER CONFIGURATION is the preferred method.

- Processor affinity ties an instance to specific processors rather than to all processors on the host server.

- A maximum memory strategy assigns each instance a maximum amount of memory. A minimum memory strategy assigns each instance a minimum amount of memory and allows instances to use available extra free memory as necessary.

- The model database serves as a template for all new databases. Use the ALTER DATABASE statement to modify the model database.

- MSDTC is required when transactions run across multiple servers. You should configure it as a cluster resource prior to installing the Database Engine on a cluster.

- Database Mail enables an instance to send email messages. You can enable Database Mail by using the sp_configure stored procedure.

Lesson Review

Answer the following questions to test your knowledge of the information in this lesson. You can find the answers to these questions and explanations of why each answer choice is correct or incorrect in the "Answers" section at the end of this chapter.

1. You have recently removed a SQL 2012 Database Engine instance from a computer running the Windows Server 2008 R2 operating system. Prior to the removal of the instance, you had configured affinity so that the default instance used CPU 0 and 1 and the second instance used CPU 2 and 3. You want to ensure that the default instance can use all processors available to the host. Which of the following commands would you use to accomplish this goal?

A. ALTER SERVER CONFIGURATION SET PROCESS AFFINITY CPU = AUTO

B. ALTER SERVER CONFIGURATION SET PROCESS AFFINITY CPU = 2,3

C. ALTER SERVER CONFIGURATION SET PROCESS AFFINITY CPU = 0,1

D. ALTER SERVER CONFIGURATION SET PROCESS AFFINITY CPU = 0,4

2. You have run the following command on a SQL Server 2012 default instance:

```
EXEC sys.sp_configure 'show advanced options', 1;
GO
```

Which of the following commands must you run to configure the instance so that the maximum amount of memory the instance uses does not exceed 4,096 MB? (Each answer presents part of a complete solution. Choose two.)

A. RECONFIGURE;
```
GO
```

B. EXEC sys.sp_configure 'min server memory', 1024;
```
GO
```

C. EXEC sys.sp_configure 'min server memory', 4096;
```
GO
```

D. EXEC sys.sp_configure 'max server memory', 4096;
```
GO
```

3. You want to ensure that disk input/output operations of an instance are bound to a specific processor. Which of the following would you configure to accomplish this goal?

A. Minimum server memory

B. Maximum server memory

C. Processor affinity

D. I/O affinity

4. You want to ensure that all future databases created on a SQL 2012 instance are configured to Auto Shrink. Which of the following system databases do you modify to accomplish this goal?

A. master

B. model

C. msdb

D. tempdb

5. Which stored procedure do you use to enable Database Mail on an instance?

A. sp_configure

B. sp_rename

C. sp_monitor

D. sp_depends

Lesson 2: Managing SQL Server Instances

This lesson covers installing additional instances of SQL Server, managing software updates for single-instance and multiple-instance deployments, managing resources within an instance by using Resource Governor, cycling error logs, and managing resources between instances by using Windows System Resource Manager.

> **After this lesson, you will be able to:**
> - Install additional instances.
> - Update management.
> - Manage resource usage by using Resource Governor.
> - Manage instance interaction.
> - Configure error log cycling.
>
> **Estimated lesson time: 60 minutes**

Installing Additional Instances

SQL Server 2012 supports up to 50 instances of the Database Engine on a single host computer and up to 25 instances on a failover cluster. Instances are functionally separate deployments of SQL Server 2012 features on the same host computer and have separate program files and data directories. Applying a service pack or software update to one instance does not update other instances unless you specify that it do so. A user or group assigned the SQL Server Administrator role for one instance might not have the role on any other instance even though the same server hosts those other instances.

Instances can host more than just separate copies of the SQL Server Database Engine. You can deploy the following features individually or together as separate instances in SQL Server 2012:

- Database Engine Services
  - SQL Server Replication
  - Full-Text and Semantic Extractions for Search
  - Data Quality Services
- Analysis Services
- Reporting Services – Native

Although it is possible to install a named instance as the first instance on a host, in most cases the first instance installed on a computer is the default instance. (The default instance has the name of the host on which it was installed.) Instance names have the following properties and limitations:

- They are not case sensitive.

- If you specify MSSQLServer as the instance name, the installation routine installs the default instance. If a default instance already exists on the host, the installer presents you with an error.

- You can't use the name DEFAULT or any other reserved keywords such as ADD, ALL, EXECUTE, ALTER, PRIMARY, or RECONFIGURE. You can find a full list of reserved keywords at *http://msdn.microsoft.com/en-us/library/ms143507.aspx*.

- Instance names can be a maximum of 16 characters.

- The first character in an instance name must be a letter. This can include letter characters from other character sets such as Cyrillic.

- You cannot use the backslash (\), comma (,), colon (:), semicolon (;), single quote ('), ampersand (&), embedded space, or at sign (@) in an instance name.

To install an additional SQL Server Database Engine instance by using the GUI, perform the following steps:

1. Open SQL Server Installation Center from the Configuration Tools folder of the Microsoft SQL Server 2012 folder in the Start menu. Click Yes when presented with the User Account Control dialog box.

2. In the SQL Server Installation Center dialog box, click Installation and then choose New SQL Server Stand-Alone Installation Or Add Features To An Existing Installation. In the Browse For Folder dialog box, specify the location of the SQL Server 2012 installation files.

3. On the Setup Support Rules page, click Show Details to verify that no problems are present, although this is unlikely because you are installing an additional instance. Click OK.

4. Installation will check for updates. Click Next. On the Setup Support Rules page, verify that all steps pass and then click Next.

5. On the Installation Type page, choose Perform A New Installation Of SQL Server 2012, as shown in Figure 2-11.

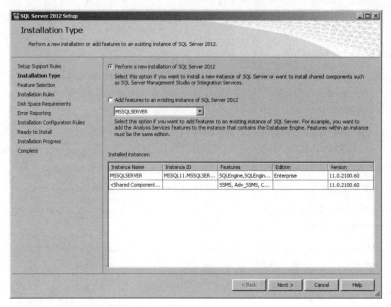

FIGURE 2-11 Installing a new instance

6. On the Product Key page, enter a product key or choose between the Evaluation or Express editions. Click Next.

7. On the License Terms page, enable I Accept The License Terms and then click Next.

8. On the Setup Role page, choose SQL Server Feature Installation and then click Next.

9. On the Feature Selection page, choose Database Engine Services and then click Next.

10. On the Installation Rules page, click Next.

11. On the Instance Configuration page, shown in Figure 2-12, enter the name for the alternate instance. You must conform to the rules about instance names described earlier in this lesson. You can also choose an alternate instance directory if necessary. Click Next.

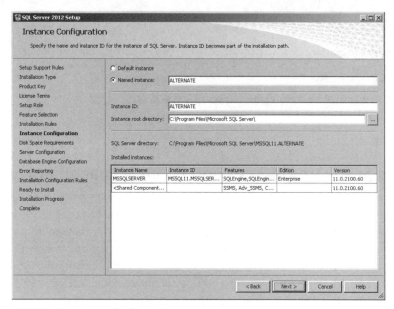

FIGURE 2-12 Instance Configuration page

12. Review the Disk Space Requirements and then click Next.

13. Review the Service Account and Collation settings and then click Next.

14. On the Database Engine Configuration page, select the authentication mode and which users will hold the role of SQL Server Administrator. You can also specify the options for instance data directories and whether FILESTREAM is enabled for the instance.

15. Click Next twice and then click Install. Click Close to dismiss the Setup Wizard.

To install an additional instance from the command line, either on a supported host with a traditional GUI or on a compatible Server Core installation of Windows Server 2008 R2, use the Setup.exe command with the /Action=Install and /Features=SQLEngine option. For example, to install an additional instance of the Database Engine named Alternate and set the Contoso\Kim_Akers user account to hold the role of SQL Server Administrator, use the following command:

```
Setup.exe /qs /Action=Install /Features=SQLEngine /InstanceName=Alternate /
SQLSYSADMINACCOUNTS="Contoso\Kim_Akers" /IAcceptSQLServerLicenseTerms
```

EXAM TIP

Although it is possible to change the default collation, this process requires substantive effort, and it is often simpler to add a new instance with a different default collation. You can create databases with different collations by using the COLLATE clause of the CREATE DATABASE statement independent of default collation.

✔ **Quick Check**

- How many instances of SQL Server 2012 can you install on a failover cluster?

Quick Check Answer

- You can install a maximum of 25 instances of SQL Server 2012 on a failover cluster.

Deploying Software Updates and Patch Management

Software update deployment and *patch management* on a computer on which you have deployed a single instance of SQL Server 2012 is straightforward: You can configure Windows Update to retrieve updates for SQL Server 2012 either from Microsoft Update or from your organization's local Windows Server Update Services (WSUS) server, or you can download and deploy the updates manually. Deploying updates on a host computer on which you have multiple instances of SQL Server 2012 installed is more complex because each instance has its own separate program files. When deploying updates, consider the following:

- You must update all features associated with a SQL Server 2012 instance at the same time. For example, if you have deployed Analysis Services with the Database Engine in an instance, you must update both.

- Shared features such as Management Tools and Integration Services must be updated to the most recent update. If you have a deployment with two instances on the same host and you want to update only one of them, you must ensure that the update applies to the shared features.

- When installing an instance, you can direct SQL Server to a folder containing update files or have the installation process retrieve updates from the Microsoft Update servers or a local WSUS server. It is also possible to slipstream updates into the SQL Server 2012 installation media.

Prior to deploying updates, you should do the following:

- Back up the master, msdb, and model databases to ensure that you can roll back to a previous configuration if problems occur.

- Back up Analysis Services databases, configuration file, and repository.

- Verify that system databases have sufficient free space if they are not configured for autogrowth. Each system database should have 500 KB or more free space. You can run the sp_spaceused stored procedure on the master and msdb databases to determine the amount of free space available.

- Stop services and applications that make connections to SQL Server 2012 such as SQL Server Management Studio and SQL Server Data Tools.

Remember that each instance on a server has its own separate program files. This means that if you have multiple instances of SQL Server 2012 deployed on the same host server, you must use care when applying updates and service packs. You will need to choose whether to update all instances or only specific instances. You can control which instances you update by using the update's graphical installer. Figure 2-13 shows the application of Service Pack 1 to a SQL Server 2008 R2 deployment when two Database Engine instances are present. SQL Server 2012 will most likely use the same interface.

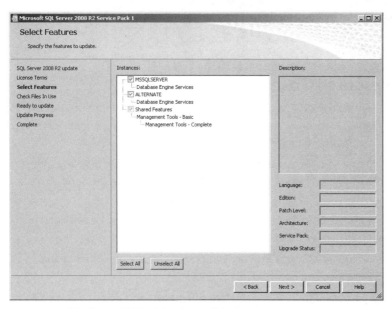

FIGURE 2-13 SQL Server 2008 R2 Service Pack 1

You can also manage which instances you update by launching the update from the command line. To update a single instance of SQL Server 2012 and all shared components, use either the InstanceName parameter or the InstanceID parameter. For example, to update instance ALTERNATE, use:

```
<package_name>.exe /qs /IAcceptSQLServerLicenseTerms /Action=Patch
/InstanceName=ALTERNATE
```

To update all instances of SQL Server 2012 on a host computer and all shared components, use the following command:

```
<package_name>.exe /qs /IAcceptSQLServerLicenseTerms /Action=Patch /AllInstances
```

To update SQL Server shared components only, without updating specific database instances, use the following command:

```
<package_name>.exe /qs /IAcceptSQLServerLicenseTerms /Action=Patch
```

You can also use the command line to remove updates from a specific instance and all shared components. For example, to remove an update from instance ALTERNATE, use:

```
<package_name>.exe /qs /IAcceptSQLServerLicenseTerms /Action=RemovePatch
/InstanceName=ALTERNATE
```

When removing updates, ensure that you remove updates in the reverse of the order in which you applied them. For example, if you applied updates in the sequence A, B, and then C, you'll need to remove them in the sequence C, B, and then A.

> **MORE INFO** **INSTALLING UPDATES**
>
> You can learn more about installing updates at *http://msdn.microsoft.com/en-us/library/dd638066.aspx*.

Configuring Resource Governor

Resource Governor is a SQL Server 2012 feature that enables you to place limits on the consumption of CPU and memory resources within a SQL Server 2012 Database Engine instance. Resource Governor has the following limitations:

- You can use it with the SQL Server Database Engine only. You cannot use Resource Governor to manage system resources for Analysis Services, Integration Services, or Reporting Services.

- You cannot use Resource Governor to perform workload monitoring or workload management between SQL Server Database Engine instances.

- Resource Governor applies only to CPU bandwidth and memory managed by the SQL Server 2012 Database Engine.

- Online transaction processing (OLTP) queries are often short and do not use the CPU long enough for Resource Governor constraints to apply.

You can enable Resource Governor by using the following methods:

- In SQL Server Management Studio, expand the Management node, edit Resource Governor properties, and choose Enable Resource Governor, as shown in Figure 2-14.

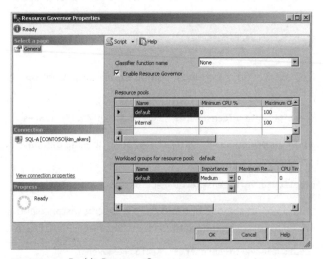

FIGURE 2-14 Enable Resource Governor

- Use the following Transact-SQL statement:

```
ALTER RESOURCE GOVERNOR RECONFIGURE;
GO
```

To disable Resource Governor by using SQL Server Management Studio, edit Resource Governor properties and clear the Enable Resource Governor check box in the Resource Governor Properties dialog box. You can also disable the Resource Governor by using the following Transact-SQL statement:

```
ALTER RESOURCE GOVERNOR DISABLE;
GO
```

> **MORE INFO**   **RESOURCE GOVERNOR**
>
> You can learn more about Resource Governor at *http://msdn.microsoft.com/en-us/library/bb933866(v=SQL.110).aspx.*

Resource Pools

Resource pools represent a subset of the physical resources available to a Database Engine instance of SQL Server 2012. Each resource pool can host one or more *workload groups*. When a session begins, the Resource Governor classifier assigns the session to a workload group. The session runs by using resources assigned to the workload group through the resource pool. SQL Server has two built-in resource pools: the internal and default resource pools. You can add additional user-defined resource pools as necessary. The internal and default resource pools have the following functions:

- *The internal pool* represents the resources the SQL Server instance uses. You cannot alter the internal pool, and the resource consumption of the internal pool is not restricted. Workloads in the internal pool are critical to server function. Resource Governor enables the internal pool to pressure other pools even if it means violating the limits set for those pools.

- The *default pool* is the first predefined user pool. You can modify the default group to add more user-defined groups, but you can't remove the default group.

A resource pool has two components. The first component is exclusive and does not overlap with other pools. This allows for minimum resource reservation for each resource pool. The second component is shared with other pools and is used to define maximum resource consumption. You assign resources by specifying either a minimum (MIN) or a maximum (MAX) for both the processor and memory resources. The sum of MIN values across all resource pools cannot exceed 100% of server resources. The MAX value must be more than the MIN value, up to a value of 100%. If any resource pool is allocated a MIN value, the MAX value for the other pools cannot exceed the sum of the MIN values across all other pools subtracted from 100%. For example, if you set the MIN value for the default pool and for the internal pool to 10%, the MAX value of a third pool would automatically be adjusted to 80% of server resources.

To create a resource pool, perform the following steps:

1. In SQL Server Management Studio, use Object Explorer; right-click the Management \Resource Governor node and choose Properties.

2. In the Resource Pools grid, click the row labeled with an asterisk (*).

3. In the Name column, enter the resource pool name. Choose a minimum or maximum CPU value and a minimum or maximum memory value. Click OK to save changes.

To create a resource pool by using Transact-SQL, use the CREATE RESOURCE POOL statement and specify the appropriate values. Then run the ALTER RESOURCE GOVERNOR RECONFIGURE statement to apply the values. For example, to create a resource pool named poolAlpha and assign it a minimum CPU allocation of 20%, use the following statement:

```
CREATE RESOURCE POOL poolAlpha
WITH (MIN_CPU_PERCENT = 20);
GO
ALTER RESOURCE GOVERNOR RECONFIGURE;
```

> **MORE INFO**   **RESOURCE POOLS**
>
> You can learn more about resource pools at *http://msdn.microsoft.com/en-us/library /hh510189(v=SQL.110).aspx*.

Workload Groups

Workload groups function as containers for session requests that share similar classification criteria. Workload groups are assigned to resource pools. There are two built-in workload groups: the internal group and the default group. It is also possible to create user-defined workload groups. These groups can be moved from the default resource group to user-created resource groups. Requests are classified into the default group under the following circumstances:

- There are no criteria to classify a request.
- A request is classified into a nonexistent workload group.
- There is a classification failure.

To create a workload group by using SQL Server Management Studio, perform the following steps:

1. Navigate to the Management\Resource Governor node in Object Explorer.

2. Right-click the Workload Groups folder under the Resource Pool that will host the workload group you are going to create and then click New Workload Group.

3. In the Workload Groups For Resource Pool grid, enter a name and then configure the values. Figure 2-15 shows a new workload group named groupAlpha. Click OK.

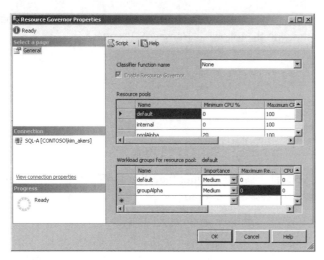

FIGURE 2-15 New Resource Governor workgroup

You can create a workload group by using the CREATE WORKLOAD GROUP Transact-SQL statement and then running the ALTER RESOURCE GOVERNOR RECONFIGURE statement. For example, use the following to create a groupBeta workload group name associated with the poolAlpha pool:

```
CREATE WORKLOAD GROUP groupBeta
USING poolAlpha;
GO
ALTER RESOURCE GOVERNOR RECONFIGURE;
GO
```

> **MORE INFO   WORKLOAD GROUPS**
>
> You can learn more about workload groups at *http://msdn.microsoft.com/en-us/library /hh510228(v=SQL.110).aspx.*

EXAM TIP

Remember the difference between resource pools and workload groups.

Resource Governor Classification

Resource Governor classification allocates incoming sessions to a workload group based on session properties. You can create *classifier functions* as a way of customizing the classification logic. For example, you might create two resource pools, Night and Day. You create similarly named workload groups associated with these resource pools. After these resource pools and workload groups are created, you create a table by which to define the times to be used so that you can allocate sessions that run during the day to Day and sessions that run during the night to Night. You could do this with the following Transact-SQL code:

```
USE master
GO
CREATE TABLE DayOrNight
(
        GroupName       sysname    not null,
        StartTime       time       not null,
        EndTime         time       not null,
)
```

After you create the table, you can insert the values that the classifier will use when assigning a workload group to a particular session. For example:

```
INSERT into DayOrNight VALUES('Day', '6:00 AM', '8:00 PM')
GO
```

When this is in place, you can create a classifier function that will use the information in the table to determine the appropriate workload group. The code for an example function is as follows:

```
CREATE FUNCTION DayNightClassifier()
RETURNS sysname
WITH SCHEMABINDING
AS
BEGIN
        DECLARE @nameGroup sysname
        DECLARE @sessionTime time
        SET @sessionTime = CONVERT(time,GETDATE())
        SELECT TOP 1 @nameGroup = GroupName
                FROM dbo.DayOrNight
                WHERE StartTime <= @sessionTime and EndTime >= @sessionTime
        IF (@nameGroup is not null)
        BEGIN
                RETURN @nameGroup

        END

--- Use default workgroup if no match is found
        RETURN N'Default'
END
GO
```

After you have created the classifier function, register it and then update the in-memory configuration. You can do this for the preceding example by using the following Transact-SQL code:

```
ALTER RESOURCE GOVERNOR with (CLASSIFIER_FUNCTION = dbo.DayNightClassifier)
ALTER RESOURCE GOVERNOR RECONFIGURE
GO
```

MORE INFO   **RESOURCE GOVERNOR CLASSIFICATION**

You can learn more about Resource Governor classification at *http://msdn.microsoft.com /en-us/library/hh510208(v=SQL.110).aspx.*

Using WSRM with Multiple Database Engine Instances

Windows System Resource Manager (WSRM), shown in Figure 2-16, enables you to allocate system resources to specific processes such as different Database Engine instances. This enables you to allocate processor resources to different instances, something you cannot do with Resource Governor because Resource Governor works on a per-instance basis only.

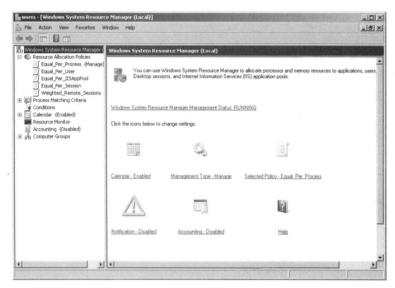

FIGURE 2-16 Windows System Resource Manager (WSRM)

You can install WSRM on computers running the Windows Server 2008 and Windows Server 2008 R2 operating systems. WSRM allows you to manage processor resources by using percent CPU targets or processor affinity rules. Microsoft recommends not using CPU affinity management through WSRM and instead using Database Engine processor affinity. You can, however, use percentage-based resource management, which is useful in situations when a host has access to only a single processor, such as when you deploy multiple instances of the SQL Server Database Engine in a virtual machine.

When you configure percent CPU targets, you allocate a minimum CPU percentage by using one of the following methods:

- **Equal Per Process**   CPU bandwidth is divided evenly across matched processes. This management rule does not allow suballocation.

- **Equal Per User** CPU bandwidth is divided equally across matched processes run by an individual user. This method of resource allocation is less appropriate for distributing CPU bandwidth across Database Engine instances.

- **Equal Per Session** This CPU bandwidth allocation scheme is used with Remote Desktop Services and allocates CPU bandwidth. This method of resource allocation is not appropriate for distributing CPU bandwidth across Database Engine instances.

You should configure per-instance memory limits by editing each instance's properties instead of configuring WSRM to configure memory limits for instances.

Although you can choose to use the Equal Per Process Resource Allocation Policy to balance bandwidth across all processes that demand CPU resources, you could instead configure a custom Resource Allocation policy to balance CPU bandwidth across only SQL Server instances or other SQL-specific processes such as Analysis Services.

To configure a WSRM Resource Allocation policy to manage CPU allocation for SQL Server instances, perform the following general steps:

1. Install the WSRM feature.

2. Open the WSRM console.

3. Select the Process Matching Criteria node. Click New Process Matching Criteria and create a new process-matching criterion for each Database Engine instance or other SQL 2012 process that you want to have WSRM balance. A single process-matching criterion can include multiple services and applications, as shown in Figure 2-17.

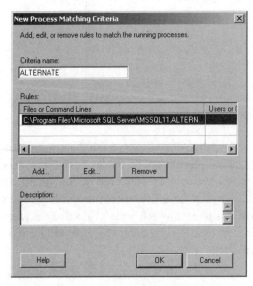

FIGURE 2-17 New Process Matching Criteria

Click Resource Allocation Policies and choose New Resource Allocation Policy. Provide a policy name and add the process-matching criteria for each SQL instance. Figure 2-18 shows a custom resource allocation policy in which the default and alternate instances have been allocated 45% CPU bandwidth.

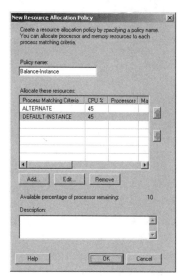

FIGURE 2-18 Custom Resource Allocation Policy page

4. Set the custom resource allocation policy as the managing policy.

MORE INFO **WINDOWS SERVER RESOURCE MANAGER**

You can learn more about WSRM at *http://technet.microsoft.com/en-us/library /cc753280(WS.10).aspx.*

Cycle SQL Server Error Logs

The SQL Server error log stores information about processes that have completed successfully such as backup operations, batch commands, and scripts. It also stores system information messages indicating issues or failures. Each time the Database Engine instance is started, the current error log cycles and is renamed errorlog.1. The file named errorlog.1 becomes errorlog.2, errorlog.2 becomes errorlog.3, and so on until errorlog.6. SQL Server 2012 default settings retain the current error log and the five most recent error logs. To modify the number of error logs stored, use SQL Server Management Studio to right-click the Management \SQL Server Logs node, select Limit The Number Of Error Logs Before They Are Cycled, and select the maximum number of error logs, as shown in Figure 2-19. The maximum number of error logs that you can keep is 99.

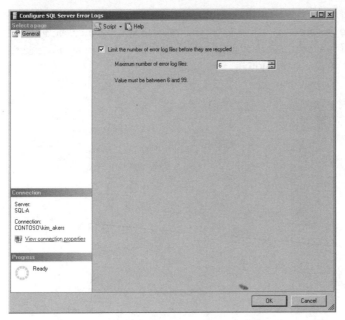

FIGURE 2-19 Error logs stored

Members of the sysadmin fixed server role are able to trigger the error log to cycle by running the sp_cycle_errorlog stored procedure. For example, you can force the error log to cycle without restarting the Database Engine instance by running the following Transact-SQL code:

```
EXEC sp_cycle_errorlog;
GO
```

A similar stored procedure exists that enables you to cycle the SQL Server Agent error log file. You must run the sp_cycle_agent_errorlog stored procedure from the msdb database. You can accomplish this by using the following Transact-SQL code:

```
USE msdb;
GO
EXEC dbo.sp_cycle_agent_errorlog;
GO
```

> **MORE INFO** **SP_CYCLE_ERRORLOG**
>
> You can learn more about sp_cycle_errorlog at *http://msdn.microsoft.com/en-us/library /ms182512(v=SQL.110).aspx.*

PRACTICE **Deploy and Configure Additional SQL Server 2012 Instances**

In this practice, apply what you learned about deploying an instance.

EXERCISE 1   Deploy Additional Instances on Computers SQL-A, SQL-B, and SQL-CORE

In this exercise, you install additional instances of the SQL Server Database Engine on computers SQL-A, SQL-B, and SQL CORE. To complete this exercise, perform the following steps:

1. Log on to computer SQL-A with the Kim_Akers user account.

2. Use SQL Server Installation Center to install a new Database Engine instance named **ALTERNATE** with the default settings.

3. Log on to computer SQL-B with the Kim_Akers user account.

4. From an elevated command prompt, install a new Database Engine instance named **ALTERNATE** with the default settings.

5. Log on to computer SQL-CORE with the Kim_Akers user account.

6. From the command prompt, install a new Database Engine instance named **ALTERNATE** with the default settings.

7. Log on to server DC. Edit the SQL-POLICY GPO. Create an inbound rule in the Windows Firewall With Advanced Security node in the Computer Configuration\Policies\Windows Settings\Security Settings node. This inbound rule should have the following properties:

    ■ Program Rule

    ■ Program Path: C:\Program Files\Microsoft SQL Server\MSSQL11.ALTERNATE \MSSQL\Binn\sqlservr.exe

    ■ Allow the connection

    ■ Domain, Private, and Public profiles

    ■ Name: SQL-AlternateManagement-Inbound

8. Right-click the SQL-AlternateManagement-Inbound rule. On the Scope tab, in the Remote IP Address section, select These IP Addresses and enter the **10.10.10.0/24** subnet.

EXERCISE 2   Resource Governor Configuration

In this exercise, you configure Resource Governor on instance SQL-A\Alternate. To complete this exercise, perform the following steps:

1. Log on to server SQL-A and use SQL Server Management Studio to connect to instance ALTERNATE.

2. Enable Resource Governor on instance ALTERNATE.

3. Use appropriate Transact-SQL code to create a resource pool named **poolAlpha**. Set the minimum CPU allocation for this pool to 5%.

4. Use appropriate Transact-SQL code to create a Workload Group named **workAlpha** associated with pool poolAlpha.

EXERCISE 3   Error Log Configuration

In this exercise, you reconfigure the properties of the SQL Server error log so that the last 20 error logs are kept and then you cycle the log. To complete this exercise, perform the following steps:

1. Connect to the SQL-A\ALTERNATE instance by using SQL Server Management Studio.

2. Configure the SQL Server error log so that 20 error log files will be kept before being recycled.

3. Use Transact-SQL to cycle the SQL Server error log.

Lesson Summary

- SQL Server 2012 supports up to 50 instances on a single host and up to 25 instances on a failover cluster.

- You must update all features associated with a SQL Server 2012 instance at the same time.

- Shared features must be updated to the most recent update.

- Run a software update with the /InstanceName parameter to update a specific instance; run the update with the /AllInstances parameter to update all instances.

- Resource Governor enables you to manage processing and memory resources within a Database Engine instance.

- You cannot use Resource Governor to manage Analysis Services, Integration Services, or Reporting Services.

- Resource pools host workload groups. The categorizer assigns particular sessions to workload groups.

- You assign resources to a resource pool by specifying either a minimum or maximum value for both the processor and memory resources.

- Windows System Resource Monitor enables you to manage and allocate processor and memory resources across instances.

- You can use the sp_cycle_errorlog stored procedure to cycle the SQL Server error log.

- You can use sp_cycle_agent_errorlog from the msdb system database to cycle the SQL Server Agent error log.

Lesson Review

Answer the following questions to test your knowledge of the information in this lesson. You can find the answers to these questions and explanations of why each answer choice is correct or incorrect in the "Answers" section at the end of this chapter.

1. You want to cycle the SQL Server Agent error log. From which of the following system databases must you run the sp_cycle_agent_errorlog stored procedure to accomplish this goal?

A. master

B. msdb

C. model

D. tempdb

2. Which feature should you enable and configure so session requests addressed to a specific instance can be allocated different processor resources based on session request properties?

   A. Resource Governor

   B. Windows System Resource Manager

   C. Processor affinity

   D. I/O affinity

3. What is the maximum number of SQL Server 2012 Enterprise edition Database Engine instances that you can deploy on a non-clustered server running Windows Server 2008 R2 Enterprise edition?

   A. 10

   B. 25

   C. 50

   D. 100

4. You have configured Resource Governor with three resource pools. You have assigned the first resource pool a minimum CPU and memory value of 20%. You have assigned the second resource pool a minimum CPU and memory value of 30%. You want to assign maximum CPU and memory values to the third resource pool. What is the maximum CPU and memory value you can assign to this resource pool?

   A. 30%

   B. 50%

   C. 70%

   D. 100%

5. A server that has four processors has three SQL Server 2012 Database Engine instances installed. Which feature should you configure to assign 60% of a host server's processor resource to the first instance, 20% to the second instance, and 15% to the third instance?

   A. Resource Governor

   B. Windows System Resource Manager

   C. Processor affinity

   D. I/O affinity

Case Scenarios

In the following case scenarios, apply what you have learned about planning server installs and upgrades. You can find answers to these questions in the "Answers" section at the end of this chapter.

Case Scenario 1: Instance Configuration

You are preparing a server running Windows Server 2008 R2 on which you have installed three SQL 2012 Database Engine instances. These are the default instance, Instance-A, and Instance-B. The host server has 32 GB of RAM. The host server has eight processor cores.

You want to ensure that Instance-A is configured in the following way:

- Minimum server memory: 512 MB
- Maximum server memory: 8,192 MB
- Affinity for CPUs 0 and 1
- Default fill factor of 95%

With this information in mind, answer the following questions:

1. What Transact-SQL code should you use to configure the minimum and maximum memory settings when connected to Instance-A in SQL Server Management Studio?

2. What Transact-SQL code should you use to configure the appropriate processor affinity when connected to Instance-A in SQL Server Management Studio?

3. What Transact-SQL code should you use to configure the appropriate fill factor when connected to Instance-A in SQL Server Management Studio?

Case Scenario 2: Additional Instances and Error Log Cycling

You are updating a computer hosting a SQL Server 2012 instance at a remote branch office. You want to add a new instance to the server and name this instance MELBOURNE. You also want to cycle the SQL Server error log and SQL Server Agent error log manually. With this in mind, answer the following questions:

1. Which command-line command would you use to add the new instance if you wanted to configure the account ADATUM\sam_abolrous as a SQL Server Administrator?

2. Which Transact-SQL statement should you use to cycle the SQL Server Agent error log?

3. Which Transact-SQL statement should you use to cycle the SQL Server error log?

Suggested Practices

To help you successfully master the exam objectives presented in this chapter, complete the following tasks.

Configure Instances

Prior to completing each task in the following practices, list the steps you would take to accomplish the task. After completing the task, assess how accurately you predicted the necessary steps.

- **Practice 1**   Configure the appropriate system database on the ALTERNATE instance on SQL-B so that newly created databases on that instance will use the simple recovery model.
- **Practice 2**   Configure the ALTERNATE instance to use a minimum server memory of 512 MB on servers SQL-A and SQL-B.

Install and Manage Multiple Instances

Prior to completing each task in the following practices, list the steps you would take to accomplish the task. After completing the task, assess how accurately you predicted the necessary steps.

- **Practice 1**   Add an additional Database Engine instance to SQL-A, SQL-B, and SQL-CORE named **DEVELOPMENT**.
- **Practice 2**   Install WSRM on SQL-B. Configure three process-matching criteria for each instance installed on the server. Create but do not apply a custom resource allocation policy that assigns 30% processor resources to each of the three process-matching criteria representing Database Engine instances.

Answers

This section contains the answers to the lesson review questions and solutions to the case scenarios in this chapter.

Lesson 1

1. **Correct Answer: A**

   A. **Correct:** The ALTER SERVER CONFIGURATION SET PROCESS AFFINITY CPU = AUTO statement will configure the instance to use all available processors.

   B. **Incorrect:** The ALTER SERVER CONFIGURATION SET PROCESS AFFINITY CPU = 2,3 statement will configure the instance to use processors 2 and 3 instead of all available processors.

   C. **Incorrect:** The ALTER SERVER CONFIGURATION SET PROCESS AFFINITY CPU = 0,1 statement will configure the instance to use processors 0 and 1 instead of all available processors.

   D. **Incorrect:** The ALTER SERVER CONFIGURATION SET PROCESS AFFINITY CPU = 0,4 statement will configure the instance to use processors 0 and 4 instead of all available processors.

2. **Correct Answers: A and D**

   A. **Correct:** You need to execute the statement:

   ```
   RECONFIGURE;
   GO
   ```

   To reconfigure the instance to use the new maximum server memory setting.

   B. **Incorrect:** You should not execute the statement:

   ```
   EXEC sys.sp_configure 'min server memory', 1024;
   GO
   ```

   This statement configures the minimum rather than the maximum instance memory.

   C. **Incorrect:** You should not execute the statement:

   ```
   EXEC sys.sp_configure 'min server memory', 4096;
   GO
   ```

   This statement configures the minimum rather than the maximum instance memory.

   D. **Correct:** You need to execute the statement:

   ```
   EXEC sys.sp_configure 'max server memory', 4096;
   GO
   ```

   This statement correctly configures the maximum instance memory.

3. **Correct Answer: D**

   A. **Incorrect:** Minimum server memory enables you to specify a minimum amount of memory allocated to the instance.

   B. **Incorrect:** Maximum server memory enables you to specify a maximum amount of memory allocated to the instance.

   C. **Incorrect:** Processor affinity enables you to bind instance CPU traffic to specific processes but not to disk I/O activity.

   D. **Correct:** I/O affinity enables you to bind disk input/output operations to a specific processor.

4. **Correct Answer: B**

   A. **Incorrect:** The master system database records all system-level information.

   B. **Correct:** The model system database is used as a template for all newly created databases.

   C. **Incorrect:** The msdb system database is used by SQL Server Agent for scheduling alerts and jobs.

   D. **Incorrect:** The tempdb system database holds temporary objects and intermediate result sets.

5. **Correct Answer: A**

   A. **Correct:** You use sp_configure to enable Database Mail on an SQL instance.

   B. **Incorrect:** Use the sp_rename stored procedure to change the name of a user-created object in the current database.

   C. **Incorrect:** Use the sp_monitor stored procedure to display statistics about SQL Server.

   D. **Incorrect:** Use the sp_depends stored procedure to display information about database object dependencies.

Lesson 2

1. **Correct Answer: B**

   A. **Incorrect:** You must run the sp_cycle_agent_errorlog stored procedure from the msdb system database rather than from the master system database.

   B. **Correct:** You must run the sp_cycle_agent_errorlog stored procedure from the msdb system database to rotate the SQL Server Agent error log file.

   C. **Incorrect:** You must run the sp_cycle_agent_errorlog stored procedure from the msdb system database rather than from the model system database.

   D. **Incorrect:** You must run the sp_cycle_agent_errorlog stored procedure from the msdb system database rather than from the tempdb system database.

2. **Correct Answer: A**

   A. **Correct:** Resource Governor enables you to allocate session requests to different resources based on the characteristics of the session request properties.

   B. **Incorrect:** WSRM enables you to allocate different resources to different instances but does not enable you to allocate different resources based on session requests.

   C. **Incorrect:** Processor affinity enables you to configure the instance to use specific processors but does not enable you to differentiate resources based on session request properties.

   D. **Incorrect:** I/O affinity enables you to configure disk I/O to occur by using a specific processor but does not allow you to differentiate resources based on session request properties.

3. **Correct Answer: C**

   A. **Incorrect:** You can deploy a maximum of 50 SQL Server 2012 Database Engine instances on a non-clustered server running Windows Server 2008 R2 Enterprise. Ten instances is fewer than 50.

   B. **Incorrect:** You can deploy a maximum of 50 SQL Server 2012 Database Engine instances on a non-clustered server running Windows Server 2008 R2 Enterprise. A 25-instance limit applies to deployment on clustered hosts. Twenty-five instances in a non-clustered environment is fewer than 50.

   C. **Correct:** You can deploy a maximum of 50 SQL Server 2012 Database Engine instances on a non-clustered server running Windows Server 2008 R2 Enterprise.

   D. **Incorrect:** You can deploy a maximum of 50 SQL Server 2012 Database Engine instances on a non-clustered server running Windows Server 2008 R2 Enterprise. One hundred instances exceeds this value.

4. **Correct Answer: B**

   A. **Incorrect:** The maximum resource value assigned to the third pool is 100%; the sum of the minimum resource values assigned to the other pools is 50%. Thirty percent is less than this value.

   B. **Correct:** The maximum resource value assigned to the third pool is 100%; the sum of the minimum resource values assigned to the other pools is 50%.

   C. **Incorrect:** The maximum resource value assigned to the third pool is 100%; the sum of the minimum resource values assigned to the other pools is 50%. You cannot assign 70% to this pool.

   D. **Incorrect:** The maximum resource value assigned to the third pool is 100%; the sum of the minimum resource values assigned to the other pools is 50%. You cannot assign 100% to this pool.

5. **Correct Answer: B**

   A. **Incorrect:** You can use Resource Governor to assign resources only from within an instance. You cannot use it to assign resources across instances.

   B. **Correct:** You can use WSRM to assign processor resources to different instances.

   C. **Incorrect:** Although you can use processor affinity to assign resources, by using processors it is only possible to assign resources to instances in lots of 25% of the total CPU bandwidth. This does not meet the requirements of the question; hence, you should use WSRM.

   D. **Incorrect:** I/O affinity enables you to assign dedicated processors to disk I/O. You can't use this for distributing CPU bandwidth across instances.

Case Scenario 1

1. Use the following Transact-SQL code when connected to Instance-A in SQL Server Management Studio to configure the instance to use a minimum server memory of 512 MB and a maximum server memory of 8192 MB.

```
EXEC sys.sp_configure 'show advanced options', 1;
GO
RECONFIGURE;
GO
EXEC sys.sp_configure 'min server memory', 512;
GO
EXEC sys.sp_configure 'max server memory', 8192;
GO
RECONFIGURE;
GO
```

2. Use the following Transact-SQL code when connected to Instance-A in SQL Server Management Studio to configure processor affinity for CPU 0 and 1.

```
ALTER SERVER CONFIGURATION SET PROCESS AFFINITY CPU = 0,1
```

3. Use the following Transact-SQL code when connected to Instance-A in SQL Server Management Studio to set the default fill factor to 95%.

```
sp_configure 'show advanced options', 1;
GO
RECONFIGURE;
GO
sp_configure 'fill factor', 95;
GO
RECONFIGURE;
GO
```

Case Scenario 2

1. Use the following command-line command to install the MELBOURNE instance and set the account ADATUM\sam_abolrous as the SQL Server Administrator:

```
Setup.exe /qs /Action=Install /Features=SQLEngine /InstanceName=Melbourne
/SQLSYSADMINACCOUNTS="adatum\sam_abolrous" /IAcceptSQLServerLicenseTerms
```

2. You should use the following statement, remembering that the stored procedure needs to be executed from the msdb system database, to cycle the agent error log:

```
USE msdb;
GO
EXEC dbo.sp_cycle_agent_errorlog;
GO
```

3. You should use the following statement to cycle the SQL Server error log:

```
EXEC sp_cycle_errorlog;
GO
```

CHAPTER 3

Configuring SQL Server 2012 Components

Exam objectives in this chapter:

- Configure additional SQL Server components.
- Manage and configure databases.

Microsoft SQL Server 2012 database administrators (DBAs) must be able to deploy not only the Database Engine but also Analysis Services and Reporting Services in either Native or SharePoint integrated mode. In this chapter, you learn about the new FileTable feature and configuring Integration Services security and support for FILESTREAM. As a DBA, you must also know how to create full-text indexes, design filegroups, partition tables and indexes, and how to configure transparent data encryption and data compression.

Lessons in this chapter:

Before You Begin

To complete the practice exercises in this chapter, you must have:

- Completed the setup tasks for installing computers DC, SQL-A, SQL-B, and SQL-CORE as outlined in the introduction of this book.
- Completed the setup tasks outlined in the end-of-lesson practice exercises in Chapter 1, "Planning and Installing SQL Server 2012," and Chapter 2, "Configuring and Managing SQL Server Instances."

No additional configuration is required for this chapter.

Lesson 1: Configuring Additional SQL Server Components

SQL Server 2012 is more than just the Database Engine. In this lesson, you learn how to deploy SQL Server 2012 Analysis Services, Reporting Services, SharePoint integration, full-text indexing, and SQL Server Integration Services and how to configure the FILESTREAM and FileTable features.

> **After this lesson, you will be able to:**
> - Deploy and configure Analysis Services.
> - Deploy and configure Reporting Services.
> - Deploy and configure SharePoint integration.
> - Manage full-text indexing.
> - Configure SQL Server Integration Services security.
> - Configure FILESTREAM and FileTable.
>
> **Estimated lesson time: 60 minutes**

Deploying and Configuring Analysis Services

When installing Analysis Services, you can choose whether to install it in *multidimensional mode* and *data mining mode* or in *tabular mode*, as shown in Figure 3-1. Mode is specific to an instance, and if you want to use more than one mode, it is necessary to install more than one Analysis Services instance. The difference between these modes is as follows:

- **Multidimensional and data mining mode**   The default Analysis Services mode. Supports online analytical processing (OLAP) databases and data mining models.
- **Tabular mode**   Supports new tabular modeling features. When installed using this mode, Analysis Services can host solutions built in the tabular model designer. Analysis Services in tabular mode is necessary when you want tabular model data access over a network.

You can install Analysis Services from the command line by using the /FEATURES=AS option. The /ASSERVERMODE can be set to MULTIDIMENSIONAL, TABULAR, or POWERPIVOT. For example, to create an instance named ASMulti with Analysis Services installed in multidimensional and data mining mode and configuring the Analysis Services service account as contoso\asaccount, and with contoso\kim_akers as the Analysis Services Administrator account, use the following command:

```
Setup.exe /q /IAcceptSQLServerLicenseTerms /Action=install /Features=AS
/ASSERVERMODE=MULTIDIMENSIONAL /INSTANCENAME=ASMulti /ASSVCACCOUNT=Contoso\kim_akers
/ASSYSADMINACCOUNTS=contoso\kim_akers
```

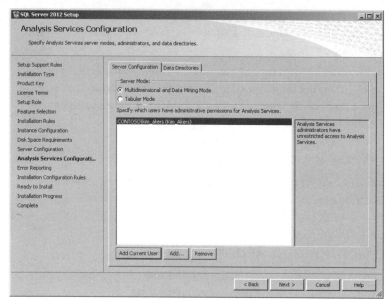

FIGURE 3-1 Multidimensional and data mining mode or tabular mode

To create an instance named ASTabular with Analysis Services installed in tabular mode, with the Analysis Services service account as NetworkService, and with contoso\kim_akers as the Analysis Services Administrator account, use the following command:

```
Setup.exe /q /IAcceptSQLServerLicenseTerms /Action=install /Features=AS
/ASSERVERMODE=TABULAR /INSTANCENAME=ASTabular /ASSVCACCOUNT=NetworkService
/ASSYSADMINACCOUNTS=contoso\kim_akers
```

Although the option isn't available in the dialog box displayed in Figure 3-1, you can also deploy Analysis Services in PowerPivot for SharePoint mode by using the /ASSSERVERMODE=POWERPIVOT installation option.

> **MORE INFO**   **INSTALLING ANALYSIS SERVICES**
>
> You can learn more about installing Analysis Services at *http://msdn.microsoft.com/en-us /library/hh231722(SQL.110).aspx*.

Analysis Services uses a managed service account when installed by default. You can also configure Analysis Services to use a domain or local user account:

- If Analysis Services will connect to network resources in the security context of the logon account, create a specific domain user account for use with Analysis Services. You can also use the NetworkService account. When you use this account, the account presents the local computer's credentials to remote servers. To grant access to this account, use the Computer account of the Analysis Server host.

- If Analysis Services will not connect to external network resources, Analysis Services can be run using a local user account, a domain user account, a virtual account, or a managed service account.

Best practice is to run Analysis Services by using an account assigned the fewest possible privileges. You should avoid using the LocalService and NetworkService accounts in high-security environments because Analysis Services connection strings and passwords can be decrypted and are accessible to the Analysis Services logon account.

> **MORE INFO**   **ANALYSIS SERVICES ACCOUNTS**
>
> You can learn more about Analysis Services accounts at *http://msdn.microsoft.com/en-us /library/ms174905(SQL.110).aspx.*

Deploying and Configuring Reporting Services

To install a SQL Server Reporting Services (SSRS) Native Mode Report Server–only instance by using SQL Server Installation Center, perform the following general steps:

1. Open SQL Server Installation Center from the Configuration Tools folder.
2. Click Installation and then choose New SQL Server Stand-Alone Installation Or Add Features To An Existing Installation. Specify the location of the SQL Server 2012 installation files.
3. Click OK after the Setup Support Rules check runs.
4. Click Next on the Product Updates page.
5. Click Next on the Setup Support Rule page.
6. On the Installation Type page, choose Perform A New Installation Of SQL Server 2012.
7. On the Product Key page, enter the product key.
8. On the License Terms page, choose I Accept The License Terms.
9. On the Setup Role page, choose SQL Server Feature Installation.
10. On the Feature Selection page, choose Reporting Services - Native And Database Engine Services shown in Figure 3-2, and then click Next.

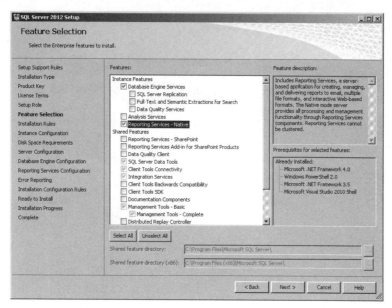

FIGURE 3-2 Install Reporting Services

11. On the Installation Rules page, click Next.

12. On the Instance Configuration page, provide a name for the Reporting Services instance.

13. On the Disk Space Requirements page, click Next.

14. On the Service Accounts page, review the Service Account configuration and then click Next.

15. On the Database Engine Configuration page, add the users who will hold the SQL Server Administrative role and then click Next.

16. On the Reporting Services Configuration page, shown in Figure 3-3, choose Install And Configure. You'll have this option only if you have already installed the necessary Web Server components.

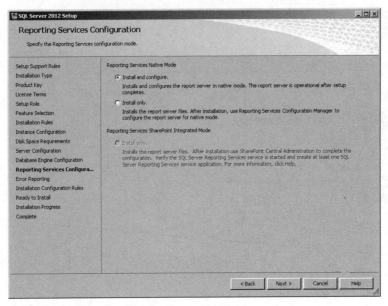

FIGURE 3-3 Install and configure Reporting Services

17. On the Error Reporting page, click Next twice and then choose Install. Click Close to dismiss the Setup Wizard.

EXAM TIP

You can choose the Install And Configure option only if you have installed the web server role prior to attempting to install the Report Server instance and you are also installing the Database Engine on the same instance.

To install Reporting Services in the default configuration for native mode from the command line from the command prompt, by using the NetworkService account for both the Reporting Services service account and the SQL Server service account and assigning members of BUILTIN\ADMINISTRATORS SQL Server system administrator access, and by using the instance named RPTSVR, use the following command:

```
setup /q /IAcceptSQLServerLicenseTerms /ACTION=install /FEATURES=SQL,RS,TOOLS
/INSTANCENAME=RPTSVR /SQLSYSADMINACCOUNTS="BUILTIN\ADMINISTRATORS"
/RSSVCACCOUNT=NetworkService /SQLSVCACCOUNT=NetworkService /AGTSVCACCOUNT=NetworkService
/RSSVCSTARTUPTYPE="Manual" /RSINSTALLMODE="DefaultNativeMode"
```

MORE INFO   REPORTING SERVICES

You can learn more about installing Reporting Services at *http://msdn.microsoft.com /en-us/library/ms143711(SQL.110).aspx.*

If you install Reporting Services Configuration Manager by using the Install And Configure option, Reporting Services is already configured for you. If you install Reporting Services by using the files-only installation option, you must run Reporting Services Configuration Manager, shown in Figure 3-4, to configure Reporting Services.

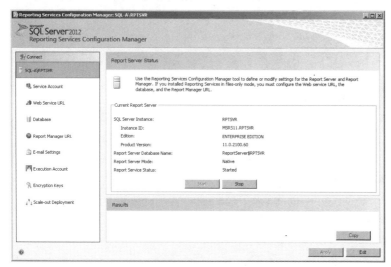

FIGURE 3-4 Reporting Services Configuration Manager

Using Reporting Services Configuration Manager, which you can launch from the Configuration menu, you can perform the following tasks:

- Configure the Reporting Services service account.

- Configure the Web Service URL, including Virtual directory, IP Address, TCP Port, SSL Certificate, and SSL Port.

- Configure the Report Server Database and database credential.

- Configure the Report Manager URL.

- Configure email settings, including Sender Address, Current SMTP Delivery Method, and SMTP Server.

- Configure the Execution Account. This is usually a domain account with minimal permissions that is used for retrieving external report data sources that do not require authentication and for unattended report processing.

- Configure Backup And Restore and update Reporting Services encryption keys.

- Configure Scale-out Deployment.

MORE INFO **REPORTING SERVICES CONFIGURATION**

You can learn more about Reporting Services Configuration at *http://msdn.microsoft.com /en-us/library/ms157412(SQL.110).aspx.*

Deploying and Configuring SharePoint Integration

You can deploy Analysis Services and Reporting Services as shared services in a SharePoint farm. Deploying Analysis Services and Reporting Services enables you to use features such as PowerPivot for Microsoft SharePoint and Power View, a Reporting Services interactive report designer.

To deploy Reporting Services, Power View, and PowerPivot for SharePoint, you must install the following products:

- SharePoint Server 2010 Enterprise edition with Service Pack 1
- SQL Server 2012 Database Engine
- SQL Server 2012 Reporting Services and Reporting Services Add-in
- SQL Server 2012 PowerPivot for SharePoint

The host computer must be joined to the domain, and you must configure domain user accounts for the following services:

- SharePoint Web Services and Administrative Services
- Reporting Services
- Analysis Services
- Microsoft Excel Services
- Secure Store Services
- PowerPivot System Service

The SQL Server 2012 Database Engine can use a Virtual or Managed service account. To configure SharePoint 2010 and SQL Server 2012 integration, perform the following general steps:

1. Install a SharePoint Server 2010 SP1 Enterprise edition farm. Choose to configure the farm later by not running the SharePoint 2010 Product Configuration Wizard. This enables you to use the SQL Server 2012 Database Engine as the farm's database server.

2. Install the SQL Server 2012 Database Engine and PowerPivot for SharePoint, as shown in Figure 3-5.

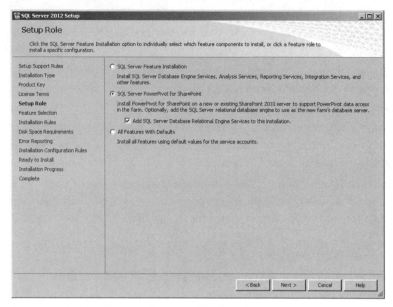

FIGURE 3-5 Install SQL Server PowerPivot for SharePoint

3. Accept the default instance ID of PowerPivot and complete the SQL Server 2012 Installation Wizard.

4. Use the PowerPivot Configuration tool, available from the Configuration Tools folder and shown in Figure 3-6, to create the farm, a default web application, and a root site collection.

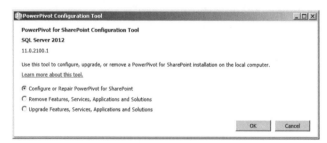

FIGURE 3-6 PowerPivot Configuration Tool

5. Verify that the farm is operational by navigating to Central Administration.

6. Run SQL Server 2012 setup again to install and configure Reporting Services and the Reporting Services Add-in.

7. SharePoint Site Administrators can extend SharePoint document libraries to use Business Intelligence (BI) content types. This can be done by performing the following steps:

   A. In Shared Documents or another document library, on the Library tab, click Library Settings. Under General Settings, click Advanced Settings. In Content Types, click Yes to enable management of content types.

   B. On the Library tab, click Library Settings. Under Content Types, click Add From Existing Site Content Types. Locate the Business Intelligence content type group and add BI Semantic Model Connection File and Report Data Source.

8. SharePoint Site Administrators create data connection files to launch Power View. This involves creating a BI semantic model connection (.bism) or a Reporting Services shared data source (.rsds) as a data source for Power View.

> **MORE INFO   SHAREPOINT INTEGRATION**
>
> You can learn more about SharePoint 2010 integration with SQL Server 2012 at
> *http://msdn.microsoft.com/en-us/library/hh231671(SQL.110).aspx.*

 Quick Check

- Which mode should you select during the installation of Analysis Services if you want to support OLAP databases?

Quick Check Answer

- You should install Analysis Services in multidimensional and data mining mode if you want to use OLAP databases.

Configuring SQL Server Integration Services Security

Integration Services enables you to run and schedule Integration Services packages in SQL Server Management Studio. You can install Integration Services only once on a computer, even if that computer hosts multiple instances. You can install Integration Services as a shared feature in the SQL Server Setup Wizard or install it from the command line by issuing the following command:

```
Setup.exe /q /IAcceptSQLServerLicenseTerms /Action=Install /Features=IS
```

In previous versions of SQL Server, all users in the Users group could access the Integration Services service. In SQL Server 2012, the service is secure by default; and, by default, only the built-in Administrators group can run Integration Services. You must use the DCOM

Configuration tool (dcomcnfg.exe) to grant specific users access to SQL Server Integration Services (SSIS). To do this, perform the following steps:

1. Run Dcomcnfg.exe from the Search Programs and Files text box.

2. Expand the Component Services, Computers, My Computer, and DCOM Config nodes.

3. Right-click Microsoft SQL Server Integration Services 11.0 and choose Properties.

4. On the Security tab, shown in Figure 3-7, click Edit in Launch And Activation Permissions.

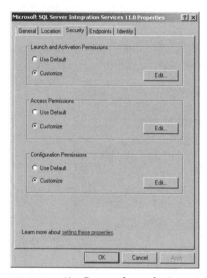

FIGURE 3-7 Use Dcomcnfg.exe for Integration Services permissions

5. Add users and assign permissions. You can assign the following permissions:

- Local Launch
- Remote Launch
- Local Activation
- Remote Activation

MORE INFO   INTEGRATION SERVICES

You can learn more about Integration Services at *http://msdn.microsoft.com/en-us/library /ms143731(SQL.110).aspx.*

Managing Full-Text Indexing

Full-text indexes store information about significant words and their location within the columns of a database table. In SQL Server 2012, the Full-Text Engine is part of the SQL Server process rather than a separate service. Only one full-text index can be created per table or indexed view. A full-text index can contain up to 1,024 columns.

To create a full-text index by using SQL Server Management Studio, perform the following steps:

1. Right-click the table on which you want to create a new full-text index and choose Design.

2. From the Table Designer menu, click Full-Text Index to open the Full-Text Index dialog box. Click Add. Configure the properties of the index as shown in Figure 3-8.

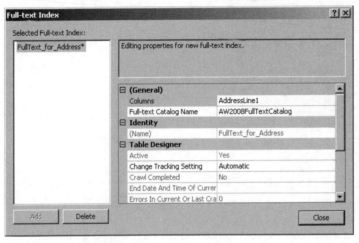

FIGURE 3-8 Full-text Index

As an alternative to using the Table Designer, you can run the Full-Text Indexing Wizard by performing the following steps:

1. Right-click the table for which you want to configure the full-text index, choosing Full-Text Index and then Define Full-Text Index. This launches the Full-Text Indexing Wizard.

2. On the Select An Index page, choose a unique index for the table.

3. On the Select Table Columns page, choose the columns you want to be eligible for full-text queries, as shown in Figure 3-9.

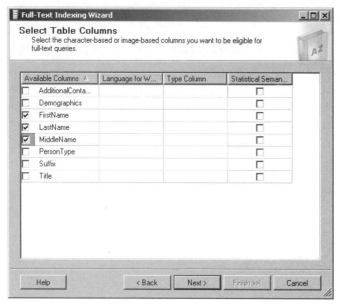

FIGURE 3-9 Full-text index columns

4. On the Select Change Tracking page, choose whether to track changes as they occur, to track them manually, or not to track changes.

5. On the Select Catalog, Index Filegroup, And Stoplist page, you can choose to use an existing full-text catalog or create a new catalog. You can also select the index file-group and the full-text stoplist. Figure 3-10 shows the creation of a new catalog named NEWCATALOG.

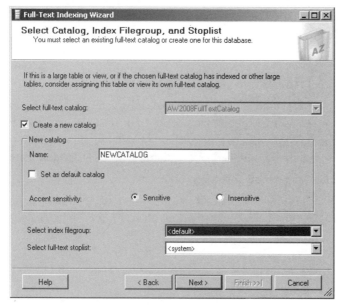

FIGURE 3-10 New full-text catalog

6. On the Define Population Schedules page, you can specify a population schedule for the full-text catalog.

7. On the Summary page, click Finish to complete creation of the new full-text index.

You can use the CREATE FULLTEXT INDEX statement to create a full-text index on a table. For example, to create a FULLTEXT index on the Production.ProductReview table in the AdventureWorks2012 database by using the ReviewerName, EmailAddress, and Comments columns in the existing unique key index PK_ProductReview_ProductReviewID while also creating a FULLTEXT catalog called production_catalog, use the following statement:

```
USE AdventureWorks2012;
GO
CREATE FULLTEXT CATALOG production_catalog;
GO
CREATE FULLTEXT INDEX ON Production.ProductReview
(
ReviewerName, EmailAddress, Comments
)
KEY INDEX PK_ProductReview_ProductReviewID
ON production_catalog;
GO
```

To delete a full-text index, right-click the table that hosts the full-text index, choose Full-Text Index, and then select Delete Full-Text Index. You can also delete a full-text index by using the DROP FULLTEXT INDEX statement. For example, to drop the index created in the previous example, use the query:

```
DROP FULLTEXT INDEX ON Production.ProductReview
```

> **MORE INFO** **FULL-TEXT INDEXES**
>
> You can learn more about full-text indexes at *http://msdn.microsoft.com/en-us/library /cc879306(v=SQL.110).aspx.*

Configuring FILESTREAM

FILESTREAM enables SQL Server–based applications to store unstructured data, such as images and documents, on the host computer's file system. To use FILESTREAM, you must create or modify a database to host a special type of filegroup, after which you can create or modify tables so that they can use the varbinary(max) column with the FILESTREAM attribute.

You should use FILESTREAM under the following conditions:

- Objects that you want to store are greater than 1 MB. The traditional varbinary(max) limit of 2 GB does not apply to BLOBs (binary large objects) stored in the file system.

- Fast read access is important.

For objects smaller than 1 MB, use the varbinary(max) BLOB data type. You can't enable FILESTREAM if you are running a 32-bit version of SQL Server 2012 on a 64-bit operating system.

To enable FILESTREAM, perform the following steps:

1. Open SQL Server Configuration Manager from the Configuration Tools folder.

2. Edit the properties of the instance on which you want to enable FILESTREAM.

3. On the FILESTREAM tab, select Enable FILESTREAM For Transact-SQL Access. You can also use this dialog box to enable FILESTREAM for file I/O streaming access and to allow remote clients access to FILESTREAM data, as shown in Figure 3-11.

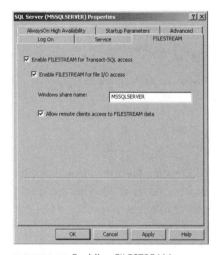

FIGURE 3-11 Enabling FILESTREAM

4. In SQL Server Management Studio, execute the following query:

```
EXEC sp_configure filestream_access_level, 2
RECONFIGURE
```

> **NOTE   FILESTREAM_ACCESS_LEVEL**
>
> Setting filestream_access_level to 0 disables FILESTREAM access. Setting level 1 allows Transact-SQL only. Setting level 2 allows Transact-SQL and Win32 streaming.

5. Restart the SQL Server Service related to the instance on which you are enabling FILESTREAM by using SQL Server Configuration Manager.

6. Create a FILESTREAM filegroup for the database. For example, to create a FILESTREAM filegroup named FileStreamFileGroup for the Litware2012 database, use the following query:

```
USE master
GO
```

```
ALTER DATABASE Litware2012 ADD
FILEGROUP FileStreamFileGroup CONTAINS FILESTREAM;
GO
```

7. Add FILESTREAM files to the FILESTREAM filegroup by specifying a folder location that does not currently exist. For example, to create and associate the C:\FSTRM directory with the FILESTREAM file named FileStrmFile in the FileStreamFileGroup FILESTREAM filegroup for the Litware2012 database, use the following query:

```
USE master
GO
ALTER DATABASE Litware2012 ADD FILE (
NAME = FileStrmFile,
FILENAME = 'C:\FSTRM')
TO FILEGROUP FileStreamFileGroup
```

> **MORE INFO   FILESTREAM**
>
> You can learn more about FILESTREAM at *http://msdn.microsoft.com/en-us/library /gg471497(SQL.110).aspx.*

Configuring FileTables

FileTables are a special type of table that enables you to store files and documents within SQL Server 2012. These files and documents can be accessed from Windows applications as though they were stored normally in the file system. For example, you can add files and folders to the FileTable by dragging and dropping them in Windows Explorer. You can remove them from the FileTable by using the same method.

A FileTable provides the following functionality:

- A FileTable provides a hierarchy of files and directories.
- Each row in a FileTable represents a file or directory.
- Each row holds the following items:
  - A FILESTREAM column for stream data and a file_id (GUID) identifier.
  - Path_locator and parent_path_locator columns. These represent the file and directory hierarchy.
  - Ten file attributes. These include creation data and modification date.
  - Type column that supports full-text and semantic search.
- You can update FileTables by using normal Transact-SQL queries.

To enable FileTables, perform the following steps:

1. Enable FILESTREAM at the instance level. You can do this with the following query:

```
EXEC sp_configure filestream_access_level, 2
RECONFIGURE
```

2. Enable Non-Transactional Access at the database level. You can do this when creating a new database by using the CREATE DATABASE statement and the FILESTREAM NON_TRANSACTED_ACCESS option. For example:

```
CREATE DATABASE database_name
WITH FILESTREAM ( NON_TRANSACTED_ACCESS = FULL, DIRECTORY_NAME = N'dir_name')
```

You can do this for an existing database by using the ALTER DATABASE statement with the SET FILESTREAM option. For example:

```
ALTER DATABASE database_name
SET FILESTREAM (NON_TRANSACTED_ACCESS = FULL, DIRECTORY_NAME = N'directory_name')
```

3. Specify a Directory for FileTables at the database level if you haven't already done so when configuring Non-Transactional Access. You can modify the directory name by using the ALTER DATABASE statement with the SET FILESTREAM option. You can also configure the directory name on the Options page of the Database Properties dialog box, as shown in Figure 3-12.

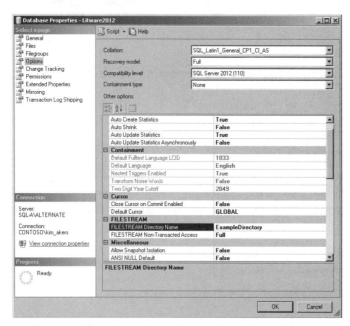

FIGURE 3-12 Configuring directory for FileTables

To create a FileTable by using SQL Server Management Studio, right-click the Tables node and choose New FileTable to open a new script window that contains a template Transact-SQL script that you can modify. You can also create a FileTable by using the CREATE TABLE statement with the AS FileTable option. For example, to create a new FileTable named DocStore, use the following query:

```
CREATE TABLE DocStore as FileTable;
GO
```

You can create FileTables subject to the following conditions:

- You cannot convert an existing table into a FileTable.
- You have specified a parent directory at the database level.
- A valid FILESTREAM filegroup exists. If you don't specify a filegroup, the default FILESTREAM filegroup will be used.
- You cannot create a table constraint when creating the table, but you can add one after the table is created.
- You cannot create a FileTable in the tempdb database.

FileTable tables have predefined and fixed schema, so it is not possible to add or change columns. It is possible to add custom indexes, triggers, and constraints to a FileTable. Dropping a FileTable also drops the directory and the subdirectories that it contained.

> **MORE INFO** **FILETABLES**
>
> You can learn more about FileTables at *http://msdn.microsoft.com/en-us/library /ff929144(SQL.110).aspx*.

PRACTICE   Install Analysis Services and Reporting Services

In this practice, you deploy two instances of Analysis Services in different configurations and deploy an instance of Reporting Services.

EXERCISE 1   Install Analysis Services

In this exercise, you install two Analysis Services instances. The first Analysis Services instance will use multidimensional and data mining modes. The second Analysis Services instance will use tabular mode. To complete this exercise, perform the following steps:

1. Log on to server SQL-A with the Contoso\Kim_Akers user account.

2. Use the command line to install a new instance of Analysis Services on server SQL-A. The server should have the following properties:
   - Installation mode: Multidimensional and data mining mode
   - Instance name: ASMulti
   - Analysis Services service account: NetworkService
   - Analysis Services Server administrator: contoso\kim_akers

3. Use the command line to install an additional new instance of Analysis Services on server SQL-A. This instance of Analysis Services should have the following properties:
   - Installation mode: Tabular mode
   - Instance name: ASTabular
   - Analysis Services service account: NetworkService
   - Analysis Services Server administrator: contoso\kim_akers

EXERCISE 2   Install Reporting Services

In this exercise, you use Windows PowerShell to install the web server role that Reporting Services uses and then deploy a new Reporting Services instance from the command line. To complete this exercise, perform the following steps:

1. On SQL-A, open an elevated PowerShell prompt and run the following command:

    ```
    Import-module ServerManager
    ```

2. Run the following command:

    ```
    Add-WindowsFeature Web-Server -IncludeAllSubFeature
    ```

3. Install a new instance of Reporting Services from the command line. Use the following options so that you don't have to perform post-installation configuration by using Reporting Services Configuration Manager.

    - Install the SQL, Reporting Services, and Tools features.
    - Use **RPTSVR** as the name of the instance.
    - Use the NetworkService account for the Reporting Services, SQL Server, and SQL Server Agent service accounts.
    - Set the Reporting Services startup type to Manual.
    - Use the Default Native Mode Reporting Services installation mode.
    - Configure the BUILTIN\ADMINISTRATORS group for the SQL sysadmin accounts.

4. When the installation has finished, open Reporting Services Configuration Manager and verify that Reporting Services has deployed correctly and the service has started.

Lesson Summary

- An Analysis Services instance in multidimensional and data mining mode supports OLAP databases.
- An Analysis Services instance in tabular mode supports the new tabular modeling feature.
- If you perform a file-only Reporting Services deployment, you must run the Reporting Services Configuration Manager.
- FILESTREAM enables you to store BLOB objects in the file system.
- FileTables are special types of tables that enable you to store files and directories directly in the database. These files and directories can be accessed through the Windows file system.
- Analysis Services and Reporting Services can be enhanced with SharePoint integration.
- You configure Integration Services security with the DCOM Configuration Tool.

Lesson Review

Answer the following questions to test your knowledge of the information in this lesson. You can find the answers to these questions and explanations of why each answer choice is correct or incorrect in the "Answers" section at the end of this chapter.

1. Which tool do you use to give a user access to Integration Services?

    A. SQL Server Management Studio

    B. SQL Server Configuration Manager

    C. SQL Server Data Tools

    D. DCOM Configuration Tool (Dcomcnfg.exe)

2. Which tool do you use to change the Reporting Services execution account?

    A. SQL Server Management Studio

    B. Reporting Services Configuration Manager

    C. SQL Server Configuration Manager

    D. SQL Server Installation Center

3. What is the maximum number of full-text indexes that you can configure for a partitioned table?

    A. 1

    B. 32

    C. 1,024

    D. 2,048

4. Which of the following steps must you take to enable FILESTREAM on a SQL Server 2012 instance that has both the Database Engine and Analysis Services features installed? (Each correct answer presents part of the solution. Choose two.)

    A. Edit the properties of the SQL Server service in SQL Server Configuration Manager.

    B. Edit the properties of the Analysis Services service in SQL Server Configuration Manager.

    C. Run sp_configure filestream_access_level, 2.

    D. Run sp_configure filestream_access_level, 0.

Lesson 2: Managing and Configuring Databases

Database administrators are often responsible for configuring and managing database infrastructure, such as the location of database files, and issues such as database encryption, which do not have a direct impact on users of the database. This lesson covers managing and configuring the properties of databases, including filegroups, database standardization, contained databases, data compression, transparent data encryption, partitioning, log file management, and database console commands.

After this lesson, you will be able to:

- Design and manage filegroups.
- Standardize and configure databases.
- Implement and configure contained databases.
- Configure data compression.
- Manage Transparent Data Encryption.
- Configure table and index partitioning.
- Manage the growth of log files.
- Use database console commands.

Estimated lesson time: 60 minutes

Designing and Managing Filegroups

Each database has a *primary filegroup*. This filegroup hosts the primary data file and any secondary files that you have not allocated to other filegroups. The system tables are hosted in the primary filegroup. You can create *filegroups* to host data files together for reasons including data allocation, administrative, and placement. Secondary data files use the .ndf extension. You can assign these secondary files to different filegroups. Secondary data files that are hosted on different volumes can be assigned to the same filegroup.

When you create a table or an index, you can configure it to use a specific filegroup. When a filegroup contains more than one file, the Database Engine will write data across the files proportionally, depending on how much free space is available in each file.

MORE INFO   FILEGROUPS

You can learn more about filegroups at *http://msdn.microsoft.com/en-us/library /ms189563(SQL.110).aspx.*

Adding New Filegroups

To add a new filegroup to a database by using SQL Server Management Studio, perform the following steps:

1. In SQL Server Management Studio, right-click the database to which you want to add the filegroup and then choose Properties.

2. On the Filegroups page, click Add and then enter the name of the new filegroup, as shown in Figure 3-13.

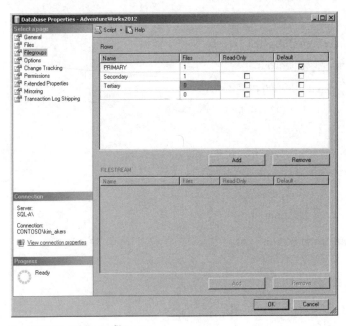

FIGURE 3-13 Adding a filegroup

3. You can add new files to a filegroup on the Files page in the Database Properties dialog box.

You can use the ALTER DATABASE statement with the ADD FILEGROUP option to add filegroups to a database. For example, to add a new filegroup named Tertiary to the AdventureWorks2012 database, use the following query:

```
USE [master]
GO
ALTER DATABASE [AdventureWorks2012] ADD FILEGROUP [Tertiary]
GO
```

Moving an Index from One Filegroup to Another

To move an index to a different filegroup or partition scheme in SQL Server Management Studio, perform the following steps:

1. In SQL Server Management Studio, right-click the index that you want to move to a new filegroup and then choose Properties.

2. On the Storage page, use the Filegroup drop-down list to select the filegroup to which you want to move the index, as shown in Figure 3-14.

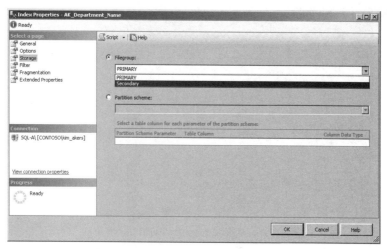

FIGURE 3-14 Moving an index

You can move indexes under the following conditions:

- You cannot move indexes created using a unique or primary key constraint through SQL Server Management Studio. You can move these indexes by using the CREATE INDEX statement with the (DROP_EXISTING=ON) option.

- If the table or index is partitioned, you must select the partition scheme in which to move the index.

- You can move clustered indexes by using online processing, allowing user access to data during the move.

To move an index by using Transact-SQL, use the CREATE INDEX statement with the DROP_EXISTING = ON option and specify the target filegroup.

> **MORE INFO** **MOVING AN EXISTING INDEX**
>
> You can learn more about moving indexes to different filegroups at *http://msdn.microsoft .com/en-us/library/ms175905(SQL.110).aspx*.

Configuring and Standardizing Databases

You can standardize the configuration of databases by configuring appropriate settings such as Auto Close, Auto Shrink, and database recovery model on the model system database. As you learned in Chapter 2, the model system database serves as a template for new databases that you create on an instance. You can configure the properties of the model database either by using SQL Server Management Studio, as shown in Figure 3-15, or by using the ALTER DATABASE statement.

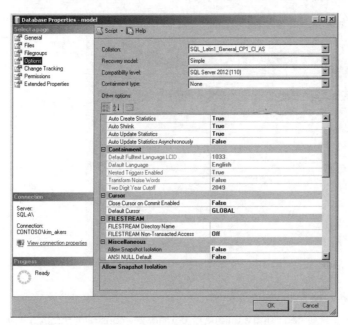

FIGURE 3-15 Model database properties

> **MORE INFO** **MODEL DATABASE**
>
> You can learn more about configuring the model database at *http://msdn.microsoft.com /en-us/library/ms186388.aspx*.

Understanding Contained Databases

Contained databases include all the settings and metadata required to define the database. Contained databases have no configuration dependencies on the Database Engine instance on which the database is deployed, so users connect to a contained database without authenticating at the Database Engine level. An advantage of contained databases is that you can easily move them to other instances or to SQL Server 2012 Azure. Having all database configuration settings within the database enables the database owners to manage all those settings for the database.

SQL Server 2012 supports *Partially Contained Databases (Partial-CDBs)*, which provide a high degree of isolation from the Database Engine instance but are not fully contained. Partial-CDBs are a transitional step toward contained databases.

The SQL Server 2012 implementation of Partial-CDBs does not allow the following:

- Numbered procedures
- Schema-bound objects that depend on built-in functions with collation changes
- Binding change resulting from collation changes, including references to objects, columns, symbols, or types
- Replication, change data capture, and change tracking

You can use the sys.dm_db_uncontained_entities and sys.sql_modules (Transact-SQL) views to find information about uncontained objects or features. Through these views, you can determine the containment status of applications and work out which objects or features you must replace or modify when transitioning to a fully contained database. You should also monitor the database_uncontained_usage event to determine whether uncontained features are used in a database.

You can enable contained databases by using SQL Server Management Studio on the Advanced page of an instance's properties by setting the Enable Contained Databases option to True, as shown in Figure 3-16.

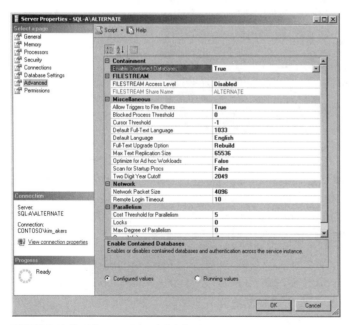

FIGURE 3-16 Enabling contained databases

To enable contained databases on an instance of SQL Server 2012 by using Transact-SQL, issue the following query:

```
sp_configure 'contained database authentication', 1;
GO
RECONFIGURE ;
GO
```

To convert a database to a Partial-CDB or contained database by using SQL Server Management Studio, edit the properties of a database and, on the Options page, change the Containment Type option to Partial or Full, as shown in Figure 3-17.

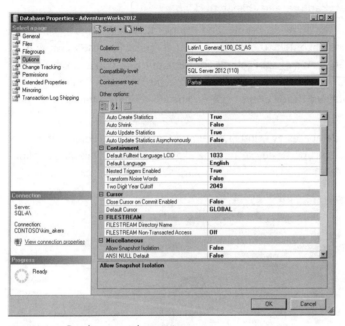

FIGURE 3-17 Database containment type

You can use the ALTER DATABASE statement with the SET CONTAINMENT option to configure containment for a database after you have enabled containment at the database instance level. For example, to set the containment of the AdventureWorks2012 database to Partial, use the following query:

```
USE [master]
GO
ALTER DATABASE [AdventureWorks2012] SET CONTAINMENT = PARTIAL
GO
```

> **MORE INFO** **PARTIALLY CONTAINED DATABASES**
>
> You can learn more about Partially Contained Databases at *http://msdn.microsoft.com /en-us/library/ff929071(SQL.110).aspx.*

Using Data Compression

Row and page compression for tables and indexes enables you to save storage space by reducing the size of the database. Data compression has the drawback of increasing CPU usage because the data must be compressed and decompressed when being accessed. You cannot use data compression with system tables, and only the Enterprise and Developer editions of SQL Server 2012 support data compression.

You can configure data compression on the following:

- Clustered tables
- Heap tables (a heap is a table without a clustered index)
- Non-clustered indexes
- Indexed views
- Individual partitions of a partitioned table or index

There are three forms of data compression you can use with SQL Server 2012: row-level compression, unicode compression, and page-level compression.

> **MORE INFO   HEAPS**
>
> You can learn more about heaps at *http://msdn.microsoft.com/en-us/library /hh213609(v=SQL.110).aspx.*

Row-Level Compression

Row-level compression works by using more efficient storage formats for fixed-length data. Row-level compression uses the following strategies to save space:

- Storing fixed-length numeric data types and CHAR data types as though they were variable-length data types
- Not storing NULL or 0 values
- Reducing metadata required to store data

Although it does reduce the amount of space that data uses, row-level compression does not provide the storage improvements of page-level compression. The advantage of row-level compression is that it requires less CPU usage than page-level compression. You use the following syntax to compress a table by using row-level compression:

```
ALTER TABLE tableName REBUILD WITH (DATA_COMPRESSION=ROW)
```

For example, to rebuild all partitions of the Sales.Customer table of the AdventureWorks2012 database by using row compression, use the following query:

```
USE [AdventureWorks2012]
ALTER TABLE [Sales].[Customer] REBUILD PARTITION = ALL
WITH (DATA_COMPRESSION = ROW)
```

You use the following syntax to configure an index with row-level compression:

```
ALTER INDEX indexName ON tableName REBUILD PARTITION = ALL WITH (DATA_COMPRESSION=ROW)
```

> **MORE INFO** **ROW-LEVEL COMPRESSION**
>
> You can learn more about row-level compression at *http://msdn.microsoft.com/en-us /library/cc280576(v=sql.110).aspx*.

Unicode Compression

Unicode compression enables the database engine to compress unicode values stored in page or row compressed objects. You can use unicode compression with the fixed-length nchar(n) and nvarchar(n) data types. Unicode compression is automatically used where appropriate when you enable row and page compression.

> **MORE INFO** **UNICODE COMPRESSION**
>
> You can learn more about unicode compression at *http://msdn.microsoft.com/en-us /library/ee240835(SQL.110).aspx*.

Page-Level Compression

Page-level compression compresses data by storing repeating values and common prefixes only once and then making references to those values from other locations within the table. When page compression is applied to a table, row compression techniques are also applied. Page-level compression uses the following strategies:

- Row-level compression is applied to maximize the number of rows stored on a page.
- Column prefix compression is applied by replacing repeating data patterns with references. This data is stored in the page header.
- Dictionary compression scans for repeating values and then stores this information in the page header.

The benefits of page compression depend on the type of data compressed. Data that involves many repeating values will be more compressed than data populated by more unique values. You use the following general syntax to apply page-level compression:

```
ALTER TABLE name REBUILD WITH (DATA_COMPRESSION=PAGE)
```

For example, to rebuild all partitions of the Sales.Customer table of the AdventureWorks2012 database by using page compression, use the following query:

```
USE [AdventureWorks2012]
ALTER TABLE [Sales].[Customer] REBUILD PARTITION = ALL
WITH
(DATA_COMPRESSION = PAGE)
```

You use the following syntax to configure an index with page-level compression:

```
ALTER INDEX indexName ON tableName REBUILD PARTITION ALL WITH (DATA_COMPRESSION=PAGE)
```

> **MORE INFO** **PAGE-LEVEL COMPRESSION**
>
> You can learn more about page-level compression at *http://msdn.microsoft.com/en-us /library/cc280464(v=sql.110).aspx*.

If tables or indexes are partitioned, you can configure compression on a per-partition basis. If you split a partition by using the ALTER PARTITION statement, the new partitions inherit the data compression attribute of the original partition. If you merge two partitions, the resulting partition has the compression attribute of the destination partition.

Although compression does allow more rows to be stored on a page, it doesn't alter the maximum row size of a table or index. You can't enable a table for compression if the maximum row size and the compression overhead exceed 8,060 bytes.

The default compression setting for indexes is NONE, and you must specify the compression property for indexes when you create them. Non-clustered indexes do not inherit the compression property of the table, but clustered indexes created on a heap inherit the compression state of the heap.

Data compression applies only at the source, so when you export data from a compressed source, SQL Server will output the data in uncompressed row format. Importing uncompressed data into a target table enabled for compression will compress the data.

> **MORE INFO** **DATA COMPRESSION**
>
> You can learn more about data compression at *http://msdn.microsoft.com/en-us/library /cc280449(v=sql.110).aspx*.

You can configure compression by using the preceding Transact-SQL statements or from SQL Server Management Studio by using the Data Compression Wizard on either tables or indexes. You can use the Data Compression Wizard to add and remove compression. To use the Data Compression Wizard to change the compression settings for both tables and indexes, perform the following steps:

1. In SQL Server Management Studio, right-click the table or index you want to compress, choose Storage, and then select Manage Compression.

2. On the Welcome To The Data Compression Wizard page, click Next.

3. On the Select Compression Type page, shown in Figure 3-18, you can choose to use the same compression type for all partitions or choose among Row, Page, and None on a per-partition basis. Click Calculate to determine the difference between current space usage and compressed usage.

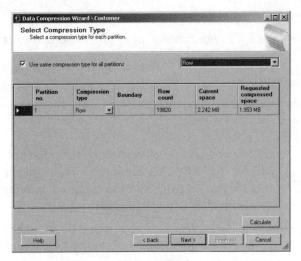

FIGURE 3-18 Data Compression Wizard

4. On the Select An Output Option page, choose whether to create a script, to perform the operation immediately, or to perform the option according to a schedule. Click Next and then click Finish to complete the wizard.

> **MORE INFO   DATA COMPRESSION WIZARD**
>
> You can learn more about the Data Compression Wizard at *http://msdn.microsoft.com /en-us/library/cc280496(v=SQL.110).aspx*.

Estimating Compression

The best way to determine the benefits of compression on an object is to use the sp_estimate_data_compression_savings stored procedure. The benefits of compression depend on factors such as the uniqueness of data. The sp_estimate_data_compression_savings stored procedure is available in the Enterprise edition of SQL Server 2012 only.

The syntax of the stored procedure is as follows:

```
sp_estimate_data_compression_savings[ @schema_name = ] 'schema_name', [ @object_name = ]
'object_name', [@index_id = ] index_id,[@partition_number = ] partition_number,
[@data_compression = ] 'data_compression'
```

For example, to configure an estimate of the compression benefits of using Row compression on the HumanResources.Employee table in the AdventureWorks2012 database, execute the following Transact-SQL statement:

```
USE AdventureWorks2012;
GO
EXEC sp_estimate_data_compression_savings 'HumanResources', 'Employee', NULL, NULL,
'ROW';
GO
```

To configure an estimate of the compression benefits of using Page compression on the same table, execute the following Transact-SQL statement:

```
USE AdventureWorks2012;
GO
EXEC sp_estimate_data_compression_savings 'HumanResources', 'Employee', NULL, NULL,
'PAGE';
GO
```

> **MORE INFO** **SP_ESTIMATE_DATA_COMPRESSION_SAVINGS**
>
> You can learn more about how to estimate compression savings at *http://msdn.microsoft
> .com/en-us/library/cc280574(v=sql.110).aspx.*

Encrypting Databases with Transparent Data Encryption

Transparent Data Encryption (TDE) enables you to encrypt an entire database. TDE protects the database against unauthorized third parties gaining access to the hard disks or backups on which the database is stored. TDE encrypts the database by using a Database Encryption Key (DEK) that is stored in the database boot record. The DEK is in turn protected by the database master key, which is in turn protected by the service master key. You can use BitLocker Drive Encryption, a full-volume encryption method supported by Windows Server 2008 and Windows Server 2008 R2, although this will not ensure that database backups are encrypted.

> **NOTE** **TDE AND TEMPDB**
>
> If any database on the instance uses TDE, the tempdb system database will also be encrypted.

To use TDE to encrypt a database, you must perform the following steps:

1. Create the master encryption key.
2. Create the certificate protected by the master key.
3. Create a DEK and protect it by using the certificate.
4. Encrypt the database.

The first step in deploying TDE involves creating a master encryption key. You do this by using the CREATE MASTER KEY ENCRYPTION BY PASSWORD statement. For example, you can accomplish that by using the following query:

```
USE master;
GO
CREATE MASTER KEY ENCRYPTION BY PASSWORD = '<MasterKeyPasswordHere>';
GO
```

After you have created the master encryption key, the next step involves creating the certificate that will be used to encrypt the database. You can accomplish this by using the CREATE CERTIFICATE statement. For example, to create a certificate named ServerCertificate that uses the subject name Server Certificate, use the following query:

```
CREATE CERTIFICATE ServerCertificate WITH SUBJECT = 'Server Certificate';
GO
```

When the master key and certificate are in place, you can create the DEK for the specific database. You do this by using the CREATE DATABASE ENCRYPTION KEY statement. For example, the following query creates a DEK for the AdventureWorks2012 database:

```
USE AdventureWorks2012;
GO
CREATE DATABASE ENCRYPTION KEY
WITH ALGORITHM = AES_128
ENCRYPTION BY SERVER CERTIFICATE ServerCertificate;
GO
```

After all the appropriate keys and certificates are in place, you can encrypt the database by using the ALTER DATABASE statement. For example, to encrypt the AdventureWorks2012 database, use the following query:

```
ALTER DATABASE AdventureWorks2012
SET ENCRYPTION ON;
GO
```

When using TDE, you should create a backup of the server certificate in the master database. If you lose the database server without backing this up, you cannot access data in a database protected by TDE. You can use the BACKUP CERTIFICATE statement to create a backup of the certificate and private key, both of which are required for certificate recovery. The private key password does not have to be the same as the database master key password. For example, the following code, when run from the master system database, creates a backup of the ServerCertificate certificate to a file called ServerCertExport and a PrivateKeyFile private key:

```
BACKUP CERTIFICATE ServerCertificate
TO FILE = 'ServerCertExport'
WITH PRIVATE KEY
(
    FILE = 'PrivateKeyFile',
    ENCRYPTION BY PASSWORD = '<PrivateKeyPasswordHere>'
);
GO
```

SQL Server will write these backup files to the \MSSQL\DATA directory of the instance.

MORE INFO   **TRANSPARENT DATA ENCRYPTION**

You can learn more about Transparent Data Encryption at *http://msdn.microsoft.com /en-us/library/bb934049(SQL.110).aspx.*

Partitioning Indexes and Tables

Partitioning divides index and table data across more than one filegroup. Data is partitioned so that groups of rows are mapped to individual partitions. All partitions of a table or index must reside in the same database. You can use partitioned indexes and tables only in the Enterprise and Developer editions of SQL Server 2012. The x64 versions of SQL Server 2012 support up to 15,000 partitions. It is possible to create more than 1,000 partitions on the x86 versions of SQL Server 2012, but this is not supported by Microsoft.

Table and index partitioning involves the following concepts:

- **Partition function**   Defines how the rows of an index or table map to specific partitions based on the values of partitioning columns
- **Partition scheme**   Maps the partitions of a partition function to a collection of filegroups
- **Partitioning column**   The column of an index or table that a partition function uses to partition the index or table
- **Aligned index**   An index that uses the same partition scheme as the table to which it belongs
- **Nonaligned index**   An index that is partitioned independently from the table to which it belongs
- **Partition elimination**   The process through which the query optimizer will access only the appropriate partitions to satisfy a query's filter criteria

When creating a partitioned table or index, follow these general steps:

1. Create the filegroup or filegroups that will host the partitions.
2. Create a partition function that assigns rows of a table or index to partitions based on the values of a specific column.
3. Create a partition scheme that maps partitions to filegroups.
4. Create or modify an index or table and specify the partition scheme.

Partitioned tables or indexes require the following permissions:

- To create a partitioned table, a user needs the CREATE TABLE permission in the database, the ALTER permission on the schema in which the table is being created, and one of the following permissions:
  - ALTER ANY DATASPACE permission
  - CONTROL or ALTER permission on the database
  - CONTROL SERVER or ALTER ANY DATABASE permission on the instance
- To create a partitioned index, a user needs the ALTER permission on the table or view that hosts the index and one of the following permissions:
  - ALTER ANY DATASPACE permission
  - CONTROL or ALTER permission on the database
  - CONTROL SERVER or ALTER ANY DATABASE permission on the instance

To create a partitioned table, perform the following steps:

1. In SQL Server Management Studio, right-click the table you want to partition, choose Storage, and then select Create Partition.

2. On the first page of the Create Partition Wizard, click Next.

3. On the Select A Partitioning Column page, shown in Figure 3-19, choose the column you will use to partition the table. You can also enable the following options:

- **Collocate This Table To The Selected Partitioned Table**   This option can improve query efficiency.

- **Storage-Align Non-Unique Indexes And Unique Indexes With Indexed Partitioning Column**   This option enables you to move partitions in and out of partitioned tables more effectively.

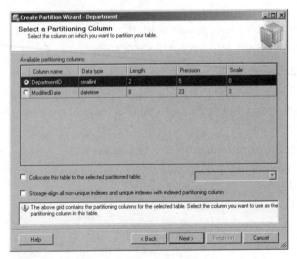

FIGURE 3-19 Select a partitioning column

4. On the Select A Partition Function page, either choose an existing partition function or specify the name of a new partition function.

5. On the Select A Partition Scheme page, either choose an existing partition scheme or enter the name of a new partition scheme.

6. On the Map Partitions page, choose Left Boundary or Right Boundary to determine whether to include the highest or lowest bounding value within each filegroup. In the Boundary column, specify the boundary value, as shown in Figure 3-20. You can also choose Set Boundaries if you want to use date values with a partitioning column. This is useful for separating table data into filegroups based on date, but it is available only if the partitioning column is of type date, datetime, smalldatetime, datetime2, or datetimeoffset.

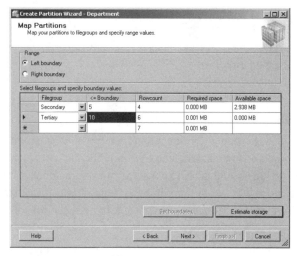

FIGURE 3-20 Map partitions

7. On the Select An Output Option page, choose between Create a Script or Run Immediately or to run on a schedule.

8. On the Review Summary page, click Finish.

You can create a partition function by using the CREATE PARTITION FUNCTION statement. For example, to create a function named PartFunction that will divide a table into two partitions by using the number 50, use the following statement:

```
CREATE PARTITION FUNCTION PartFunction (int)
as RANGE LEFT FOR VALUES (50);
```

You can create a partition scheme with the CREATE PARTITION SCHEME statement. For example, to create a partition scheme named PartScheme that applies the partition function PartFunction to the filegroups FgOne and FgTwo, use the following query:

```
CREATE PARTITION SCHEME PartScheme
    AS PARTITION PartFunction
```

```
        TO (FgOne, FgTwo);
GO
```

You can create a partitioned table by referencing the partition scheme. For example, to create a table called Exemplar that uses the PartScheme partition scheme to partition col1, use the following query:

```
CREATE TABLE Exemplar (col1 int, col2 char(20))
        ON PartScheme (col1);
GO
```

You can use the ALTER PARTITION FUNCTION statement to modify an existing partition function by either splitting one partition into two or merging two partitions into one. You can use the ALTER PARTITION SCHEME statement to modify an existing partition scheme.

> **MORE INFO** **PARTITIONED INDEXES AND TABLES**
>
> You can learn more about partitioned tables and indexes at *http://msdn.microsoft.com /en-us/library/ms190787(SQL.110).aspx.*

Managing Log Files

Transaction log files use the .ldf extension. Although a database might have multiple log files, SQL Server treats these multiple log files as a single contiguous-file virtual log file. If log records were never deleted, the logs would grow to consume the volume on which they were hosted. Log truncation is the process by which the Database Engine frees space in the logical log for reuse by the transaction log. Log truncation occurs automatically in the following situations:

- When a database uses the simple recovery model, the Database Engine truncates the transaction log after a checkpoint. Automatic checkpoints are triggered each time the number of log records reaches the number that the Database Engine determines it can process during the *recovery interval* server configuration option. The Database Engine triggers an automatic checkpoint under the simple recovery model when the virtual log becomes 70 percent full. You can trigger checkpoints manually by using the CHECKPOINT statement.

- When a database uses the full recovery model or bulk-logged recovery model, the Database Engine truncates the transaction log after a log backup as long as a check-point has occurred since the previous backup. You will learn more about backing up transaction logs in Chapter 11, "Backup and Restore."

You can use the DBCC SQLPERF (LOGSPACE) command to monitor the amount of log space used. Figure 3-21 shows the output of this command.

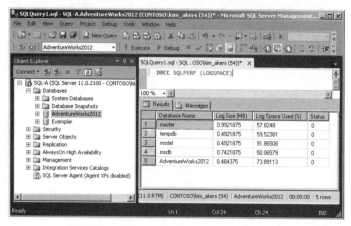

FIGURE 3-21 DBCC SQLPERF (LOGSPACE)

You can add log files to the database by using the ALTER DATABASE statement with the ADD LOG FILE option. You can modify the size of a transaction log file by using the ALTER DATABASE statement with the MODIFY FILE option and specifying a SIZE and MAXSIZE figure. By default, SQL Server 2012 transaction log files are configured to autogrow by 10 percent to a maximum of 2,097,152 MB.

> **MORE INFO** **TRANSACTION LOG FILES**
>
> You can learn more about the transaction log at *http://msdn.microsoft.com/en-us/library /ms190925(SQL.110).aspx*.

Using Database Console Commands

Database console commands (DBCC) enable you to perform SQL Server 2012 administration tasks by using queries rather than by using the SQL Server Management Studio graphical user interface (GUI). DBCC commands are grouped into the following categories:

- **Maintenance** Commands that perform maintenance tasks on databases, indexes, or filegroups
- **Informational** Commands that display SQL Server information
- **Validation** Commands that enable you to validate operations on databases, tables, indexes, catalogs, or filegroups
- **Miscellaneous** Commands that enable you to perform tasks such as enabling trace flags or modifying which dynamic-link libraries (DLLs) are loaded into memory

Maintenance Statements

DBCC maintenance statements, their functions, and the permissions required to run them are as follows:

- **DBCC CLEANTABLE**   Reclaims space from dropped variable-length columns in indexed views or tables. The user must own the table or indexed view or be a member of the sysadmin fixed server role or the db_owner or db_ddladmin fixed database roles.

- **DBCC DBREINDEX**   Rebuilds one or more indexes for a table. The user must be a member of the sysadmin fixed server role or the db_owner or db_ddladmin fixed database roles. This statement is deprecated in this version of SQL Server, and you should use ALTER INDEX to perform this task.

- **DBCC DROPCLEANBUFFERS**   Removes all clean buffers from the buffer pool. The user must be a member of the sysadmin fixed server role.

- **DBCC FREEPROCCACHE**   Removes all elements from the plan cache, specific plan from the plan cache, or all cache entries related to a specific resource pool. The user must have ALTER SERVER STATE permission in the Database Engine.

- **DBCC INDEXDEFRAG**   Defragments indexes. This feature will be removed in future versions of SQL Server, and you should use ALTER INDEX instead. The user must be a member of the sysadmin fixed server role or the db_owner or db_ddladmin fixed database roles.

- **DBCC SHRINKDATABASE**   Shrinks the size of all data and log files of the specified database. The user must be a member of the sysadmin fixed server role or the db_owner fixed database role.

- **DBCC SHRINKFILE**   Shrinks a specified data or log file. The user must be a member of the sysadmin fixed server role or the db_owner fixed database role.

- **DBCC UPDATEUSAGE**   Updates page and row count data for catalog views to remove inaccuracies. The user must be a member of the sysadmin fixed server role or the db_owner fixed database role. This statement is provided for backward compatibility.

Informational Statements

DBCC informational statements, their functions, and the permissions required to run them are as follows:

- **DBCC INPUTBUFFER**   Shows the last statement forward from a client to the Database Engine. The user must be a member of the sysadmin fixed server role or have the VIEW SERVER STATE permission.

- **DBCC OPENTRAN**   Shows information about the oldest running transaction, oldest running distributed transaction, and oldest running non-distributed transaction. The user must be a member of the sysadmin fixed server role or the db_owner fixed database role.

- **DBCC OUTPUTBUFFER**   Displays the current output buffer in hexadecimal and ASCII format for a specific session_id. The user must be a member of the sysadmin fixed server role.

- **DBCC PROCCACHE**   Provides information about the procedure cache. The user must be a member of the sysadmin fixed server role or the db_owner fixed database role.

- **DBCC SHOW_STATISTICS**   Provides current query optimization statistics for a table or indexed view. The user must be a member of the sysadmin fixed server role or the db_owner or db_ddladmin fixed database roles.

- **DBCC SHOWCONTIG**   Provides fragmentation information for tables, views, or indexes. The user must be a member of the sysadmin fixed server role or the db_owner or db_ddladmin fixed database roles. This statement is deprecated, and you should migrate to using appropriate dynamic management views for this information.

- **DBCC SQLPERF**   Displays transaction log space usage statistics for all databases hosted by an instance. Access requires the VIEW SERVER STATE permission on the server.

- **DBCC TRACESTATUS**   Provides information about trace flags. The user must be a member of the public role.

- **DBCC USEROPTIONS**   Provides information about currently set options on the connection. The user must be a member of the public role.

Validation Statements

DBCC validation statements, their functions, and the permissions required to run them are as follows:

- **DBCC CHECKALLOC**   Performs a consistency check of disk space allocation structures. The user must be a member of the sysadmin fixed server role or the db_owner fixed database role.

- **DBCC CHECKCATALOG**   Checks catalog consistency of online databases. The user must be a member of the sysadmin fixed server role or the db_owner fixed database role.

- **DBCC CHECKCONSTRAINTS**   Verifies the integrity of a specific constraint or all constraints on a table within the current database. The user must be a member of the sysadmin fixed server role or the db_owner fixed database role.

- **DBCC CHECKDB**   Checks the physical and logical integrity of all objects in a specific database; runs DBCC CHECKALLOC, DBCC CHECKTABLE, and DBCC CHECKCATALOG; validates the contents of every indexed view, link-level consistency between table metadata, file system directories, and files when storing varbinary(max) data on the file system using FILESTREAM; and checks Service Broker data. The user must be a member of the sysadmin fixed server role or the db_owner fixed database role.

- **DBCC CHECKFILEGROUP** Verifies the allocation and structural integrity of indexed views and tables in a specific filegroup. The user must be a member of the sysadmin fixed server role or the db_owner fixed database role.

- **DBCC CHECKIDENT** Verifies and, if necessary, changes the identity value for a specific table. The user must be a member of the sysadmin fixed server role or the db_owner or db_ddladmin fixed database roles.

- **DBCC CHECKTABLE** Verifies the integrity of all pages and structures that make up a table or indexed view. The user must be a member of the sysadmin fixed server role or the db_owner or db_ddladmin fixed database roles.

EXAM TIP

Be familiar with the functionality of DBCC CHECKDB prior to taking the 70-462 exam.

Miscellaneous Statements

Miscellaneous DBCC statements, their functions, and the permissions required to run them are as follows:

- **DBCC dllname (FREE)** Unloads a specific extended stored procedure DLL from memory. The user must be a member of the sysadmin fixed server role or the db_owner fixed database role.

- **DBCC FREESESSIONCACHE** Flushes the distributed query connection cache. The user must be a member of the sysadmin fixed server role.

- **DBCC FREESYSTEMCACHE** Flushes all unused cache entries from all caches. Access requires the ALTER SERVER STATE permission.

- **DBCC HELP** Provides information on a specific DBCC command. The user must be a member of the sysadmin fixed server role.

- **DBCC TRACEOFF** Disables specific trace flags. The user must be a member of the sysadmin fixed server role.

- **DBCC TRACEON** Enables specific trace flags. The user must be a member of the sysadmin fixed server role.

Table Partitioning, Compression, Encryption, and Log Files

In this practice, you partition tables, configure encryption and compression, and manage SQL Server log files.

EXERCISE 1   Partition Tables

In this exercise, add filegroups and files to the WingTipToys2012 database. You create a partition function and a partition scheme and then create a table that uses that partition scheme. To complete this exercise, perform the following steps:

1. Log on to server SQL-A with the Kim_Akers user account.

2. Using SQL Server Management Studio, create a database named **WingTipToys2012** on instance SQL-A.

3. Add filegroups **FgOne**, **FgTwo**, and **FgThree** to database WingTipToys2012.

4. Add a database file named **file1** to FgOne, a database file named **file2** to FgTwo, and a database file named **file3** to FgThree.

5. Use Transact-SQL on the WingTipToys2012 database to create a partition function named **WTPartFunction** for the integer data type for RANGE LEFT values of 30 and 60.

6. Use Transact-SQL to create a partition scheme named **WTPartScheme** for WTPartFunction for FgOne, FgTwo, and FgThree.

7. Create a table named **Toys,** in which column 1 uses the integer data type and column 2 uses the char(30)data type, by using the WTPartScheme on column 1.

EXERCISE 2   Configure Encryption and Compression

In this exercise, connect to the SQL-A\ALTERNATE instance, create a new database, encrypt that new database, and then create new tables and configure them with compression. To complete this exercise, perform the following steps:

1. Use SQL Server Management Studio to connect to instance SQL-A\Alternate.

2. Create a new database named **WingTipToys2012** by using the default settings.

3. Use appropriate Transact-SQL queries to encrypt the WingTipToys2012 database by using Transparent Database Encryption.

4. Create a table in the WingTipToys2012 database named **Aeroplanes**. The table should have a single column named **Model** and should use the varchar(max) data type.

5. Configure the Aeroplanes table to use row-level compression.

6. Create a table in the WingTipToys2012 database named **Helicopters**. The table should have a single column named **Model** and should use the varchar(max) data type.

7. Configure the Helicopters table to use page-level compression.

EXERCISE 3 Manage Transaction Log Files

In this exercise, you manage transaction log files. To complete this exercise, perform the following steps:

1. On the default instance on SQL-A, add a file to the transaction log in the WingTipToys2012 database.

2. Trigger a transaction log file checkpoint in the WingTipToys2012 database.

3. Use the appropriate Transact-SQL code to determine how much free space is available in transaction logs.

Lesson Summary

- Filegroups are collections of database files that enable you to implement partitioning of tables and indexes.
- Configure the model system database as a template when standardizing databases on an instance.
- Contained databases are databases that have no dependencies on the Database Engine. This makes it easy to move databases between instances and to cloud-based deployments such as SQL Azure.
- Row-level compression modifies data types to reduce the amount of storage space used. Page-level compression uses dictionary compression techniques and provides greater space savings, but at the cost of CPU usage.
- Transparent Data Encryption (TDE) enables you to encrypt an entire database. The database will remain encrypted even when backed up.
- Transaction log truncation depends on the configured recovery model. You can force a checkpoint by using the CHECKPOINT statement.

Lesson Review

Answer the following questions to test your knowledge of the information in this lesson. You can find the answers to these questions and explanations of why each answer choice is correct or incorrect in the "Answers" section at the end of this chapter.

1. Which statement would you use to add a filegroup to an existing database?

   A. ALTER DATABASE

   B. CREATE DATABASE

   C. ALTER TABLE

   D. CREATE TABLE

2. The STUDENTS table contains name, address, and contact information for students at a local college. Columns include Student_Name, DOB, Telephone, Email, Street_Address, Town, State, and Zip Code. IDX1 is an index on the Student_Name column. Given this

information, which of the following statements will provide the greatest reduction in the amount of space required to store data for the STUDENTS table?

A. ALTER TABLE STUDENTS REBUILD WITH (DATA_COMPRESSION=ROW)

B. ALTER TABLE STUDENTS REBUILD WITH (DATA_COMPRESSION=PAGE)

C. ALTER INDEX IDX1 ON STUDENTS REBUILD PARTITION ALL WITH (DATA_COMPRESSION=ROW)

D. ALTER INDEX IDX1 ON STUDENTS REBUILD PARTITION ALL WITH (DATA_COMPRESSION=PAGE)

3. Which of the following must you do before enabling Transparent Data Encryption for a database? (Each correct answer presents part of the complete solution. Choose three.)

A. Create a master encryption key.

B. Create a certificate.

C. Create a database encryption key.

D. Enable page-level compression.

4. Which command would you run if you wanted to check the physical and logical integrity of all objects within a specific database?

A. DBCC CHECKFILEGROUP

B. DBCC CHECKDB

C. DBCC SQLPERF

D. DBCC SHRINKDATABASE

Case Scenarios

In the following case scenarios, apply what you have learned about configuring additional SQL Server components and managing and configuring databases. You can find answers to these questions in the "Answers" section at the end of this chapter.

Case Scenario 1: Configuring FILESTREAM and FileTable

You have recently deployed SQL Server 2012 on a server named SYDNEY-DB. You want to use this server to store a large number of image files, most of which are between 10 MB and 20 MB in size. In view of this goal, you want to configure the default instance on SYDNEY-DB to support FILESTREAM. You also want to configure FileTables to simplify the process of adding image files to the database. With this information in mind, answer the following:

1. What general steps must you take to enable FILESTREAM on the default instance of server SYDNEY-DB?

2. After FILESTREAM is enabled on the default instance of server SYDNEY-DB, what general steps must you take to create a FileTable?

Case Scenario 2: Deploying Transparent Data Encryption

You want to deploy Transparent Data Encryption (TDE) to protect the ContosoCars2012 database hosted on one of your organization's SQL Server 2012 Database Engine instances. With that in mind, answer the following questions:

1. Which query would you use to create a master encryption key with the password **P@ssw0rd**?

2. Which query would you use to create the certificate that encrypts the database if the certificate name is ServerCertA and the subject name is Server Certificate A?

3. Which query would you use to create a Database Encryption Key (DEK) for the ContosoCars2012 database if you were using the AES_128 encryption algorithm and ServerCertA?

4. Which query would you use to encrypt the ContosoCars2012 database?

5. Which query would you use to back up the server certificate to a file named CertExport and the private key to a file named PrivateKey with the password **P@ssw0rd**?

Suggested Practices

To help you successfully master the exam objectives presented in this chapter, complete the following tasks.

FILESTREAM and FileTable

Prior to completing each task in the following practices, list the steps you would take to accomplish the task. After completing the task, assess how accurately you predicted the necessary steps.

- **Practice 1** Enable FILESTREAM on the ALTERNATE instance hosted on server SQL-A.
- **Practice 2** Create a new custom database on the ALTERNATE instance on server SQL-A. Create and populate a FileTable in this database.

Transparent Data Encryption and Table Partitioning

Prior to completing each task in the following practices, list the steps you would take to accomplish the task. After completing the task, assess how accurately you predicted the necessary steps.

- **Practice 1** Encrypt the new database on the ALTERNATE instance of SQL-A by using TDE.
- **Practice 2**   Add a second filegroup and files to the new custom database. Create a partitioned table that uses the primary and second filegroup.

Answers

This section contains the answers to the lesson review questions and solutions to the case scenarios in this chapter.

Lesson 1

1.   **Correct Answer: D**

     A.   **Incorrect.** You cannot use SQL Server Management Studio to give a user access to Integration Services.

     B.   **Incorrect.** You cannot use SQL Server Configuration Manager to give a user access to Integration Services.

     C.   **Incorrect.** SQL Server Data Tools enables you to create Analysis Services, Integration Services, and Report Server projects, but it cannot be used to give a user access to Integration Services.

     D.   **Correct.** Dcomcnfg.exe is the tool you can use to give non-administrative users access to Integration Services.

2.   **Correct Answer: B**

     A.   **Incorrect.** You cannot use SQL Server Management Studio to change the Reporting Services execution account.

     B.   **Correct.** You use Reporting Services Configuration Manager to change the Reporting Services execution account.

     C.   **Incorrect.** You cannot use SQL Server Configuration Manager to change the Reporting Services execution account.

     D.   **Incorrect.** You cannot use SQL Server Installation Center to change the Reporting Services execution account.

3.   **Correct Answer: A**

     A.   **Correct.** The maximum number of full-text indexes for a table is 1.

     B.   **Incorrect.** The maximum number of full-text indexes for a table is 1. You cannot have 32 full-text indexes for a partitioned table.

     C.   **Incorrect.** The maximum number of full-text indexes for a table is 1. You cannot have 1,024 full-text indexes for a partitioned table.

     D.   **Incorrect.** The maximum number of full-text indexes for a table is 1. You cannot have 2,048 full-text indexes for a partitioned table.

4.   **Correct Answers: A and C**

     A.   **Correct.** To enable FILESTREAM, you must edit the properties of the SQL Server service in SQL Server Configuration Manager.

     B.   **Incorrect.** You do not have to edit the properties of the Analysis Services service in SQL Server Configuration Manager to enable FILESTREAM.

C. **Correct.** You must run the sp_configure filestream_access_level, X, with a non-zero value of X to enable FILESTREAM.

D. **Incorrect.** Running sp_configure filestream_access_level, 0, disables FILESTREAM.

Lesson 2

1. **Correct Answer: A**

   A. **Correct.** You can add a filegroup to an existing database by using the ALTER DATABASE statement.

   B. **Incorrect.** The CREATE DATABASE statement enables you to create a new database but not to alter an existing database.

   C. **Incorrect.** The ALTER TABLE statement enables you to modify a table but not a database.

   D. **Incorrect.** The CREATE TABLE statement enables you to create a table but not to modify a database.

2. **Correct Answer: B**

   A. **Incorrect.** Implementing page-level compression will provide a greater reduction in the amount of space used than implementing row-level compression will, given the properties of the table.

   B. **Correct.** Unless the table data is unique, page-level compression provides the greatest compression but has a cost in CPU usage.

   C. **Incorrect.** In this case, compressing the index using row compression will not provide the space savings that compressing the entire table will.

   D. **Incorrect.** In this case, compressing the index using page compression will not provide the space savings that compressing the entire table will.

3. **Correct Answers: A, B, and C**

   A. **Correct.** You must create a master encryption key prior to enabling TDE on a database.

   B. **Correct.** You must create a certificate prior to enabling TDE on a database.

   C. **Correct.** You must create a database encryption key prior to enabling TDE on a database.

   D. **Incorrect.** You do not need to enable page-level compression prior to enabling TDE on a database.

4. **Correct Answer: B**

   A. **Incorrect.** DBCC CHECKFILEGROUP verifies the allocation and structural integrity of indexed views and tables for a specific filegroup but not for the entire database.

   B. **Correct.** DBCC CHECKDB checks the physical and logical integrity of all objects within a specific database.

C. **Incorrect.** DBCC SQLPERF provides transaction log space statistics.

D. **Incorrect.** DBCC SHRINKDATABASE shrinks the size of all data and log files for the specified database.

Case Scenario 1

1. To enable FILESTREAM on the default instance of server SYDNEY-DB, you must perform the following general steps:

    A. Edit the properties of the SQL Server Service to enable FILESTREAM.

    B. Run the sp_configure filestream_access_level, X, stored procedure, where X is 1 or 2.

    C. Restart SQL Server Services.

    D. Create a FILESTREAM filegroup.

    E. Add a file to the FILESTREAM filegroup.

2. After FILESTREAM is enabled on the default instance of server SYDNEY-DB, you must take the following general steps to deploy a FileTable:

    A. Enable Non-Transactional Access at the database level.

    B. Specify a directory for FileTables at the database level.

    C. Create a table as a FileTable.

Case Scenario 2

1. Use the following query to create a master encryption key with the password **P@ssw0rd**:

```
USE master;
GO
CREATE MASTER KEY ENCRYPTION BY PASSWORD = 'P@ssw0rd';
GO
```

2. Use the following query to create the certificate ServerCertA with the subject name **'Server Certificate A':**

```
CREATE CERTIFICATE ServerCertA WITH SUBJECT = 'Server Certificate A';
GO
```

3. Use the following query to create a DEK for database ContosoCars2012 by using the AES_128 encryption algorithm and certificate ServerCertA:

```
USE ContosoCars2012;
GO
CREATE DATABASE ENCRYPTION KEY
WITH ALGORITHM = AES_128
ENCRYPTION BY SERVER CERTIFICATE ServerCertA;
GO
```

4. Use the following statement to encrypt the ContosoCars2012 database:

```
ALTER DATABASE ContosoCars2012
SET ENCRYPTION ON;
GO
```

5. Use the following statement to back up the server certificate to a file named CertExport with a private key file named PrivateKey with the password **P@ssw0rd**:

```
BACKUP CERTIFICATE ServerCertA
TO FILE = 'CertExport'
WITH PRIVATE KEY
(
    FILE = 'PrivateKeyFile',
    ENCRYPTION BY PASSWORD = 'P@ssw0rd'
);
GO
```

CHAPTER 4

Migrating, Importing, and Exporting

Exam objectives in this chapter:

- Implement a migration strategy.
- Import and export data.

In this chapter, you learn about the methods you can use to upgrade a Database Engine instance from a previous version of Microsoft SQL Server to SQL Server 2012. To cover those situations when a Database Engine upgrade is not possible or desirable, you learn how to migrate an existing database to a new instance, located on either the same or a different host system. You learn how to copy large amounts of data from one table or set of tables to other databases on the same and on different instances, and about the different techniques you can use to perform bulk import and export operations.

Lessons in this chapter:

Before You Begin

To complete the lessons in this chapter, make sure that you have:

- Completed the setup tasks outlined in the introduction.
- Completed the end-of-lesson exercises for Chapter 1, "Planning and Installing SQL Server 2012," through Chapter 3, "Configuring SQL Server 2012 Components."

Lesson 1: Migrating to SQL Server 2012

This lesson covers migrating to SQL Server 2012 from previous versions of SQL Server, including other SQL Server 2012 instances. Migration includes not only moving or copying databases but also moving security principals such as SQL logins. You also learn about the circumstances under which you can upgrade an instance of SQL Server 2005, SQL Server 2008, or SQL Server 2008 R2 to SQL Server 2012.

> **After this lesson, you will be able to:**
> - Upgrade an instance to SQL Server 2012.
> - Copy a database from one instance to another.
> - Migrate SQL logins to SQL Server 2012.
> - Migrate to SQL Server 2012 from a previous version.
> - Migrate data to SQL Server 2012 from other sources.
>
> **Estimated lesson time: 60 minutes**

Upgrading an Instance to SQL Server 2012

Upgrading an instance is the process by which you upgrade the SQL Server program files from a previous version of SQL Server to SQL Server 2012. The upgrade process can minimize the complexity of transitioning to SQL Server 2012 because all databases and security settings are moved to the new platform when you perform an upgrade. Whether you are able to perform an upgrade depends on the answers to the following questions.

- From which edition of SQL Server are you upgrading? This will limit the editions of SQL Server 2012 to which you can upgrade.
- From which SQL instance processor architecture are you upgrading? You can upgrade only to a SQL Server 2012 instance that uses the same processor architecture.
- The host operating system, including processor architecture (x86 or x64), will influence whether the desired upgrade is possible.

 Previous versions of SQL Server support the *Itanium* architecture, a special 64-bit processor architecture that is different from the x64 architecture supported by SQL Server 2012. The Itanium architecture is not supported by SQL Server 2012, and you cannot upgrade any Itanium edition of a previous version of SQL Server to SQL Server 2012. If you have a database hosted on an Itanium-architecture SQL Server instance, you must perform a migration rather than an upgrade to SQL Server 2012.

Upgrading from SQL Server 2005

The key to upgrading from SQL Server 2005 to SQL Server 2012 is ensuring that the host operating system supports SQL Server 2012. For example, you can't deploy SQL Server 2012 on Microsoft Windows Server 2003 or Windows Server 2003 R2, which are supported plat-forms for SQL Server 2005. The only operating systems that support both SQL Server 2005 and SQL Server 2012 are Windows Server 2008 and Windows Vista. Although it is possible to upgrade a Windows Server 2003 host to Windows Server 2008 and then perform an upgrade of SQL Server 2005 to SQL Server 2012, it takes substantially less effort to migrate databases hosted on a SQL Server 2005 on Windows Server 2003 instance to SQL Server 2012 running on a different host operating system.

Prior to performing an upgrade, ensure that SQL Server 2005 Service Pack 4 has been applied to the SQL Server 2005 instance. When planning an upgrade, keep in mind that the edition from which you are upgrading limits the edition to which you can upgrade. These limitations are as follows:

- **SQL Server 2005 SP4 Enterprise** Can upgrade to SQL Server 2012 Enterprise and Business Intelligence editions

- **SQL Server 2005 SP4 Developer** Can upgrade to SQL Server 2012 Developer edition

- **SQL Server 2005 SP4 Standard** Can upgrade to SQL Server 2012 Enterprise, Business Intelligence, and Standard editions

- **SQL Server 2005 SP4 Workgroup** Can upgrade to SQL Server 2012 Enterprise, Business Intelligence, Standard, and Web editions

- **SQL Server 2005 SP4 Express (Express with Tools, Express with Advanced Services)** Can upgrade to SQL Server 2012 Enterprise, Business Intelligence, Standard, Web, and Express editions

Upgrading from SQL Server 2008

You can upgrade SQL Server 2008 to SQL Server 2012. You must apply Service Pack 2 for SQL Server 2008 before you can upgrade to SQL Server 2012. You can perform the following upgrades:

- **SQL Server 2008 SP2 Enterprise** Can upgrade to SQL Server 2012 Enterprise or Business Intelligence editions
- **SQL Server 2008 SP2 Developer** Can upgrade to SQL Server 2012 Developer edition
- **SQL Server 2008 SP2 Standard** Can upgrade to SQL Server 2012 Enterprise, Business Intelligence, or Standard editions
- **SQL Server 2008 SP2 Web** Can upgrade to SQL Server 2012 Enterprise, Business Intelligence, Standard, or Web editions
- **SQL Server 2008 SP2 Workgroup** Can upgrade to SQL Server 2012 Enterprise, Business Intelligence, Standard, or Web editions
- **SQL Server 2008 SP2 Express (Express with Tools, Express with Advanced Services)** Can upgrade to SQL Server 2012 Enterprise, Business Intelligence, Standard, Web, or Express editions

Upgrading from SQL Server 2008 R2

You can upgrade SQL Server 2008 R2 to SQL Server 2012. You must apply Service Pack 1 to SQL Server 2008 R2 before you can upgrade to SQL Server 2012. You can perform the following upgrades:

- **SQL Server 2008 R2 SP1 Datacenter** Can upgrade to SQL Server 2012 Enterprise and Business Intelligence editions
- **SQL Server 2008 R2 SP1 Enterprise** Can upgrade to SQL Server 2012 Enterprise and Business Intelligence editions
- **SQL Server 2008 R2 SP1 Developer** Can upgrade to SQL Server 2012 Developer edition
- **SQL Server 2008 R2 SP1 Standard** Can upgrade to SQL Server 2012 Enterprise, Business Intelligence, and Standard editions
- **SQL Server 2008 R2 SP1 Web** Can upgrade to SQL Server 2012 Enterprise, Business Intelligence, Standard, and Web editions
- **SQL Server 2008 R2 SP1 Workgroup** Can upgrade to SQL Server 2012 Enterprise, Business Intelligence, Standard, and Web editions
- **SQL Server 2008 R2 SP1 Express (Express with Tools, Express with Advanced Services)** Can upgrade to SQL Server 2012 Enterprise, Business Intelligence, Standard, Web, and Express editions

Intra-Edition Upgrades

It is also possible to perform an intra-edition upgrade. This might be necessary if you find that you deployed an edition that does not have all the features you need. You can perform an intra-edition upgrade only from certain editions, within the same processor architecture, and it is not possible to perform a downgrade to a "lower" edition.

You can perform the following SQL Server 2012 intra-edition upgrades:

- SQL Server 2012 Enterprise can be upgraded to the Business Intelligence edition.
- SQL Server 2012 Business Intelligence edition can be upgraded to the Enterprise edition.
- SQL Server 2012 Standard edition can be upgraded to the Enterprise or Business Intelligence editions.
- SQL Server 2012 Developer edition can be upgraded to the Enterprise, Business Intelligence, Standard, or Web editions.
- SQL Server 2012 Web edition can be upgraded to the Enterprise, Business Intelligence, and Standard editions.
- SQL Server 2012 Express edition can be upgraded to the Enterprise, Business Intelligence, Standard, and Web editions.
- SQL Server 2012 Evaluation edition can be upgraded to the Enterprise, Business Intelligence, Standard, and Web editions.

When performing an upgrade, remember that the version numbers of the Database Engine, Analysis Services, and Reporting Services features of an instance must be the same. For example, if a SQL Server 2008 R2 instance hosts the Database Engine and Analysis Services feature, you cannot upgrade only the Database Engine to SQL Server 2012. You must also upgrade the Analysis Services feature of the instance as well. It is possible to install a SQL Server 2012 instance on the same host server as SQL Server 2005, SQL Server 2008, or SQL Server 2008 R2.

> **MORE INFO** **SUPPORTED EDITION AND VERSION UPGRADES**
>
> You can learn more about the versions and editions of SQL Server you can upgrade to SQL Server 2012 at *http://msdn.microsoft.com/en-us/library/ms143393(SQL.110).aspx*.

Upgrade Advisor

Upgrade Advisor is a tool included with the SQL Server 2012 installation media that enables you to identify issues that will potentially block an upgrade. You can run Upgrade Advisor against SQL Server 2005, SQL Server 2008, and SQL Server 2008 R2 instances. Upgrade Advisor enables you to check the following SQL Server features:

- Database Engine
- Analysis Services

- Reporting Services
- Integration Services

You cannot use Upgrade Advisor to check the compatibility of desktop applications or encrypted stored procedures. You can run Upgrade Advisor only on host operating systems that support SQL Server 2012. When running Upgrade Advisor, you select which SQL Server components on the instance you want it to check, as shown in Figure 4-1.

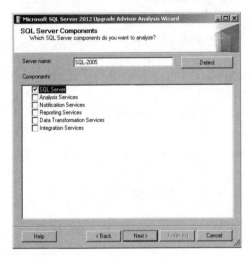

FIGURE 4-1 Upgrade Advisor

To run Upgrade Advisor, perform the following general steps:

1. Ensure that Microsoft .NET Framework 4.0 and Transact-SQL ScriptDom are installed on the server on which you want to install the upgrade advisor. You can download these components from the Microsoft website.

2. Install SQL Server 2012 Upgrade Advisor from SQL Server Installation Center by clicking Install Upgrade Advisor from the Planning section.

3. Run SQL Server 2012 Upgrade Advisor from the Microsoft SQL Server 2012 folder on the Program Files menu.

4. On the Welcome To SQL Server 2012 Upgrade Advisor page, click Launch Upgrade Advisor Analysis Wizard. On the first page of the wizard, click Next.

5. On the SQL Server Components page, click Detect to determine automatically which components are installed on the local server.

6. On the Connection Parameters page, choose the instance name and the authentication method. Use the drop-down menu to select the instance name. MSSQLSERVER represents the default instance.

7. On the SQL Server Parameters page, shown in Figure 4-2, choose which databases to analyze. You can also select trace files and SQL batch files to analyze.

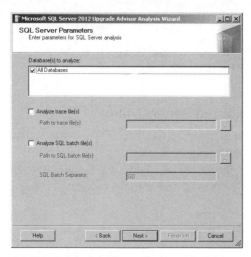

FIGURE 4-2 Select databases for Upgrade Advisor

8. On the Confirm Upgrade Advisor Settings page, review the chosen settings and then click Run.

9. After the analysis completes, click Launch Report to view the report. Figure 4-3 shows a sample Microsoft SQL Server 2012 Upgrade Advisor report.

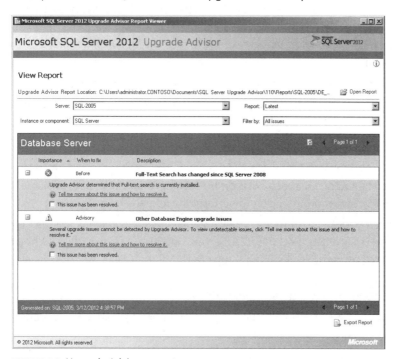

FIGURE 4-3 Upgrade Advisor report

Preparing for Upgrade with Distributed Replay Utility

The *Distributed Replay utility* enables you to simulate mission-critical workloads. You can use it to determine how a test server will function before upgrading it to SQL Server 2012. You can also use it to determine whether any incompatibilities might occur between the application and SQL Server 2012. You learn more about the Distributed Replay utility in Chapter 9, "Troubleshooting SQL Server 2012."

Performing an Upgrade

An upgrade overwrites the existing version of SQL Server with SQL Server 2012. If you are upgrading a 64-bit version of SQL Server 2005, SQL Server 2008, or SQL Server 2008 R2, it is necessary to upgrade Analysis Services before upgrading the Database Engine. If you are upgrading an instance that has both these components by using the setup wizard, this will happen automatically.

You should take the following steps prior to upgrading to SQL Server 2012:

- Ensure that databases are in a consistent state by running appropriate database console commands (DBCC).
- Verify that the system databases are configured with AutoGrow enabled.
- Disable startup stored procedures and replication.
- Ensure that enough disk space exists on the system volume and on the volume that will host the SQL Server program files to perform the upgrade.

You can launch an upgrade from the Installation page of SQL Server Installation Center by clicking Upgrade From SQL Server 2005, SQL Server 2008, Or SQL Server 2008 R2. You can upgrade from the command line by using setup.exe with the /ACTION=UPGRADE parameter.

Migrating a Database to a SQL Server 2012 Instance

When you *migrate* a database, the database is no longer hosted on the original instance. You might use migration if you have installed a SQL Server 2012 instance alongside a SQL Server 2005, SQL Server 2008, or SQL Server 2008 R2 instance. If you have a large number of databases hosted on a previous version of SQL Server, running different versions of SQL Server in parallel on the same host gives you the opportunity to migrate databases from the previous version of SQL Server to SQL Server 2012 gradually. You can also use this method to migrate from an x86 to an x64 version of SQL Server.

Detach a Database

Detaching a database removes it from the original instance of SQL Server but keeps the database and transaction log files intact. It is possible to *detach* a database only in the following circumstances:

- The database is not replicated and published. If you want to detach a database that is replicated, you must unpublish the database prior to attempting to detach the database. You learn more about replication in Chapter 7, "Mirroring and Replication."

- The database is not mirrored. If the database you want to detach is being mirrored, you must terminate the mirroring session. You learn more about mirroring databases in Chapter 7.

- The database must have no snapshots. Prior to detaching the database, you must drop all existing database snapshots.

- You cannot detach system databases.

You can attach a database only if all data files are available. You can specify alternate locations for files when attaching a database to a new instance. You cannot attach a database created on a more recent version of SQL Server to an earlier version. For example, you cannot detach a database from a SQL Server 2012 instance and then attach it to a SQL Server 2005 instance.

To detach a database by using SQL Server Management Studio, right-click the database, choose Tasks, and then click Detach. This brings up the Detach Database dialog box, shown in Figure 4-4. Choose whether to drop connections and update statistics and then click OK.

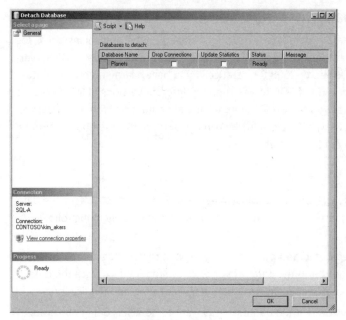

FIGURE 4-4 Detach Database dialog box

To detach a database by using Transact-SQL, execute the sp_detach_db stored procedure. For example, to detach the SpaceElevator database, execute the following statement:

```
USE master;
GO
EXEC sp_detach_db @dbname = [SpaceElevator];
GO
```

After the database has been detached, you can copy the database and log files to a new location. If you intend to attach the database to an alternate instance on the same server, you can keep the files in their original location.

Attach a Database

To *attach* a database to a new instance, right-click the Databases node in SQL Server Management Studio and then click Attach. This opens the Attach Databases dialog box, shown in Figure 4-5. Click Add to add the database file. If the log files are not located at the same path, you can use the ellipsis button (...) to specify an alternate path. Click OK to attach the database.

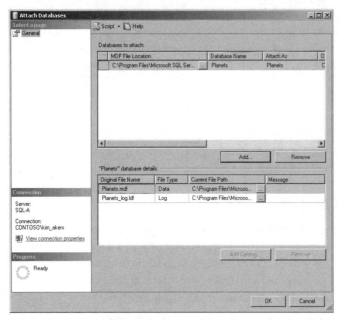

FIGURE 4-5 Attach Databases dialog box

You can attach a database by using the CREATE DATABASE statement with the FOR ATTACH option. For example, to attach the SpaceElevator database, where the mdf and log file are located in the C:\SpaceElevator directory, execute the following statement:

```
USE master;
GO
CREATE DATABASE SpaceElevator ON (Filename = 'C:\SpaceElevator\SpaceElevator.mdf'),
(FILENAME = 'C:\SpaceElevator\SpaceElevator_log.ldf') FOR ATTACH;
GO
```

When you attach a database from a previous version of SQL Server, full-text indexes will be imported, reset, or rebuilt, depending on the upgrade_option Database Engine property. The default setting for a SQL Server 2012 Database Engine instance is to import full-text catalogs. You can change this by altering the Full-Text Upgrade option on the Advanced page of the Server Properties dialog box or by using the sp_fulltext_service stored procedure.

Attaching a database to a SQL Server 2012 Database Engine instance sets the database compatibility level to 90 if it was 80 or less prior to the upgrade. If the database compatibility level was set to 90 or 100 prior to the upgrade, it remains at its original level.

> **MORE INFO** **DETACH AND ATTACH DATABASES**
>
> You can learn more about detaching and attaching databases at *http://msdn.microsoft*
> *.com/en-us/library/ms190794(SQL.110).aspx*.

> **Quick Check**
>
> - Which stored procedure should you call from a Transact-SQL statement if you want to detach a database from a SQL Server 2012 Database Engine instance?
>
> **Quick Check Answer**
>
> - You call the sp_detach_db stored procedure from a Transact-SQL statement when you want to detach a database from a SQL Server 2012 Database Engine instance.

Copying Databases to Other Servers

When you *copy* a database, the original instance retains a copy of that database while allowing you to deploy a copy of that instance on the target server. Copying a database has the advantage of allowing the original database to remain available to clients. You can copy a database to an instance hosted on new hardware and perform tests against the database without having an impact on clients of the database on the existing instance.

There are three general methods you can use to copy databases to other servers:

- Copy Database Wizard
- Backup and Restore database
- Publish Database by using Generate and Publish Scripts Wizard

> **MORE INFO   COPY DATABASES TO OTHER SERVERS**
>
> You can learn more about copying databases to other servers at *http://msdn.microsoft.com/en-us/library/ms189624(SQL.110).aspx*.

Copy Database Wizard

The *Copy Database Wizard* simplifies the process of copying databases from previous versions of SQL Server to SQL Server 2012 Database Engine instances. When you use the Copy Database Wizard, the database becomes available immediately on the target instance after the transfer completes and is automatically upgraded. The default configuration of SQL Server 2012 has full-text indexes imported, and these indexes will be unavailable during the upgrade process. Importing full-text indexes can take a substantial amount of time, but rebuilding full-text indexes usually takes even longer.

The Copy Database Wizard enables you to:

- Choose the source and destination instance. The destination instance must be running SQL Server 2012.
- Copy databases and move them. Choosing the Move option deletes the database on the source instance after a successful transfer.

- Choose database file locations on the destination instance.
- Migrate SQL logins to the destination instance, as shown in Figure 4-6.
- Migrate jobs, user-defined stored procedures, and custom error messages.
- Schedule what time the copy or move occurs.

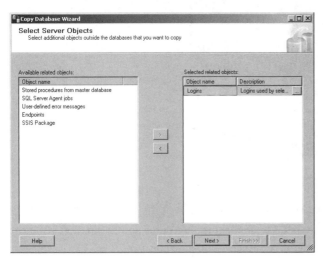

FIGURE 4-6 Migrate objects, including logins

You can't use the Copy Database Wizard to copy the system databases across to a new instance. You also cannot use the Copy Database Wizard to copy databases that are being replicated or databases that are marked as Inaccessible, Loading, Offline, Recovering, Suspect, or in Emergency mode. When using the Copy Database Wizard, the user performing the copy or move must be a member of the sysadmin fixed server role on both the source and destination instances. To use the Copy Database Wizard successfully, SQL Server Agent must be started on the destination instance.

When using the Copy Database Wizard, you must specify a transfer method, as shown in Figure 4-7. The difference between these methods is as follows:

- **Detach and Attach method** This method is faster, but the database on the source instance is taken offline. This method is suitable for moving large databases between instances. The database is reattached to the source instance when performing a copy operation.
- **SQL Management Object method** This method is slower but enables the database on the source instance to remain online.

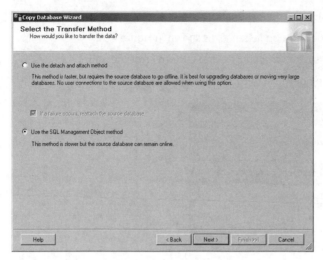

FIGURE 4-7 Database copy transfer method

To copy a database by using the Copy Database Wizard, perform the following steps:

1. Use SQL Server Management Studio to connect to the source and destination instances with a user account that is a member of the sysadmin fixed server role.

2. Ensure that the SQL Server Agent is started on the destination instance.

3. On the source instance, right-click the database you want to copy, click Tasks, and then click Copy Database. This starts the Copy Database Wizard. Click Next.

4. On the Source Server page, specify the source instance and click Next.

5. On the Select A Destination Server page, specify the destination instance, as shown in Figure 4-8.

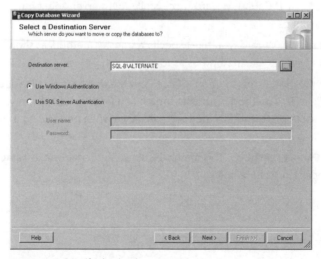

FIGURE 4-8 Specify destination server

6. Choose whether to use the detach and attach method or the SQL Management Object method.

7. On the Select Databases page, choose which databases you want to migrate from the source instance to the destination instance. You also choose whether to perform a move or a copy operation on this page.

8. On the Configure Destination Database page, shown in Figure 4-9, specify the name of the database on the destination instance. You can also specify the destination file location of the database and transaction log files.

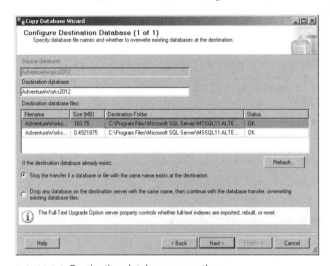

FIGURE 4-9 Destination database properties

9. On the Select Server Objects page, you can choose which objects to migrate, including logins used by security principals related to the databases that you want to migrate.

10. If you are using the detach and attach method, on the Location Of Source Database Files page, specify a file share that is configured for the location of the source database files.

11. Choose a name for the Integration Services package that will be created to assist with the migration.

12. On the Schedule page, choose whether to perform the transfer immediately or at a later point in time. Here you must also select an Integration Services Proxy account that has access to the file system on both the source and destination instances.

    You can create an Integration Services Proxy account by first creating a credential under the Security node mapped to a user that has the appropriate permissions on the destination instance. The second step requires that you add an SSIS Package Execution Proxy mapped to the newly created credential.

Copying Databases with Backup and Restore

You can *restore* backups taken of databases hosted on SQL Server 2005, SQL Server 2008, SQL Server 2008 R2, and SQL Server 2012 on a SQL Server 2012 instance. Prior to performing this task, you should create the same *backup devices* on the destination instance as you use on the source instance.

The general steps involved in using the backup and restore method are as follows:

1. Use either SQL Server Management Studio or Transact-SQL to back up the database that you want to copy on the source instance.

2. Transfer the backup file to the destination instance.

3. Restore the backup on the destination instance.

EXAM TIP

SQL Server 2012 uses different default paths than SQL Server 2005, SQL Server 2008, and SQL Server 2008 R2. When restoring a database backup taken from a previous version, remember to use the MOVE option.

When performing a restore operation, you might need to restore to an alternate location, especially if the destination instance doesn't have the same volume configuration as the source instance. Depending on the configuration of the destination instance, it also might be necessary to restore by using a different name. When you perform a restore operation, the principal who performs the restore operation becomes the owner of the restored database. Performing a backup of a database does not back up all metadata for the database. For example, you must migrate logins and jobs from the original server instance when using the backup and restore method of migrating or copying a database. You learn more about backup devices, backup, and restore in Chapter 11, "SQL Server Agent, Backup, and Restore."

Publishing a Database by Using Generate and Publish Scripts Wizard

You can use the Generate and Publish Scripts Wizard to publish a database to a web hosting provider. You can also use this wizard to produce a script that enables you to transfer a database.

To publish a database to a web service, perform the following steps:

1. In SQL Server Management Studio, right-click the database you want to publish to the web service, click Tasks, and then click Generate Scripts. This launches the Generate and Publish Scripts Wizard.

2. On the Choose Objects page, choose Script Entire Database And All Database Objects and click Next.

3. On the Set Scripting Options page, shown in Figure 4-10, specify the provider and target database.

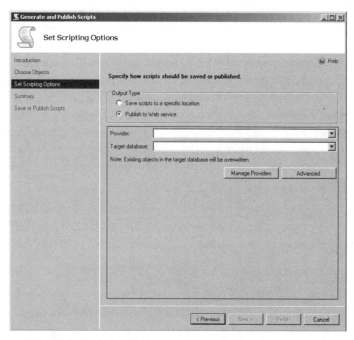

FIGURE 4-10 Set Scripting Options page

4. On the Summary page, review options.

5. On the Save And Publish Scripts page, verify that all actions have completed successfully and click Finish.

Migrating SQL Logins

SQL logins enable users to connect to the Database Engine instance. SQL logins can use
Windows security accounts, SQL Server, certificates, or asymmetric keys for authentication.
Except in the case of contained databases, database users map to logins. When you migrate a
database from one SQL Server instance to another, you must make sure that you also migrate
logins; otherwise, database users you have configured for the databases you are migrating
will become orphaned. An orphaned user is a database user who has no corresponding SQL
login. You learn more about SQL logins and database users in Chapter 5, "SQL Server Logins,
Roles, and Users."

In addition to the Copy Database Wizard that you learned about earlier, there are two
other methods that you can use to migrate SQL logins from one instance to another. The
first method is to use the Generate A Script function in SQL Server Management Studio to
re-create an object in the database. Using scripts is a simple way of transferring Windows-
authenticated SQL logins between instances. You can also use this method to migrate
other objects and the permissions associated with those objects. To create a script that will
re-create a SQL login on a new instance, perform the following general steps.

1. In SSMS, expand the Security\Logins node of the Database Engine instance.

2. Right-click the SQL login you wish to migrate, choose Script Login As, select CREATE To,
    and then choose New Query Editor Window, as shown in Figure 4-11. Doing this cre-
    ates a script that you can run on the destination instance that will re-create the login.

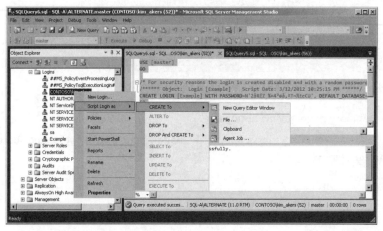

FIGURE 4-11 Script Login

You can use this method to create scripts to re-create multiple logins. After you have performed this for all the logins you want to migrate, save the script and then run it on the destination instance.

> **MORE INFO** **MANAGING DATABASE METADATA**
>
> You can find out more about managing database metadata when performing database copy and migration at *http://msdn.microsoft.com/en-us/library/ms187580(SQL.110).aspx*.

The drawback of generating a script is that although it enables the simple transfer of Windows-authenticated SQL logins, this method creates SQL-authenticated SQL logins on the new instance. These logins are in disabled state and will be assigned a random password. You can't use this method to export the passwords associated with SQL-authenticated SQL logins. If you use this method, it will be necessary to reset the password associated with the login before the principal associated with the login is able to connect.

In Knowledge Base article KB918992, Microsoft provides a script that database administrators can use to export SQL logins from SQL Server 2005, SQL Server 2008, and SQL Server 2008 R2. This script creates two stored procedures in the master database, named sp_hexadecimal and sp_help_revlogin. The database administrator executes the sp_help_revlogin stored procedure, the output of which is a script. The database administrator then executes the script on the destination instance. This script re-creates the logins exported from the source Database Engine instance and migrates the passwords associated with those logins. Consider using this script if you need to migrate databases that have database users associated with a large number of SQL-authenticated logins.

> **MORE INFO** **MIGRATE SQL LOGINS**
>
> You can find the script that enables you to migrate logins between instances at *http://support.microsoft.com/kb/918992*.

PRACTICE Migrate and Copy Databases

In this practice, you use the backup and restore and detach and attach methods of migrating databases.

EXERCISE 1 Copy a Database by Using Backup and Restore and Copy Database Wizard

In this exercise, you use the backup and restore method to copy the AdventureWorks2012 database from the default instance on SQL-A to the Alternate instance of SQL-A. To complete this exercise, perform the following steps:

1. Log on to the domain controller with the Kim_Akers user account and edit the SQL-POLICY Group Policy Object (GPO).

2. On the Inbound Rules node of the Windows Firewall With Advanced Security node, create a new Inbound rule allowing traffic on UDP ports 137, 138, and 1434 for all network profiles.

3. Log on to server SQL-A with the Kim_Akers user account.

4. Create a database named **Neptune** on the default SQL-A instance.

5. Use the backup and restore method to transfer the database to the SQL-A\ALTERNATE instance.

6. Create a credential mapped to the contoso\kim_akers account on the SQL-A\Alternate instance. Create a new SSIS Package Execution Proxy mapped to the new contoso \kim_akers credential.

7. Copy the AdventureWorks2012 database from the Default instance of SQL-A to the SQL-A\ALTERNATE instance by using the Copy Database Wizard.

EXERCISE 2   Migrate a Database by Using Detach and Attach

In this exercise, you migrate a database from one instance to another instance on the same server by using the Detach and Attach method. To complete this exercise, perform the following steps:

1. Log on to server SQL-A with the Kim_Akers user account.

2. On SQL-A, create the **C:\SpaceElevator** directory.

3. In SQL Server Management Studio, connect to the default instance on SQL-A and create a database named **SpaceElevator**. Store the database file and the transaction log file in the C:\SpaceElevator directory.

4. Using Transact-SQL, detach the SpaceElevator database from the SQL-A instance.

5. In SQL Server Management Studio, connect to the SQL-A\Alternate instance.

6. Use SQL Server Management Studio to attach the SpaceElevator database to the SQL-A\Alternate instance.

EXERCISE 3   Migrate Logins

In this exercise, you create and migrate a Windows-authenticated SQL login and a SQL-authenticated SQL login from one Database Engine instance to another. To complete this exercise, perform the following steps:

1. On the domain controller, create a new user account named **Cassie_Hicks**. Set the password to **Pa$$w0rd** and configure it so that it neither expires nor must be changed at the next login.

2. On the default instance of SQL-A, execute the following Transact-SQL statements to create the two SQL logins that you will migrate.

```
CREATE LOGIN "CONTOSO\Cassie_Hicks" FROM WINDOWS;
CREATE LOGIN Ben_Andrews WITH PASSWORD = 'Pa$$w0rd';
```

3. Use the Script Login As functionality in SQL Server Management Studio to script both logins to a new query window.

4. Execute the script generated in step 3 on the SQL-A\ALTERNATE instance to migrate the two logins to the ALTERNATE instance.

> **NOTE** **PASSWORD COMPLEXITY**
>
> You might need to alter the random password generated by the script for the Ben_Andrews login to ensure that it meets password complexity requirements.

Lesson Summary

- You can upgrade from SQL Server 2005, SQL Server 2008, and SQL Server 2008 R2 if the appropriate service packs have been applied, you are upgrading within the same processor architecture, and you are attempting a supported edition upgrade path.

- You can migrate a database from one instance to another instance by using the detach and attach method. You can't detach a database that is being mirrored or replicated or that has a snapshot.

- You can copy a database to another instance by using the Copy Database Wizard or by backing up and then restoring the database. The advantage of using the Copy Database Wizard is that it also enables you to migrate database metadata, such as logins, to the new instance.

- You can migrate SQL logins by using the Generate A Script function in SQL Server Management Studio.

Lesson Review

Answer the following questions to test your knowledge of the information in this lesson. You can find the answers to these questions and explanations of why each answer choice is correct or incorrect in the "Answers" section at the end of this chapter.

1. Which of the following can you upgrade to SQL Server 2012 Standard edition without having to apply additional service packs? (Each correct answer presents a complete solution. Choose all that apply.)

    A. SQL Server 2005 SP4 Standard edition installed on Windows Server 2008 with Service Pack 2

    B. SQL Server 2008 SP2 Standard edition installed on Windows Server 2003 R2

    C. SQL Server 2008 SP2 Enterprise edition installed on Windows Server 2008 R2 SP1

    D. SQL Server 2008 R2 SP1 Standard edition installed on Windows Server 2008 R2 SP1

2. To which of the following editions and versions of SQL Server 2012 can you upgrade SQL Server 2008 R2 Datacenter edition (x64)? (Each correct answer presents a complete solution. Choose all that apply.)

   A. SQL Server 2012 Enterprise edition (x86)

   B. SQL Server 2012 Enterprise edition (x64)

   C. SQL Server 2012 Business Intelligence edition (x64)

   D. SQL Server 2012 Standard edition (x64)

3. Which of the following tools can you use to migrate Windows-authenticated SQL logins from an x86 instance of SQL Server 2012 to an x64 instance of SQL Server 2012 if contained databases are not in use? (Each correct answer presents a complete solution. Choose all that apply.)

   A. Copy Database Wizard

   B. Import and Export Wizard

   C. Backup and Restore Database

   D. Generate A Script

4. You want to migrate a database, including logins and user-defined error messages, from one SQL Server 2012 instance to another. Which of the following tools can you use to accomplish this goal?

   A. Copy Database Wizard

   B. BACKUP DATABASE Transact-SQL statement

   C. Import and Export Wizard

   D. sp_detach_db stored procedure

5. You want to use the detach and attach method of migrating a database to another SQL Server 2012 Database Engine instance. The database is currently published and replicated. Which of the following steps must you take prior to detaching the database from the source instance? (Each correct answer presents part of a complete solution. Choose all that apply.)

   A. Drop database snapshots.

   B. Unpublish the database.

   C. Create a format file.

   D. Create a database snapshot.

Lesson 2: Exporting and Importing Data

At times, it is necessary to import or export large amounts of data into or out of a database. Large-scale import and export operations are termed bulk import and export operations. In this lesson, you learn about the tools you can use to import data from and export data to databases hosted in a SQL Server 2012 instance.

After this lesson, you will be able to:

- Transfer data.
- Perform a bulk copy operation.
- Perform a bulk insert operation.

Estimated lesson time: 60 minutes

Copying and Exporting Data

SQL Server 2012 provides several tools that you can use to perform bulk copy and bulk export and import operations. These tools are as follows:

- Use the bcp command to export data to or import data from files. The bcp command is a command-line utility.

- Use the BULK INSERT Transact-SQL statement to import data from a file stored on the file system. You can execute this statement from within the Database Engine.

- Use the OPENROWSET(BULK) function to import data from an OLE DB data source.

- Use the Integration Services Import And Export Wizard to migrate data from SQL Server and OLE DB providers such as Microsoft Access and Microsoft Excel.

- Use the SELECT INTO statement to create a new table and populate it with data based on the results of a SELECT query.

You learn more about each of these tools throughout the rest of the lesson.

MORE INFO **COPYING DATA BETWEEN SERVERS**

You can learn more about copying data between servers at *http://msdn.microsoft.com /en-us/library/ms190923(SQL.110).aspx.*

Using the SQL Server Import and Export Wizard

The *SQL Server Import and Export Wizard* (*DTSWizard.exe*) is a component of Integration Services. The SQL Server Import and Export Wizard enables you to migrate data to and from the following sources:

- .NET Framework Data Provider for SQLServer
- Flat File Source
- Microsoft Access
- Microsoft Excel
- Microsoft OLE DB Provider for Analysis Services 11.0
- Microsoft OLE DB Provider for Oracle
- Microsoft OLE DB Provider for SQL Server
- SQL Server Native Client 11.0

The Import and Export Wizard works by creating an Integration Services package. Integration Services enables you to perform complex data transformation tasks that are beyond the scope of the 70-462 exam. The benefit of an Integration Services package, though, is that you can schedule it to run on a regular basis and modify it as necessary by using SQL Server Data Tools.

The following permissions are required to use the SQL Server Import and Export Wizard:

- Permission to read from the source database or file.
- Permission to write data to the destination database or file.
- To save the Integration Services package created by the wizard, the security principal requires INSERT permission on the msdb database.
- If it is necessary to create a new database or table to complete the wizard, the appropriate permissions are required on the destination database instance.

When you deploy Integration Services on a computer that has a 64-bit operating system, Integration Services installs an x64 version of the SQL Server Import and Export Wizard. In some cases, this might cause problems when connections are made to data sources that use 32-bit providers, such as a 32-bit version of Microsoft Access. To resolve this issue, choose to install either the Client Tools or SQL Server Data Tools (SSDT) shared features during the SQL Server setup process.

To use the SQL Server Import and Export Wizard to export data from a database hosted on a SQL Server 2012 Database Engine instance, perform the following steps:

1. In SQL Server Management Studio, right-click the database from which you want to export data. Choose Tasks and then select Export Data. This launches the SQL Server Import and Export Wizard.

2. On the Choose A Data Source page, shown in Figure 4-12, choose the data source from which you want to export data. If necessary, provide alternate authentication credentials.

FIGURE 4-12 Choose A Data Source page

3. On the Destination page, choose the destination type, server name, authentication credentials, and, if the destination type supports it, a target database or a new database.

4. On the Specify Table Copy Or Query page, shown in Figure 4-13, choose whether you want to copy data from one or more tables or views within the source database or want to create a custom query to limit the source data that you export by using the wizard. You can choose all tables and views in the source database.

FIGURE 4-13 Specify Table Copy Or Query page

5. You can select a table or view and click Edit Mappings to modify the properties of the destination table on a per-column basis, as shown in Figure 4-14. Note that you cannot perform column transformations by using the Import and Export Wizard. If you must perform transformations when exporting data, you should create an Integration Services package.

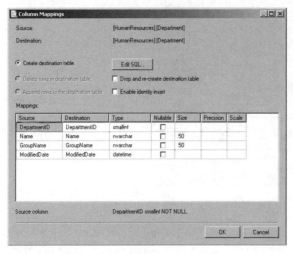

FIGURE 4-14 Column mappings

6. On the Save And Run Package page, choose whether to run the package immediately. You can also save the Integration Services package generated by the wizard to either the SQL Server instance or the file system.

> **MORE INFO**   **SQL SERVER IMPORT AND EXPORT WIZARD**
>
> You can learn more about the SQL Server Import and Export Wizard at *http://msdn*
> *.microsoft.com/en-us/library/ms141209(SQL.110).aspx.*

Using BCP to Import and Export Data

The *bcp* utility is a command-line utility that enables you to bulk export data from a database to a file or bulk import data from a file into tables in a database. You can use bcp with XML format files only if you have installed the SQL Server Native Client feature. To use bcp to perform a bulk export operation, the security principal using the utility must have SELECT permission on the source table. When you use bcp to export data to a file, the utility either creates a new file by using the specified filename or overwrites the contents of an existing file.

EXAM TIP

The bcp utility can export data to a file or import data from a file. It cannot transfer data directly from one database to another.

SQL Server 2012 uses parallel scans to retrieve data, which means that, unless you take precautions, exported data will not be written using a specific order in the data file. You can ensure that data in a file created by using the bcp utility is in a specific order by using the queryout option and the ORDER BY clause. For example, to export a list of products and product numbers ordered alphabetically by product name to the products.txt file from the AdventureWorks2012 database, use the following bcp command.

```
bcp "SELECT Name, ProductNumber FROM AdventureWorks2012.Production.Product ORDER BY
NAME" queryout products.txt -c -T
```

The -T option specifies a trusted connection. This means that bcp uses the credentials of the currently logged on user. If you do not specify the -T option, you must specify a username and password by using the -U and -P options. The -c option specifies that bcp is being used with character data.

Prior to importing data, ensure that the destination table has columns configured that are compatible with the data type you intend to import. The table must exist prior to attempting the import. To insert the data exported in the previous example into a table named ExampleDatabase.dbo.TableBeta, which is configured with two columns that use the *nvarchar(max)* data type, run the following command.

```
bcp ExampleDatabase.dbo.TableBeta in products.txt -T -c
```

You can use a format file with the bcp utility by specifying the -f option. You learn about format files later in this lesson.

> **MORE INFO** **THE BCP UTILITY**
>
> You can find out more about the bcp utility at *http://msdn.microsoft.com/en-us/library /ms162802(SQL.110).aspx.*

Importing Data by Using BULK INSERT

Use the *BULK INSERT* statement to load data into a table from a file. Unlike the bcp utility, which you run from the operating system, the BULK INSERT statement is run from within the Database Engine. When using the BULK INSERT statement, specify the table into which you want to insert the data and the location of the file from which to import the data. As is the case with the bcp utility, you must ensure that the table into which you are importing data already exists and has column types that are compatible with the type of data you are importing. For example, you create a table named TableAlpha in the dbo schema of the ExampleDatabase database that has two columns of data type *nvarchar(max)*. To use the BULK INSERT statement to import the data from the products.txt file that was exported in the earlier example, where that file is hosted on the \\SQL-A\DATA share, execute the statement:

```
BULK INSERT ExampleDatabase.dbo.TableAlpha FROM '\\SQL-A\DATA\products.txt';
GO
```

Importing Data by Using OPENROWSET(BULK)

OPENROWSET(BULK) enables you to connect to an OLE DB data source to retrieve data. You use OPENROWSET(BULK...) when using an INSERT statement with a SELECT...FROM clause. You provide the full details of how to connect to the data source as parameters for the OPENROWSET function. This function provides you with an alternative to accessing tables on a linked server and is suitable when you need to perform one-off importation of data from a remote source. You reference OPENROWSET(BULK) in a FROM clause of a query in the same way that you would reference a table name: for example: SELECT * FROM OPENROWSET(BULK...).

Using Format Files

Format files map data file fields to the columns of a table. You use a format file with bcp, BULK INSERT, or OPENROWSET(BULK...) when importing data from a file that uses fixed-width or character-terminated fields. SQL Server 2012 supports two types for format files. Previous versions of SQL Server support non-XML format files, and Microsoft recommends that you use XML syntax for new format files.

You use the bcp utility to create a format file. Instead of specifying a data file path, use nul. You use the -x extension to specify that the XML format is being used. You specify the field terminator by using the -t option. In the following example, a format file is being created for the AdventureWorks2012.HumanResources.Employee table in which the field terminator will be the comma (,) character.

```
bcp AdventureWorks2012.HumanResources.Employee format nul -c -x -f Employee-c.xml -t, -T
```

> **Quick Check**
>
> - Which statement or function would you use if you wanted to import data into a table from a remote data file through an OLE DB provider?
>
> **Quick Check Answer**
>
> - You can use the OPENROWSET(BULK) function to import data into a table by connecting to a remote data source through an OLE DB provider.

Preparing Data for Bulk Operations

When preparing a bulk import operation, remember the following:

- Columns in the table that you are targeting with the bulk import operation must be compatible with the fields in the data file.

- You must use a format file if you are performing a bulk import of data from a data file with a fixed-length or fixed-width field.

- Although not supported, comma separated values (CSV) files can be used as the data file for a bulk import. You can use CSV files if none of the values in a data field are enclosed in quotation marks and data fields never contain the field-terminator character (usually a comma).

- A user performing the bulk import operation needs the SELECT and INSERT permissions on the table.

- If a user must be able to disable constraints or use other options that use data definition language (DDL) operations, he or she needs the ALTER TABLE permission on the target table.

- A user performing the bulk operation needs read access to the file on the file system and the ADMINISTER BULK OPERATIONS permission.

- You cannot perform a bulk import operation into a partitioned view.

> **MORE INFO PREPARING DATA FOR BULK OPERATIONS**
>
> You can learn more about preparing data for bulk import and export operations at
> *http://msdn.microsoft.com/en-us/library/ms188609(SQL.110).aspx.*

You can improve the speed at which bulk import operations are performed by using the bcp utility, BULK INSERT statement, or OPENROWSET (BULK...) function by taking the following general steps:

- Change the logging model if the database uses the full recovery model. If you perform a bulk insert operation on a database configured to use the full recovery model, all row-insert operations are written in their entirety to the transaction log. Prior to performing a bulk insert operation, switch the database to use the bulk logged recovery model and perform the bulk import operation. After the bulk import operation has completed, return the database to the full recovery model.

- You can perform bulk import operations in parallel. The bcp utility, the BULK INSERT statement, and the OPENROWSET (BULK...) function all support parallel import of data. If the destination table has no indexes, specify the TABLOCK option when performing the bulk-import operation. If the TABLOCK operation is not specified, the Database Engine does not use bulk optimization, and blocking issues can occur when obtaining locks on individual rows or pages.

- Disabling triggers and constraints can improve the performance of bulk import operations.

- If the destination table has a clustered index, you can improve bulk import operation performance by importing data from the data file by using the same ordering as used in the table.

> **MORE INFO** **IMPROVING BULK IMPORT PERFORMANCE**
>
> You can learn more about improving the performance of bulk import operations at *http://msdn.microsoft.com/en-us/library/ms190421(SQL.105).aspx.*

SELECT INTO

The INTO clause, when used with the SELECT statement, enables you to create a new table by using the results of a select statement. The columns in the newly created table use the same name, data type, nullability, and value as the columns output from the select query. Assuming that you have the appropriate permissions, you can use the SELECT statement with the INTO clause to create a new table on another database hosted on the same instance. A security principal must have been assigned the CREATE TABLE permission to use the SELECT statement with the INTO clause.

For example, to create a copy of the HumanResources.Department table of the AdventureWorks2012 database named HumanResourcesDepartmentCopy in the dbo schema of the ExampleDatabase database on the same instance, issue the query:

```
SELECT * INTO ExampleDatabase.dbo.HumanResourcesDepartmentCopy FROM AdventureWorks2012.
HumanResources.Department;
```

Although it is not possible to use the SELECT statement with the INTO clause to create a new table on a remote server, you can include remote data sources in the SELECT statement if there is an existing link to the remote data source. You can also use the OPENQUERY or OPENDATASOURCE functions in the SELECT query FROM clause when specifying the remote data source.

Any indexes, triggers, and constraints that are present on the source table will not transfer across to the new table. You must create indexes, triggers, and constraints after the SELECT... INTO query has executed.

The column in the newly created table will inherit the IDENTITY property of the column output by the query except under the following circumstances:

- The SELECT statement uses a join, GROUP BY clause, or an aggregate function.
- The UNION clause is used to join multiple SELECT statements.
- The identity column is from a remote data source, is part of an expression, or is used more than once.

You cannot use the INTO clause with the SELECT statement to create a partitioned table. If you want to create a partitioned table, it is necessary to create the partitioned table first and then insert rows into the table by using the INSERT INTO...SELECT FROM statement.

> **MORE INFO SELECT INTO**
>
> You can learn more about using he SELECT statement with the INTO clause at *http://msdn .microsoft.com/en-us/library/ms188029(SQL.110).aspx.*

PRACTICE Bulk Export and Import of Data

In this practice, you use several SQL Server 2012 tools to transfer data, perform a bulk export, and perform a bulk import.

EXERCISE 1 Export Data from AdventureWorks

In this exercise, use the SQL Server Import and Export Wizard to transfer data to another instance. You also use the SELECT...INTO statement to create a copy of the contents of a table. To complete this exercise, perform the following steps:

1. Create a new database on the SQL-CORE default instance named **AdventureExport**.
2. Use the SQL Server Import and Export Wizard to export data from all tables and views of the AdventureWorks2012 database hosted on the default instance of SQL-A to the AdventureExport database on SQL-CORE.
3. Use the SELECT...INTO statement to create a copy of the AdventureWorks2012. HumanResources.Employee table in the dbo schema of the AdventureExport database.

EXERCISE 2 Use bcp to Transfer Data

In this exercise, you use bcp to export data from one table in one database and then use it to insert data into a table in another database. To complete this exercise, perform the following steps:

1. On the default instance of SQL-A, create a database named **AdventureContacts.**
2. Create two tables in the AdventureContacts database named **TableAlpha** and **TableBeta**. Both tables should have two columns named **FirstName** and **LastName** and should use the *nvarchar(max)* datatype.

3. Create the **C:\Data** directory on server SQL-A.

4. Share this directory.

5. Use the bcp utility to export data from the Person.Person table in the AdventureWorks2012 database hosted on the default instance of SQL-A to a file named contacts.txt in the C:\Data directory. The exported data should contain a person's first name and last name and should be sorted on the basis of last name and then first name.

6. Use the BULK INSERT statement to import the data from the \\SQL-A\data\contacts.txt file into TableAlpha in the AdventureContacts database.

7. Use the bcp utility to perform a bulk insert of the data in the c:\data\contacts.txt file into the TableBeta table in the AdventureContacts database.

Lesson Summary

- The bcp utility is a command-line utility you can use to export data from a database or to perform a bulk import of data into a preexisting table.

- The BULK INSERT Transact-SQL statement enables you to import data from a file into a preexisting table.

- You can use the OPENROWSET(BULK) function to import data from an OLE DB data source.

- You can use the Integrations Services Import and Export Wizard to migrate data to and from OLE DB providers. The wizard enables you to save an import or an export task as an Integration Services package, which you can execute later according to a schedule.

- The SELECT INTO statement enables you to create a new table on a database hosted on the current instance based on the results of a SELECT query.

- You use a format file when you are performing a bulk import of data from a file that uses a fixed-length or fixed-width field.

Lesson Review

Answer the following questions to test your knowledge of the information in this lesson. You can find the answers to these questions and explanations of why each answer choice is correct or incorrect in the "Answers" section at the end of this chapter.

1. You must create an XML format file based on a database table to use later when bulk importing data on other instances. Which of the following tools would you use to accomplish this goal?

   A. bcp utility

   B. Import and Export Wizard

   C. BULK INSERT statement

   D. OPENROWSET function

2. Which of the following tools can you use to create an Integration Services package that enables you to repeat a specific data import or export operation?

    A. OPENROWSET function

    B. BULK INSERT statement

    C. Import and Export Wizard

    D. bcp utility

3. You must copy the complete contents of a table in the Hovercraft database into a new table in the Watercraft database. The destination table does not currently exist in the Watercraft database. The Watercraft and Hovercraft databases are hosted on the same SQL Server 2012 instance. Which of the following tools can you use to accomplish this goal? (Each correct answer presents a complete solution. Choose all that apply.)

    A. bcp utility

    B. SELECT...INTO Transact-SQL statement.

    C. Import and Export Wizard

    D. Copy Database Wizard

4. You must connect to a remote OLE DB data source and import a substantial amount of data into a table hosted on a local database. Which of the following tools can you use to accomplish this goal? (Each correct answer presents a complete solution. Choose all that apply.)

    A. Import and Export Wizard

    B. Copy Database Wizard

    C. bcp utility

    D. OPENROWSET(BULK) function

5. You have a table that contains 20,000 customer records. Which of the following tools can you use to export these records to a file? (Each correct answer presents a complete solution. Choose all that apply.)

    A. bcp utility

    B. BULK INSERT Transact-SQL statement

    C. Import and Export Wizard

    D. Copy Database Wizard

Case Scenarios

In the following case scenarios, apply what you have learned about planning server installs and upgrades. You can find answers to these questions in the "Answers" section at the end of this chapter.

Case Scenario 1: Consolidation at Contoso

Contoso has 20 database servers running a mix of SQL Server 2005 and SQL Server 2008. All existing database servers are running x86 versions of SQL Server. Contoso has recently deployed 20 virtual machines that have the x64 version of SQL Server 2012 Enterprise edition in their private cloud. You want to start by deploying databases from 10 instances to an instance hosted in the private cloud used for development work. During the development phase of the project, these databases should also remain hosted on their original parent instances. Each database instance has between 10 and 100 SQL logins, which all use Windows authentication.

With this information in mind, answer the following questions:

1. What steps should you take to migrate the databases during the development phase of the project?

2. Describe the steps that you would take to migrate the SQL logins from the original instances to the new instances.

3. What factors will influence whether you perform a backup and restore method or a detach and attach method when it comes to migrating the databases prior to deploying them in the private cloud environment?

Case Scenario 2: Tailspin Toys Bulk Data

Tailspin Toys has a number of SQL Server 2012 instances deployed on traditional hardware. It is necessary to export a substantial amount of data from the database on a regular basis. The data is the entire contents of specific tables and must be written to Excel format. It is also necessary on occasion to import a substantial amount of customer data from a specially prepared file into one of the databases.

With this information in mind, answer the following questions.

1. You have a file that contains customer names, phone numbers, and addresses. Which command-line utility would you use to import this data into a table on a database instance?

2. Every week, you must perform a bulk export of data from the database. What steps could you take to automate this process?

3. You must copy the contents of several large tables to new tables on a different database hosted on the same instance. Which method could you use to accomplish this goal?

Suggested Practices

To help you successfully master the exam objectives presented in this chapter, complete the following tasks.

Implement a Migration Strategy

Prior to completing each task in the following practices, list the steps you would take to accomplish the task. After completing the task, assess how accurately you predicted the necessary steps.

- **Practice 1**   On the default instance of SQL-A, create a database named **Neptune**. Use the backup and restore method to copy this database to the default instance of SQL-B.

- **Practice 2**   On the default instance of SQL-A, create three SQL-authenticated logins. Use the script published in Knowledge Base article KB918992 to migrate these logins from the default instance of SQL-A to the default instance on SQL-B.

Import and Export Data

Prior to completing each task in the following practices, list the steps you would take to accomplish the task. After completing the task, assess how accurately you predicted the necessary steps.

- **Practice 1**   Use the bcp utility to export the contents of the Production.Document table in the AdventureWorks2012 database to a file named proddocs.txt. Ensure that the data in the file is sorted by the document title.

- **Practice 2**   Use the SQL Server Import and Export Wizard to export the Person. Address table to a newly created database on the default instance of SQL-CORE.

Answers

This section contains the answers to the lesson review questions and solutions to the case scenarios in this chapter.

Lesson 1

1. **Correct Answers: A and D**

    A. **Correct:** You can upgrade SQL Server 2005 SP4 to SQL Server 2012 if the host operating system is running Windows Server 2008 with Service Pack 2.

    B. **Incorrect:** You cannot install SQL Server 2012 on a computer running the Windows Server 2003 R2 operating system.

    C. **Incorrect:** You cannot upgrade the Enterprise edition of SQL Server 2008 with Service Pack 2 to the Standard edition of SQL Server 2012. You can upgrade it to the Enterprise or Business Intelligence editions.

    D. **Correct:** You can upgrade SQL Server 2008 R2 SP1 Standard edition to SQL Server 2012 Standard edition on a host running Windows Server 2008 R2 SP1.

2. **Correct Answers: B and C**

    A. **Incorrect:** You cannot upgrade an x64 version of SQL Server 2008 R2 to an x86 version of SQL Server 2012.

    B. **Correct:** You can upgrade the Datacenter edition of SQL Server 2008 R2 to the Enterprise edition of SQL Server 2012 if they share the same processor architecture.

    C. **Correct:** You can upgrade the Datacenter edition of SQL Server 2008 R2 to the Business Intelligence edition of SQL Server 2012 if they share the same processor architecture.

    D. **Incorrect:** You cannot upgrade the Datacenter edition of SQL Server 2008 R2 to the Standard edition of SQL Server 2012.

3. **Correct Answers: A and D**

    A. **Correct:** You can use the Copy Database Wizard to migrate SQL logins from an x86 instance of SQL Server 2012 to an x64 instance of SQL Server 2012; however, this will also copy the entire database, not just the logins.

    B. **Incorrect:** You cannot use the Import and Export Wizard to copy logins from one SQL Server instance to another.

    C. **Incorrect:** Backing up and restoring a database does not copy login data because this is stored outside the database. Contained databases are the exception to this.

    D. **Correct:** You can use the Generate A Script option to create a script that enables you to re-create a Windows-authenticated SQL login on another instance.

4. **Correct Answer: A**

   A. **Correct:** You can use the Copy Database Wizard to migrate a database, including logins and user-defined error messages, from one SQL Server 2012 instance to another.

   B. **Incorrect:** You can use this statement to back up a database, but it will not back up logins and user-defined error messages, which are stored outside the database.

   C. **Incorrect:** You cannot use the Import and Export Wizard to migrate a database including logins and user-defined error messages.

   D. **Incorrect:** You use the sp_detach_db stored procedure to detach a database. You cannot use this stored procedure to migrate logins and user-defined error messages.

5. **Correct Answers: A and B**

   A. **Correct:** You must drop any database snapshots prior to detaching the database.

   B. **Correct:** You must unpublish the database from replication prior to detaching the database.

   C. **Incorrect:** Format files are used when performing bulk imports of data. You do not need to create a format file prior to detaching a database.

   D. **Incorrect:** You must remove database snapshots prior to detaching a database, not create additional snapshots.

Lesson 2

1. **Correct Answer: A**

   A. **Correct:** You use the bcp utility to create XML format files. These files are used when importing files that use fixed-width fields.

   B. **Incorrect:** You cannot use the Import and Export Wizard to create an XML format file. You use the bcp utility to create this type of file.

   C. **Incorrect:** You cannot use the BULK INSERT statement to create an XML format file. You use the bcp utility to create this type of file.

   D. **Incorrect:** You cannot use the OPENROWSET function to create an XML format file. You use the bcp utility to create this type of file.

2. **Correct Answer: C**

   A. **Incorrect:** You cannot use the OPENROWSET function to save an export or import configuration as an Integration Services package for later use.

   B. **Incorrect:** You cannot use the BULK INSERT statement to save an export or import configuration as an Integration Services package for later use.

   C. **Correct:** When you use the Import and Export Wizard to import or export data, you can save the import or export configuration as an Integration Services package that you can use later.

D. Incorrect: You cannot use the bcp utility to save an export or import configuration as an Integration Services package for later use.

3. **Correct Answers: B and C**

    A. Incorrect: Although the bcp utility can export the contents of an entire table and then insert that data into another table, the destination table must already exist.

    B. Correct: You can use the SELECT...INTO Transact-SQL statement to copy the contents of one table to another table in a separate database on the same instance while having the destination table automatically created during the process.

    C. Correct: You can use the Import and Export Wizard to copy the contents of one table to another table in a separate database on the same instance while having the destination table automatically created during the process.

    D. Incorrect: Although you can use the Copy Database Wizard to copy an entire database, you cannot use this wizard to copy a single table.

4. **Correct Answers: A and D**

    A. Correct: You can use the Import and Export Wizard to connect to a remote OLE DB data source when you need to import a substantial amount of data.

    B. Incorrect: Although you can use the Copy Database Wizard to copy an entire SQL Server database, you do not use this tool to import data from an OLE DB data source.

    C. Incorrect: You can use the bcp utility only to import and export data from a local SQL Server instance.

    D. Correct: You can use the OPENROWSET(BULK) function as part of a statement that imports a substantial amount of data from a remote OLE DB data source.

5. **Correct Answers: A and C**

    A. Correct: You can use the bcp utility to perform a bulk export of data from a table to a file.

    B. Incorrect: You can use the BULK INSERT Transact-SQL statement only to import data from a file. You cannot use this statement to export data to a file.

    C. Correct: You can use the Import and Export Wizard to export all the data hosted in a table to a file.

    D. Incorrect: You can use the Copy Database Wizard to copy a database from one instance to another. You cannot use this wizard to export data from a table to a file.

Case Scenario 1

1. You should copy the databases from the production hosts to the virtual machines in the development private cloud. You could use the backup and restore method of copying the databases or the Copy Database Wizard by using the object model to

perform the copy. The key is that your strategy should ensure that the databases on the production server remain online.

2. You should use the Script Login As method of migrating the SQL logins because the problem statement says that all logins use Windows authentication. You might also consider using the script published with Knowledge Base article KB918992, which enables you to automate the migration of both SQL Server–authenticated and Windows-authenticated SQL logins, although in this case, because you don't have to worry about migrating passwords, the Script Login As method might be simpler. You can also use the Copy Database Wizard to migrate the logins.

3. A detach operation takes the database offline from its current instance. Although you can make a copy of the files and then reattach on the original instance and the destination instance, using the Backup and Restore method of copying a database ensures that the database remains online on the original host during the migration.

Case Scenario 2

1. You use the bcp utility to import data into the database from the command line.

2. Use the SQL Server Import and Export Wizard to create an Integration Services package. Schedule the package to execute on a periodic basis.

3. You could use the SELECT...INTO statement to copy the contents of existing tables quickly into new tables if the new tables are associated with a different database hosted on the same instance.

CHAPTER 5

SQL Server Logins, Roles, and Users

Exam objectives in this chapter:

- Manage logins and server roles.
- Manage users and database roles.

Understanding how to assign appropriate permissions to security principals is critical for database administrators. Many find understanding the differences among SQL logins, users, and roles to be difficult. This is because many have come from a background in server administration in which the terms *login* and *user* are used interchangeably. In this chapter, you learn about the difference between logins and users and between database roles and server roles. You also learn about contained users, a feature new in SQL Server 2012, and why you might want to implement this new feature.

Lessons in this chapter:

Before You Begin

To complete the practice exercises in this chapter, make sure that you have:

- Completed the setup tasks for installing computers DC, SQL-A, SQL-B, and SQL-CORE as outlined in the introduction of this book.
- Completed the setup tasks outlined in the end-of-lesson practice exercises in Chapter 1, "Planning and Installing SQL Server 2012," through Chapter 4, "Migrating, Importing, and Exporting."

No additional configuration is required for this chapter.

Lesson 1: Managing Logins and Server Roles

This lesson covers managing security principals at the instance level. Security principals at this level allow access to the instance and serve as a gateway to the security principals that allow access to databases hosted on the instance. In this lesson, you learn about the different kinds of authentication you can use to support logins to SQL Server, how to use fixed server roles, and how to create user-defined server roles, a feature new in SQL Server 2012.

After this lesson, you will be able to:

- Create SQL Server–authenticated SQL Server logins.
- Administer Windows-authenticated SQL Server logins.
- Create SQL logins authenticated by certificate and asymmetric key.
- Manage fixed server roles.
- Create user-defined server roles.
- Grant and deny access to the Database Engine instance.

Estimated lesson time: 60 minutes

SQL Logins

Logins are the credentials that authenticate connections to an instance. Except in the case of an instance configured to support contained databases, a database user must map to an existing SQL Server login. You can differentiate SQL Server logins based on the type of authentication method used. SQL Server 2012 supports the following login types:

- Windows-authenticated login
- SQL Server–authenticated login
- Certificate
- Asymmetric key

A security principal must have the ALTER ANY LOGIN permission to be able to create SQL logins.

EXAM TIP

It is important to remember the difference between logins and users.

Windows-Authenticated SQL Server Logins

Windows-authenticated SQL Server logins are instance logins in which the operating system handles authentication. You can map a Windows-authenticated SQL Server login to a local user account, a local security group, a domain user account, or a domain security group. The type of authentication you use depends on your organization's needs. Controlling access by using local computer-based or domain-based groups can reduce the number of SQL logins required but requires giving database administrators the ability to manage membership of these groups. Password complexity and expiration policies are determined by either the local security policy or domain-based Group Policy settings.

To create a Windows-authenticated SQL Server login by using SQL Server Management Studio, perform the following steps:

1. Open SQL Server Management Studio and connect to the Database Engine instance on which you want to create the Windows-authenticated SQL Server login.

2. Right-click the Security node, click New, and then click Login. This opens the Login - New dialog box. Ensure that Windows Authentication is selected and then click Search.

3. The Select User Or Group dialog box defaults to the local host server's security account database. If you want to use a group account, you must click the Object Types button and select the Groups object, as shown in Figure 5-1.

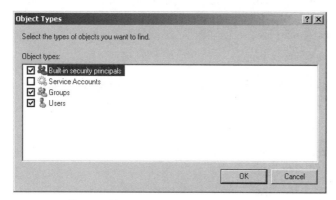

FIGURE 5-1 Choose object type

4. If you want to use a security principal from the host computer's local account database, enter either the user or group name and then click OK. If you want to create a Windows-authenticated SQL Server login that uses a domain security principal, click Locations and then select the domain that hosts the security principal. Click OK, enter the user or group name, and then click OK.

5. On the Login - New page, verify that the appropriate security principal is selected, as shown in Figure 5-2, and then click OK.

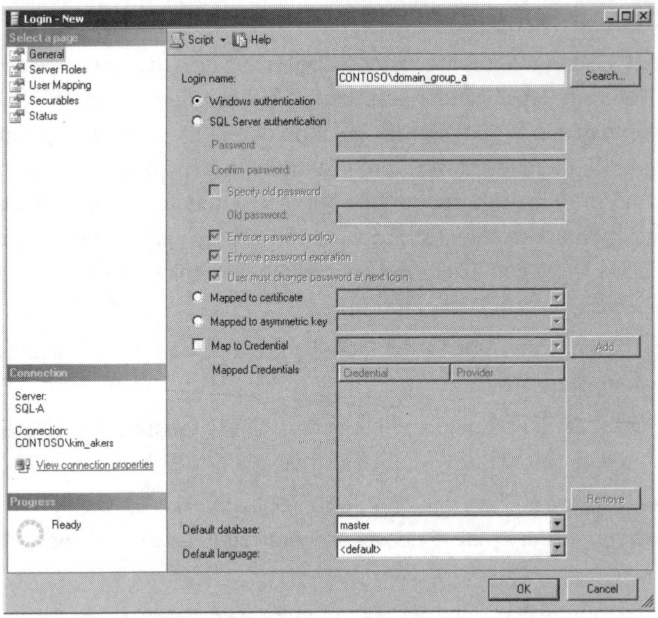

FIGURE 5-2 New domain group SQL login

To create a Windows-authenticated SQL Server login, use the CREATE LOGIN Transact-SQL statement with the FROM WINDOWS option. For example, to create a SQL Server login by using the local account Local_One on the server SQL-A, use the Transact-SQL statement:

```
CREATE LOGIN "SQL-A\Local_One" FROM WINDOWS;
```

To create a SQL Server login using the local security group Group_One on the server SQL-A, use the Transact-SQL statement:

```
CREATE LOGIN "SQL-A\Group_One" FROM WINDOWS;
```

To create a SQL Server login using the domain account Account_Two from the domain Contoso, use the Transact-SQL statement:

```
CREATE LOGIN "CONTOSO\Account_Two" FROM WINDOWS;
```

To create a SQL Server login using the domain security group Group_Two from the domain Contoso, use the Transact-SQL statement:

```
CREATE LOGIN "CONTOSO\Group_Two" FROM WINDOWS;
```

> **MORE INFO** **CREATING LOGINS**
>
> To learn more about creating logins, consult the following page: *http://msdn.microsoft .com/en-us/library/aa337562(SQL.110).aspx.*

SQL Server–Authenticated Logins

SQL Server–authenticated logins are authenticated by the Database Engine instance rather than through the host operating system or a domain controller. SQL Server–authenticated login passwords are stored within the master database. If the SQL Server authentication option button is disabled, you must configure the instance to support mixed-mode authentication.

To create a SQL Server–authenticated login by using SQL Server Management Studio, perform the following steps:

1. Open SQL Server Management Studio, right-click the Security node, click New, and then click Login.

2. In the Login - New dialog box, enter a login name, ensure that SQL Server Authentication is selected, and then enter and confirm a password for the SQL Server–authenticated login.

3. Choose whether to enforce password policy and password expiration and whether the user must change the password at the next login, as shown in Figure 5-3. Click OK.

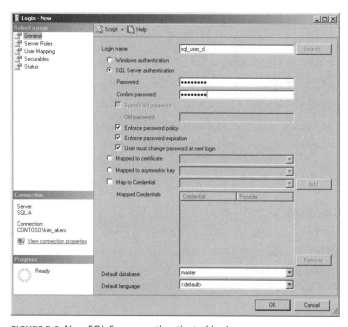

FIGURE 5-3 New SQL Server–authenticated login

You can create a new SQL Server–authenticated login using the CREATE LOGIN statement and the WITH PASSWORD option. For example, to create a SQL Server–authenticated login named sql_user_a with the password Pa$$w0rd, execute the following statement:

```
CREATE LOGIN sql_user_a WITH PASSWORD = 'Pa$$w0rd';
```

You can create a SQL Server–authenticated login to use the password expiration and complexity policies that apply to the host operating system by using the following options with the CREATE LOGIN statement:

- CHECK_EXPIRATION   Enables you to configure SQL Server–authenticated logins so that the password expiration policy that applies to the host operating system applies to the login. This option can be set to ON or OFF with the default value of OFF.

- CHECK_POLICY   Enables you to configure SQL Server–authenticated logins so that the password complexity policy that applies to the host operating system applies to the login. Password complexity policy includes minimum and maximum password lengths and whether the password must contain a mix of uppercase, lowercase, numeric, and symbol characters. This option can be set to ON or OFF with the default value of ON.

> **MORE INFO   CREATE LOGIN**
>
> To learn more about the CREATE LOGIN Transact-SQL statement, consult *http://msdn .microsoft.com/en-us/library/ms189751(SQL.110).aspx*.

 Quick Check

- Which security principals can you use with a SQL Server login that uses Windows authentication?

Quick Check Answer

- You can use a local user account, a local security group, a domain user account, or a domain security group as the basis for a Windows-authenticated SQL Server login.

Certificate Authentication

You can create a certificate to be associated with a login if a database master key is present by using the CREATE CERTIFICATE statement. For example, to create a certificate to be associated with the login that you want to use with a SQL Server login for Dan Bacon and which expires on the first of January 2018, issue the following Transact-SQL statement:

```
CREATE CERTIFICATE Dan_Bacon
WITH SUBJECT = 'Dan Bacon certificate in master database',
EXPIRY_DATE = '01/01/2018';
```

After the certificate is present, you can create a login based on the certificate by using the CREATE LOGIN statement. For example, to create a login for Dan_Bacon using the Dan_Bacon certificate created in the earlier example, issue the following Transact-SQL statement:

```
CREATE LOGIN Dan_Bacon FROM CERTIFICATE Dan_Bacon;
```

Asymmetric Key Authentication

You can also use an asymmetric key to authenticate SQL logins. Unlike certificates, asymmetric keys contain both a public key and a private key. If there is no database master key, you must provide a password when creating an asymmetric key. You create asymmetric keys with the CREATE ASYMMETRIC KEY Transact-SQL statements. For example, to create an asymmetric key named sql_user_e by using the RSA_2048 algorithm on a database that has an existing master key, issue the following Transact-SQL statement:

```
CREATE ASYMMETRIC KEY sql_user_e WITH ALGORITHM = RSA_2048;
```

You can create a login that uses an asymmetric key by using the CREATE LOGIN statement with the ASYMMETRIC KEY option. For example, to create a SQL Server login that uses the asymmetric key created in the previous example, execute the following statement:

```
CREATE LOGIN sql_user_e FROM ASYMMETRIC KEY sql_user_e;
```

> **MORE INFO** **CREATE ASYMMETRIC KEY**
>
> You can learn more about creating an asymmetric key at *http://msdn.microsoft.com/en-us /library/ms174430.aspx.*

Altering Existing Logins

You can alter existing logins using SQL Server Management Studio to edit the properties of the login. You can also alter existing logins by using the ALTER LOGIN Transact-SQL statement. You can disable a login by using the DISABLE keyword or enable a disabled login by using the ENABLE keyword. For example, to disable the sql_user_a login, use this statement:

```
ALTER LOGIN sql_user_a DISABLE;
```

If the login uses SQL Server authentication, you can use the MUST_CHANGE or UNLOCK options with this statement to configure the login so that the password must be changed at next login or to unlock a locked login.

> **MORE INFO** **ALTER LOGIN**
>
> You can find out more about the ALTER LOGIN statement at *http://msdn.microsoft.com /en-us/library/ms189828(SQL.110).aspx.*

Login-Related Catalog Views

You can query several catalog views to view the properties of SQL Server logins. You can generate a list of SQL logins either by looking at the Security\Logins node in SQL Server Management Studio or by querying the sys.server_principals catalog view. This catalog view provides you with information about the login creation date, modification date, whether the login has been disabled, and whether the login type is SQL_LOGIN, SERVER_ROLE, WINDOWS_LOGIN, or CERTIFICATE_MAPPED_LOGIN.

> **MORE INFO** **SYS.SERVER_PRINCIPALS**
>
> You can learn more about the sys.server_principals catalog view on the following page: *http://msdn.microsoft.com/en-us/library/ms188786(SQL.110).aspx*.

You can generate a list of SQL Server–authenticated logins by querying the sys.sql_logins catalog view. This catalog view details information about SQL Server–authenticated logins only. It also enables you to determine whether the SQL Server–authenticated login is configured with password expiration and password complexity policies.

> **MORE INFO** **SYS.SQL_LOGINS**
>
> You can learn more about the sys.sql_logins catalog view at *http://msdn.microsoft.com/en-us/library/ms174355(SQL.110).aspx*.

Removing Logins

You can remove a login by using SQL Server Management Studio, right-clicking the login, and clicking Delete. You can also remove a login by using the DROP LOGIN Transact-SQL statement. You cannot drop a login while that login has an active connection to the database instance. You cannot drop a login that owns a SQL Server Agent job, a server-level object, or a securable. Although it is possible to drop logins that are mapped to database users, this creates orphaned users, which you learn more about in the next lesson. It is often prudent to disable rather than drop a login because it is simpler to re-enable a login that is mapped to multiple database users than it is to re-create a login if circumstances change.

> **MORE INFO** **DROP LOGIN**
>
> You can learn more about the DROP LOGIN Transact-SQL statement at *http://msdn .microsoft.com/en-us/library/ms188012(SQL.110).aspx*.

Denying Server Access

Denying permission to connect to the database enables you to block specific Windows security principals from making connections to the Database Engine. You can configure the Deny permission on the Status page of the Login properties dialog box, as shown in Figure 5-4.

To deny access by using Transact-SQL, use the DENY CONNECT statement from the master database. For example, to deny the contoso\domain_user_b login access to the Database Engine instance, use the following Transact-SQL statement:

```
USE [master]
GO
DENY CONNECT SQL TO "contoso\domain_user_b";
GO
```

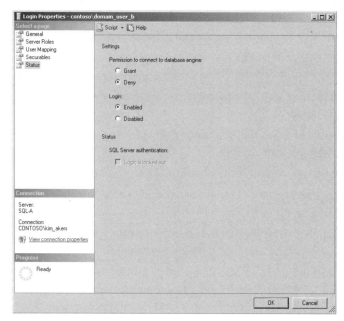

FIGURE 5-4 Deny permission to connect to the Database Engine

Server Roles

Server roles enable you to simplify the assignment of permissions at the database instance level. Although it is possible to assign permissions to SQL logins, this can be difficult to manage in all but the smallest environments. Permissions are assigned to server roles rather than to individual SQL logins. To grant a set of permissions to a specific SQL login, add the login to a server role. SQL Server 2012 ships with nine built-in server roles. These built-in server roles are fixed and, other than the public role, it is not possible to modify the permissions assigned to these roles. In SQL Server 2012, you can modify the permissions assigned to a new type of server role known as a user-defined server role. You learn about user-defined server roles later in this lesson.

The nine fixed server-level roles are as follows:

- **sysadmin** Role members can perform all activities possible on the Database Engine instance. You specify initial membership of this role when performing installation of the Database Engine feature.

- **serveradmin**   Role members can perform instance-wide configuration tasks. Members of this role can shut down the instance.

- **securityadmin**   Assign this role to logins that must be able to manage instance-level permissions. Because this role can configure permissions at the instance level, membership in this role allows the elevation of privileges on logins and user-defined server roles to the equivalent of those assigned to the sysadmin fixed server role.

- **processadmin**   Role members can terminate processes running on a Database Engine instance.

- **setupadmin**   Role members can add linked servers to and remove linked servers from the Database Engine instance.

- **bulkadmin**   Assign this role to logins that you want to allow to use the BULK INSERT statement on databases hosted on an instance.

- **diskadmin**   Role members can manage instance-related files.

- **dbcreator**   Role members are able to create, alter, drop, and restore databases hosted on the Database Engine instance.

- **public**   All SQL Server logins are members of this role. You can alter the permissions assigned to this role, but you cannot alter the membership of the role.

You can use the ALTER SERVER ROLE Transact-SQL statement to modify the membership of a server role. You use the ADD MEMBER option to add a server principal and the DROP MEMBER option to remove a server principal. For example, to add the contoso\domain _group_b login to the serveradmin fixed server role, execute this statement:

```
ALTER SERVER ROLE serveradmin ADD MEMBER "contoso\domain_group_b";
```

You can use the following commands, views, and functions to learn more about the properties of specific server roles:

- **sp_helpsrvrole**   Provides a list of fixed server roles

- **sp_helpsrvrolemember**   Provides fixed server role membership

- **sp_srvrolepermission**   Provides fixed server role permissions

- **IS_SRVROLEMEMBER**   Enables you to check whether a SQL Server login is a member of a specific fixed or user-defined server role

- **sys.server_role_members**   Provides information about role members, displayed as role and member id

---

MORE INFO   **SERVER-LEVEL ROLES**

You can learn more about server-level roles at *http://msdn.microsoft.com/en-us/library /ms188659(SQL.110).aspx.*

User-Defined Server Roles

User-defined server roles are a new SQL Server 2012 feature. You can use user-defined server roles to create custom server roles when using one of the existing server roles does not suit your specific requirements. Creating a user-defined server role involves performing the following steps:

- Creating the user-defined server role
- Granting server-level permissions to the role
- Adding SQL Server logins to the role

You can create a user-defined server role by using SQL Server Management Studio and performing the following steps:

1. In SQL Server Management Studio, right-click the Security\Server Roles node and then click New Server Role.

2. In the New Server Role dialog box, shown in Figure 5-5, enter a server role name. Expand the securables that you want to assign to the user-defined server role and then select the permissions that you want to assign.

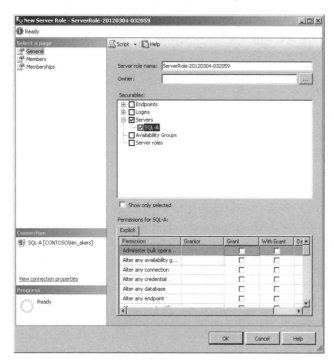

FIGURE 5-5 Creating a user-defined server role

3. On the Members page, click Add. In the Select Server Login Or Role dialog box, click Browse to browse through the SQL logins you can add to the user-defined server role.

You can create user-defined server roles by using the CREATE SERVER ROLE statement.

For example, to create a new user-defined server role named Modify_Databases, execute this statement:

```
CREATE SERVER ROLE Modify_Databases;
```

When you use the CREATE SERVER ROLE statement with the AUTHORIZATION option, you grant ownership of the server role to the principal specified by using the AUTHORIZATION clause. If you do not use the AUTHORIZATION clause, the role will be owned by the security principal that executed the CREATE SERVER ROLE statement.

You can use the GRANT statement to grant permissions to the user-defined server role. For example, to grant the ALTER ANY DATABASE permission to the Modify_Databases role, execute the following Transact-SQL statement:

```
GRANT ALTER ANY DATABASE TO Modify_Databases;
```

You can use the DENY statement to apply a DENY permission to a user-defined server role. You can use the REVOKE statement to remove a GRANT or DENY permission from a user-defined server role.

You can use the ALTER SERVER ROLE statement to modify which logins are members of the server role. You can use the ADD MEMBER option to add a server principal and the DROP MEMBER option to remove a server principal.

Credentials

Credentials store the authentication information that facilitates a connection to a resource external to the Database Engine instance. You can map a single credential to multiple SQL logins, but it is only possible to map a single SQL login to one credential.

You can create a credential in SQL Server Management Studio by navigating to the Security node, right-clicking the Credentials node, and choosing New Credential. In the New Credential dialog box, shown in Figure 5-6, enter the credential name, the credential identity, and the password associated with the credential and choose whether to associate the credential with a specific encryption provider.

You can also use the CREATE CREDENTIAL Transact-SQL statement to create a credential. For example, to create a credential named RemoteFTP that uses the FTP_Login identity and the password Pa$$w0rd, execute the following statement:

```
CREATE CREDENTIAL RemoteFTP with IDENTITY = 'FTP_Login', SECRET = 'Pa$$w0rd';
```

> **MORE INFO** **CREDENTIALS**
>
> You can learn more about credentials at *http://msdn.microsoft.com/en-us/library /ms161950(SQL.110).aspx.*

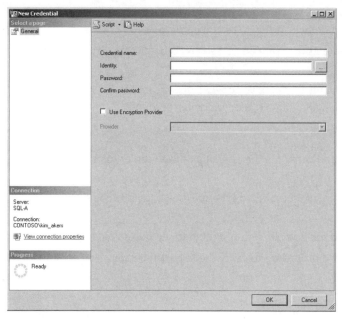

FIGURE 5-6 New credential

PRACTICE **SQL Server Logins and Server Roles**

In this practice, you create SQL Server logins that use both Windows and SQL Server authentication, add SQL logins to fixed server roles, and create a user-defined server role.

EXERCISE 1 Create SQL Logins

In this exercise, you create different SQL logins that use a variety of authentication methods. To complete this exercise, perform the following steps:

1. Use the computer management console on SQL-A to create a local security group named *local_group_b*.

2. Use the computer management console to create a local user account named *local_account_b* and assign this account the password *Pa$$w0rd*.

3. Use the Active Directory Users And Computers console on the domain controller (DC) to create a global security group named *domain_group_b* in the Users container.

4. Use the Active Directory Users And Computers console on the domain controller to create a user account named *domain_user_b* in the Users container with the password *Pa$$w0rd*.

5. Use SQL Server Management Studio to create a SQL Server–authenticated login named *sql_user_b* with the password *Pa$$w0rd*.

6. Use SQL Server Management Studio to create Windows-authenticated logins based on the local_account_b and domain_group_b security principals.

7. Use Transact-SQL statements to create a SQL Server–authenticated login named *sql_user_c.*

8. Use Transact-SQL statements to create Windows-authenticated logins based on the local_group_b local group and domain_user_b domain account.

EXERCISE 2   Server Roles

In this exercise, you configure and verify the membership of fixed server roles. To complete this exercise, perform the following steps:

1. Use SQL Server Management Studio to add the sql_user_b login to the setupadmin fixed server role.

2. Use Transact-SQL to add the domain_group_b login to the bulkadmin fixed server role.

3. Use an appropriate stored procedure to verify the role memberships you configured in steps 1 and 2.

EXERCISE 3   User-Defined Server Roles

In this exercise, you create user-defined server roles. To complete this exercise, perform the following steps:

1. Use SQL Server Management Studio to create a user-defined server role named *Login_Manager.*

2. Grant the Login_Manager user-defined server role the Alter Any Login permission.

3. Add the contoso\domain_group_b SQL login to this user-defined server role.

4. Use Transact-SQL to create a user-defined server role named *Database_Creator.*

5. Use Transact-SQL to grant the Database_Creator user-defined server role the Create Any Database permission.

6. Use Transact-SQL to add the login associated with domain_user_b to the Database_Creator user-defined server role.

Lesson Summary

- SQL Server logins allow access at the instance level. You can create SQL Server logins that are mapped to local or domain-based user accounts or to local or domain-based security groups. You can also create SQL Server logins that are authenticated by SQL Server or that use certificate or asymmetric keys for authentication.

- Nine fixed server roles are associated with a SQL Server 2012 Database Engine instance. You cannot alter the permissions assigned to eight of these roles, but you can modify the membership of these roles.

- You can alter the permissions assigned to the public fixed server role, but you cannot modify the membership of the public fixed server role.

- User-defined server roles are a feature new in SQL Server 2012. You can assign customized permissions to user-defined server roles.
- You can grant or deny access on the basis of SQL Server login.

Lesson Review

Answer the following questions to test your knowledge of the information in this lesson. You can find the answers to these questions and explanations of why each answer choice is correct or incorrect in the "Answers" section at the end of this chapter.

1. Which permission must a security principal have at the instance level to be able to create SQL logins?
   A. ALTER ANY LOGIN
   B. ALTER ANY CREDENTIAL
   C. ALTER ANY ENDPOINT
   D. ALTER SETTINGS

2. You are managing a SQL Server 2012 instance installed on a server named SQL-SYD. You want to create a SQL Server login that is mapped to the Research security group in the CONTOSO domain. Which of the following statements would you use to accomplish this goal?
   A. CREATE LOGIN [Research] WITH PASSWORD = 'Pa$$w0rd'
   B. CREATE USER [Research] WITH PASSWORD = 'Pa$$word'
   C. CREATE LOGIN "CONTOSO\Research" FROM WINDOWS
   D. CREATE USER "CONTOSO\Research"

3. You want to create an instance-level security principal named Development on server SQL-A. This security principal should use the password Pa$$w0rd and should be authenticated by the SQL Server 2012 instance. Which of the following Transact-SQL statements would you use to accomplish this goal?
   A. CREATE LOGIN "SQL-A\Development" FROM WINDOWS
   B. CREATE USER "SQL-A\Development"
   C. CREATE LOGIN [Development] WITH PASSWORD = 'Pa$$w0rd'
   D. CREATE USER [Development] WITH PASSWORD = 'Pa$$word'

4. Following the principle of least privilege, to which of the following fixed server-level roles would you add a SQL Server login if you wanted the user to be able to drop and restore databases?
   A. sysadmin
   B. securityadmin
   C. setupadmin
   D. dbcreator

5. You want to configure SQL Server so that the Database Engine instance can automatically authenticate against a remote FTP server. Which of the following should you create to accomplish this goal?

   A. Database User

   B. SQL Login

   C. Credential

   D. User-defined server role

Lesson 2: Managing Users and Database Roles

This lesson covers managing security principals at the database level, including database user accounts and fixed and flexible database roles. You learn about configuring contained users, a new feature of SQL Server 2012 granting database access with least privilege, and application roles.

> **After this lesson, you will be able to:**
> - Administer database user accounts.
> - Manage database roles.
> - Configure contained users.
> - Grant database access with least privilege.
>
> **Estimated lesson time: 60 minutes**

Database Users

Database users represent the identity of a SQL Server login when connected to a database. Each database user maps to a SQL Server login except in the special case of contained databases. You learn more about contained databases later in this lesson. You can configure a database user to use the same name as a login to simplify the process of quickly identifying the relationship between a database user and a SQL Server login. You can map a SQL Server login to only one database user in each database. You can map a single login to different users in different databases if you follow the "one database user per SQL Server login per database" rule. You can assign database-level permissions directly to database users. It is best practice to assign database-level permissions to database-level roles and then add database users to those roles.

A security principal requires the ALTER ANY USER permission on the database to be able to create database users. To create a database user by using SQL Server Management Studio when there is an existing SQL Server login, perform the following steps:

1. In SQL Server Management Studio, expand the Security node under the database in which you want to create the database user.

2. Right-click the Users node and click New User.

3. On the User Type drop-down menu, ensure that SQL User With Login is selected. Click the ellipsis (...) button next to Login Name and then click Browse. In the Browse For Objects dialog box, select the SQL login that you want to map to the database user and then click OK. Click OK again to close the Select Login dialog box.

4. In the Database User - New dialog box, shown in Figure 5-7, enter a user name and then click OK.

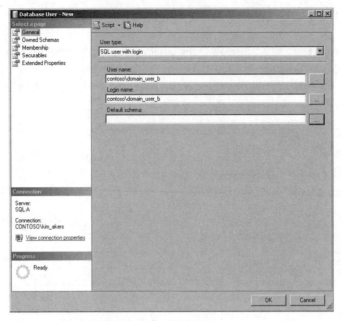

FIGURE 5-7 New database user for SQL login

You can create a database user for an existing SQL login by using the CREATE USER Transact-SQL statement with the FOR LOGIN option. For example, to create a database login named contoso\domain_group_a in the AdventureWorks2012 database for the Windows-authenticated SQL login contoso\domain_group_a, execute the following statement:

```
USE [AdventureWorks2012]
GO
CREATE USER "contoso\domain_group_a" FOR LOGIN "contoso\domain_group_a";
GO
```

> **MORE INFO** **DATABASE USERS**
>
> You can learn more about creating database users at *http://msdn.microsoft.com/en-us
> /library/aa337545(SQL.110).aspx*.

You can remove a database user by right-clicking the user in SQL Server Management Studio and clicking Delete. You can use the DROP USER statement to remove a database user account. Dropping a database user account does not remove the SQL login associated with the user.

 An *orphaned user* is a database user whose corresponding SQL login has been dropped or the database is restored or attached to a different instance of SQL Server. You can detect orphaned users in a database by using the sp_change_users_login stored procedure with the @Action='Report' option. For example, to check for orphaned users in the AdventureWorks2012 database, execute the following Transact-SQL statement:

```
USE [AdventureWorks2012]
GO;
sp_change_users_login @Action='Report';
GO;
```

You can use the sp_change_users_login stored procedure to relink a database user with a SQL login.

> **MORE INFO** **ORPHANED USERS**
>
> You can learn more about orphaned users at *http://msdn.microsoft.com/en-us/library /ms175475(SQL.110).aspx.*

 Quick Check

- What is the maximum number of database users that can exist in a database for a specific SQL Server login?

Quick Check Answer

- You can have only one database user mapped to a SQL Server login in any specific database.

Database Roles

Database roles enable you to assign permissions to database users on a collective basis. Rather than assigning permissions to each individual database user, you assign permissions to database roles and then add database users to those roles. There are nine fixed database-level roles. All databases use these fixed database-level roles. You can also create custom database-level roles, known as flexible database roles.

Fixed Database-Level Roles

Fixed database-level roles have specific permissions assigned to them that you cannot alter. The fixed database roles are as follows:

- **db_owner**   Assign this role to principals who need to perform all database configuration and management tasks. Role members are able to drop the database.
- **db_securityadmin**   Members of this role are able to manage the membership of fixed and flexible database-level roles. Principals who are members of this role can elevate their privileges to those functionally equivalent to the db_owner role.
- **db_accessadmin**   Assign this role to security principals who need to manage database access for logins.
- **db_backupoperator**   Members of this role can back up the database.

- **db_ddladmin** Adding a principal to this role enables him or her to run any Data Definition Language (DDL) command in the database.
- **db_datawriter** Assign this role when you want to enable the principal to insert, delete, or modify data in a database's user tables.
- **db_datareader** Members of this role can read all data from all user tables in a database.
- **db_denydatawriter** Assign this role when you want to block a principal from inserting, altering, or deleting data from a database's user tables.
- **db_denydatareader** Assign this role when you want to block a principal from reading data stored within a database's user tables.

To add a database user or role to a fixed database-level role by using SQL Server Management Studio, perform the following steps:

1. Right-click the role and click Properties.
2. In the Database Role Properties dialog box, on the General page, click Add in the Members Of This Role section.
3. In the Select Database User Or Role dialog box, click Browse.
4. Select the database user or role you want to add to the fixed database-level role and then click OK. Click OK again to close the Select Database User Or Role dialog box.
5. In the Database Role Properties dialog box, shown in Figure 5-8, click OK.

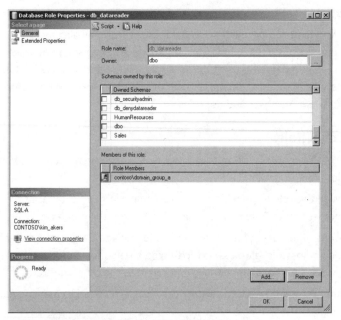

FIGURE 5-8 Add database user to fixed database role

You can also use the sp_addrolemember stored procedure to add database users to fixed database roles. For example, to add the contoso\domain_user_b database user to the db_datawriter role in the AdventureWorks2012 database, execute the following Transact-SQL statement:

```
USE [AdventureWorks2012];
GO
EXEC sp_addrolemember 'db_datawriter', "contoso\domain_user_b";
GO
```

You can remove users from a database role in SQL Server Management Studio by editing the properties of that role, selecting the database user you want to remove, and then clicking Remove. You can also use the sp_droprolemember stored procedure to accomplish the same goal.

> **MORE INFO** **FIXED DATABASE-LEVEL ROLES**
>
> You can find out more about the permissions assigned to fixed database-level roles at *http://msdn.microsoft.com/en-us/library/ms189121.aspx*.

Flexible Database-Level Roles

Flexible database-level roles enable you to create roles with custom database-level permissions. You can use them to apply permissions to collections of database users if one of the fixed database-level roles is not appropriate for your organization's circumstances. To create a role, a principal either needs the CREATE ROLE permission on the database or must be a member of the db_securityadmin fixed database role.

EXAM TIP

Remember that the CREATE ROLE statement is used to create a flexible database-level role, and the CREATE SERVER ROLE statement is used to create a user-defined server role.

To create a flexible database role by using SQL Server Management Studio, perform the following steps:

1. Locate the database for which you want to create the flexible database role in SQL Server Management Studio, expand the Security node and the Roles node, and then right-click the Database Roles node. Click New Database Role.

2. In the Database Role - New dialog box, shown in Figure 5-9, enter a name for the role and then click OK.

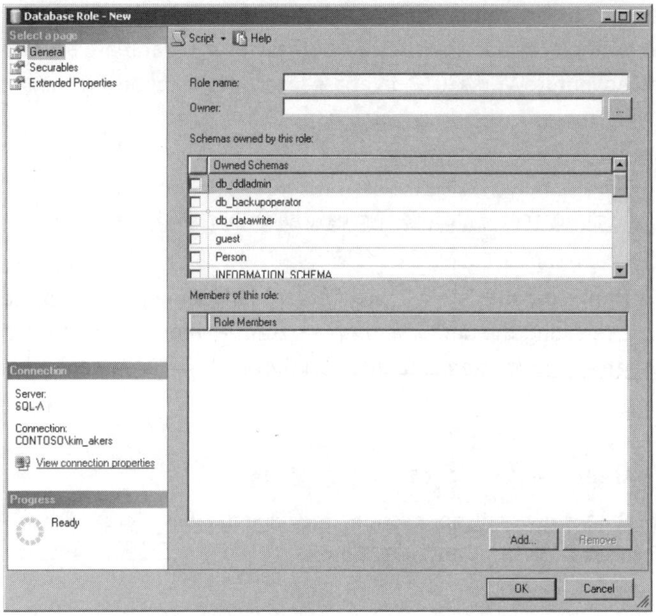

FIGURE 5-9 New database role

When you use the CREATE ROLE statement with the AUTHORIZATION option, you grant ownership of the role to the principal specified by using the AUTHORIZATION clause. If you do not use the AUTHORIZATION clause, the role will be owned by the security principal who executed the CREATE ROLE statement. For example, to create a flexible database role named TableCreator in the AdventureWorks2012 database that is owned by the contoso\kim_akers database user, execute the following Transact-SQL statement:

```
USE [AdventureWorks2012];
GO
CREATE ROLE TableCreator AUTHORIZATION "contoso\kim_akers";
GO
```

To grant permissions to a role by using SQL Server Management Studio, edit the role's properties and, on the Securables page, choose the specific securables for which you want to configure permissions and then choose the explicit permissions that you want to grant, as shown in Figure 5-10.

You can use the GRANT statement to grant permissions to a flexible database role. For example, to grant the CREATE TABLE permission to the TableCreator role in the AdventureWorks2012 database, execute the following Transact-SQL statement:

```
USE [AdventureWorks2012];
GO
GRANT CREATE TABLE TO TableCreator;
GO
```

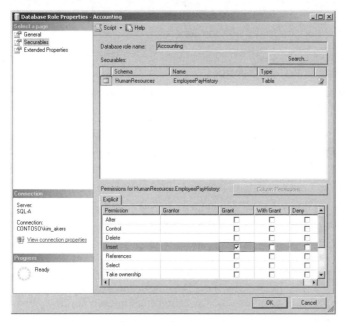

FIGURE 5-10 Grant permissions on database role

To assign database users to the flexible database role by using SQL Server Management Studio, edit the role properties. On the General page, in the Members Of This Role area, click Add. On the Select Database User Or Role page, click Browse. In the Browse For Objects dialog box, choose which objects you want to add to the role. Click OK three times.

You can also use the sp_addrolemember stored procedure to add a principal to a flexible database role. For example, to add the contoso\domain_user_b database login to the TableCreator role in the AdventureWorks2012 database, execute the following Transact-SQL statement:

```
USE [AdventureWorks2012];
GO
EXEC sp_addrolemember 'TableCreator', "contoso\domain_user_b";
GO
```

msdb Roles

The msdb system database has a set of special database roles in addition to the nine fixed database-level roles. These roles enable you to assign permissions associated with Integration Services, Data Collector, Server Groups, database mirroring, and Policy-Based Management.

- The db_ssisadmin, db_ssisoperator, and db_ssisltduser msdb database roles enable you to assign permissions to principals for Integration Services.
- The dc_admin, dc_operator, and dc_proxy msdb database roles enable you to assign permissions to principals for the Data Collector.
- The ServerGroupAdministratorRole and ServerGroupReaderRole msdb database roles enable you to assign permissions to principals for creating Server Groups.
- Use the dbm_monitor msdb database role when working with the Database Mirroring Monitor. This role does not exist until a database is registered with Database Mirroring Monitor.
- The PolicyAdministratorRole msdb database role enables you to assign permissions to principals for administering Policy-Based Management policies and conditions.
- The SQLAgentOperatorRole, SQLAgentReaderRole, and SQLAgentUser msdb database roles enable you to assign permissions to principals for the SQL Server Agent.

> **MORE INFO**   **DATABASE ROLES**
>
> You can find out more about database-level roles at *http://msdn.microsoft.com/en-us /library/ms189121(SQL.110).aspx.*

User and Role Catalog Views

You can use the following security catalog views to determine information about users, roles, and permissions at the database level:

- **sys.database_principals**   This catalog view provides you with information about database principals, including database roles, application roles, SQL Users, and Windows Users.
- **sys.database_role_members**   This catalog view provides you with information about roles and the security principals who are members of those roles.
- **sys.database_permissions**   This catalog view provides you with information about permissions assigned to security principals at the database level.

Contained Users

Contained databases have no external dependencies. The primary benefit of a contained database is that you can move it to another instance, or even to an appropriately configured cloud provider, and have the database work without requiring additional configuration. Contained databases do not use SQL logins but instead use contained users. A *contained user* is a database user who does not have a SQL Server login. Contained users can connect to the contained database by specifying credentials in the connection string.

You can create contained users only after you enable contained database authentication at the instance level. You can do this by executing the following Transact-SQL statement:

```
sp_configure 'show advanced', 1;
RECONFIGURE WITH OVERRIDE;
GO
sp_configure 'contained database authentication', 1;
RECONFIGURE WITH OVERRIDE;
GO
```

After you have configured the instance to support contained database authentication, you can create a database that supports containment. SQL Server 2012 supports partial database containment. You can create a partially contained database by using the CREATE DATABASE statement with the CONTAINMENT = PARTIAL option. For example, to create a partially contained database named partially_contained_db, execute the following Transact-SQL statement:

```
CREATE DATABASE partially_contained_db
CONTAINMENT = PARTIAL;
```

After you have created the partially contained database, you can use the CREATE USER Transact-SQL statement without having to specify an existing SQL Server login. For example, to create a partially contained database user named contained_user who uses SQL Server for authentication, from the partially contained database, execute the statement:

```
CREATE USER contained_user WITH PASSWORD = 'Pa$$w0rd';
```

You can also create partially contained users who use Windows authentication. For example, to create a partially contained database user mapped to the contoso\contained_user_a domain account, execute the statement:

```
CREATE USER [contoso\contained_user_a];
```

When connecting to a contained database, you must specify the database in the connection properties of the Connect To Server dialog box, as shown in Figure 5-11, or in the connection string.

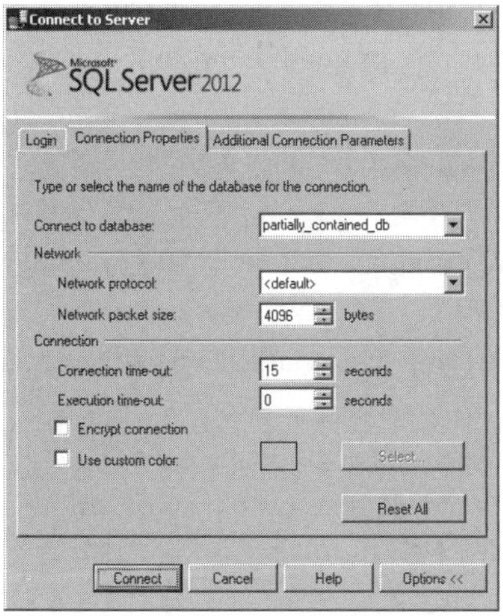

FIGURE 5-11 Connecting by using a contained user

Least Privilege

The *principle of least privilege* is a principle of information security that dictates granting a security principal only those privileges that are necessary to perform required tasks. When applied to SQL Server 2012, this means that rather than using the built-in server and database roles, which have a mixture of privileges granted to them, you should determine the specific privileges needed by each security principal and grant only those privileges rather than those that you would apply more generally by adding the principal to a fixed role. For example, rather than giving a database user the ability to insert data into any table in a specific database, you would grant permissions to insert data on only a limited number of tables in the database. Correctly applying the principle of least privilege requires a thorough understanding of the tasks that must be performed by each security principal and tailoring roles at the instance and database levels that allow those tasks, and only those tasks, to be performed.

Application Roles

Application roles enable you to grant permissions to a specific application. For example, you might have a web application that needs to interact with a database hosted on a back-end SQL Server 2012 instance. Rather than have the user access the database with a database user permission, the user accesses the data by using the permissions assigned to the application role. This happens in the following general way:

1. A user interacts with a client application that connects to an instance with the user's credentials.

2. The application executes the sp_setapprole stored procedure, authenticating by using a password configured to be used by the application.

3. When authenticated, the application role is enabled, and the connection uses the permissions assigned to the application role.

You can create a new application role in SQL Server Management Studio by right-clicking the Application Roles node under the Security\Roles node of a database and then choosing New Application Role. This opens the Application Role - New dialog box, shown in Figure 5-12.

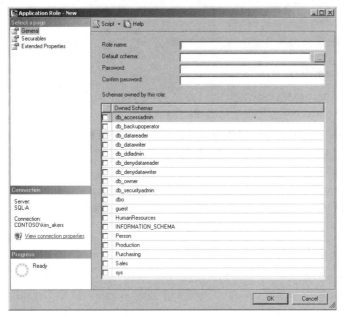

FIGURE 5-12 New application role

On the General page, provide the application role with a name and a password. On the Securables page, choose the securables and the explicit permissions to which you want to grant the application role access.

You use the CREATE APPLICATION ROLE Transact-SQL statement. When you use this statement, you must provide a password for the application role. The password you use for the application role must meet the complexity requirements that apply to passwords on the host operating system. For example, to create an application role named app_role_alpha in the AdventureWorks2012 database with the password Pa$$w0rd, execute the statement:

```
USE [AdventureWorks2012]
GO
CREATE APPLICATION ROLE app_role_alpha WITH PASSWORD = 'Pa$$w0rd';
GO
```

You can use the ALTER APPLICATION ROLE Transact-SQL statement to change the name, password, or default schema applied to an application role. You can use the DROP APPLICATION ROLE statement to remove an existing application role.

MORE INFO **APPLICATION ROLES**

You can learn more about application roles at *http://msdn.microsoft.com/en-us/library /ms190998(SQL.110).aspx.*

PRACTICE **Database Users and Roles**

In this practice, you create database users and roles.

EXERCISE 1 Create Database Users

In this exercise, you create database users based on the logins you created in the previous lesson. To complete this exercise, perform the following steps:

1. Use SQL Server Management Studio to create a database user named contoso \domain_group_b based on the contoso\domain_group_b SQL login in the AdventureWorks2012 database.

2. Use Transact-SQL to create database users named *SQL-A\local_account_b* and *sql_user_c* in the AdventureWorks2012 database. These database users should be mapped to the SQL-A\local_account_b and sql_user_c SQL logins.

EXERCISE 2 Administer Database Roles

In this exercise, you add database users to existing fixed database roles, create a flexible database role, assign permissions to the new database role, and add database users to this role. To complete this exercise, perform the following steps:

1. Add the contoso\domain_group_b user to the db_datareader fixed database role in the AdventureWorks2012 database by using SQL Server Management Studio.

2. Use Transact-SQL to create a flexible database role named *TableAdmin* in the AdventureWorks2012 database.

3. Use Transact-SQL to grant the CREATE TABLE and CREATE SCHEMA permissions to the TableAdmin flexible database role.

4. Use the appropriate stored procedure to add the sql_user_c user to the *TableAdmin* flexible database role.

EXERCISE 3 Create a Partially Contained Database and Users

In this exercise, you create a partially contained database and users. To complete this exercise, perform the following steps:

1. Create a user account in the CONTOSO domain named *contained_user_b*. Assign the password *Pa$$w0rd*.

2. Use the sp_configure stored procedure to enable contained database authentication on the SQL-A\Alternate instance.

3. Use Transact-SQL to create a database with partial containment named *partial_containment_db*.

4. Use Transact-SQL to create a contained database user that uses the contoso \contained_user_b domain account.

5. Use Transact-SQL to create a contained database user that uses SQL authentication. The username should be *contained_user_c* and the password should be set to *Pa$$w0rd.*

Lesson Summary

- In uncontained databases, database user accounts map to existing SQL logins.
- In contained databases, database user accounts do not need to map to existing SQL logins.
- Orphaned users are users in uncontained databases in which there is no corresponding SQL Server login.
- There are nine fixed database-level roles. You cannot alter the permissions assigned to these roles.
- You can create flexible database-level roles and assign custom permissions to these roles so you can be more specific with the assignment of permissions rather than using the more general fixed database-level roles.
- An application role is a special role used by an application to access a database. Application roles are secured by passwords.

Lesson Review

Answer the following questions to test your knowledge of the information in this lesson. You can find the answers to these questions and explanations of why each answer choice is correct or incorrect in the "Answers" section at the end of this chapter.

1. You have created a database instance security principal that maps to a domain-based user account. Which of the following should you create at the database level so that you can grant the database instance security principal the appropriate privileges to create and drop tables in the database?

   A. Login

   B. Server role

   C. Credential

   D. User

2. You want to create a security principal at the database level, add existing database users to this security principal, and assign permissions to it. Which of the following Transact-SQL statements would you use to accomplish this goal?

   A. CREATE ROLE

   B. CREATE SERVER ROLE

   C. ALTER ROLE

   D. ALTER SERVER ROLE

3. Which of the following statements or stored procedures do you use to add database users to a fixed database role?

   A. ALTER SERVER ROLE

   B. ALTER ROLE

   C. sp_addrolemember

   D. CREATE ROLE

4. To which of the following fixed database roles should you add a database user if you want to grant the ability to manage database access for logins without assigning unnecessary privileges?

   A. db_owner

   B. db_accessadmin

   C. db_securityadmin

   D. db_ddladmin

5. Which of the following steps must you take before you can create a database that allows database logins that do not map to a SQL Server login?

   A. Enable contained database authentication at the instance level.

   B. Disable contained database authentication at the instance level. Create a user-defined server role.

   C. Create a flexible database role.

   D. Create a user-defined server role.

Case Scenarios

In the following case scenarios, you apply what you have learned about managing logins, users, roles, and contained databases. You can find answers to these questions in the "Answers" section at the end of this chapter.

Case Scenario 1: Instance-Level Permissions for Contoso's Accountants

You are the database administrator at Contoso, and you are deploying an instance of SQL Server 2012 that members of the accounting and finance departments will use. All members of the accounting and finance departments have accounts in the Contoso Active Directory domain. There are no accounting or finance-based domain security groups. In the accounting department are 20 users who require access to the SQL Server 2012 instance. These users require specific permissions that differ from those available in the fixed server-level roles. In the next few months, members of the finance department might need similar access and permissions. You want to configure security so that the number of SQL logins is minimized but also so that members of the accounting department do not share a SQL login with members of the finance department. With this in mind, answer the following questions:

1. What steps should you take to minimize the number of SQL Server logins when granting access to the 20 accounting users?

2. What approach should you take when granting the custom permissions at the Database Engine instance level?

Case Scenario 2: Contained Databases at Fabrikam

You are the SQL Server 2012 database administrator at Fabrikam, and you are planning a new database. One of the goals in developing this new database is for you to be able to attach and detach the database as necessary from different instances without creating orphaned users. All instances that host the database will be running SQL Server 2012. All users who will access the database have accounts in the Fabrikam Active Directory domain. They should be able to connect to the database without entering a separate password. Each user might require different permissions on the database.

With this information in mind, answer the following questions:

1. Prior to creating the database, what steps should you take to prepare the instance?

2. What type of security principal should you configure in the database?

Suggested Practices

To help you successfully master the exam objectives presented in this chapter, complete the following tasks.

Manage Logins and Server Roles

Prior to completing each task in the following practices, list the steps you would take to accomplish the task. After completing the task, assess how accurately you predicted the necessary steps.

■ **Practice 1**   On server SQL-B's default instance, create SQL Server logins that use certificates and asymmetric keys for authentication.

■ **Practice 2**   On server SQL-B's default instance, create a user-defined server role that enables members to create and manage SQL Server logins.

Manage Users and Database Roles

Prior to completing each task in the following practices, list the steps you would take to accomplish the task. After completing the task, assess how accurately you predicted the necessary steps.

- **Practice 1** Create a partially contained database on the default instance of server SQL-B. Populate this instance with contained users that use both Windows and SQL Server authentication.

- **Practice 2** Create a flexible database role in the partially contained database that you created in Practice 1. Grant the role the ability to create, manage, and drop database users. Add the contained users that you created in Practice 1 to this role.

Answers

This section contains the answers to the lesson review questions and solutions to the case scenarios in this chapter.

Lesson 1

1. **Correct Answer: A**

   A. **Correct:** A security principal must have the ALTER ANY LOGIN permission to be able to create SQL Server logins.

   B. **Incorrect:** The ALTER ANY CREDENTIAL permission allows for the creation of credentials rather than logins.

   C. **Incorrect:** The ALTER ANY ENDPOINT permission allows for the creation of endpoints rather than logins.

   D. **Incorrect:** The ALTER SETTINGS permission allows for the modification of Database Engine settings rather than creation of SQL Server logins.

2. **Correct Answer: C**

   A. **Incorrect:** The CREATE LOGIN [Research] WITH PASSWORD = 'Pa$$w0rd' statement creates a SQL-authenticated login rather than one mapped to a domain security group.

   B. **Incorrect:** You would use the CREATE USER [Research] WITH PASSWORD = 'Pa$$w0rd' statement to create a contained user rather than a SQL Server login.

   C. **Correct:** You use the CREATE LOGIN "CONTOSO\Research" FROM WINDOWS statement to create a SQL Server login that is mapped to the Research security group in the CONTOSO domain.

   D. **Incorrect:** You would use the CREATE USER "Contoso\Research" statement to create a contained database user who uses the Research security group in the Contoso domain. This will not create a login that uses this security group at the database-instance level.

3. **Correct Answer: C**

   A. **Incorrect:** You should not execute the CREATE LOGIN "SQL-A\Development" FROM WINDOWS statement. This statement will create a Windows-authenticated login based on a local account named Development.

   B. **Incorrect:** You should not execute the CREATE USER "SQL-A\Development" statement. This statement creates a contained user based on a local account named Development.

   C. **Correct:** You should execute the statement "CREATE LOGIN [Development] WITH PASSWORD = 'Pa$$w0rd'" because this will create a SQL Server–authenticated login named Development that uses the password Pa$$w0rd.

D. **Incorrect:** You should not execute the CREATE USER [Development] WITH PASSWORD = 'Pa$$word' statement because it creates a contained database user named Development that uses SQL authentication rather than a SQL Server login that users SQL authentication.

4. **Correct Answer: D**

    A. **Incorrect:** You would not add the SQL login to the sysadmin role. This role enables members to perform all activities possible on the Database Engine instance.

    B. **Incorrect:** You would not add the SQL login to the securityadmin fixed server role. This role enables management of instance-level permissions.

    C. **Incorrect:** You would not add the SQL login to the setupadmin fixed server role. This role allows for the adding and removing of linked servers.

    D. **Correct:** You would assign the dbcreator role. This allows the SQL Server login to perform tasks of dropping and restoring databases without assigning unnecessary permissions.

5. **Correct Answer: C**

    A. **Incorrect:** You should not create a database user. Database users are security principals used at the database level for assigning database permissions.

    B. **Incorrect:** You should not create a SQL Server login. SQL Server logins enable access to the instance. You need to configure a credential that enables access to a remote resource.

    C. **Correct:** Credentials enable the SQL Server 2012 Database Engine instance to connect to remote resources that require authentication, such as FTP servers.

    D. **Incorrect:** You should not create a user-defined server role. User-defined server roles enable you to apply permissions at the Database Engine–instance level.

Lesson 2

1. **Correct Answer: D**

    A. **Incorrect:** Logins are Database Engine instance–level security principals. You need to create a user mapped to the existing login to accomplish your goal.

    B. **Incorrect:** Server roles are Database Engine–level security principals. You need to create a user mapped to the existing login to accomplish your goal.

    C. **Incorrect:** Credentials allow the Database Engine access to external resources that require authentication. You need to create a user mapped to the existing login to accomplish your goal.

    D. **Correct:** You can create database users that are mapped to SQL logins when you want to assign permissions at the database level. You can also create flexible database roles, add the database user to the role, and assign the appropriate permissions to the role.

2. **Correct Answers: A and C**

   A. **Correct:** You use the CREATE ROLE statement to create a flexible database role and assign permissions to that role.

   B. **Incorrect:** You should not use the CREATE SERVER ROLE statement because this creates a user-defined server role at the instance rather than at the database level.

   C. **Correct:** You use the ALTER ROLE statement to add and remove members from a database role.

   D. **Incorrect:** You use the ALTER SERVER ROLE statement to alter user-defined server roles at the instance rather than at the database level.

3. **Correct Answers: B and C**

   A. **Incorrect:** The ALTER SERVER ROLE statement enables you to add security principals at the instance level to a user-defined server role rather than to a flexible database role.

   B. **Correct:** The ALTER ROLE statement enables you to change the name of a flexible database role and allows you to alter the membership of a flexible database role.

   C. **Correct:** You use the sp_addrolemember stored procedure to add members to a flexible database role.

   D. **Incorrect:** You use the CREATE ROLE statement to create flexible database roles. You can't use this statement to modify the membership of a flexible database role.

4. **Correct Answer: B**

   A. **Incorrect:** You should not add the user to the db_owner role. This role is granted all permissions at the database level.

   B. **Correct:** You should add the user to the db_accessadmin role because this will grant the ability to manage database access for logins without conferring unnecessary privileges.

   C. **Incorrect:** You should not add the user to the db_securityadmin role because members of this role can manage the membership of other roles and can grant themselves almost any privilege at the database level.

   D. **Incorrect:** You should not add the user to the db_ddladmin role because members of this role can run any Data Definition Language (DDL) command in the database.

5. **Correct Answer: A**

   A. **Correct:** You must enable contained database authentication at the instance level before you can create a database that allows database logins that do not map to a SQL Server login.

   B. **Incorrect:** You can use database logins that do not map to a SQL Server login only if contained database authentication is enabled at the instance level.

C. Incorrect: The existence of flexible database roles does not influence whether you can create databases that support contained users.

D. Incorrect: The existence of user-defined server roles does not influence whether you can create databases that support contained users.

Case Scenario 1

1. Create a domain group and add the 20 users in the accounting department to this group. Create a SQL Server login that uses the Windows authentication type and is mapped to this domain group.

2. Create a user-defined server role. Grant the custom permissions to this user-defined server role. Add the SQL Server login mapped to the group holding the accounting department user accounts to this user-defined server role. In the future, you will be able to add other logins to this role, such as a login relating to the finance users.

Case Scenario 2

1. You should configure the instance to support contained database authentication. This enables you to attach and detach the database from different instances without creating orphaned users.

2. You should create contained database users that map to domain-based user accounts.

CHAPTER 6

Securing SQL Server 2012

Exam objectives in this chapter:

- Manage database permissions.
- Troubleshoot security.
- Audit SQL Server instances.

M icrosoft SQL Server 2012 databases hold information that is critical for an organization. Databases can host confidential customer information or organizational information not for public disclosure. This chapter covers how to set up database permissions to ensure that database principals have appropriate rights. You learn how to troubleshoot security settings to ensure that appropriate access is possible and how to track specific actions that occur at the instance and database level by using SQL Server Audit.

Lessons in this chapter:

Before You Begin

To complete the practice exercises in this chapter, make sure that you have:

- Completed the setup tasks for installing computers DC, SQL-A, SQL-B, and SQL-CORE as outlined in the introduction of this book.
- Completed the setup tasks outlined in the end-of-lesson practice exercises in Chapter 1, "Planning and Installing SQL Server 2012," through to Chapter 5, "SQL Server Logins, Roles, and Users."

No additional configuration is required for this chapter.

Lesson 1: Managing Database Permissions

Database permissions enable you to control which actions can and cannot be performed by security principals at the database level. Configuring database permissions involves understanding which permissions are available at the database level and how those permissions can be granted, denied, and revoked.

After this lesson, you will be able to:

- Configure database security.
- Manage database-level permissions.
- Protect database objects from modification.

Estimated lesson time: 60 minutes

Understanding Securables

A *securable* is an item in SQL Server for which you can assign permissions. Securables can be contained within other securables; the term for these nested hierarchies is *scope*. SQL Server 2012 has the following securables at the database scope:

- User
- Database role
- Application role
- Assembly
- Message type
- Route
- Service
- Remote service binding
- Full-text catalog
- Certificate
- Asymmetric key
- Symmetric key
- Contract
- Schema

The schema scope contains the following securables:

- Type
- XML schema collection
- Object

The Object class has the following members:

- Aggregate
- Function
- Procedure
- Queue
- Synonym
- Table
- View

When you apply a permission at the scope level, that permission is inherited by the objects within that scope.

> **MORE INFO** **SECURABLES**
>
> You can learn more about securables at *http://msdn.microsoft.com/en-us/library /ms190401.aspx.*

Specific keywords identify permissions. Some of the most common permissions configured when securing a database include:

- **ALTER** Provides the ability to modify the properties of a securable; does not allow change in ownership of the securable; grants the ability to alter, create, or drop any securable within the scope
- **BACKUP/DUMP** Permission to back up or dump the securable
- **CONTROL** Gives all defined permissions on the securable; can grant permissions on the securable; grants CONTROL permissions on all securables within the scope
- **CREATE** Permission to create the securable
- **DELETE** Permission to delete the securable
- **EXECUTE** Permission to execute the securable
- **IMPERSONATE** Permission to impersonate the securable principal
- **INSERT** Permission to insert data into the securable
- **RECEIVE** Permission to receive messages from service broker
- **REFERENCE** Permission to reference the securable
- **RESTORE/LOAD** Permission to restore the securable
- **SELECT** Permission to view data in the securable
- **TAKE OWNERSHIP** Permission to take ownership of the securable
- **UPDATE** Permission to modify the data stored in the securable
- **VIEW DEFINITION** Permission to view the securable definition

Assigning Permissions on Objects

You use the GRANT, DENY, and REVOKE statements to manage permissions on objects: GRANT to allow the permission to be used; DENY to block the permission from being used; and REVOKE to remove an existing GRANT or DENY permission.

You can use Transact-SQL statements to assign permissions directly to objects. For example, to grant the INSERT permission to the Alpha-Role role on the Person.Address table in the AdventureWorks2012 database, issue the following Transact-SQL statement:

```
USE [AdventureWorks2012]
GO
GRANT INSERT ON [Person].[Address] TO [Alpha-Role]
GO
```

To deny the INSERT permission on the Person.Address table to the Alpha-Role role, issue the following Transact-SQL statement:

```
Use [AdventureWorks2012]
GO
DENY INSERT ON [Person].[Address] TO [Alpha-Role]
GO
```

To revoke the INSERT permission from the Alpha-Role role on the Person.Address table, issue the following Transact-SQL statement:

```
Use [AdventureWorks2012]
GO
REVOKE INSERT ON [Person].[Address] TO [Alpha-Role]
GO
```

 Quick Check

- Which Transact-SQL statement do you use to remove a DENY permission from a securable?

Managing Permissions by Using Database Roles

Database roles simplify the management of permissions. Rather than assign permissions on securables to individual security principals, you can add database users to a flexible database-level role and assign permissions on securables to that role. SQL Server 2012 also includes fixed database roles that are assigned a fixed set of permissions. You learned about database users and roles in Chapter 5.

Assigning Fixed Database Roles

Fixed database roles provide a simple way of assigning common permissions to a database. Each fixed database role has a specific set of permissions that cannot be altered. The fixed database roles are as follows:

- **db_owner**   Role members can perform any configuration or maintenance activity on the database. Role members can also drop the database.

- **db_securityadmin**   Role members can modify role membership and manage role permissions. Members of this role can escalate their privilege, so you should treat adding a user to this role as functionally similar to adding the user to the db_owner role in production environments.

- **db_accessadmin**   Role members can add or remove database access for Windows logins, Windows groups, and SQL Server logins.

- **db_backupoperator**   Role members can back up the database.

- **db_ddladmin**   Role members can run any Data Definition Language (DDL) command on the database.

- **db_datawriter**   Role members can add, delete, and change data in all user tables.

- **db_datareader**   Role members can read all data stored in user tables.

- **db_denydatawriter**   Role members are blocked from adding, modifying, or deleting any data stored in user tables.

- **db_denydatareader**   Role members are blocked from reading any data stored in user tables.

Except for the Public database role, you cannot modify the permissions assigned to a fixed database role.

You can add a security principal, including another role, to a database role by using the sp_addrolemember stored procedure. For example, to add the Chicken role to the db_datawriter fixed database role, execute the statement:

```
EXEC sp_addrolemember [db_datawriter], [Chicken];
```

You can also use the ALTER ROLE statement to accomplish the same goal. For example, to add the Egg role to the db_datawriter fixed database role, execute the following Transact-SQL statement from the relevant database:

```
ALTER ROLE [db_datawriter] ADD MEMBER [Egg];
```

You cannot add any of the fixed database roles except the Public role to a fixed or flexible database role.

> **MORE INFO   DATABASE ROLES**
>
> You can learn more about database roles at *http://msdn.microsoft.com/en-us/library/ms189121(SQL.110).aspx*.

Using Flexible Database Roles

Flexible database roles enable you to use roles with a custom set of permissions. You can nest flexible database roles in a manner similar to the way you nest security groups in Active Directory. To create a flexible database role by using SQL Server Management Studio and to grant that role permissions, perform the following steps:

1. Locate the database in which you want to create the flexible database role.

2. Right-click the Roles node and click New Database Role.

3. On the Database Role dialog box General page, provide a name for the database role and specify a role owner.

    The role owner can manage the role. The default role owner is the security principal who created the role. You can also choose the schemas owned by the role and the principals who are members of the role.

4. On the Securables tab, click Search to find a particular securable.

    You can search for a specific object, specify a type of object, as shown in Figure 6-1, or choose all objects in a particular schema.

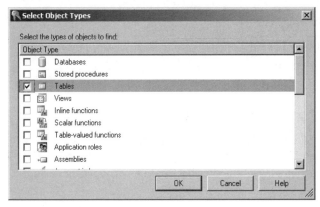

FIGURE 6-1 Select Object Types page

5. In the Securables box, choose a securable. In the Permissions area, specify the permissions you want to grant on the securable. For example, in Figure 6-2, the Alter, Insert, and Select privileges have been granted on the Person.Address table.

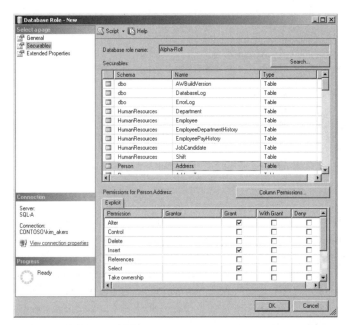

FIGURE 6-2 Role securables

You use the CREATE ROLE statement to create flexible roles. For example, to create a role named Beta-Role in the AdventureWorks2012 database, issue the statement:

```
CREATE ROLE [Beta-Role]
```

Protecting Objects from Modification

Protecting objects from modification involves configuring permissions so that only authorized principals can make modifications. The most basic way to do this is by adding security principals to the db_denydatawriter role. The drawback of this method is that it applies to the entire database.

You can protect specific database objects from modification by using the DENY setting with the ALTER, CONTROL, DELETE, INSERT, TAKE OWNERSHIP, and UPDATE permissions. When granting, denying, or revoking permissions from a securable, you should perform one operation at a time. For example, to deny the ALTER, INSERT, and UPDATE permissions to the Gamma-Role role on the Person.Address table, issue the following statement:

```
use [AdventureWorks2012]
GO
DENY ALTER ON [Person].[Address] TO [GAMMA-ROLE]
DENY INSERT ON [Person].[Address] TO [GAMMA-ROLE]
DENY UPDATE ON [Person].[Address] TO [GAMMA-ROLE]
GO
```

NOTE   **READ-ONLY FILEGROUPS**

Placing objects such as tables in read-only filegroups doesn't stop all forms of modification. For example, it is possible to drop columns from tables stored in read-only filegroups.

Using Schemas

Schemas simplify the application of permissions by enabling you to collect securables into containers. Objects belong to schemas, and schemas belong to security principals. You can create a flexible database role and then create a schema owned by that role, adding security principals to that role as necessary to grant them permissions over the objects within that schema. For example, you want to grant one group of principals the ability to perform any actions on the database's user tables but not allow that group of principals the ability to alter or drop those user tables. You want to allow this same group of principals to create application-related objects such as views, stored procedures, and functions.

To accomplish this goal, perform the following steps:

1.   Create a new role. Add all the security principals to whom you want to give the ability to perform all actions except alter and drop on user tables to this role.

2.   Create a new schema for the user tables. Move all the user tables to this schema.

3. Grant the role created in Step 1 SELECT, REFERENCES, INSERT, UPDATE, DELETE, and VIEW DEFINITION permissions on the new schema created in Step 2.

4. Create a second new schema for views, stored procedures, and functions. Grant the role created in Step 1 the CREATE TABLE permission on the second schema.

You can create a new schema by using the CREATE SCHEMA statement. You can create a new schema in SQL Server Management Studio by performing the following steps:

1. Expand the Security node under the user database in which you want to create the schema.

2. Right-click the Schemas node and click New Schema.

3. On the General page, provide a name for the schema and a schema owner.

4. On the Permissions page, shown in Figure 6-3, configure appropriate permissions on the schema for each role.

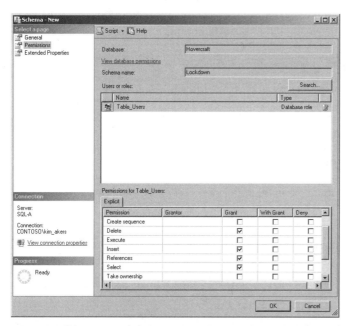

FIGURE 6-3 Schema permissions

You can use the ALTER SCHEMA Transact-SQL statement to move securables between schemas in the same database. For example, to move the Engines table from the dbo schema to the Lockdown schema, execute the following statement:

```
ALTER SCHEMA Lockdown TRANSFER dbo.Engines;
```

MORE INFO **USING SCHEMAS TO SECURE DATABASE OBJECTS**

You can learn more about using schemas to secure database objects at *http://msdn .microsoft.com/en-us/library/dd283095(SQL.100).aspx*.

Determining Effective Permissions

You can use the HAS_PERMS_BY_NAME function to determine a specific principal's effective permission on a certain securable. An effective permission can be one of the following:

- Permission is granted directly to the security principal.
- Permission is granted to a role of which the security principal is a member.
- Permission is implied by a higher-level permission held by the security principal.
- Permission is not denied to the principal directly or indirectly through role membership.

The HAS_PERMS_BY_NAME function returns a result of 1 if the principal has an effective permission on the securable and returns 0 if the principal has no effective permission on the securable. The function returns NULL if neither the permission nor securable class is valid. The HAS_PERMS_BY_NAME function runs in the context of the current principal. To use the HAS_PERMS_BY_NAME function to determine the effective permission of another security principal, the caller must have the IMPERSONATE permission on that security principal.

> **MORE INFO** **HAS_PERMS_BY_NAME**
>
> You can learn more about the HAS_PERMS_BY_NAME function at *http://msdn.microsoft .com/en-us/library/ms189802.aspx*.

PRACTICE **Configuring Database Permissions**

In this practice, you configure database permissions, schemas, and roles.

EXERCISE 1   Create Schema, Roles, and Permissions

In this exercise, you create database objects and then assign them permissions. To complete this exercise, perform the following steps:

1. Log on to the default instance on SQL-A with the Kim_Akers user account.
2. Create a new database named **Saturn**.
3. Create a new role named **Moon_Table_Editors**.
4. Create three tables in the default location, named **Mimas**, **Thethys**, and **Hyperion**.
5. Create a new schema named **Orbits**.
6. Grant the Moon_Table_Editors role SELECT, REFERENCES, INSERT, UPDATE, DELETE, and VIEW DEFINITION privileges on the Orbits schema.

EXERCISE 2   Modify Privileges by Using Transact-SQL

In this exercise, you use Transact-SQL to configure additional permissions on the Orbits schema. To complete this exercise, perform the following steps:

1. Use Transact-SQL to configure the Moon_Table_Editors role with only SELECT and REFERENCES permissions on the Orbits schema.

2. Use Transact-SQL to create a new role named **Moon_Table_Designers**.

3. Use Transact-SQL to assign the Moon_Table_Designers the ability to create new tables in the Orbits schema but ensure that they cannot create tables in other schemas in the Saturn database.

Lesson Summary

- A securable is an item for which you can assign permissions. Securables can be contained within other securables.

- A scope is a container. Permissions assigned at the scope level are inherited by objects within that scope.

- The GRANT, DENY, and REVOKE statements are used to manage permissions on objects.

- Roles enable you to simplify the management of permissions. Assign permissions to roles and then add principals to roles.

- Fixed database roles have fixed permissions. Flexible database roles enable you to assign custom permissions.

- Schemas enable you to collect objects to simplify the process of assigning permissions.

Lesson Review

Answer the following questions to test your knowledge of the information in this lesson. You can find the answers to these questions and explanations of why each answer choice is correct or incorrect in the "Answers" section at the end of this chapter.

1. Which permission must you assign on a table if you want to allow a database user to view the information in that table?

   A. REFERENCE

   B. INSERT

   C. UPDATE

   D. SELECT

2. You want to configure permissions on a table so that members of a database role are allowed to insert data into a table but cannot change existing data in that table. Which of the following permissions should you assign?

   A. REFERENCE

   B. INSERT

   C. RECEIVE

   D. UPDATE

3. Which of the following Transact-SQL statements removes the INSERT permission from the Person.Address table for the Sydney_Users role?

    A. GRANT INSERT ON [Person].[Address] to [Sydney_Users]

    B. GRANT SELECT ON [Person].[Address] to [Sydney_Users]

    C. DENY INSERT ON [Person].[Address] to [Sydney_Users]

    D. REVOKE INSERT ON [Person].[Address] to [Sydney_Users]

4. To which fixed database role would you add a security principal to ensure that he or she cannot add, modify, or delete any data stored in user tables in the database?

    A. db_datawriter

    B. db_denydatawriter

    C. db_denydatareader

    D. db_owner

Lesson 2: Troubleshooting SQL Server Security

Troubleshooting SQL Server security involves ensuring that the security settings configured for an instance or database match the security requirements for that instance or database. In this lesson, you learn how to configure security settings for authentication and learn the catalog views and Transact-SQL statements you can use to resolve problems with SQL Server security.

> **After this lesson, you will be able to:**
> - Troubleshoot authentication.
> - Troubleshoot certificates and keys.
> - Troubleshoot endpoints.
>
> **Estimated lesson time: 60 minutes**

Troubleshooting Authentication

The most common authentication problem is a *security principal* being unable to access the Database Engine instance, or a specific database in the case of contained databases, because of a forgotten password. Forgotten passwords must be reset, which is usually triggered by a call to the service desk.

When SQL Server authentication is enabled, Group Policy controls how long an account is locked out, how many failed logins trigger a lockout, and the duration over which the logins must occur to trigger a lockout. These factors depend on the configuration of the following three Group Policy items, found in the Computer Configuration\Policies\Windows Settings \Security Settings\Account Policies\Account Lockout Policy Group Policy node:

- **Account Lockout Duration**   The length of time an account is locked out
- **Account Lockout Threshold**   The number of failed logins that must occur to trigger a lockout
- **Reset Account Lockout Counter After**   The duration in which the failed logins must occur to trigger a lockout

The default configuration of Active Directory does not define an account lockout policy.

If some connections can be established while others cannot be established, check the Status page of the login's properties, as shown in Figure 6-4, to verify the following:

- Does the login have permission to connect to the Database Engine?
- Is the login disabled?
- If the login uses SQL Server authentication, has the login been locked out?

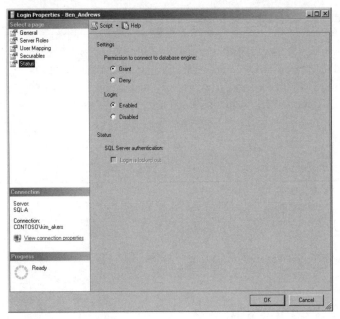

FIGURE 6-4 Check login status

You can query the sys.server_principals catalog view to determine whether a login is disabled.

You can use the ALTER LOGIN Transact-SQL statement with the MUST_CHANGE parameter to force a password change the next time a SQL Server–authenticated login is used to connect to the Database Engine instance. You can use the ALTER LOGIN Transact-SQL statement with the UNLOCK parameter to unlock a locked SQL Server–authenticated login.

> **MORE INFO** **ALTER LOGIN**
>
> You can learn more about the ALTER LOGIN statement at *http://msdn.microsoft.com/en-us /library/ms189828.aspx*.

Using Authentication Modes

SQL Server 2012 supports two authentication modes: Windows authentication mode and mixed authentication mode. When Windows authentication mode is enabled, as shown in Figure 6-5, SQL Server authentication is disabled and cannot be used. If mixed authentication mode is enabled, both forms of authentication are used. If you choose to enable mixed authentication mode during setup, you must provide a strong password for the built-in SQL Server system administrator account, sa. If you choose Windows authentication mode, the sa account is created but disabled. If you choose to switch to mixed mode and enable the sa account, you must also configure the account with a strong password.

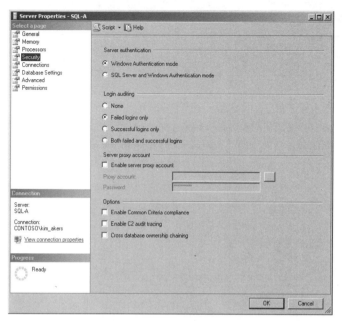

FIGURE 6-5 Windows Authentication mode

MORE INFO **AUTHENTICATION MODES**

You can learn more about authentication modes at *http://msdn.microsoft.com/en-us /library/ms144284.aspx.*

 Quick Check

- Which Transact-SQL statement can you use to unlock a locked-out login?

Quick Check Answer

- Use the ALTER LOGIN statement to unlock a locked-out login.

Resolving Client Connection Problems

In some cases, authentication issues are not related to login and password but are caused by the client being unable to connect to a named instance because the SQL Server Browser service is disabled or is stopped, as shown in Figure 6-6. The browser service helps clients connect to instances that are not using fixed ports. You can resolve this problem by ensuring that the SQL Server Browser service is running.

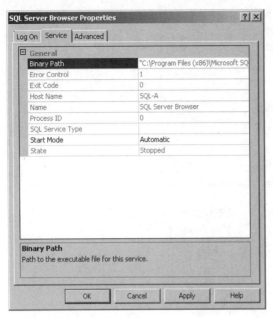

FIGURE 6-6 Browser service

Troubleshooting Certificates and Keys

A common cause of problems related to keys is that the certificate used in key generation might have expired. You must also ensure that keys and certificates are regularly backed up because encrypted data might be unrecoverable if keys or certificates become corrupt. You can use the following security catalog views to view information about certificates and keys at the instance and database levels:

- **sys.asymmetric_keys** Provides information about each asymmetric key, including how the key is encrypted, how the private key is encrypted, the key length, and the algorithm used.

- **sys.certificates** Provides information on each certificate stored in the database, including certificate name, how the private key is encrypted, certificate serial number, certificate login security identifier (SID), certificate expiration, and the date when the private key was last backed up.

- **sys.key_encryptions** Provides information about each symmetric encryption specified when using the CREATE SYMMETRIC KEY statement with the ENCRYPTION BY parameter. Options include encryption by symmetric key, password, certificate, asymmetric key, and master key.

- **sys.symmetric_keys** Provides information for every symmetric key that has been created by using the CREATE SYMMETRIC KEY statement, including the database principal who owns the key, key length, and key generation algorithm.

Troubleshooting Endpoints

The first step in troubleshooting endpoints is to understand the precise configuration of the endpoint that is causing the issue you must resolve. You can query the following catalog views to determine more about the configuration of endpoints configured on a Database Engine instance:

- **sys.database_mirroring_endpoints** Provides information on endpoints used for database mirroring and AlwaysOn Availability Groups. You can use this catalog view to determine the connection authentication type and the properties of any certificate used to secure the endpoint.

- **sys.endpoints** Provides information about each endpoint created on the instance. Includes information on endpoint protocol, payload type, and endpoint state.

- **sys.http_endpoints** Provides information on each endpoint that uses the HTTP protocol. Enables you to determine whether Secure Sockets Layer (SSL) is in use and the type of authentication method that has been configured for the endpoint.

- **sys.service_broker_endpoints** Provides information on service broker endpoints, including authentication configuration, encryption algorithm, and the identifier of any certificate used for authentication.

- **sys.tcp_endpoints** Provides information about the TCP endpoints in the system, including port number, IP address, and whether the port is dynamic.

When troubleshooting the security endpoint, you might need to alter the authentication or encryption settings. It is also possible that the endpoint is in a stopped state. You can configure an existing endpoint by using the ALTER ENDPOINT Transact-SQL statement. For example:

- To start a stopped endpoint, use the ALTER ENDPOINT statement with the STATE parameter.

- You can change the endpoint authentication by using the ALTER ENDPOINT statement with the AUTHENTICATION parameter.

- You can enable, disable, or require encryption by using the ALTER ENDPOINT statement with the ENCRYPTION parameter.

If there is a problem making a connection between endpoints, use the GRANT statement to grant permissions on an endpoint to a LOGIN. For example, to allow a login to connect to an endpoint, grant the CONNECT permission on the endpoint. When configuring permissions on endpoints, you must ensure that the remote instance has some way of authenticating with the local instance. If both instances are members of the same domain, you can accomplish this by using Windows-authenticated logins. You can also use certificates to authenticate endpoints.

You use the ALTER AUTHORIZATION Transact-SQL statement to change the ownership of an endpoint. Endpoints must be owned by logins, and you must have the TAKE OWNERSHIP permission on an endpoint to change ownership of the endpoint. If you are setting the Ownership permission of an endpoint to a login that is different from the one you are using to perform the operation, you need the IMPERSONATE permission on the login to which you are assigning permission.

Using Security Catalog Views

You can use security catalog views to view the properties of server and database security. SQL Server provides the following catalog views for viewing security information at the Database Engine instance level. To use these views, the security principal must have the VIEW SERVER STATE permission:

- **sys.server_permissions**   Provides information about permissions configured at the Database Engine instance level
- **sys.server_principals**   Provides information on server-level principals, including principal type, whether the principal is disabled, creation date, and modification date
- **sys.server_role_members**   Provides information on role membership
- **sys.sql_logins**   Provides information on whether a login is subject to password policy and is configured with an expiration date

- **sys.system_components_surface_area_configuration** Provides information about each executable system object that you can enable or disable by using surface-area configuration

You can use the following catalog views to learn more about security configuration at the individual database level. To use these views, the security principal must have the VIEW DATABASE STATE permission:

- **sys.database_permissions** Provides information about permissions at the database level

- **sys.database_principals** Provides information about principal type, including authentication type (instance, database, or Windows) and creation date

- **sys.database_role_members** Provides information about role membership at the database level

- **sys.master_key_passwords** Provides information on database master key passwords, including the credential with which the master key password is associated

> **MORE INFO** **SECURITY CATALOG VIEWS**
>
> You can learn more about security catalog views at *http://technet.microsoft.com/en-us /library/ms178542.aspx.*

PRACTICE **Troubleshooting Security**

In this practice, you view security settings for the AdventureWorks2012 database.

EXERCISE 1 **Review Permissions and Security Settings**

In this exercise, you review permissions and security settings. To complete this exercise, perform the following steps:

1. Review the permissions assigned to the Person, Production, and Purchasing schemas in the AdventureWorks2012 database.

2. Query the sys.database_permissions catalog view to determine permissions assigned to the AdventureWorks2012 database.

3. Query the sys.database_principals catalog view for the AdventureWorks2012 database to determine the security principals at the database level for this database.

Lesson Summary

- Group Policy items determine account lockout settings.
- The ALTER LOGIN Transact-SQL statement can unlock locked SQL Server–authenticated logins and force password changes.

- Windows authentication mode disables SQL Server authentication mode. Mixed authentication mode uses both Windows authentication and SQL Server authentication.
- Verify the expiry dates of certificates when troubleshooting certificate-based security. Use the sys.certificates catalog view to view certificate properties.
- Use the sys.endpoints catalog view to view endpoint information.
- Use the sys.server_principals catalog view to determine whether a principal is disabled.

Lesson Review

Answer the following questions to test your knowledge of the information in this lesson. You can find the answers to these questions and explanations of why each answer choice is correct or incorrect in the "Answers" section at the end of this chapter.

1. You have configured the default, ALPHA, BETA, GAMMA, and DELTA instances on a single host server so that users can connect by using their Active Directory domain credentials. This morning, users can connect to the default instance but report that they cannot connect to the ALPHA, BETA, GAMMA, and DELTA instances. Which of the following should you do when attempting to resolve this problem?

   A. Configure the default instance to use mixed authentication.

   B. Start the SQL Server Agent service on the default instance.

   C. Start the SQL Server Browser service.

   D. Restart the SQL Server service on the default instance.

2. A colleague in the Finance department cannot connect to the Database Engine, although other workers in the finance department can connect. You suspect that the user's login is disabled. Which of the following catalog views can you query to determine whether this is the case?

   A. sys.sql_logins

   B. sys.server_permissions

   C. sys.server_principals

   D. sys.server_role_members

3. You are determining which SQL Server–authenticated logins on an instance are configured without a password expiration date. Which of the following SQL catalog views could you query to make this determination?

   A. sys.server_permissions

   B. sys.sql_logins

   C. sys.server_role_members

   D. sql.server_principals

4. You are resolving a problem a database user is having. You must determine whether instance, database, or Windows authentication is being used. Which of the following security catalog views can you query to determine this information?

   A. sys.database_principals

   B. sys.database_permissions

   C. sys.server_principals

   D. sys.sql_logins

Lesson 3: Auditing SQL Server Instances

Auditing enables you to track activity on a SQL Server instance. This could be as simple as determining which security principal updated a table or which administrator altered important permissions.

> **After this lesson, you will be able to:**
> - Configure server audits.
> - Track object modification.
> - Monitor elevated privileges.
> - Audit unsolicited connection attempts.
> - Create, maintain, and monitor policy-based management.
>
> **Estimated lesson time: 60 minutes**

Using SQL Server Audit

SQL Server Audit enables you to configure sophisticated auditing at the instance and database levels. SQL Server Audit forwards audit results to a target, which can be either a flat file or the Windows Security or Windows Application event logs on the host computer. When choosing between the Security and Application logs, remember that access to the Security log is limited to users with appropriate permissions, who are usually members of the local Administrators group on the host computer. The Application log can be written to and read by any authenticated user, which can present a security risk, depending on the types of actions you are auditing. Only SQL Server 2012 Enterprise edition supports database-level auditing in production environments.

If you want to use the Windows Security log as the target, you must perform the following steps:

- Add the SQL Server service account to the Generate Security Audits policy. This policy is located on the Computer Configuration\Policies\Windows Settings\Security Settings \Local Policies\User Rights Assignment Group Policy node. The Network Service, Local System, and Local Service accounts have this permission by default. This policy is shown in Figure 6-7.
- Configure the Audit Object Access policy for both Success and Failure. This policy is located on the Computer Configuration\Policies\Windows Settings\Security Settings \Local Policies\Audit Policy Group Policy node.

FIGURE 6-7 Generate Security Audits policy

When using a file as a target, take the following steps:

1. Configure the SQL Server service account with Read and Write permissions on the file.

2. Users assigned the Audit Administrators role require Read and Write permissions on the file.

3. Users assigned the Audit Reader role must have Read permission on the file.

Microsoft recommends that you send audit data to a separate instance from the one you are auditing to minimize the chance that administrators of the audited instance can tamper with the results. Configure the destination instance so that only Audit Administrators and Audit Readers have access. One of the most important functions of auditing is to provide a record of administrator activity. By using a separate instance, you can minimize the chance that administrators of important Database Engine instances can tamper with auditing data.

> **MORE INFO** **SQL SERVER AUDIT**
>
> You can learn more about using SQL Server Audit at *http://msdn.microsoft.com/en-us /library/cc280386(SQL.110).aspx.*

Creating a Server Audit

Before you can create an audit specification at the instance or the database level, you must create a *server audit*, which involves specifying the following items:

- **Audit Name** A name for the server audit.
- **Queue Delay** The delay in milliseconds before audit actions must be processed. Default value is 1,000 milliseconds.

- **On Audit Log Failure**   What to do when there is an audit log failure. The options are that operations continue, the Database Engine instance is shut down, or the audit simply fails and no event is written.

- **Audit Destination**   Enables you to specify the Application log, Security log, or a file destination. If you specify a file destination, you must specify the file path, maximum number of files, and the maximum file size.

To create a server audit, perform the following steps:

1. In SQL Server Management Studio, right-click the Audits node under the Security node and choose New Audit. This opens the Create Audit dialog box.

2. In the Create Audit dialog box, shown in Figure 6-8, specify the settings for the Audit.

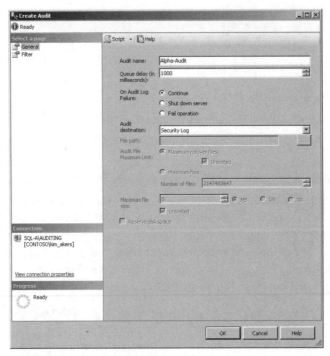

FIGURE 6-8 Creating a server audit

You can create a server audit by using the CREATE SERVER AUDIT Transact-SQL statement. For example, to create a server audit named BETA-AUDIT that writes events to the Application log, has a queue delay of 1,000 milliseconds, and will shut down the Database Engine instance in the event of audit failure, execute the following Transact-SQL statement from the MASTER database:

```
CREATE SERVER AUDIT [BETA-AUDIT]
TO APPLICATION_LOG
WITH
( QUEUE_DELAY = 1000
  ,ON_FAILURE = SHUTDOWN
)
```

You can enable an audit by right-clicking the audit and choosing Enable.

If the On Audit Log Failure option is set to Shutdown, an audit failure will cause the Database Engine instance to shut down. After the instance is shut down, it is possible that the Database Engine instance will be unable to start unless you start it using the -f option from the command line, which enables you to override the audit-triggered shutdown. You can also start an instance that has been shut down by SQL Server Audit in Single User mode. This is because, in single user mode, a server audit configured with the Shutdown option functions as though you had set the Continue option. When an audit is bypassed in this manner, the Database Engine writes a MSG_AUDIT_SHUTDOWN_BYPASSED message to the error log.

> **MORE INFO** **CREATE SERVER AUDIT**
>
> You can learn more about the CREATE SERVER AUDIT statement at *http://msdn.microsoft .com/en-us/library/cc280448.aspx*.

SQL Server Audit Action Groups and Actions

When you create a *server audit specification*, as shown in Figure 6-9, or a database audit specification, you choose action groups and actions, which determine the type of actions SQL Server Audit records.

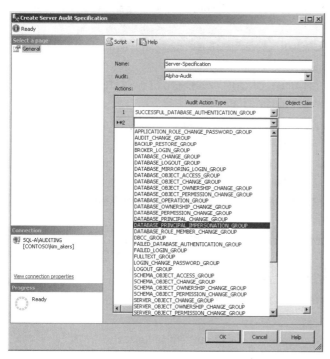

FIGURE 6-9 Server-level audit action types

When configuring a server audit specification, you can choose from the following:

- **APPLICATION_ROLE_CHANGE_PASSWORD_GROUP** Audit the application role password changes.
- **AUDIT_CHANGE_GROUP** Audit the creation and modification of audit specifications.
- **BACKUP_RESTORE_GROUP** Audit backup and restore operations.
- **BROKER_LOGIN_GROUP** Audit service broker transport security operations.
- **DATABASE_CHANGE_GROUP** Audit the creation, modification, or deletion of databases.
- **DATABASE_LOGOUT_GROUP** Audit the logout of contained database users.
- **DATABASE_MIRRORING_LOGIN_GROUP** Audit database mirroring transport security.
- **DATABASE_OBJECT_ACCESS_GROUP** Audit database access. This type can lead to large audit records.
- **DATABASE_OBJECT_CHANGE_GROUP** Audit CREATE, ALTER, or DROP statements used on database objects.
- **DATABASE_OBJECT_OWNERSHIP_CHANGE_GROUP** Audit object ownership changes within a database.
- **DATABASE_OBJECT_PERMISSION_CHANGE_GROUP** Audit permission changes within a database.
- **DATABASE_OPERATION_GROUP** Audit database checkpoint and subscription operations.
- **DATABASE_OWNERSHIP_CHANGE_GROUP** Audit use of the ALTER AUTHORIZATION statement to modify database ownership.
- **DATABASE_PERMISSION_CHANGE_GROUP** Audit the use of GRANT, REVOKE, or DENY statements to modify permissions on a database.
- **DATABASE_PRINCIPAL_CHANGE_GROUP** Audit the creation, deletion, and modification of database security principals.
- **DATABASE_PRINCIPAL_IMPERSONATION_GROUP** Audit the use of the EXECUTE AS or SETPRINCIPAL statements.
- **DATABASE_ROLE_MEMBER_CHANGE_GROUP** Audit the modification of database roles.
- **DBCC_GROUP** Audit use of DBCC commands.
- **FAILED_DATABASE_AUTHENTICATION_GROUP** Audit failed authentication for a contained database.
- **FAILED_LOGIN_GROUP** Audit failed instance authentication.
- **FULLTEXT_GROUP** Audit full-text events.
- **LOGIN_CHANGE_PASSWORD_GROUP** Audit login password changes.

- **LOGOUT_GROUP**   Audit logouts at the instance level.
- **SCHEMA_OBJECT_ACCESS_GROUP**   Audit use of object permissions within a schema.
- **SCHEMA_OBJECT_CHANGE_GROUP**   Audit CREATE, ALTER, or DROP operations on any schema in any database on the instance.
- **SCHEMA_OBJECT_OWNERSHIP_CHANGE_GROUP**   Audit ownership change on any schema object on any schema in any database on the instance.
- **SCHEMA_OBJECT_PERMISSION_CHANGE_GROUP**   Audit permission change on any schema object on any schema in any database on the instance.
- **SERVER_OBJECT_CHANGE_GROUP**   Audit the creation, alteration, or deletion of server objects.
- **SERVER_OBJECT_OWNERSHIP_CHANGE_GROUP**   Audit ownership changes of any server objects.
- **SERVER_OBJECT_PERMISSION_CHANGE_GROUP**   Audit permission changes of any server objects.
- **SERVER_OPERATION_GROUP**   Audit modification of settings, resources, external access, or authorization at the server level.
- **SERVER_PERMISSION_CHANGE_GROUP**   Audit assignment of permissions at the server level.
- **SERVER_PRINCIPAL_CHANGE_GROUP**   Audit creation, modification, or deletion of server principals.
- **SERVER_PRINCIPAL_IMPERSONATION_GROUP**   Audit use of the EXECUTE AS statement at the server level.
- **SERVER_ROLE_MEMBER_CHANGE_GROUP**   Audit changes to fixed server roles.
- **SERVER_STATE_CHANGE_GROUP**   Audit changes to the SQL Server service.
- **SUCCESSFUL_DATABASE_AUTHENTICATION_GROUP**   Audit successful contained database authentication.
- **SUCCESSFUL_LOGIN_GROUP**   Audit successful instance logins.
- **TRACE_CHANGE_GROUP**   Audit use of the ALTER TRACE permission.
- **USER_CHANGE_PASSWORD_GROUP**   Audit password changes of contained database users.
- **USER_DEFINED_AUDIT_GROUP**   Audit events generated by the sp_audit_write Transact-SQL statement.

If you are using SQL Server 2012 Enterprise edition, you can also configure audit specifications at the database level. The advantage of this is that you can configure auditing for specific databases rather than auditing for all databases. If you configure certain audit action groups at the instance level, SQL Server records actions performed on all databases, not just on specific databases. You can use both audit action groups and audit actions with database audit specifications. When creating a database-level audit specification, you can use the following audit action groups:

- **APPLICATION_ROLE_CHANGE_PASSWORD_GROUP** Audit modification of application role passwords.

- **AUDIT_CHANGE_GROUP** Audit modification of database audit specifications.

- **BACKUP_RESTORE_GROUP** Audit backup and restore operations.

- **DATABASE_CHANGE_GROUP** Audit database creation, alteration, or deletion.

- **DATABASE_LOGOUT_GROUP** Audit contained database user logout.

- **DATABASE_OBJECT_ACCESS_GROUP** Audit database object access.

- **DATABASE_OBJECT_CHANGE_GROUP** Audit modification of database objects, including use of CREATE, ALTER, and DROP statements.

- **DATABASE_OBJECT_OWNERSHIP_CHANGE_GROUP** Audit modification of database object ownership.

- **DATABASE_OBJECT_PERMISSION_CHANGE_GROUP** Audit modification of permissions on database objects.

- **DATABASE_OPERATION_GROUP** Audit database operations, including checkpoint and subscribe queries.

- **DATABASE_OWNERSHIP_CHANGE_GROUP** Audit modification of database ownership.

- **DATABASE_PERMISSION_CHANGE_GROUP** Audit modification of database permissions.

- **DATABASE_PRINCIPAL_CHANGE_GROUP** Audit modification of database principals.

- **DATABASE_PRINCIPAL_IMPERSONATION_GROUP** Audit use of EXECUTE AS or SETUSER statements.

- **DATABASE_ROLE_MEMBER_CHANGE_GROUP** Audit modifications to database roles.

- **DBCC_GROUP** Audit use of DBCC commands.

- **FAILED_DATABASE_AUTHENTICATION_GROUP** Audit failed contained database user logins.

- **SCHEMA_OBJECT_ACCESS_GROUP** Audit when object permissions are used in a schema.

- **SCHEMA_OBJECT_CHANGE_GROUP** Audit ALTER, CREATE, and DROP operations on a schema.

- **SCHEMA_OBJECT_OWNERSHIP_CHANGE_GROUP** Audit schema ownership permission changes.

- **SCHEMA_OBJECT_PERMISSION_CHANGE_GROUP** Audit schema object permission changes.

- **SUCCESSFUL_DATABASE_AUTHENTICATION_GROUP** Audit contained database user login.
- **USER_CHANGE_PASSWORD_GROUP** Audit contained database user password change.
- **USER_DEFINED_AUDIT_GROUP** Audit use of the sp_audit_write Transact-SQL statement.

You can also audit the use of specific actions directly on database schema and schema objects with database audit specifications. For example, you could use a database audit specification to audit the use of UPDATE statements on a specific table. You can use the following audit actions when creating a database audit specification:

- **SELECT** Audit use of SELECT on specific database schema and schema objects.
- **UPDATE** Audit use of UPDATE on specific database schema and schema objects.
- **INSERT** Audit use of INSERT on specific database schema and schema objects.
- **DELETE** Audit use of DELETE on specific database schema and schema objects.
- **EXECUTE** Audit use of EXECUTE on specific database schema and schema objects.
- **RECEIVE** Audit use of RECEIVE on specific database schema and schema objects.
- **REFERENCES** Audit use of REFERENCES on specific database schema and schema objects.

> **MORE INFO** **AUDIT ACTION GROUPS AND ACTIONS**
>
> You can learn more about SQL Server Audit action groups and actions at *http://msdn .microsoft.com/en-us/library/cc280663.aspx.*

Creating a Server Audit Specification

You can create a server audit specification only after a server audit is present. The general process of using SQL Server Audit to audit activities at the instance level involves the following steps:

1. Verify that a server audit is present.
2. Create a server audit specification that maps to the audit.
3. Enable the audit specification.

To create a server audit specification in SQL Server Management Studio, perform the following steps:

1. In SQL Server Management Studio, right-click the Server Audit Specifications node under the Security node and then choose New Server Audit Specification.
2. In the Create Server Audit Specification dialog box, shown in Figure 6-10, provide a name for the server audit specification and use the drop-down list to select an existing server audit to use with the specification.

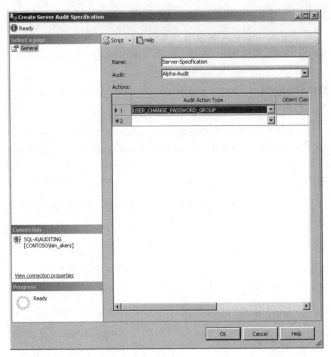

FIGURE 6-10 The Create Server Audit Specification dialog box

3. Use the Audit Action Type list to specify the server-level audit action groups you want to audit.

4. Enable the specification.

You can create a server audit specification by using the CREATE SERVER AUDIT SPECIFICATION Transact-SQL statement. For example, to create a server specification named BETA-SPECIFICATION that uses the BETA-AUDIT server audit and audits database creation, alteration, and deletion actions, execute the following statement:

```
CREATE SERVER AUDIT SPECIFICATION [BETA-SPECIFICATION]
  FOR SERVER AUDIT [BETA-AUDIT]
  ADD (DATABASE_CHANGE_GROUP)
```

If you must modify an existing server audit specification, you can edit the properties of the specification by using SQL Server Management Studio or by using the ALTER SERVER AUDIT SPECIFICATION statement. For example, to add the DATABASE_LOGOUT_GROUP server-level audit action group to the BETA-SPECIFICATION group created in the previous example, execute the statement:

```
ALTER SERVER AUDIT SPECIFICATION [BETA-SPECIFICATION]
ADD (DATABASE_LOGOUT_GROUP)
```

To create, alter, or drop a Server Audit or a Server Audit specification, security principals must be assigned the ALTER ANY SERVER AUDIT or CONTROL SERVER permission.

MORE INFO   **CREATING SERVER AUDITS AND SERVER AUDIT SPECIFICATIONS**

You can learn more about creating server audits and server audit specifications at
http://msdn.microsoft.com/en-us/library/cc280525.aspx.

✔ Quick Check

- What must you create before creating a server audit specification?

Quick Check Answer

- You must create a server audit before creating a server audit specification.

Creating a Database Audit Specification

Database audit specifications enable you to perform targeted auditing of specific databases and objects rather than more general auditing of a specific type of object across all databases on the instance. A server audit must exist before you create a database audit specification.

The general process of using SQL Server Audit to audit activities at the database level involves performing a few steps. To create a database audit specification by using SQL Server Management Studio, perform the following steps:

1. Expand the Security node under the database for which you want to create the Database Audit specification.

2. Right-click Database Audit Specification and choose New Database Audit Specification.

3. In the Create Database Audit Specification dialog box, provide the following information:

   - Name: Type the database audit specification name.

   - Server Audit: Choose the existing server audit for this database audit specification.

   - Audit Actions: Choose from the audit action groups and the audit actions you want to audit. You can also choose the object you want to audit and the principal you want to audit. Figure 6-11 shows a database audit specification that records INSERT operations on a specific table.

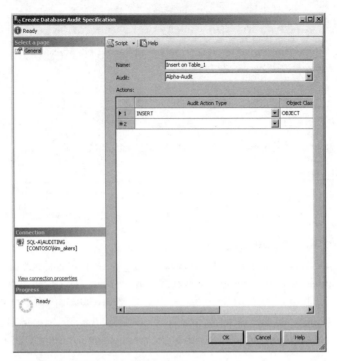

FIGURE 6-11 Database audit specification

Another way to create a database audit specification is by using the CREATE DATABASE AUDIT SPECIFICATION Transact-SQL statement. For example, to create a database audit specification named Audit_Spec_1 that uses existing server audit Srv_Audit_1 to audit INSERT operations by members of the Exemplar role on the Paradigm table, execute the statement:

```
CREATE DATABASE AUDIT SPECIFICATION [Audit_Spec_1]
FOR SERVER AUDIT [Srv_Audit_1]
ADD (INSERT ON OBJECT::[dbo].[Paradigm] BY [Exemplar])
```

You can enable the database audit specification by right-clicking it and choosing Enable Database Audit Specification or by using the ALTER DATABASE AUDIT SPECIFICATION statement with the WITH (STATE = ON) parameter.

 EXAM TIP

To create, alter, or drop a database audit specification, security principals must have permission to connect to the database and be assigned either the ALTER ANY DATABASE AUDIT permission or the ALTER or CONTROL permissions on the database.

If you attach a database with a database audit specification to another instance with a different audit specification, SQL Server Audit will not record audit events because the database audit specification will be in an orphaned state. For example, you have an audit specification on the Hovercraft database. You then detach and reattach the Hovercraft database to a different instance. The Hovercraft database audit specification will be in an orphaned state. You can resolve an orphaned audit specification in one of two ways:

- If the instance has an existing server audit, use the ALTER DATABASE AUDIT SPECIFICATION statement to connect the orphaned database audit specification to the existing server audit.

- If the instance does not have an existing server audit, you can use the CREATE SERVER AUDIT statement and specify the GUID of the original host instance's server audit.

If you are using database mirroring with a database that has a database audit defined, you must ensure the following:

- The mirror instance must have an audit that uses the same GUID. This enables the database audit to write audit records during the mirroring process.

- If you are using a file-based target to record audit events, you must ensure that the SQL Server service account on the mirror instance has read/write permission to the file that serves as the target.

- If you are using a Windows event log target, you must configure Group Policy so that the SQL Server service account on the mirror instance has permission to access the event logs.

> **MORE INFO** **DATABASE AUDIT SPECIFICATION**
>
> You can learn more about creating a database audit specification at *http://msdn.microsoft.com/en-us/library/cc280424.aspx*.

Viewing SQL Server Audit Views and Functions

The following dynamic views, catalog views, and functions enable you to view audit configuration information:

- **sys.dm_audit_actions**   Stores information on each audit action and each audit action group that you can use with SQL Server Audit

- **sys.server_audits**   Enables you to see information about each SQL Server audit configured on an instance

- **sys.dm_server_audit_status**   Enables you to see information about currently configured audits

- **sys.server_audit_specifications**   Enables you to see information about server audits

- **sys.server_audit_specification_details**   Enables you to see information about actions that are audited at the server level

- **sys.database_audit_specifications**   Enables you to see information about currently configured database audit specifications

- **sys.database_audit_specifications_details** Enables you to see information about actions that are audited at the database level
- **fn_get_audit_file** Enables you to query a file-based target for audit information

Configuring Login Auditing

You can configure login auditing on the Security page of the Server Properties dialog box, as shown in Figure 6-12. You can configure the following options:

- None: Login auditing is disabled.
- Failed logins only: Only failed logins are written to the error log.
- Successful logins only: Only successful logins are written to the error log.
- Both failed and successful logins: Both failed and successful logins are written to the error log.

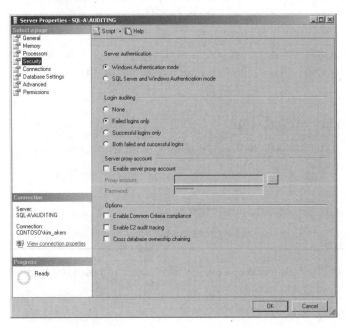

FIGURE 6-12 Login auditing

MORE INFO **LOGIN AUDITING**

You can learn more about login auditing at *http://msdn.microsoft.com/en-us/library /ms175850.aspx.*

Using c2 Audit Mode

c2 audit mode configures the instance to record both successful and failed attempts to access statements and objects as defined by the c2 security standard. You can configure c2 audit mode by using the Enable c2 Audit Tracing option in the Server Properties dialog box, as shown in Figure 6-13. You can also use the following Transact-SQL statement to enable c2 audit mode:

```
sp_configure "show advanced options", 1;
GO
RECONFIGURE;
GO
sp_configure "c2 audit mode", 1;
GO
RECONFIGURE;
GO
```

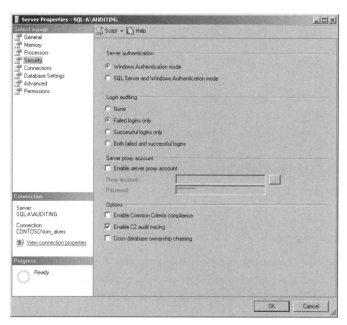

FIGURE 6-13 c2 audit tracing

c2 audit mode data is stored in a file in the default instance data directory. The Database Engine rotates the file after it reaches 200 MB. The Database Engine continues to create files until the volume hosting the data directory reaches capacity or c2 audit mode is disabled. The c2 audit mode feature will be removed in a future version of SQL Server and has been superseded by common criteria certification. If the volume hosting the Database Engine fills and the instance halts, you must make space available on the host volume and then restart the Database Engine either by using -f or in single-user mode.

Common Criteria Compliance

Common criteria compliance supersedes c2 audit mode and enables certain security options on a Database Engine instance, including login auditing information. You can access this login information by querying the sys.dm_exec_sessions dynamic management view and enabling common criteria compliance on the Security page of the Server Properties dialog box.

You can also enable common criteria compliance by executing the following Transact-SQL statement:

```
sp_configure "show advanced options", 1;
GO
RECONFIGURE;
GO
sp_configure "common criteria compliance enabled", 1;
GO
RECONFIGURE;
GO
```

Policy-Based Management

Policy-based management provides you with a method of managing more than one instance across multiple servers. You can use policy-based management to manage instances, databases, and other objects such as backup devices. You can use policies to enforce configuration standards such as blocking anyone from enabling Auto Shrink and Auto Close on databases.

You use the following objects to configure policy-based management:

- **Facet**   A collection of properties that can be configured.
- **Condition**   The settings that can be configured for the property. Available conditions depend on the properties of a facet.
- **Policy**   A condition that should be enforced. Blocking Auto Shrink from being enabled on databases could be one policy; blocking Auto Close on databases could be another.
- **Category**   A collection of policies that should be enforced together, such as the Block Auto Shrink and Block Auto Close policies.

- **Target** Defines the scope of policy application. It can include instances, databases, or database objects.

You can create a policy by performing the following general steps:

1. In SQL Server Management Studio, under the Management node, choose a policy-based management facet that includes the properties that you want to configure. When configuring a policy that blocks Auto Shrink, choose the Database facet.

2. Right-click the facet and then choose New Condition. For example, Figure 6-14 shows the creation of a new condition for Auto Shrink.

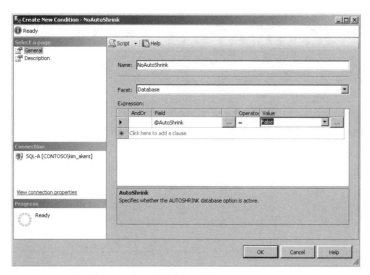

FIGURE 6-14 Creating an Auto Shrink condition

3. Define a policy that includes the condition by right-clicking the Policy node and clicking New Policy. In the Create New Policy dialog box, shown in Figure 6-15, add a check condition, a set of targets, an evaluation mode, and a server restriction. Evaluation can be performed on demand according to a schedule. Server restriction enables you to limit the scope of the policy.

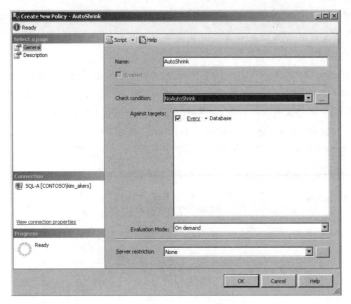

FIGURE 6-15 The Create New Policy dialog box

EXAM TIP

There is an existing policy named Database Auto Shrink that you can use instead of creating your own.

To work with policy-based management, a principal must be a member of the PolicyAdministratorRole database role in the msdb database. Policy information is stored in the msdb database, and you should back up this database after making substantial changes to policy-based management configuration.

You can transfer policies between instances by using the import and export functionality. You can also configure a central management server and have the policies on one instance apply directly to other instances. You specify a central management server by performing the following steps:

1. Click Registered Servers in the View menu in SQL Server Management Studio.

2. Right-click the Central Management Servers node and choose Register Central Management Server.

3. In the New Server Registration dialog box, shown in Figure 6-16, specify the name of the instance that will function as the central management server. Click Test to verify the connection and then click Save.

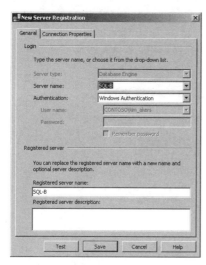

FIGURE 6-16 Central management server

To register subordinate servers, right-click the central management server and then click New Server Registration. Enter the details of the server that will function as a subordinate to the central management server. You can also create new server groups that are collections of subordinate servers. You can execute queries against the subordinate servers by right-clicking the central management server and choosing New Query.

You evaluate policies to determine whether objects comply with those policies. For example, you can evaluate the policy related to the Auto Shrink setting to determine if databases are configured with the Auto Shrink option. To evaluate an object to determine whether it complies with a particular policy, perform the following steps:

1. Right-click the item in SQL Server Management Studio, choose Policies, and then click Evaluate.

2. In the Evaluate Policies dialog box, shown in Figure 6-17, select which policies you want to evaluate and then click Evaluate. On the Evaluation page, you can view the results of the evaluation.

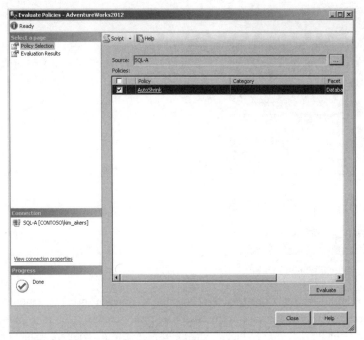

FIGURE 6-17 The Evaluate Policies dialog box

You can use the following views to discover information about policy-based management policies, expressions, conditions, filters, and groups:

- **syspolicy_conditions** Provides one row for each policy-based management condition on the instance

- **syspolicy_policies** Provides one row for each policy-based management policy on the instance

- **syspolicy_policy_execution_history** Lists times when policies were executed and the results of those actions

- **syspolicy_policy_execution_history_details** Provides detailed information on the execution of policies, including targets and results

- **syspolicy_policy_group_subscriptions** Provides one row for each policy-based management subscription on the instance

- **syspolicy_policy_categories** Provides one row for each policy-based management policy on the instance

- **syspolicy_system_health_state** Provides one row for each combination of policy-based management policy and target query expression

MORE INFO POLICY-BASED MANAGEMENT

You can learn more about policy-based management at *http://msdn.microsoft.com/en-us /library/bb510667.aspx*.

PRACTICE   Configuring SQL Server Audit

In this practice, you configure SQL Server Audit.

EXERCISE 1   Prepare for Auditing

In this exercise, you create a service account, configure appropriate permissions, and deploy a new instance on which you perform auditing tasks. To complete this exercise, perform the following steps:

1. Log on to DC with the Kim_Akers user account.

2. Create a new service account named **SQL-SVC-A** with password **Pa$$w0rd.**

3. Edit the SQL-POLICY GPO and configure the following settings:

    ■ Grant the SQL-SVC-A user account the Log On As A Service right.

    ■ Add the SQL-SVC-A user account to the Generate Security Audits policy.

4. Log on to server SQL-A with the Kim_Akers user account and run **gpupdate /force** from a command prompt.

5. Install a new instance on SQL-A named **AUDITING** by using the following command:

    ```
    setup.exe /qs /ACTION=Install /FEATURES=SQLEngine /INSTANCENAME=AUDITING
    /SQLSVCACCOUNT="CONTOSO\SQL-SVC-A" /SQLSVCPASSWORD="Pa$$w0rd" /
    SQLSYSADMINACCOUNTS="Contoso\Kim_Akers" /AGTSVCACCOUNT="CONTOSO\SQL-SVC-A" /
    AGTSVCPASSWORD="Pa$$w0rd" /IACCEPTSQLSERVERLICENSETERMS
    ```

EXERCISE 2   Create a SQL Server Audit

In this exercise, you create a SQL server audit that writes audit events to the Security log. To complete this exercise, perform the following steps:

1. Log on to SQL-A\AUDITING with the Kim_Akers user account.

2. Create an audit with the following properties:

    ■ Name: ALPHA-AUDIT

    ■ Queue Delay: 1000 MS

    ■ On Audit Log Failure: Continue

    ■ Audit Destination: Security Log

3. Enable this server audit.

EXERCISE 3 Create a Server Audit Specification

In this exercise, you create a Server Audit specification and then test the audit specification and verify the audit specification details. To complete this exercise, perform the following steps:

1. Configure a server audit specification that tracks the creation, deletion, and modification of a database.

2. Enable this server audit specification.

3. Create a new database on the AUDITING instance named **Hovercraft**.

4. Check the Security log to verify that the database creation event has been recorded.

5. Query the following views for information about the audit and audit specification created in Exercises 2 and 3:

   - sys.server_audits
   - sys.server_audit_specifications
   - sys.server_audit_specification_details

Lesson Summary

- SQL Audit enables you to track specific actions on the instance or database level.
- SQL Audit can write audit data to the Windows Security or Windows Application log. Audit data can also be written to a normal file.
- An audit can be configured so that the instance shuts down in the event of an audit failure.
- Action groups and actions determine which activity is audited.
- You can create a server or database audit specification only after a server audit has been configured.

Lesson Review

Answer the following questions to test your knowledge of the information in this lesson. You can find the answers to these questions and explanations of why each answer choice is correct or incorrect in the "Answers" section at the end of this chapter.

1. You are configuring the Windows Security log as an audit target on the default instance of server SYD-SQL-A. The SQL Server service uses the contoso\SYD-SQL-SRV account as its service account. The SQL Server Agent service uses the contoso \SYD-SQL-AGT account as its service account. Which of the following policies must you configure to accomplish this goal? (Each correct answer presents part of a complete solution. Choose all that apply.)

A. Add the contoso\SYD-SQL-SRV account to the Generate Security Audits policy.

B. Add the contoso\SYD-SQL-AGT account to the Generate Security Audits policy.

C. Enable success and failure audits on the Audit Object Access policy.

D. Enable success and failure audits on the Audit Privilege Use policy.

2. You must perform database-level audits in a production environment. Which of the following SQL Server editions supports this functionality?

   A. Enterprise

   B. Business Intelligence

   C. Standard

   D. Web

3. An audit failure has caused the Database Engine to shut down. What steps can you take to restart the Database Engine so that you can modify the server audit and resolve the issue? (Each correct answer presents a complete solution. Choose all that apply.)

   A. Restart the SQL Server Agent service.

   B. Start SQL Server by using the -f option.

   C. Start SQL Server in single-user mode.

   D. Restart the SQL Server Browser service.

4. SQL Server Audit has not been configured on a Database Engine instance. You will use SQL Server audit to track insert activity on specific tables in the Hovercraft database. You do not want to track insert activity on any other user databases hosted on the instance. Which of the following Transact-SQL statements would you use to configure SQL Server Audit to accomplish this goal? (Each correct answer presents part of a complete solution. Choose all that apply.)

   A. CREATE SERVER AUDIT

   B. CREATE SERVER AUDIT SPECIFICATION

   C. CREATE DATABASE AUDIT SPECIFICATION

   D. ALTER DATABASE AUDIT SPECIFICATION

Case Scenarios

In the following case scenarios, you apply what you have learned about securing SQL Server 2012. You can find answers to these questions in the "Answers" section at the end of this chapter.

Case Scenario 1: Configuring Database Permissions

You are developing permissions for the Production database. This database has two schema, named Accounts and Manufacturing. The database has three roles, named Finance, DataProtection, and Engineering.

1. You must ensure that principals in the Finance role can add and change data on tables in the Accounts schema. Which permissions must you grant to accomplish this goal?

2. Members of the DataProtection role must be able to back up and recover data stored in the Protection database. Which permissions must you assign this role?

3. Which permission must the Engineering role have on the Manufacturing schema if members of that role must be able to create and drop tables in the schema?

Case Scenario 2: Troubleshooting Security

You are auditing the security of a subsidiary company's SQL Server 2012 databases. A previous database administrator implemented certificates and asymmetric keys for database authentication and authorization. The database administrator has since moved on, and you must determine the properties of certificates and keys, including when certificates will expire, when private keys were last backed up, and the key lengths used when generating asymmetric keys. With these requirements in mind, answer the following questions:

1. Which security catalog view would you query to determine the expiration dates of database certificates?

2. Which security catalog view would you query to determine when the private key for a specific certificate was last backed up?

3. Which security catalog view would you query to determine the key length of the asymmetric keys?

Case Scenario 3: Auditing at Fabrikam

You are configuring auditing for several databases hosted on the default instance of server SYD-SQL-A. You are working on this configuration with a colleague. With this situation in mind, answer the following questions:

1. Which permissions do you need to be able to create a database audit specification?

2. Which step should you take to ensure that both successful and failed logins are audited on the default instance on SYD-SQL-A?

3. You want to check how your colleague has configured auditing. Which catalog view would you query to determine which actions are audited at the database level?

Suggested Practices

To help you successfully master the exam objectives presented in this chapter, complete the following tasks.

Manage Database Permissions

Prior to completing each task in the following practices, list the steps you would take to accomplish the task. After completing the task, assess how accurately you predicted the necessary steps.

- **Practice 1**   Create a new schema in the Saturn database on the default instance of SQL-A. Create two new flexible roles.
- **Practice 2**   Configure permissions so that members of the first role have only read access to the objects in the new schema. Configure permissions so that members of the second role can perform any action on objects in the schema except modifying permissions, creating new objects, or dropping existing objects.

Troubleshoot Security

Prior to completing each task in the following practices, list the steps you would take to accomplish the task. After completing the task, assess how accurately you predicted the necessary steps.

- **Practice 1**   Create a new database on the Alternate instance of SQL-A named **Pluto**. Create a certificate, an asymmetric key, and a symmetric key. Query the appropriate catalog views to determine key properties of each of these objects.
- **Practice 2**   Configure account lockout policies to lock out any user who enters an incorrect password three times in succession in a ten-minute period.

Audit SQL Server Instances

Prior to completing each task in the following practices, list the steps you would take to accomplish the task. After completing the task, assess how accurately you predicted the necessary steps.

- **Practice 1**   Configure a database audit specification for the Hovercraft database that tracks the creation of objects.
- **Practice 2**   Create a table in the Hovercraft database and verify that the CREATE TABLE event has been recorded in the Security event log.

Answers

This section contains the answers to the lesson review questions and solutions to the case scenarios in this chapter.

Lesson 1

1. **Correct Answer: D**

   A. Incorrect. The REFERENCE permission enables a principal to reference the securable.

   B. Incorrect. The INSERT permission enables a principal to add data to the securable.

   C. Incorrect. The UPDATE permission enables a principal to modify the data stored in an executable.

   D. Correct. The SELECT permission enables a principal to view data stored in the securable.

2. **Correct Answer: B**

   A. Incorrect. The REFERENCE permission enables a principal to reference the securable.

   B. Correct. The INSERT permission enables a principal to add data to the securable.

   C. Incorrect. The RECEIVE permission enables a principal to receive messages from the service broker.

   D. Incorrect. The UPDATE permission enables a principal to modify the data stored in an executable.

3. **Correct Answer: D**

   A. Incorrect. This statement grants the INSERT permission rather than revoking it.

   B. Incorrect. This statement grants the SELECT permission on the table.

   C. Incorrect. This statement applies the DENY INSERT permission rather than revoking the INSERT permission.

   D. Correct. This statement revokes the INSERT permission on the table.

4. **Correct Answer: B**

   A. Incorrect. This role enables members to add, delete, and change data in user tables in the database.

   B. Correct. This role blocks members from adding, modifying, or deleting any data stored in user tables in the database.

   C. Incorrect. This role blocks members from reading data stored in user tables in the database.

   D. Incorrect. This role enables members to perform any maintenance or configuration activity on the database.

Lesson 2

1. **Correct Answer: C**

   A. Incorrect. Clients must able to connect successfully to the default instance by using Windows authentication, so it is not necessary to configure mixed authentication to resolve this problem.

   B. Incorrect. No problem is described that relates to the SQL Server Agent service on the default instance. Starting this service will not resolve this problem.

   C. Correct. Clients cannot connect to named instances that do not use fixed ports if the SQL Server Browser service is not running.

   D. Incorrect. No problem is described that relates to the SQL Server service on the default instance. Restarting this service will not resolve this problem.

2. **Correct Answers: A and C**

   A. Correct. You can use the sys.sql_logins catalog view to determine whether a SQL Server–authenticated login is configured to use a password policy and has an expiration date. Through inheritance this view also displays whether a login is disabled.

   B. Incorrect. The sys.server_permissions catalog view provides information about server-level permissions. You cannot use this catalog view to determine whether a login is disabled.

   C. Correct. You can query the sys.server_principals catalog view to determine whether a login is disabled.

   D. Incorrect. This catalog view provides information about role membership. You cannot use this catalog view to determine whether a login is disabled.

3. **Correct Answer: B**

   A. Incorrect. The sys.server_permissions catalog view provides information about server-level permissions. You cannot use this catalog view to determine whether a SQL Server–authenticated login is configured with an expiration date.

   B. Correct. You can use the sys.sql_logins catalog view to determine whether a SQL Server–authenticated login is configured with an expiration date.

   C. Incorrect. The sys.server_role_members catalog view provides information about role membership. You cannot use this catalog view to determine whether a SQL Server–authenticated login is configured with an expiration date.

   D. Incorrect. You cannot use the sql.server_principals catalog view to determine whether a SQL Server–authenticated login is configured with an expiration date.

4. **Correct Answer: A**

   A. Correct. You can query the sys.database_principals catalog view to determine which authentication type a database principal uses.

B. Incorrect. You cannot use the sys.database_permissions catalog view to determine which authentication type a database principal uses.

C. Incorrect. You cannot use the sys.server_principals catalog view to determine which authentication type a database principal uses.

D. Incorrect. You cannot use the sys.sql_logins catalog view to determine which authentication type a database principal uses.

Lesson 3

1. **Correct Answers: A and C**

   A. Correct. If you want to use the local Security log as a target, you must add the SQL Server service account to the Generate Security Audits policy.

   B. Incorrect. You must add the SQL Server service account, not the agent account, to this policy.

   C. Correct. You must enable success and failure audits on the audit object access policy when using the local Security log as a target.

   D. Incorrect. You must enable success and failure audits for the Audit Object Access policy but not the Audit Privilege Use policy when using the Security log as a target.

2. **Correct Answer: A**

   A. Correct. Only the Enterprise edition of SQL Server 2012 supports database-level audits in a production environment.

   B. Incorrect. The Business Intelligence edition of SQL Server 2012 does not support database-level audits in a production environment.

   C. Incorrect. The Standard edition of SQL Server 2012 does not support database-level audits in a production environment.

   D. Incorrect. The Web edition of SQL Server 2012 does not support database-level audits in a production environment.

3. **Correct Answers: B and C**

   A. Incorrect. Restarting the Agent service will not enable you to resolve server audit issues when an audit failure has caused shutdown.

   B. Correct. You can restart the Database Engine by using the -f option so that you can resolve server audit issues when an audit failure has caused shutdown.

   C. Correct. You can restart the Database Engine in single-user mode to resolve server audit issues when an audit failure has caused shutdown.

   D. Incorrect. Restarting the browser service will not enable you to resolve server audit issues when an audit failure has caused shutdown.

4. **Correct Answers: A and C**

   A. **Correct.** You must create a SQL Server Audit before you can create a database audit specification.

   B. **Incorrect.** You do not need to create a SQL Server Audit specification. You need to create a SQL Server Audit specification only if you are performing auditing at the Database Engine instance level rather than at the level of a specific database.

   C. **Correct.** After you have created a SQL Server Audit, you can create a database audit specification to track insert activities on a specific database without tracking the same activity on other databases hosted on the instance.

   D. **Incorrect.** You use the ALTER DATABASE AUDIT SPECIFICATION statement only to modify an existing database audit specification. Because no such audit specification exists, you should not use this statement.

Case Scenario 1

1. They will need SELECT permission to view the data, INSERT permission to add data, and UPDATE permission to modify data.

2. Backup permission grants permission to back up a securable. Restore permission allows a securable to be recovered from backup.

3. They must be assigned the ALTER permission to create and drop tables in the schema.

Case Scenario 2

1. You can query the sys.certificates catalog view to determine the expiration date of database certificates.

2. You can query the sys.certificates catalog view to determine the most recent date on which a certificate's private key was backed up.

3. You can query the sys.asymmetric_keys catalog view to determine the key length of asymmetric keys.

Case Scenario 3

1. You need either the ALTER ANY DATABASE AUDIT permission or the ALTER or CONTROL permissions on the database.

2. Configure Login Auditing at the instance level. Enabling common criteria compliance and c2 audit tracing also accomplishes this goal.

3. You can query the sys.database_audit_specifications_details catalog view to learn detailed information about auditing at the database level.

CHAPTER 7

Mirroring and Replication

Exam objectives in this chapter:

- Implement database mirroring.
- Implement replication.

Database mirroring is a solution for increasing the availability of databases, enabling a mirror database to function as a substitute if the primary database becomes unavailable. The amount of data lost and how automatically the switch occurs between the primary and the mirror depends on the configuration of the mirroring session. Replication is a method of transmitting database data and objects between database servers. Microsoft SQL Server 2012 supports four primary methods of replication, and the ability to determine the situations in which each replication method is appropriate comprises part of the 70-462 exam.

Lessons in this chapter:

Before You Begin

To complete the practice exercises in this chapter, make sure that you have:

- Completed the setup tasks for installing computers DC, SQL-A, SQL-B, and SQL-CORE as outlined in the introduction of this book.
- Completed the setup tasks outlined in the end-of-lesson practice exercises in Chapter 1, "Planning and Installing SQL Server 2012," through Chapter 4, "Migrating, Importing, and Exporting."

No additional configuration is required for this chapter.

Lesson 1: Mirroring Databases

Database mirroring is the process of creating and maintaining an always up-to-date copy of a database on another SQL Server instance. Transactions applied to the database on the principal instance are also applied to the database on the mirrored instance. If you configure the mirroring session with a witness instance, automatic failover to the mirrored instance is possible if the principal instance becomes unavailable.

> **After this lesson, you will be able to:**
> - Prepare a database for mirroring.
> - Mirror a database.
> - Configure high-safety and high-performance mode.
> - Configure automatic failover with a witness server.
> - Perform failover from principal to mirrored instance.
> - Monitor a mirrored database.
>
> **Estimated lesson time: 60 minutes**

Database Mirroring

 Database mirroring is a strategy for increasing the availability of a database. *Database mirrors* are paired copies of a single database that are hosted on separate instances of SQL Server. Although it is possible to use mirroring with instances installed on the same hosts, you should use separate hosts to ensure that the mirrored database remains available in the event of host operating system failure.

Clients interact with the database hosted on the principal server. When you configure mirroring, every insert, update, and delete operation performed against the principal database is redone on the mirror database through a stream of active transaction logs that the Database Engine instance applies in sequence immediately after it receives them.

> **NOTE FUTURE OF MIRRORING**
>
> Microsoft intends to remove mirroring in a future version of SQL Server. Plan on implementing AlwaysOn availability groups, which you learn about in Chapter 8, "Clustering and AlwaysOn," to accomplish the availability objectives you currently achieve through database mirroring.

Depending on how you configure mirroring, the mirror instance functions in either high-safety or high-performance mode.

- **High-safety mode** enables failover to occur without data loss from committed transactions. Hot standby is possible when you are using the high-safety mode. In high-safety mode, transactions are committed on both partners after they are synchronized. The drawback of high-safety mode is an increase in transaction latency. If a witness server is present, you can enable automatic failover with this mode.

- **High-performance mode** enables failover to occur, but data loss is possible. In high-performance mode, the primary instance does not wait for the mirror instance to confirm that it has received the log record.

EXAM TIP

You can mirror some or all the user databases on an instance. However, you can mirror only databases that are configured to use the full recovery model. Database mirroring supports only a single principal instance and a single mirror instance.

MORE INFO   **DATABASE MIRRORING**

Learn more about database mirroring at *http://msdn.microsoft.com/en-us/library /ms189852(SQL.110).aspx.*

Mirroring Prerequisites

Before you create a new mirroring session, ensure that your environment will support mirroring. The primary, mirror, and witness instances must run the same version of SQL Server. The primary and the mirror instances must run the same edition, whereas the witness instance must run only an edition of SQL Server that supports witnessing. Mirroring support on a per-edition basis in SQL Server 2012 is as follows:

- **Enterprise**   Supports high-performance, high-safety, and witness modes
- **Business Intelligence**   Supports high-safety and witness modes
- **Standard**   Supports high-safety and witness modes
- **Web**   Supports witness mode only
- **Express (all versions)**   Supports witness mode only

Database mirroring on SQL Server 2012 has the following restrictions:

- You can mirror only user databases. It is not possible to mirror the master, msdb, tempdb, or model databases.

- You cannot rename mirrored databases.

- You cannot configure database mirroring for a database that contains FILESTREAM filegroups. You cannot create FILESTREAM filegroups on the principal server.

- Cross-database and distributed transactions are not supported for mirrored databases.

The principal and mirroring instance should be hosted on servers that can tolerate similar workloads. The normal load on the principal and mirroring instance should not regularly exceed 50 percent of CPU usage when deploying in high-safety mode with automatic failover because an inability to contact other partners can cause unnecessary failover.

It is best practice to use the same paths on the principal and the mirror instance. If the principal and mirror instances use different paths, it might be necessary to suspend mirroring if adding files to the database.

> **MORE INFO** **MIRRORING PREREQUISITES**
>
> Learn more about mirroring prerequisites at *http://msdn.microsoft.com/en-us/library /ms366349(SQL.110).aspx.*

Full Recovery Model

You must configure a database to use the full recovery model before you can mirror it. You can view the recovery model of a database on the Options page of the Database Properties dialog box, as shown in Figure 7-1.

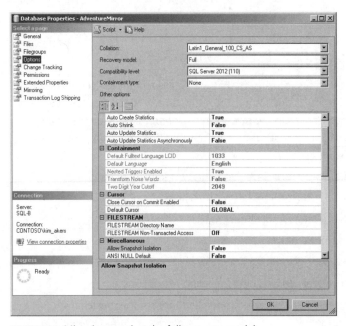

FIGURE 7-1 Mirroring requires the full recovery model

You can configure the recovery model by using the ALTER DATABASE statement with the SET RECOVERY option. For example, to configure the EXEMPLAR database to use the FULL recovery model, execute the following Transact-SQL statement:

```
USE MASTER;
ALTER DATABASE Exemplar SET RECOVERY FULL;
```

Recover by Using NO RECOVERY

Prior to commencing a mirroring session, you must restore a database by using the NO RECOVERY option on the mirror instance. To do this, you need a full backup of the database that you mirror. You can create a full backup either by using SQL Server Management Studio, as shown in Figure 7-2, or by using the BACKUP DATABASE Transact-SQL statement.

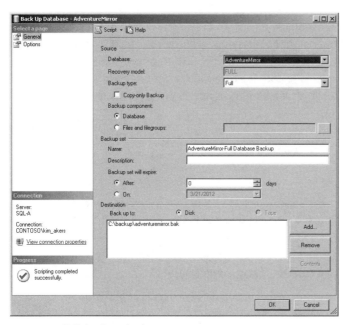

FIGURE 7-2 Full database backup

For example, to perform a full backup of the AdventureMirror database to the c:\backup\adventuremirror.bak location, overwriting any existing backup file, execute the statement:

```
BACKUP DATABASE [AdventureMirror] TO DISK = N'C:\backup\adventuremirror.bak' WITH
FORMAT;
```

You must then restore the database backup on the mirror instance by using the NO RECOVERY option. You can configure this option on the Options page of the Restore Database dialog box. You can also do this by using the RESTORE DATABASE Transact-SQL statement with the WITH NORECOVERY option. For example, to restore the AdventureMirror database from the c:\backup\adventuremirror.bak backup file by using the WITH NORECOVERY option, execute the statement:

```
RESTORE DATABASE AdventureMirror
        FROM DISK = 'C:\backup\adventuremirror.bak'
        WITH NORECOVERY
GO
```

After you have performed these steps, go back to the principal database and perform a transaction log backup. You can do this from SQL Server Management Studio or by using the BACKUP LOG statement. For example, to perform a transaction log backup of the AdventureMirror database to the c:\backup\adventuremirror.trn location, execute this statement:

```
BACKUP LOG AdventureMirror
      TO DISK = 'C:\backup\adventuremirror.trn'
GO
```

You then must apply this transaction log backup to the database that you restored by using the WITH NORECOVERY option on the mirroring instance. You can do this by using SQL Server Management Studio or by using the RESTORE LOG statement with the WITH NORECOVERY option. For example, to restore the c:\backup\adventuremirror.trn transaction log backup file to the AdventureMirror database by using the WITH NORECOVERY option, execute the statement:

```
RESTORE LOG AdventureMirror
      FROM DISK = 'C:\backup\adventuremirror.trn'
      WITH FILE=1, NORECOVERY
GO
```

You must also restore any other transaction log backups that were taken prior to enabling mirroring. You learn about backup and recovery in detail in Chapter 11, "SQL Server Agent, Backup, and Restore."

> **MORE INFO**   **PREPARE MIRROR DATABASE FOR MIRRORING**
>
> You can learn more about preparing a mirror database for mirroring at *http://msdn .microsoft.com/en-us/library/ms189053(v=sql.110).aspx.*

Endpoint Firewall Rules

When configuring a mirroring session, you must configure firewall rules to allow traffic through on the endpoint. For example, to support the mirroring configuration shown in Figure 7-3, it is necessary to allow traffic on TCP port 7024.

 Quick Check

■ What recovery model must a database be set to use before you can mirror it?

Quick Check Answer

■ A database must be set to use the full recovery model before you can mirror it.

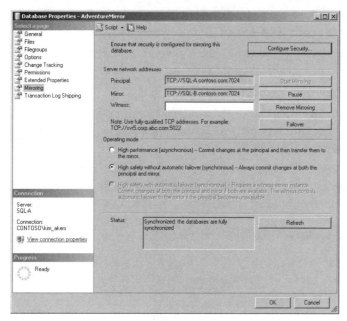

FIGURE 7-3 TCP Port 7024 used for endpoint

Configuring Mirroring with Windows Authentication

You can configure mirroring with Windows-based authentication if the SQL Server service accounts on the principal, mirror, and witness are members of the same Active Directory domain or trusted domains. You can configure mirroring with Windows-based authentication by using SQL Server Management Studio or Transact-SQL.

If you are using a separate domain account for the SQL Server Service on each instance, you must create a login in the master database for the accounts associated with the other instances. For example, if you are using the SQL-A-SVC domain account for the SQL Server Service on server SQL-A and you want to configure SQL-B as a mirrored instance, you must create a login for SQL-A-SVC on instance SQL-B. You must also create a login on instance SQL-A for whatever domain account is associated with the SQL Server Service for SQL-B.

To configure mirroring using high-safety mode with a witness server, using Windows authentication, perform the following steps:

1. Ensure that you have performed the prerequisite steps, including restoring a backup of the database and transaction log on the mirror instance by using the WITH NORECOVERY option.

2. Ensure that necessary logins have been created if different domain accounts are used for the SQL Server service on each instance that will participate in the mirroring. You must also perform this step on the witness server.

3. In SQL Server Management Studio, connect to the primary instance, right-click the database that you want to mirror, choose Tasks, and then choose Mirror.

4. On the Mirroring page of Database Properties, click Configure Security to open the Configure Database Mirroring Security Wizard. Click Next.

5. On the Include Witness Server page, choose Yes and click Next.

6. On the Choose Servers To Configure page, choose whether to save security configuration information on the Witness server instance. Security configuration information is saved by default on the Principal and Mirror server instances.

7. On the Principal Server Instance page, shown in Figure 7-4, either accept the default listener port or configure an alternate port. You can also accept the default endpoint name or configure an alternate endpoint name.

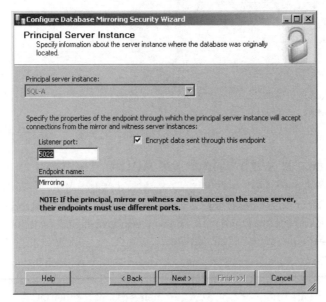

FIGURE 7-4 Principal server instance

8. On the Mirror Server Instance page, click Connect to open the Connect To Server dialog box. You must make this connection to the mirror instance by using a login or account that has the CREATE ENDPOINT permission or membership in the sysadmin fixed server role on the mirror instance. Note and, if necessary, alter the assigned listener port and endpoint name and then click Next.

9. On the Witness Server Instance page, shown in Figure 7-5, choose a third instance to function as the witness server. Click Connect to open the Connect To Server dialog box.

   As with connecting to the mirror server, you must connect with an account that has the CREATE ENDPOINT permission or is a member of the sysadmin fixed server role on the witness instance.

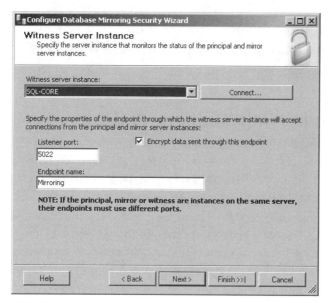

FIGURE 7-5 Witness setup

10. On the Service Accounts page, shown in Figure 7-6, enter the domain service accounts that are used for the SQL Server service on each instance. Click Next and then click Finish to complete the wizard.

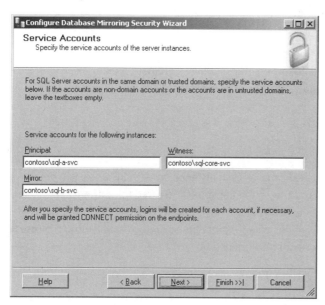

FIGURE 7-6 Mirroring service accounts

<table>
<tr><td>MORE INFO MIRRORING WITH WINDOWS AUTHENTICATION</td></tr>
<tr><td>For more information about mirroring, visit http://msdn.microsoft.com/en-us/library/ms188712(SQL.110).aspx.</td></tr>
</table>

Configuring Mirroring with Certificate Authentication

You use certificate-based authentication when configuring mirroring between instances when a domain-based account is not used as the service account for SQL Server. You cannot configure certificate-based authentication for mirroring by using SQL Server Management Studio; you must perform this operation by using Transact-SQL.

In the following example, the AdventureMirror database is mirrored with SQL-A serving as the principal instance and SQL-B serving as the mirror instance. The AdventureMirror database is already configured to use the full recovery model, and the database has already been backed up on SQL-A and restored with NO RECOVERY on SQL-B. A transaction log backup has then been taken on the SQL-A instance and that log backup restored by using NO RECOVERY on the SQL-B instance.

Query the sys.symmetric_keys catalog view to determine whether a database master key exists. If no key exists, use the following Transact-SQL statement to create a database master key on both SQL-A and SQL-B:

```
USE master;
CREATE MASTER KEY ENCRYPTION BY PASSWORD = 'Pa$$w0rd';
GO
```

After the master key exists on each instance, use it to create a certificate for each instance on that instance. The following Transact-SQL statement creates a certificate named SQL_A_cert on the SQL-A instance for the SQL-A instance:

```
USE master;
CREATE CERTIFICATE SQL_A_cert
   WITH SUBJECT = 'SQL_A certificate';
GO
```

After you have created a certificate for each instance on each instance, you create endpoints on each instance that use the certificate you just created for authentication. You can choose any available TCP port for mirroring. The following Transact-SQL statement, when executed on instance SQL-A, creates an endpoint named Endpoint_Mirroring that uses port 7024 and certificate SQL_A_cert for authentication:

```
CREATE ENDPOINT Endpoint_Mirroring
   STATE = STARTED
   AS TCP (
     LISTENER_PORT=7024
     , LISTENER_IP = ALL
   )
   FOR DATABASE_MIRRORING (
     AUTHENTICATION = CERTIFICATE SQL_A_cert
```

```
      , ENCRYPTION = REQUIRED ALGORITHM AES
      , ROLE = ALL
   );
GO
```

After the endpoints have been created on the primary and mirror instances, it is necessary to back up the certificates so that they can then be imported on the partner instance. The following Transact-SQL statement backs up the SQL_A_cert to the c:\backup\SQL_A_cert.cer file:

```
BACKUP CERTIFICATE SQL_A_cert TO FILE = 'C:\BACKUP\SQL_A_cert.cer';
GO
```

After the certificates have been backed up on each instance, copy them across to the partner instance so you can create logins and users based on those certificates. For example, to create a login on instance SQL-A by using the SQL_B_cert.cer certificate, first create the login, then the user, and then a certificate based on the backed-up certificate by executing the following Transact-SQL code:

```
USE master;
CREATE LOGIN SQL_B_login WITH PASSWORD = 'Pa$$w0rd';
GO
CREATE USER SQL_B_user FOR LOGIN SQL_B_login;
GO
CREATE CERTIFICATE SQL_B_cert
   AUTHORIZATION SQL_B_user
   FROM FILE = 'C:\backup\SQL_B_cert.cer'
GO
```

After the login, user, and certificate for the partner instance have been created, grant permissions to the login on the endpoint. For example, the following code, when run on instance SQL-A, grants the login associated with SQL-B permission on the endpoint:

```
GRANT CONNECT ON ENDPOINT::Endpoint_Mirroring TO [SQL_B_login];
GO
```

Repeat this step on the mirror instance but, in this case, grant permission to the login associated with the primary instance. After these steps have been completed, you can configure mirroring on the actual databases. Start by configuring the database on the mirrored instance. In the following Transact-SQL statement, run on instance SQL-B, the partner for the AdventureMirror database is configured as sql-a.contoso.com:

```
ALTER DATABASE AdventureMirror
   SET PARTNER = 'TCP://sql-a.contoso.com:7024';
GO
```

You then repeat the process on the primary instance with the address of the mirror instance endpoint:

```
ALTER DATABASE AdventureMirror
   SET PARTNER = 'TCP://sql-b.contoso.com:7024';
GO
```

After you successfully perform this step, the database is mirrored in high-safety mode.

Changing Operating Modes

You can change database mirroring operating mode on the Mirroring page of the database's
properties. You can change to the high safety with automatic failover mode only if a witness
server is present. Automatic failover occurs when the mirror instance and the witness server
are able to contact each other but are unable to contact the primary instance.

You can configure the operating mode in Transact-SQL by using the ALTER DATABASE with
the SAFETY option:

- Setting the SAFETY option to FULL will configure the database for high-safety mode.
  When you configure database mirroring, the session automatically starts in high-safety
  mode.

- Setting the SAFETY option to OFF will configure the database for high-performance
  mode.

You can add a witness to an existing session by creating the necessary endpoint on the
witness, creating logins for the principal and mirror instance service accounts, and granting CONNECT privileges on the endpoint to that login. You must also create a login on the
principal and mirror instances for the domain account used for the SQL Server service on the
witness. If you are using certificate-based authentication, you must configure the appropriate
certificates rather than the logins associated with domain accounts, as described earlier in the
section on certificate-based authentication.

After you have taken these steps, you can specify the witness on the Mirroring page of
the mirrored database's properties on the principal instance. You can also use the ALTER
DATABASE Transact-SQL statement with the SET WITNESS option. For example, to configure
server SQL-CORE as the witness server for the AdventureMirror database when an endpoint
has been configured that uses TCP port 7024, execute the statement:

```
ALTER DATABASE AdventureMirror
     SET WITNESS = 'TCP://SQL-CORE:7024'
```

Role Switching and Failover

Depending on the mode that the mirrored session is configured to use, three types of role switching are available:

- **Manual failover** Manual failover is available if the mirroring session is configured in high-safety mode, shown in Figure 7-7. You can initiate manual failover when the mirroring session is synchronized. Database administrators often perform manual failover when they need to apply updates or service packs that require a restart.

- **Automatic failover** If a witness is present and the mirroring session is configured for high-safety mode, automatic failover can occur when the witness and mirror are still connected, but the principal server cannot be contacted.

- **Forced service (with possible data loss)** Forced service can be used in high-safety mode when no witness is present or in high-performance mode. In this mode, the administrator forces the mirror to become the principal when the original principal instance becomes unavailable.

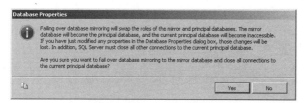

FIGURE 7-7 Manual failover

You can trigger manual failover by clicking the Failover button on the Mirroring page of the mirrored database properties on the primary server. You can also trigger manual failover by using the ALTER DATABASE statement with the SET PARTNER FAILOVER option. For example, to trigger manual failover of the AdventureMirror database, execute the following statement on the principal instance:

```
USE master;
ALTER DATABASE AdventureMirror SET PARTNER FAILOVER;
```

Automatic failover can occur under the following conditions:

- The mirroring session is configured for high-safety mode and has a witness.

- The mirror is in a synchronized state.

- The principal instance is unavailable while the mirror and witness instances retain quorum. If all instances lose communication, automatic failover will not occur even if the witness and the mirror reestablish communication.

A forced service switchover enables you to switch from the principal to the mirror. You can perform a forced service switchover only if the mirror cannot contact the principal server. Forced service switchovers can result in data loss. Microsoft does not recommend performing a forced service switchover except when it is necessary to restore the service and you accept the possibility of data loss. You can perform a forced service failover by issuing the ALTER DATABASE Transact-SQL statement with the SET PARTNER FORCE_SERVICE_ALLOW_DATA_LOSS option against the mirror database. For example, to configure forced service switchover on the AdventureMirror database, connect to the mirror instance and execute the following statement:

```
USE master;
ALTER DATABASE AdventureMirror SET PARTNER FORCE_SERVICE_ALLOW_DATA_LOSS;
```

> **MORE INFO**   **ROLE SWITCHING**
>
> You can learn more about role switching at *http://msdn.microsoft.com/en-us/library /ms189850(SQL.110).aspx.*

Monitoring Mirrored Databases

There are several tools you can use to monitor mirrored databases. You can determine the operating mode of a mirroring session by querying the *sys.database_mirroring catalog view* on either the principal or mirror instance. The key columns to examine are:

- **mirroring_safety_level_desc**   Describes the mirroring safety level as FULL, OFF, UNKNOWN, or NULL if the database is offline.

- **mirroring_witness_name**   Describes the name of the witness instance. A value of NULL indicates that no witness is configured.

- **mirroring_witness_state_desc**   Describes the state of the witness instance. States include CONNECTED, DISCONNECTED, UNKNOWN, and NULL.

Figure 7-8 shows the results of this query against a mirrored database configured to use high-safety mode.

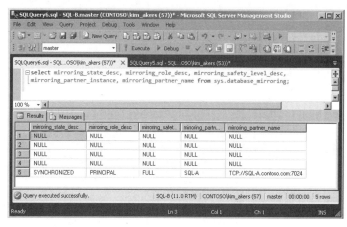

FIGURE 7-8 sys.database_mirroring catalog view

Database Mirroring Monitor

The Database Mirroring Monitor, shown in Figure 7-9, enables you to monitor how data is being transmitted between the primary and mirrored instances in a mirroring session. You must register a database with the Database Mirroring Monitor before you can monitor that database. You can use this tool to determine the size of unsent logs, the data transfer rate, the oldest unsent transaction, the current restore rate, and the mirror commit overhead. The Database Mirroring Monitor can also provide the status of the connection to the witness if one is present, the witness address, and the operating mode.

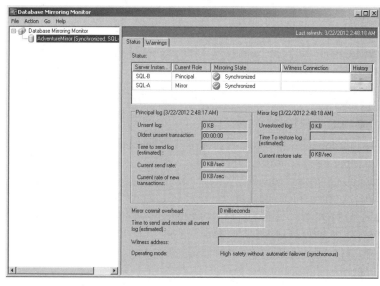

FIGURE 7-9 Database Mirroring Monitor

To launch the Database Mirroring Monitor from within SQL Server Management Studio, perform the following steps:

1. Connect to the principal server instance by using SQL Server Management Studio.

2. Right-click the mirrored database that you want to monitor, choose Tasks, and select Launch Database Mirroring Monitor.

3. In the Database Mirroring Monitor dialog box, click Register Mirrored Database.

> **MORE INFO**   **DATABASE MIRRORING MONITOR**
>
> You can learn more about the Database Mirroring Monitor at *http://msdn.microsoft.com /en-us/library/ms365809(SQL.110).aspx*.

Monitoring Mirroring by Using Stored Procedures

You can use the following stored procedures, which work independently of the Database Mirroring Monitor, to manage the monitoring of mirrored databases:

- **sp_dbmmonitoraddmonitoring**   Enables you to create a job that updates status information of all databases mirrored on the instance

- **sp_dbmmonitordropmonitoring**   Deletes the mirror monitoring job for all databases mirrored on an instance

- **sp_dbmmonitorchangemonitoring**   Enables you to modify the value of a database mirroring parameter

- **sp_dbmmonitorresults**   Enables you to view the status of monitored databases

> **MORE INFO**   **MONITORING MIRRORING**
>
> You can learn more about monitoring database mirrors at *http://msdn.microsoft.com /en-us/library/ms365781(SQL.110).aspx*.

Upgrading Mirrored Databases

You can establish a mirror session between instances running different versions of SQL Server only when you are upgrading an existing set of mirrored instances. For example, if you are upgrading a database mirrored between SQL Server 2008 instances, you can have a period when the primary and witness instances are running SQL Server 2008 and the mirror instance is running SQL Server 2012. Although it is possible to run a mix of versions, you should upgrade all instances as soon as possible so that they are running the same version of SQL Server.

When performing an upgrade, you should:

1. If necessary, modify the mirroring session safety mode so that you are using high safety without automatic failover. This involves either switching from high performance or removing the witness server if you are using high safety with automatic failover.

2. Perform a full backup of the principal database.

3. Run DBCC CHECKDB on the principal server.

4. Upgrade the mirror server to SQL Server 2012.

5. Manually fail over to the upgraded mirror server running SQL Server 2012.

6. Upgrade the witness server to SQL Server 2012 if you were originally using high safety with automatic failover.

7. Resume mirroring the database.

8. Switch back to the original safety mode.

9. Upgrade the new mirror instance to SQL Server 2012.

> *MORE INFO*   **UPGRADING MIRRORED DATABASES**
>
> You can learn more about upgrading mirrored databases at *http://msdn.microsoft.com /en-us/library/bb677181(SQL.110).aspx*.

PRACTICE   **Mirroring a Database**

In this practice, you configure a database so that it is mirrored with high safety but without automatic failover.

EXERCISE 1   Prepare a Database for Mirroring

In this exercise, you make a copy of the AdventureWorks2012 database and prepare that copy so it can be used in a mirroring session between instances SQL-A and SQL-B. To complete this exercise, perform the following steps:

1. Log on to server SQL-A with the Kim_Akers user account and connect to the default Database Engine instance by using SQL Server Management Studio.

2. Use the Database Copy Wizard to make a copy of the AdventureWorks2012 database on the default instance. Name this copy **AdventureMirror**.

3. Configure AdventureMirror so that it uses the full recovery model.

4. Create the c:\backup directory. Back up the AdventureMirror database to the c:\backup\adventuremirror.bak file.

5. Log on to SQL-B with the Kim_Akers user account and create the c:\backup directory.

6. Copy the adventuremirror.bak file from SQL-A to the c:\backup directory of SQL-B.

7. On SQL-A, connect to SQL-B by using SQL Server Management Studio. Restore adventuremirror.bak on SQL-B with NO RECOVERY.

8. Perform a transaction log backup of the AdventureMirror database on SQL-A to the file c:\backup\adventuremirror.trn.

9. Copy adventuremirror.trn from SQL-A to the c:\backup directory of SQL-B.

10. On SQL-A, use the connection to SQL-B to restore adventuremirror.trn on that instance with NO RECOVERY.

EXERCISE 2 Prepare Firewall Rules, Certificates, and Endpoints for Mirroring

In this exercise, you create a firewall rule to support the endpoints that you configure. You also create the necessary certificates to support endpoint authentication. To complete this exercise, perform the following steps:

1. On the domain controller, edit the SQL-POLICY GPO. Add a firewall rule that allows traffic on TCP port 7024.

2. In SQL Server Management Studio, use appropriate Transact-SQL queries to create database master keys for SQL-A and SQL-B if none already exist.

3. On SQL-A, create a certificate named **SQL_A_cert**. On SQL-B, create a certificate named **SQL_B_cert**.

4. On SQL-A, create an endpoint named **Endpoint_Mirroring** that listens on all IPs on port 7024. Configure authentication to use SQL_A_cert.

5. On SQL-B, create an endpoint named **Endpoint_Mirroring** that listens on all IPs on port 7024. Configure authentication to use SQL_B_cert.

6. On SQL-A, back up the SQL_A_cert certificate to c:\backup\SQL_A_cert.cer.

7. On SQL-B, back up the SQL_B_cert certificate to c:\backup\SQL_B_cert.cer.

EXERCISE 3 Configure Logins, Users, Endpoint Permissions, and Database Mirroring

In this exercise, you configure logins and users for each instance and then configure partnerships for the database, which enable mirroring. To complete this exercise, perform the following steps:

1. On SQL-A, create a login named **SQL_B_login** that uses the password **Pa$$w0rd**.

2. On SQL-A, create a user named **SQL_B_user** for the SQL_B_login.

3. On SQL-A, create a certificate for SQL_B_user that uses the backed up certificate SQL_B_cert.cer that you exported from instance SQL-B.

4. On SQL-B, create a login named **SQL_A_login** that uses the password **Pa$$w0rd**.

5. On SQL-B, create a user named **SQL_A_user** for the SQL_A_login.

6. On SQL-B, create a certificate for SQL_A_user that uses the backed up certificate SQL_A_cert.cer that you exported from instance SQL-A.

7. On instance SQL-A, grant CONNECT on the Endpoint_Mirroring endpoint to the SQL_B_login.

8. On instance SQL-B, grant CONNECT on the Endpoint_Mirroring endpoint to the SQL_A_login.

9. On instance SQL-B, use the ALTER DATABASE statement to set the partner as TCP://
sql-a.contoso.com:7024.

10. On instance SQL-A, use the ALTER DATABASE statement to set the partner as
TCP://sql-b.contoso.com:7024.

EXERCISE 4   **Perform Failover and Change Operating Mode**

In this exercise, you perform failover so that instance SQL-B is the principal instance for the AdventureMirror database. To complete this exercise, perform the following steps:

1. On SQL-A, open SQL Server Management Studio and edit the properties of the AdventureMirror database.

2. Perform failover so that instance SQL-B is the primary instance.

3. View the properties of the AdventureMirror database on instance SQL-B. Verify that they match Figure 7-10.

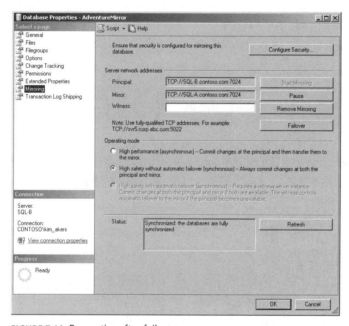

FIGURE 7-10 Properties after failover

4. Use an appropriate Transact-SQL statement to switch the operating mode from high safety to high performance.

5. Use the Database Mirroring Monitor to verify that these changes have been made and that the principal and the mirror are synchronized.

Lesson Summary

- A database must use the full recovery model before it can be mirrored.
- Only one principal and one mirror instance can participate in a mirroring session.
- High-safety mode, also known as synchronous mode, commits transactions when they are synchronized on both partners. This mode has higher transaction latency.
- High-performance mode, also known as asynchronous mode, has lower transaction latency because transactions are committed before partner synchronization. This mode can lead to data loss if the primary fails.
- The principal, mirror, and witness instance must be running the same version of SQL Server when configuring a new mirroring session.
- If the SQL Server service is not associated with a domain-based account but a local account or virtual account, you must configure certificate-based authentication.
- Automatic failover is possible only if the mirroring session is in high-safety mode with a witness.

Lesson Review

Answer the following questions to test your knowledge of the information in this lesson. You can find the answers to these questions and explanations of why each answer choice is correct or incorrect in the "Answers" section at the end of this chapter.

1. You are preparing an instance that will function as a mirror server. You must restore a backup of the database that will be mirrored to this instance. Which of the following restoration options must you use when performing this operation?

   A. WITH RECOVERY

   B. WITH NORECOVERY

   C. WITH STANDBY

   D. WITH KEEP_REPLICATION

2. In which of the following situations must you use certificate-based authentication when configuring database mirroring?

   A. SQL Server service accounts are members of an Active Directory domain.

   B. You are configuring a witness server on a Server Core–host operating system.

   C. SQL Server service accounts are managed service accounts.

   D. SQL Server service accounts are virtual accounts.

3. Which of the following editions of SQL Server 2012 support high-performance mode for database mirroring?

   A. Web edition

   B. Standard edition

C. Enterprise edition

   D. Business Intelligence edition

4. The AdventureWorks database is participating in a high-safety mirroring session. The principal instance is hosted on server SQL-A. The mirror instance is hosted on SQL-B. You must configure an instance hosted on server SQL-CORE as a witness for this mirror. The endpoint that supports mirroring on each instance uses TCP port 7024. You have configured the appropriate permissions on each endpoint. Which of the following steps should you take to configure the SQL-CORE instance as the witness?

   A. Execute the following statement on SQL-A: ALTER DATABASE AdventureWorks2012 SET WITNESS = 'TCP://SQL-CORE:7024';

   B. Execute the following statement on SQL-B: ALTER DATABASE AdventureWorks2012 SET WITNESS = 'TCP://SQL-CORE:7024';

   C. Execute the following statement on SQL-CORE: ALTER DATABASE AdventureWorks2012 SET WITNESS = 'TCP://SQL-A:7024';

   D. Execute the following statement on SQL-CORE: ALTER DATABASE AdventureWorks2012 SET WITNESS = 'TCP://SQL-B:7024';

Lesson 2: Database Replication

This lesson covers the different types of replication that you can configure for SQL Server 2012 databases. You also learn about the tools you can use to troubleshoot replication problems.

> **After this lesson, you will be able to:**
> - Implement replication.
> - Identify appropriate replication strategy.
> - Troubleshoot replication problems.
>
> **Estimated lesson time: 60 minutes**

Replication Architecture

SQL Server 2012 replication uses specific terminology to describe how components interact in the replication topology. The important terms are as follows:

- **Publisher** An instance that makes data available through publication.
- **Article** A published object. Can be a table, a stored procedure, a view, an indexed view, or a user-defined function. The Articles page of the New Publication Wizard is shown in Figure 7-11.
- **Publication** A collection of articles.
- **Distributor** An instance that manages the transmission from publisher to subscriber. A distributor on the same LAN as the publisher is a local distributor. A distributor on a network remote from the publisher is a remote distributor.
- **Subscriber** An instance that receives publications.
- **Agent** A service that enables the publisher, distributor, or subscriber to perform replication-related tasks.

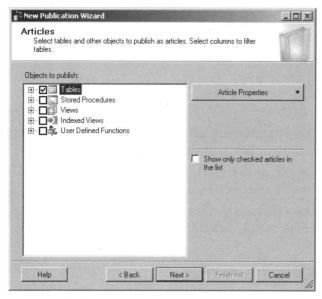

FIGURE 7-11 Articles page

Prior to configuring replication, you must ensure that the SQL Server Replication feature is installed on the instances you configure with the publisher, distributor, and subscriber roles, as shown in Figure 7-12.

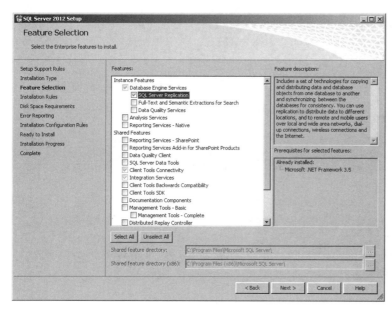

FIGURE 7-12 SQL Server Replication feature

Replication Types

Replication enables SQL Server 2012 to distribute and synchronize data and database objects from one database to another. As Figure 7-13 shows, SQL Server 2012 supports the following types of replication:

- **Snapshot replication**   Enables complete refreshes of data rather than updating the database on an incremental basis.

- **Transactional replication**   Suited for instance-to-instance situations that require subscriber databases to stay up to date with changes on the publishing database.

- **Peer-to-Peer replication**   Enables peer nodes to read and write changes and have those changes propagate to other nodes in the replication topology.

- **Merge replication**   Suited for mobile and distributed server applications when data conflict is possible and any node may issue data changes that will eventually be consistent across all nodes.

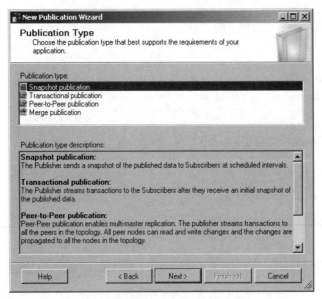

FIGURE 7-13 Replication types

***MORE INFO* REPLICATION TYPES**

You can find out more about replication types at *http://msdn.microsoft.com/en-us/library /ms152531(SQL.110).aspx.*

Snapshot Replication

When you configure a database for snapshot replication, the publisher synchronizes with subscribers by creating and transmitting a database snapshot. Snapshot replication is suitable when:

- Data changes infrequently.
- Most of the changes to the database occur over a short period.
- Only a small volume of data needs to be replicated.

Snapshot replication uses a snapshot folder. You must ensure that the replication agents you configure have the appropriate permissions to the shared folder. The publisher must be able to write the snapshots to that location, and the subscriber must be able to read snapshots at that location. If you do not specify a network share or a network drive, replication will not support pull subscriptions created at the subscriber, so you can use only push subscriptions.

When determining a schedule for snapshot replication, you must estimate how long it takes the Snapshot Agent to complete a snapshot. The Snapshot Agent uses the bcp utility to generate a snapshot. You learned about the bcp utility in Chapter 4. When configuring the publication, you can set snapshots to be compressed. Compressing snapshots takes additional time and processing resources and, due to limitations of the CAB file format used for snapshots, you cannot compress snapshot files larger than 2 GB.

Configuring Snapshot Replication

To configure snapshot replication of all tables, stored procedures, views, indexed views, and user-defined functions in a database by using the host instance as distributor, perform the following steps:

1. On the node that hosts the database you want to configure as the publisher, expand the Replication node, right-click Local Publications, and then choose New Publication. This launches the New Publication Wizard.

2. On the Distributor page, choose to use the local instance as distributor and then click Next.

3. On the SQL Server Agent Start page, configure the SQL Server Agent service to start automatically and click Next.

4. On the Snapshot Folder page, shown in Figure 7-14, specify a network share on which to store the snapshots.

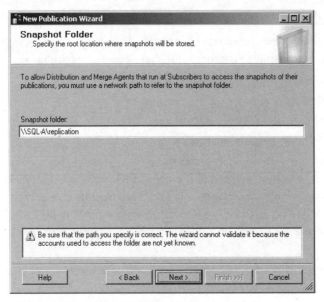

FIGURE 7-14 Snapshot replication snapshot shared folder

5. On the Publication Database page, choose the database you are publishing.

6. On the Publication Type page, choose Snapshot Publication.

7. On the Articles page, select Tables, Stored Procedures, Views, Indexed Views, and User Defined Functions.

8. Review the Article Issues page.

9. On the Filtered Table Rows page, click Next. You use this page if you want to filter the content of tables in the publication.

10. On the Snapshot Agent page, shown in Figure 7-15, choose to create a snapshot immediately and then configure a snapshot creation schedule. The default schedule is a new snapshot every hour.

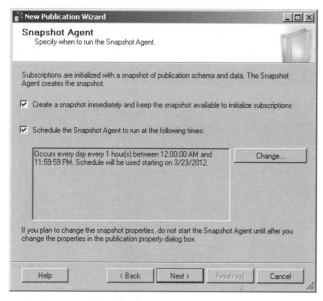

FIGURE 7-15 Snapshot schedule

11. On the Agent Security page, click Security Settings to choose the snapshot agent security account.

   You can choose to run under a Windows Account or the SQL Server Agent service account, which is not a recommended best practice for security reasons. You can also configure the account that connects to the Publisher instance. The default is to impersonate the process account, but you can also specify the credentials of a SQL Server login.

12. On the Wizard Actions page, you can choose to create the publication and generate a script file with steps to create the publication.

13. On the Complete The Wizard page, enter a name for the publication and click Finish.

Configuring a Subscription

To configure a subscription to a snapshot replication, connect to the subscriber instance and perform the following steps:

> **NOTE   SUBSCRIPTION PROCESS**
>
> You use a similar process to subscribe to different types of publications.

1. Right-click the Replication\Local Subscriptions node on the instance that will function as the subscriber and click New Subscription.

2. On the first page of the New Subscription Wizard, click Next.

3. On the Publication page, use the drop-down list to select the publisher. In the Connect To Server dialog box, select the instance that hosts the publisher and click Connect. Select the database and publication, as shown in Figure 7-16.

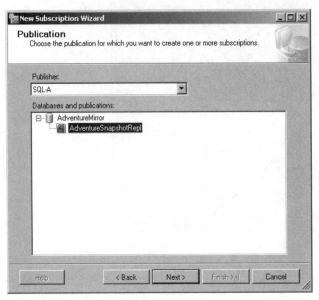

FIGURE 7-16 Select database and publication

4. On the Distribution Agent Location page, choose to run each agent at its subscriber. This configures pull subscriptions.

5. On the Subscribers page, use the drop-down list to select <New database>, as shown in Figure 7-17. In the New Database dialog box, provide the name of the subscriber database and then click OK.

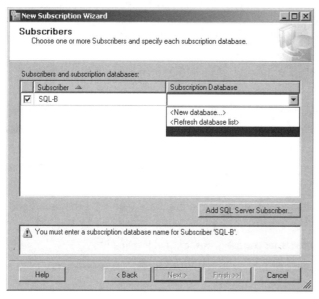

FIGURE 7-17 New Subscription Wizard

6. On the Distribution Agent Security page, click the ellipsis (...) and then enter the credentials the Distribution Agent process will use.

7. On the Synchronization Schedule page, choose Run Continuously for the Agent Schedule.

8. On the Initialize Subscriptions page, choose Immediately under Initialize When.

9. On the Wizard Actions page, choose Create The Subscription(s).

10. On the Complete The Wizard page, click Finish.

> **MORE INFO** **SNAPSHOT REPLICATION**
>
> You can learn more about snapshot replication at *http://msdn.microsoft.com/en-us/library /ms151832(SQL.110).aspx*.

Transactional Replication

Transactional replication is a suitable solution when you want changes to the publisher database to propagate to the subscriber databases as they occur. Transactional replication occurs in one direction, from the publisher to the subscriber. (Peer-to-peer transactional replication is a different form of replication.) The Database Engine initiates transactional replication by creating a snapshot of the data you want to replicate and applying that snapshot to the subscriber. Transactional replication is suitable in the following scenarios:

- Subscribers must apply incremental changes to data very soon after they are applied at the publisher.

- Updates occur at the publisher.
- The publisher is not a SQL Server 2012 instance. (SQL Server 2012 can subscribe to a publication from an Oracle database.)
- Changes must be applied at the subscriber in the same order in which they occurred at the publisher.

To use transactional replication to publish all tables, stored procedures, views, indexed views, and user-defined functions and to use the local instance as the distributor, perform the following steps:

1. In SQL Server Management Studio, right-click the Replication\Local Publication node and choose New Publication.

2. On the Publication Database page, select the database that hosts the tables and objects you will replicate.

3. On the Publication Type page, choose Transactional Publication.

4. On the Articles page, choose Tables, Stored Procedures, Views, Indexed Views, and User Defined Functions.

5. Review the Article Issues page.

6. On the Filter Table Rows page, shown in Figure 7-18, click Add if you want to filter table row data.

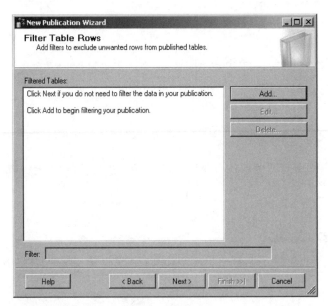

FIGURE 7-18 The Filter Table Rows page

7. On the Snapshot Agent page, choose Create A Snapshot Immediately And Keep The Snapshot Available To Initialize Subscriptions.

8. On the Agent Security page, click Security Settings to specify the credentials of the Snapshot Agent and the Log Reader Agent.

9. On the Wizard Actions page, choose Create The Publication.

10. On the Complete The Wizard page, provide a publication name.

After the snapshot is created, you can subscribe to the transactional publication through the Local Subscriptions node on the instance you want to configure with the Subscriber role.

Peer-to-Peer Transactional Replication

Peer-to-peer transactional replication enables transactions performed by subscribers to be synchronized with other nodes in the replication topology. Rather than use a conflict detection agent, like you do when you implement merge replication, when you implement peer-to-peer transactional replication, you must prevent conflicts by partitioning the data so that the same row will not be updated at separate locations. If the data isn't partitioned properly and a conflict occurs, the replication will fail or the changes will not replicate.

You should consider peer-to-peer transactional replication when:

- The data is partitioned in a way that matches the proposed replication topology.
- Conflicts are likely to be rare, such as when specific rows would be updated only by a single instance in the replication topology.

Peer-to-peer transactional replication has the following requirements:

- All instances that participate in the replication topology must be running SQL Server 2012 Enterprise edition.
- You cannot use row and column filtering.
- Publication names must be identical on all instances participating in the replication.
- Each participating instance should use its own distribution database to ensure that there is no single point of failure.
- You cannot include tables in multiple peer-to-peer publications in the same publication database.

- You cannot reinitialize peer-to-peer subscriptions. You must restore a backup at a node if you must force an update of data.

- If you add nodes to a peer-to-peer topology and have to perform a restoration, you must restore only from backups created with the new nodes participating in the topology.

To create a peer-to-peer publication that replicates all tables, stored procedures, views, indexed views, and user-defined functions and uses the local instance as the distributor, perform the following steps:

1. On the computer that will function as the publisher, in SQL Server Management Studio, right-click Replication\Local Publications and choose New Publication to launch the New Publication Wizard.

2. On the Distributor page, choose the local instance as the distributor.

3. On the SQL Server Agent Start page, configure the SQL Server Agent service to start automatically.

4. On the Snapshot Folder page, provide the location of a network share that the other agents participating in the replication can access.

5. On the Publication Database page, choose the database that hosts the data or objects you will replicate.

6. On the Publication Type page, choose Peer-to-Peer Publication.

7. On the Articles page, select Tables, Stored Procedures, Views, Indexed Views, and User Defined Functions.

8. On the Article Issues page, review the article issues.

9. On the Agent Security page, shown in Figure 7-19, click Security Settings and then specify the credentials of the Log Reader Agent.

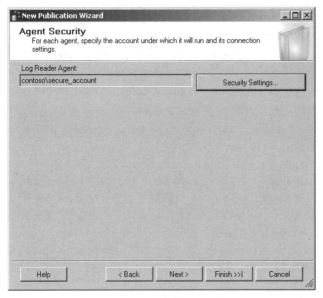

FIGURE 7-19 Log Reader Agent account

10. On the Wizard Actions page, ensure that Create The Publication is selected.

11. Provide the publication name and then create the publication.

> **MORE INFO**   **PEER-TO-PEER TRANSACTIONAL REPLICATION**
>
> You can learn more about peer-to-peer transactional replication at *http://msdn.microsoft*
> *.com/en-us/library/ms151196(SQL.110).aspx.*

Merge Replication

Merge replication enables databases hosted on instances at separate locations to be updated and those changes replicated to all other databases participating in the replication topology. When you configure merge replication, the publisher and subscribers track changes made by using triggers. When a subscriber synchronizes with the publisher, they exchange all rows that have changed between the publisher and subscriber since the last synchronization.

You can choose to implement merge replications when you meet the following requirements:

- You have the database updated at multiple locations. Those changes must be propagated to other databases participating in the replication.

- You have enabled subscribers to make offline changes to data and then to synchronize those changes back when they next connect.

- You are able to detect and resolve update conflicts.

- Your configuration supports non–SQL Server nodes participating in the replication.

- Applications do not require tables to be transactionally consistent.

Merge replication uses the SQL Server Snapshot Agent and the Merge Agent. If the Merge Agent detects a conflict, such as the same row being updated with different values at different locations, the conflict resolver determines which data is accepted. Peer-to-peer replication does not use a conflict agent or provide conflict resolution.

When you are configuring a subscription in merge replication, you specify a subscription type and a conflict resolution priority, as shown in Figure 7-20. A server subscription enables you to set a conflict resolution priority, which is a figure between 0 and 99.99, with servers assigned a higher priority overriding servers assigned a lower priority. When you configure the Client subscription type, the priority for conflict resolution is "first to publisher wins." The default type is Server, and the default priority is 75. You can view conflicts by right-clicking the merge publication and selecting View Conflicts. You can view conflicts only if conflicts have occurred. When a conflict occurs between a publisher and subscriber, the publisher change is kept, and the subscriber change is dropped.

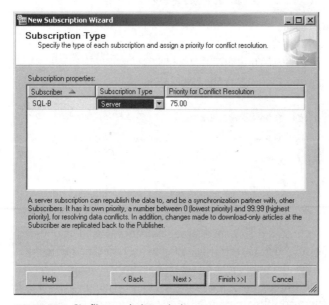

FIGURE 7-20 Conflict resolution priority

MORE INFO **ADVANCED MERGE REPLICATION CONFLICT MANAGEMENT**

You can learn about advanced merge replication conflict resolution technologies, including COM-base custom resolvers, at *http://msdn.microsoft.com/en-us/library /ms151257(SQL.110).aspx*.

To configure a merge replication publication of all tables, stored procedures, views, indexed views, and user-defined functions, using the local instance as a distributor, and supporting only subscribers running SQL Server 2008 or later, perform the following steps:

1. Right-click the Replication\Local Publications node and choose New Publication to launch the New Publication Wizard.

2. On the Distributor page, choose the instance that hosts the database to function as its own distributor.

3. On the Snapshot Folder page, specify a network location as a snapshot folder.

4. On the Publication Database page, specify the database that hosts the objects you are publishing.

5. On the Publication Type page, choose Merge Publication.

6. On the Subscriber Types page, shown in Figure 7-21, choose SQL Server 2008 or later.

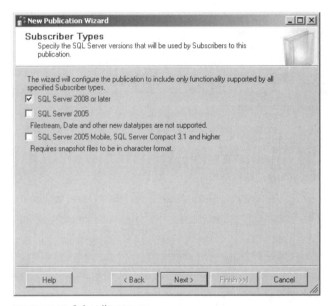

FIGURE 7-21 Subscriber types

7. On the Articles page, select Tables, Stored Procedures, Views, Indexed Views, and User Defined Functions.

8. On the Article Issues page, review the items presented.

9. On the Filter Table Rows page, choose not to filter table rows.

10. On the Snapshot Agent page, choose to create a snapshot immediately and accept the default schedule for the Snapshot Agent.

11. On the Agent Security page, click Security Settings and provide the credentials the Snapshot Agent will use, as shown in Figure 7-22.

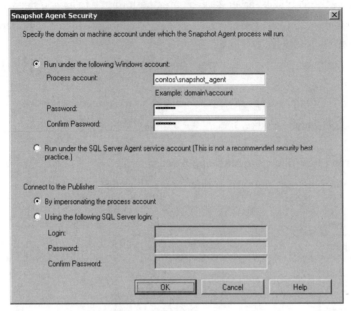

FIGURE 7-22 Snapshot agent security account

12. Create and name the publication.

> **MORE INFO   MERGE REPLICATION**
>
> You can learn more about merge replication at *http://msdn.microsoft.com/en-us/library /ms152746(SQL.110).aspx*.

 Quick Check

- Which type of replication would you configure if you had to allow updates from multiple sites with conflict resolution?

Quick Check Answer

- Merge replication offers updates from multiple sites and has a conflict resolution mechanism.

Replication Monitor

Replication Monitor, shown in Figure 7-23, is a tool available in SQL Server Management Studio that enables you to monitor replication. Users are able to monitor replication only if they are members of the sysadmin fixed server role on the Distributor instance or have been assigned membership of the replmonitor fixed database role in the distribution database.

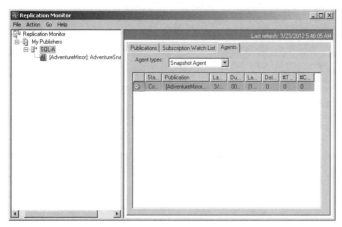

FIGURE 7-23 Replication Monitor

To add a publisher to Replication Monitor, right-click the Replication Monitor node and then choose Add Publisher to bring up the Add Publisher dialog box shown in Figure 7-24. You can choose to add a SQL Server publisher or an Oracle publisher or specify Distributor and Add Its Publishers. This final option enables you to view all publications associated with a specific distributor.

FIGURE 7-24 The Add Publisher dialog box

You can use Replication Monitor to configure alerts based on performance benchmarks. When a monitored value exceeds the benchmark, Replication Monitor displays an alert in the Status column for the subscription and the publication with which it synchronizes. You can also configure an alert to send an email or run a job. You can configure the alerts shown in Figure 7-25.

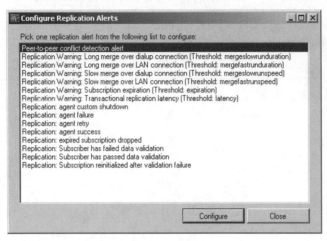

FIGURE 7-25 Replication alerts

Replication Monitor also provides performance-quality information for transactional replication and merge replication. To set a threshold, select the publication you will monitor, click the Warnings tab, choose the warning, and set the threshold value.

- For transactional replication performance, quality is determined on the basis of latency threshold, with possible values of Excellent (0–34 percent), Good (35%–59 percent), Fair (60–84 percent), Poor (85–99 percent), and Critical (exceeds latency threshold).

- For merge replication, Replication Monitor determines performance quality based on historical performance, with possible values of Excellent (151+ percent of historical performance), Good (76–150 percent), fair (26–75 percent), and poor (0–25 percent).

To configure an alert for a publication, on the Warnings tab, click Configure Alerts. Select the alert you will configure and click Configure. In the Alert Properties dialog box, shown in Figure 7-26, configure the properties of the alert. You learn more about configuring alerts in Chapter 11.

> **MORE INFO**   **REPLICATION MONITOR**
>
> You can learn more about Replication Monitor at *http://msdn.microsoft.com/en-us/library /ms151780(SQL.110).aspx.*

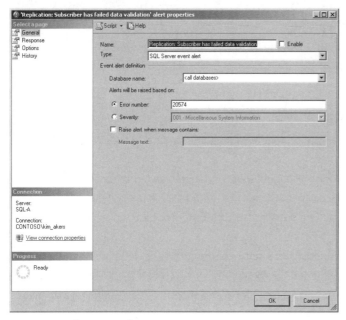

FIGURE 7-26 Alert properties

The following maximum sizes and numbers apply to SQL Server 2012 replication:

- Merge publication articles   256
- Snapshot or transactional publication articles   32,767
- Merge publication columns in a table   246
- Snapshot or transactional publication columns in a table   1,000
- Merge replication bytes for a column used in a row filter   1,024
- Snapshot or transactional publication bytes for a column used in a row filter   8,000

Controlling Replication of Constraints, Columns, and Triggers

The NOT FOR REPLICATION option enables you to configure foreign key constraints, check constraints, identity columns, and triggers to behave differently when an insert, update, or delete operation is performed by a replication agent than they behave in normal operation. If you configure the NOT FOR REPLICATION option on these items and a replication agent performs an insert, update, or delete operation on them, the following happens:

- Foreign key constraints will not be enforced on that specific operation.
- Check constraints will not be enforced on that specific operation.
- Identity column values are not incremented on that specific operation.
- Triggers will not be executed by that specific operation.

Heterogeneous Data

You can use SQL Server 2012 replication to integrate data from Oracle and IBM DB2 databases in the following ways:

- An Oracle database can serve as a publisher for data replicated to databases hosted on SQL Server 2012.

- SQL Server 2012 can serve as a publisher or distributor for data replicated to Oracle and IBM DB2 databases.

- When SQL Server 2012 functions as a subscriber to an Oracle database, that data can in turn be published to other databases running Oracle, IBM DB2, or SQL Server.

Although SQL Server 2012 supports transactional and snapshot replication, heterogeneous replication has the following constraints:

- Merge replication is not supported.

- Peer-to-peer replication is not supported.

- SQL Server 2012 cannot subscribe to an IBM DB2 publication.

PRACTICE   **Configuring Replication**

In this practice, you configure snapshot and transaction replication for copies of the AdventureWorks database.

EXERCISE 1   **Prepare to Implement Database Replication**

In this exercise, you prepare SQL-A and SQL-B for database replication. To complete this exercise, perform the following steps:

1. Log on to server SQL-B with the Kim_Akers user account.

2. Use SQL Server Installation Center to add the SQL Server Replication feature to the default instance on SQL-B.

3. Log on to server SQL-A with the Kim_Akers user account.

4. In SQL Server Management Studio, connect to the default instance on SQL-A and SQL-B. On each instance, start SQL Server Agent.

5. Use the Database Copy Wizard to make two copies of the AdventureWorks2012 database that are hosted on the SQL-A default instance. Name the first copy **AdvWrksSnapshotRepl** and the second copy **AdvWrksTransRepl**.

EXERCISE 2 Configure Snapshot Replication

In this exercise, you configure the AdvWrksSnapshotRepl database to be published by using Snapshot replication. You then configure the default instance of SQL-B to subscribe to this publication. To complete this exercise, perform the following steps:

1. Use SQL Server Management Studio to configure a publication that uses snapshot replication for the AdvWrksSnapshotRepl database. The publication should have the following properties:

   - Use snapshot publication.
   - Use SQL-A as distributor.
   - Publish all tables in the database.
   - Do not filter table rows.
   - Create a snapshot immediately and schedule a snapshot to be generated every two hours.
   - Use the Contoso\Kim_Akers user account for the Snapshot Agent.

2. Subscribe to this publication on the SQL-B default instance by using the following properties:

   - Run all agents at the distributor.
   - New subscription database.
   - Use the Contoso\Kim_Akers account for Distribution Agent security credential.
   - Configure the Synchronization Schedule to run continuously.
   - Initialize the subscription immediately.

EXERCISE 3 Configure Transactional Replication

In this exercise, configure transactional replication for the AdvWrksTransRepl database. To complete this exercise, perform the following steps:

1. Use SQL Server Management Studio to configure a publication that uses transactional replication for the AdvWrksTransRepl database. The publication should have the following properties:

   - Use transactional replication.
   - Use SQL-A as distributor.
   - Publish all tables in the database.
   - Do not filter table rows.

- Create a snapshot immediately and every two hours.
- Use the Contoso\Kim_Akers account for Distribution Agent security credential.

2. Subscribe to this publication on the SQL-B default instance by using the following properties:
   - Run all agents at the Distributor.
   - New subscription database.
   - Use the Contoso\Kim_Akers account for Distribution Agent security credential.
   - Set the Synchronization Schedule to run continuously.
   - Initialize the subscription immediately.

EXERCISE 4   Monitor Replication

In this exercise, use Replication Monitor to view the publications and subscriptions you created in Exercises 2 and 3. To complete this exercise, perform the following steps:

1. Open the Replication Monitor on SQL-A.
2. Add SQL-A as a publisher.
3. Monitor the replication of the publications created in Exercises 2 and 3.

Lesson Summary

- Snapshot replication enables complete refreshes of all data rather than refreshing on an incremental basis. This is suitable when data changes infrequently and small volumes must be replicated.
- Transactional replication is suitable when a subscriber database must be up to date with the publisher but does not need to update the publisher.
- Merge replication is suitable for distributed server applications when conflict is possible.
- Peer-to-peer replication is a form of transactional replication by which nodes can read and write changes, but you must partition data to avoid conflicts. You cannot use filtering with peer-to-peer replication.
- You must use a shared folder to publish snapshots if distribution and merge agents are running at the subscriber instance rather than at the publisher instance.
- Replication Monitor enables you to monitor replication and configure replication alerts.
- SQL Server 2012 can subscribe to an Oracle publication and can function as a publisher to Oracle and IBM DB2 transactional and snapshot replication.

Lesson Review

Answer the following questions to test your knowledge of the information in this lesson. You can find the answers to these questions and explanations of why each answer choice is correct or incorrect in the "Answers" section at the end of this chapter.

1. You have a database that is updated only between 1:00 A.M. and 1:30 A.M. each day. Updates occur only at your organization's head office site. This database must be available on local SQL Server 2012 instances at five branch office sites. Which type of replication would you use to support this configuration?

   A. Snapshot publication

   B. Transactional publication

   C. Peer-to-Peer publication

   D. Merge publication

2. You are responsible for designing the replication topology of a database that will have hosted instances in six cities. Updates occur constantly and are processed only on the database hosted at the central site, but the databases in the other cities must be kept as up to date as possible. Which form of replication should you use to support this configuration?

   A. Peer-to-peer publication

   B. Snapshot publication

   C. Transactional publication

   D. Merge publication

3. Which publication type would you choose if you needed to allow updates to occur at 10 SQL Server 2012 database instances spread across Australia and New Zealand, to allow updates to any row in published tables from any site, and to enable conflict resolution to occur with a minimum of administrator intervention?

   A. Transactional publication

   B. Snapshot replication

   C. Peer-to-peer publication

   D. Merge publication

4. Which forms of heterogeneous replication does SQL Server 2012 support?

   A. Snapshot replication from an IBM DB2 publisher

   B. Merge replication from an Oracle publisher

   C. Transactional replication from an Oracle publisher

   D. Peer-to-peer replication from an IBM DB2 publisher

Case Scenarios

In the following case scenarios, you apply what you have learned about planning server installs and upgrades. You can find answers to these questions in the "Answers" section at the end of this chapter.

Case Scenario 1: Database Mirroring at Coho Vineyard

You are the database administrator at Coho Vineyard. You have just migrated the Winery database from a host server running SQL Server 2005 to a new server named Sydney-SQL-A running SQL Server 2012. Your organization has purchased two additional servers, named Sydney-SQL-B and Sydney-SQL-C. You have installed SQL Server 2012 on both of these servers, which will host their own databases, but you will also use them to support the Winery database in a mirrored configuration. You want to configure the mirroring session in the following ways:

- The default instance on Sydney-SQL-A will serve as the principal instance.
- The default instance on Sydney-SQL-B will serve as the mirroring instance.
- The default instance on Sydney-SQL-C will serve as the witness instance.

You have configured the SQL Server service accounts on each instance as follows:

- The SQL Server Service uses a domain account named cohovineyard\syd-sql-a.
- The SQL Server Service uses a domain account named cohovineyard\syd-sql-b.
- The SQL Server Service uses a domain account named cohovineyard\syd-sql-c.

With this information in mind, answer the following questions:

1. Which logins must you create on instance Sydney-SQL-B?
2. Which mode would you set to ensure that automatic failover can occur if instance Sydney-SQL-A becomes unavailable?
3. Which Transact-SQL statement would you use to make Sydney-SQL-B the primary instance when you must apply software updates that require restarting server Sydney-SQL-A?

Case Scenario 2: Database Replication at Tailspin Toys

Tailspin Toys has offices in the cities of Melbourne, Sydney, Perth, Adelaide, Brisbane, and Hobart. Each office has its own SQL Server 2012 Enterprise edition instance. Tailspin Toys has three databases, which must be hosted in each of these cities. These databases have the following properties:

- **Airplanes**   Is updated frequently at the Melbourne office. Is not updated at any other office. Other offices must stay up to date with the changes made at the Melbourne office.

- **Hovercraft** Is updated between 6:00 P.M. and 7:00 P.M. each weekday at the Brisbane office. Is not updated at any other office. Other offices need the updates before start of business the next morning.

- **Multicopters** All sites must be able to update this database. If conflicts occur when the same row is updated at different offices, updates applied at the Adelaide office should take precedence.

With this information in mind, answer the following questions:

1. Which type of replication should you use for the Airplanes database?
2. Which type of replication should you use for the Hovercraft database?
3. Which type of replication should you use for the Multicopters database?

Suggested Practices

To help you successfully master the exam objectives presented in this chapter, complete the following tasks.

Implement Database Mirroring

Prior to completing each task in the following practices, list the steps you would take to accomplish the task. After completing the task, assess how accurately you predicted the necessary steps.

- **Practice 1** Use the appropriate stored procedures to configure mirror monitoring on the SQL-A and SQL-B instances.

- **Practice 2** Configure instance SQL-CORE to function as a witness server for the AdventureMirror database mirroring session.

Implement Replication

Prior to completing each task in the following practices, list the steps you would take to accomplish the task. After completing the task, assess how accurately you predicted the necessary steps.

- **Practice 1** Create a copy of the AdventureWorks2012 database called **AdvWksMergeRepl** on the default instance of SQL-A. Create a merge replication publication of this database. Subscribe to this publication on the default instance of SQL-B.

- **Practice 2** Create a copy of the AdventureWorks2012 database called **AdvWksP2PRepl** on the default instance of SQL-A. Create a peer-to-peer replication publication of this database. Subscribe to this publication on the default instance of SQL-B.

Answers

This section contains the answers to the lesson review questions and solutions to the case scenarios in this chapter.

Lesson 1

1. **Correct Answer: B**

   A. **Incorrect:** You should not use the WITH RECOVERY option. You must use the WITH NORECOVERY option when restoring a backed-up database when preparing a mirror instance.

   B. **Correct:** You must restore the database by using the WITH NORECOVERY option when preparing a mirror instance.

   C. **Incorrect:** You should not use the WITH STANDBY option. You must use the WITH NORECOVERY option when restoring a backed-up database when preparing a mirror instance.

   D. **Incorrect:** You should not use the WITH KEEP_REPLICATION option. You must use the WITH NORECOVERY option when restoring a backed-up database when preparing a mirror instance.

2. **Correct Answer: D**

   A. **Incorrect:** You must use certificate authentication when the SQL Server service accounts are not members of an Active Directory domain.

   B. **Incorrect:** Both domain-based and local accounts can be used for the SQL Server service account, so using a Server Core host operating system is not enough to require certificate authentication.

   C. **Incorrect:** Managed Service Accounts are domain accounts. You must use certificate authentication when the SQL Server Agent accounts are not members of an Active Directory domain.

   D. **Correct:** Virtual accounts are local accounts that can be used with service accounts. You must use certificate authentication when the SQL Server service accounts are not members of an Active Directory domain.

3. **Correct Answer: C**

   A. **Incorrect:** SQL Server Web edition can function as a witness instance, but this edition does not support high-performance mode.

   B. **Incorrect:** SQL Server Standard edition supports high-safety and witness modes. This edition does not support high-performance mode.

   C. **Correct:** SQL Server Enterprise edition supports high-safety, high-performance, and witness modes.

D. Incorrect: SQL Server Business Intelligence edition supports high-safety and witness modes but does not support high-performance mode.

4. **Correct Answer: A**

   A. Correct: You must run the ALTER DATABASE statement with the SET WITNESS option on the principal instance, specifying the endpoint on the witness server.

   B. Incorrect: You should not run the ALTER DATABASE AdventureWorks2012 SET WITNESS = 'TCP://SQL-CORE:7024'; statement on the mirror instance. You must run the ALTER DATABASE statement with the SET WITNESS option on the principal instance, specifying the endpoint on the witness server.

   C. Incorrect: You should not run the ALTER DATABASE AdventureWorks2012 SET WITNESS = 'TCP://SQL-A:7024'; statement on SQL-CORE. You must run the ALTER DATABASE statement with the SET WITNESS option on the principal instance, specifying the endpoint on the witness server.

   D. Incorrect: You should not run the ALTER DATABASE AdventureWorks2012 SET WITNESS = 'TCP://SQL-B:7024'; statement on SQL-CORE. You need to run the ALTER DATABASE statement with the SET WITNESS option on the principal instance, specifying the endpoint on the witness server.

Lesson 2

1. **Correct Answer: A**

   A. Correct: Snapshot replication is suitable when the database you will make available in multiple locations has the majority of its updates occur over a short period.

   B. Incorrect: Transactional publication is suitable when subscribers must be kept up to date with constant changes that occur on the publisher.

   C. Incorrect: Peer-to-peer publication is suitable when all subscribers must be able to perform updates, and data has been partitioned to ensure that conflicts do not occur.

   D. Incorrect: Merge publication is suitable when subscribers might be offline but must be able to accept and forward updates to the publisher while having a robust conflict resolution mechanism.

2. **Correct Answer: C**

   A. Incorrect: Peer-to-peer publication is suitable when all subscribers must be able to perform updates, and data has been partitioned to ensure that conflicts do not occur.

   B. Incorrect: Snapshot replication is suitable when the database you will make available in multiple locations has the majority of its updates occur over a short period.

   C. Correct: Transactional publication is suitable when subscribers must be kept up to date with constant changes that occur on the publisher.

D. Incorrect: Merge publication is suitable when subscribers might be offline but must be able to accept and forward updates to the publisher while having a robust conflict resolution mechanism.

3. **Correct Answer: D**

   A. Incorrect: Transactional publication is unidirectional and does not support updates from subscribers.

   B. Incorrect: Snapshot replication is unidirectional and does not support updates from subscribers.

   C. Incorrect: Peer-to-peer replication does not include a conflict resolution mechanism and requires data to be partitioned so that conflicts between subscribers do not occur.

   D. Correct: Merge publication allows updates to be processed at subscribers and includes conflict resolution mechanisms.

4. **Correct Answer: C**

   A. Incorrect: SQL Server 2012 cannot replicate data from an IBM DB2 publisher.

   B. Incorrect: SQL Server 2012 does not support heterogeneous merge replication.

   C. Correct: SQL Server 2012 supports functioning as a subscriber to transactional replication from an Oracle publisher.

   D. Incorrect: SQL Server 2012 cannot replicate data from an IBM DB2 publisher. SQL Server 2012 does not support heterogeneous peer-to-peer replication.

Case Scenario 1

1. You must create logins for accounts cohovineyard\syd-sql-a and cohovineyard\syd-sql-c so that the principal instance and the witness instance can be granted permissions on the endpoint.

2. You must set high-safety mode with a witness present to enable automatic failover.

3. Use the ALTER DATABASE Winery SET PARTNER FAILOVER; statement to make the mirror instance the primary instance when applying software updates.

Case Scenario 2

1. Transactional replication is suitable in this circumstance because updates occur at one location but must propagate quickly to other locations.

2. Snapshot replication is appropriate in this circumstance because updates occur at one location over a brief span of time, and a substantial amount of time elapses before other branch offices must be updated.

3. Merge replication is appropriate in this circumstance because each office can update the database, and automatic conflict resolution is required.

CHAPTER 8

Clustering and AlwaysOn

Exam objectives in this chapter:

- Implement a SQL Server clustered instance.
- Implement AlwaysOn.

Failover clustering instances and AlwaysOn Availability Groups are two strategies for making Microsoft SQL Server 2012 databases highly available. Failover clustering is a more traditional approach to ensuring that a database remains available in the event of server failure. If you are planning to deploy a failover cluster instance, you must first deploy the cluster and then install SQL Server 2012 by using a method that differs from a traditional installation.

AlwaysOn Availability Groups are a technology new in SQL Server 2012 that also rely on failover clustering technologies. AlwaysOn Availability Groups are a replacement technology for database mirroring and have the benefit of allowing clients read-only access to the secondary replica. In this chapter, you learn about how to deploy both of these SQL Server 2012 high-availability technologies.

Lessons in this chapter:

Before You Begin

To complete the practice exercises in this chapter, make sure that you have:

- Completed the setup tasks for installing computers DC, SQL-A, SQL-B, and SQL-CORE as outlined in the introduction of this book.
- Completed the setup tasks outlined in the end-of-lesson practice exercises in Chapter 1, "Planning and Installing SQL Server 2012," through Chapter 7, "Mirroring and Replication."
- Deployed two new servers, named SQL-C and SQL-D, in the CONTOSO domain. Instructions for configuring these servers are outlined in the introduction of this book.

No additional configuration is required for this chapter.

Lesson 1: Clustering SQL Server 2012

A SQL Server 2012 failover cluster instance is a special deployment of SQL Server 2012 that stores database files on a shared storage device. If the server that hosts one Database Engine instance fails, another Database Engine instance in the failover cluster takes control of the database files and seamlessly continues to service client requests.

> **After this lesson, you will be able to:**
>
> - Prepare the host operating system for the installation of a failover cluster instance of SQL Server 2012.
> - Deploy a failover cluster instance.
> - Manage multiple instances on a cluster.
> - Deploy multi-subnet failover clusters.
> - Troubleshoot failover clusters.
>
> **Estimated lesson time: 60 minutes**

Fulfilling Edition Prerequisites

You can deploy failover cluster instances only on specific editions of the host operating system and SQL Server. When planning the deployment of a failover cluster instance, remember that:

- SQL Server 2012 Enterprise edition supports up to 16 cluster nodes. This edition of SQL Server is the only one that you can deploy in a production environment that supports multi-subnet failover clustering.
- SQL Server 2012 Business Intelligence edition supports a two-node maximum for failover clusters.
- SQL Server 2012 Standard edition supports a two-node maximum.
- Windows Server 2008 R2 Enterprise and Datacenter editions support failover clustering. These editions also support multi-subnet failover clustering.
- Windows Server 2008 Enterprise and Datacenter editions support failover clustering but do not support multi-subnet failover clustering.

You must have a functional Windows Server failover cluster prior to deploying SQL Server as a failover cluster instance. Only then can you install SQL Server as a failover cluster instance.

> ***MORE INFO*** **WINDOWS SERVER FAILOVER CLUSTERING WITH SQL SERVER 2012**
>
> You can learn more about Windows Server failover clustering with SQL Server 2012 at *http://msdn.microsoft.com/en-us/library/hh270278.aspx.*

Windows Server 2008 R2 as Shared Storage

Except in the case of multi-subnet failover clusters, SQL Server failover cluster instances require shared storage to host the database and log files. In production situations, you use a dedicated storage area network (SAN) device for this task. If you are using a fiber channel SAN, you use vendor software to make the connection between Microsoft Windows Server 2008 or Windows Server 2008 R2 and the SAN. If you are using iSCSI, you can use the vendor-supplied software or the iSCSI initiator that is included with the server operating system. Connecting by using the iSCSI initiator is covered in the next section, "Connecting to the SAN with iSCSI Initiator."

If you don't have access to a SAN, you can use Windows Storage Server 2008 R2 as an iSCSI target by installing the iSCSI Software Target, which you can download from the Microsoft website. You can use this software to simulate an iSCSI storage device on a SAN when running virtual machines within a Hyper-V environment without actually having to connect to a traditionally deployed SAN.

> **MORE INFO** **DOWNLOAD iSCSI SOFTWARE TARGET**
>
> You can download the iSCSI Software Target at *http://www.microsoft.com/download/en /details.aspx?id=19867.*

After you have installed the iSCSI Software Target on a computer running Windows Server 2008 R2, you must perform several steps to configure the server so other computers can connect and use a specially configured virtual hard disk file as a SAN storage device.

> **NOTE** **iSCSI TARGET**
>
> Configuring the iSCSI target is unlikely to be covered directly on the 70-462 exam, but this is a necessary step to complete the clustering-related practice exercises in this chapter.

The first step you must take to configure the iSCSI Software Target is to configure Windows Firewall with Advanced Security rules on the computer on which you've installed the iSCSI Software Target. You can do this by running the following commands from an elevated command prompt:

```
netsh advfirewall firewall add rule name="Microsoft iSCSI Software Target Service-
TCP-3260" dir=in action=allow protocol=TCP localport=3260

netsh advfirewall firewall add rule name="Microsoft iSCSI Software Target Service-
TCP-135" dir=in action=allow protocol=TCP localport=135

netsh advfirewall firewall add rule name="Microsoft iSCSI Software Target Service-
UDP-138" dir=in action=allow protocol=UDP localport=138

netsh advfirewall firewall add rule name="Microsoft iSCSI Software Target Service"
dir=in action=allow program="%SystemRoot%\System32\WinTarget.exe" enable=yes

netsh advfirewall firewall add rule name="Microsoft iSCSI Software Target Service Status
Proxy" dir=in action=allow program="%SystemRoot%\System32\WTStatusProxy.exe" enable=yes
```

After you have configured the computer that will function as the iSCSI target with the appropriate firewall rules, you can configure the iSCSI Software Target application by performing the following steps:

1. Open the iSCSI Software Target application from the Administrative Tools menu.

2. Right-click the iSCSI Targets node, shown in Figure 8-1, and choose Create iSCSI Target. Click Next.

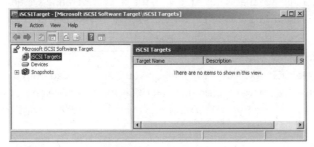

FIGURE 8-1 iSCSI Target console

3. On the iSCSI Target Identification page, enter a name for the target.

4. On the iSCSI Initiators Identifiers page, click Advanced. On the Advanced Identifiers page, click Add.

5. On the Add/Edit Identifiers page, enter the IP address or fully qualified domain name (FQDN) of the hosts that will be accessing the iSCSI target from the network. The wizard presents a warning when adding multiple initiators. Figure 8-2 shows sql-c.contoso .com and sql-d.contoso.com configured as identifiers. Return to the iSCSI Initiators Identifiers page by clicking OK; click Next and then click Finish.

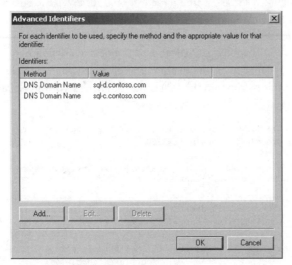

FIGURE 8-2 Advanced identifiers

To create an iSCSI logical unit number (LUN), you create a virtual hard disk (VHD) and make it available. Remember that you must provide a LUN to store quorum information and a LUN to store database files. To provide a LUN by using the iSCSI Software Target, perform the following steps:

1. In the iSCSI Software Target console, right-click Device and choose Create Virtual Disk.

2. On the File page of the Create Virtual Disk Wizard, specify the path to a VHD file that will serve as the storage device for SAN client, for example, d:\SAN\disk-one.vhd.

3. On the Access page, shown in Figure 8-3, click Add to add the iSCSI targets to allow connection to the virtual disk over the network. Click Next and then click Finish.

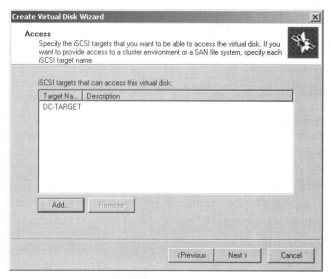

FIGURE 8-3 Access iSCSI target

Connecting to the SAN by Using iSCSI Initiator

iSCSI Initiator is a component built into the Windows Server 2008 R2 and Windows 7 operating systems that you can use to connect to an iSCSI LUN by using an iSCSI target. When preparing two servers that will function as cluster nodes in a SQL Server 2012 failover cluster, you can configure each server to connect to the same iSCSI LUN for the purposes of shared storage. To connect to an iSCSI LUN by using an iSCSI initiator, perform the following steps:

1. Open iSCSI Initiator from the Administrative Tools menu. If prompted to configure the iSCSI service to start automatically, click Yes.

2. On the Targets tab of the iSCSI Initiator properties, enter the IP address or FQDN of the iSCSI target and click Quick Connect. Verify that the discovered target is correct, as shown in Figure 8-4, and click Done.

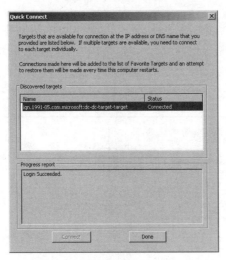

FIGURE 8-4 Discovered target

3. On the Volumes And Devices tab, click Auto Configure and then click OK.

4. Verify that the volumes are available to be brought online and formatted in the Disk Management node of the Server Manager console.

> ***MORE INFO*** **BEFORE DEPLOYING A FAILOVER CLUSTER INSTANCE**
>
> You can learn more about the steps you must take before deploying a SQL Server failover cluster instance at *http://msdn.microsoft.com/en-us/library/ms189910(SQL.110).aspx.*

Creating a Windows Server 2008 R2 Failover Cluster

The first step in creating a Windows Server 2008 R2 failover cluster to host a SQL Server 2012 failover cluster is to install the Failover Clustering feature. You can do this through the Server Manager console, as shown in Figure 8-5, or by using the following Windows PowerShell command when the ServerManager module is loaded:

```
Add-WindowsFeature Failover-Clustering
```

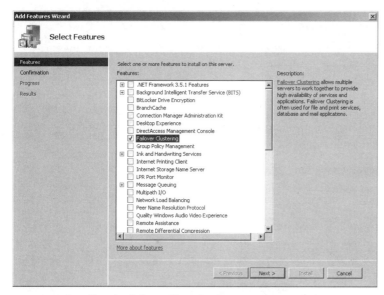

FIGURE 8-5 Installing the Failover Clustering feature

To configure a failover cluster, perform the following steps:

1. When you have connected each potential node to the shared storage device and installed the Failover Clustering feature, open the Failover Cluster Manager from the Administrative Tools menu.

2. In the Failover Cluster Manager console, click Create A Cluster in the Actions menu.

3. On the Select Servers page, shown in Figure 8-6, enter the names of the nodes that will participate in the cluster.

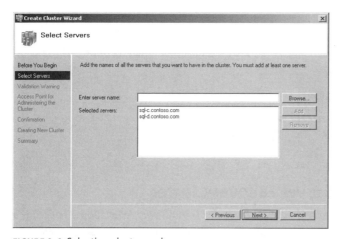

FIGURE 8-6 Selecting cluster nodes

4. Choose whether to perform validation tests.

5. On the Access Point For Administering The Cluster page, enter a name and IP address of the cluster, as shown in Figure 8-7.

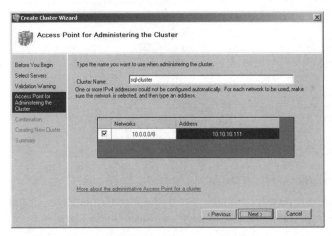

FIGURE 8-7 Cluster administration point

6. On the Confirmation page, verify the settings and click Next to have the wizard create the cluster.

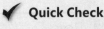 **Quick Check**

- Which editions of SQL Server 2012 support more than two-node failover clusters?

Quick Check Answer

- Only SQL Server 2012 Enterprise edition supports more than two-node failover clusters.

Installing a SQL Server Failover Cluster

Installing a SQL Server failover cluster involves performing two installation steps from SQL Server Installation Center. You must first run the Advanced Cluster Preparation Wizard. When this first wizard is complete, you must then run the Advanced Cluster Completion Wizard. You might need to restart the host server between running the first and the second wizards.

If you want to support protocol encryption on a failover cluster instance, you must install a certificate that uses the instance name as a fully qualified domain name on each of the nodes that will host the failover cluster instance prior to running the Advanced Cluster Preparation Wizard.

To prepare a SQL Server failover cluster, perform the following steps:

1. Ensure that the Microsoft .NET Framework 3.5.1 feature is installed.

2. On the first node in the cluster, run setup.exe from the installation media.

3. In the Advanced area of SQL Server Installation Center, shown in Figure 8-8, click Advanced Cluster Preparation.

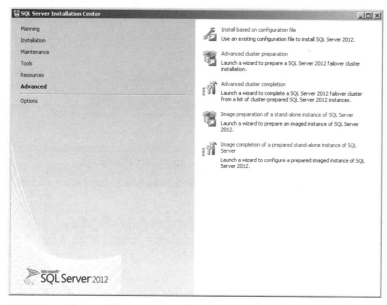

FIGURE 8-8 Advanced cluster preparation

4. On the Product Key page, enter the product key or specify that you use the Evaluation edition. On the License Terms page, select I Accept The License Terms, install any necessary updates, and review the Setup Support Rules warnings.

5. On the Feature Selection page, choose which SQL Server features you want to install on the failover cluster.

6. On the Instance Configuration page, choose the properties of the instance.

7. Review the Disk Space Requirements.

8. On the Server Configuration page, specify a specially configured domain account to be used for the Service Accounts.

9. Review the Error Reporting page.

10. On the Ready To Install page, shown in Figure 8-9, click Install.

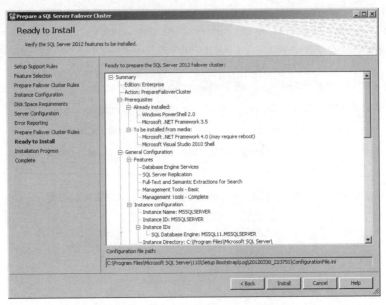

FIGURE 8-9 Preparing failover cluster installation

11. When the process completes, you might need to restart the server.

12. Repeat this process on each node that will participate in the cluster.

Complete the Installation

When you have completed the advanced cluster preparation process on each node that will participate in the failover cluster, return to the cluster node that has ownership of the shared disk and perform the following steps:

1. On the Advanced page of SQL Server Installation Center, click Advanced Cluster Completion. After the setup support rules have run, click OK and then click Next.

2. On the Cluster Node Configuration page, shown in Figure 8-10, specify the SQL Server Instance Name and the SQL Server Network Name that will identify the failover cluster on the network. This network name must be different from any preexisting cluster resource name. Click Next.

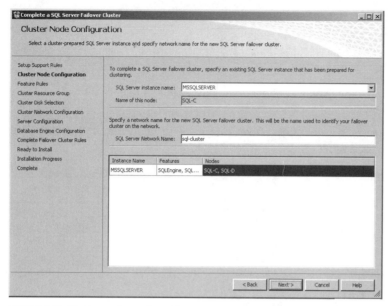

FIGURE 8-10 Cluster node configuration

3. On the Cluster Resource Group page, enter a new name for a new Cluster Resource Group.

4. On the Cluster Disk Selection page, shown in Figure 8-11, specify the disk that will be used as the default drive for databases.

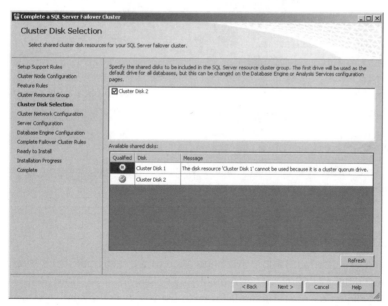

FIGURE 8-11 Cluster disk selection

5. On the Cluster Network Configuration page, specify an IP address for the cluster resource.

6. On the Server Configuration page, verify that the correct collation is set and then click Next.

7. On the Database Engine Configuration page, specify Authentication Mode and the SQL Server administrator.

8. On the Ready To Install page, shown in Figure 8-12, verify the configuration settings and then click Install.

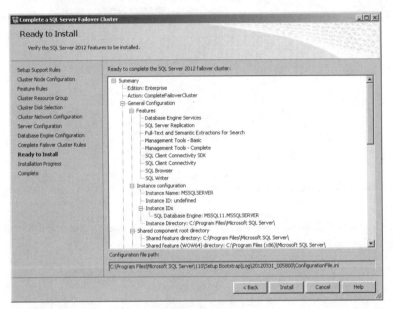

FIGURE 8-12 Final cluster configuration

You must run the Advanced Cluster Completion Wizard only once because this configures all the nodes that you prepared by using the Advanced Cluster Preparation Wizard.

> **MORE INFO** **SQL SERVER FAILOVER CLUSTER INSTALLATION**
>
> You can learn more about the specifics of SQL Server failover cluster instance deployment at *http://msdn.microsoft.com/en-us/library/hh231721(SQL.110).aspx*.

Multi-Subnet Failover Clustering

Multi-subnet failover clustering is a special configuration where each node in the failover cluster is located on a different TCP/IP subnet. A multi-subnet failover cluster does not use shared storage. When configuring a multi-subnet failover cluster, you must use another solution to replicate data between the instances on separate subnets.

NOTE **STRETCH CLUSTERS**

Stretch cluster is a term for a geographically dispersed cluster.

Multi-subnet failover clustering is supported only in production environments in SQL Server 2012 Enterprise edition and Windows Server 2008 R2 Enterprise or Datacenter editions. You cannot deploy multi-subnet failover clustering if the host operating system is running Windows Server 2008. When running the Create A New SQL Server Failover Cluster (Setup) Wizard while configuring a multi-subnet failover cluster, you must ensure that the IP address resource dependency is set to OR.

You can deploy stand-alone instances on servers that also host multi-subnet failover cluster instances. One of the challenges of this configuration is ensuring that communication occurs seamlessly and that no conflicts occur between the multi-subnet failover cluster instance and any stand-alone instances installed on the same host. You can minimize the chance of a conflict occurring by configuring stand-alone instances to use non-default fixed ports and leaving the multi-subnet failover cluster instance to use port 1433.

MORE INFO **MULTI-SUBNET FAILOVER CLUSTERING**

You can learn more about multi-subnet failover clustering at *http://msdn.microsoft.com /en-us/library/ff878716.aspx.*

Performing Manual Failover

You can use the Failover Cluster Manager to perform failover of the cluster resource from one node to another. For example, to perform failover of the SQLCRG resource from SQL-C to SQL-D, perform the following steps:

1. Open Failover Cluster Manager from the Administrative Tools menu.

2. Click the SQLCRG node. On the Actions pane, click Move This Service Or Application To Another Node and then click Move To Node SQL-D.

3. In the Please Confirm Action dialog box, shown in Figure 8-13, click Move SQLCRG To SQL-D.

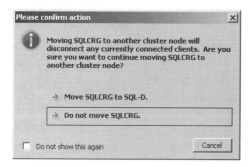

FIGURE 8-13 Moving the cluster resource

4. Verify that SQLCRG comes online on the other node.

Troubleshooting Failover Clusters

If failover occurs because the primary node suffers irreparable hardware failure, you should perform the following steps:

1. Evict the failed node from the failover cluster instance. You can do this from the Failover Cluster Manager by right-clicking the failed node, choosing Move Actions, and then selecting Evict Node.

2. Verify that the failed node has been successfully evicted from the failover cluster.

3. Replace the hardware that has failed and then use the Failover Cluster Manager console to add the failed node back to the original cluster.

4. After the node has been added to the original cluster, run SQL Server setup to readmit the failed node to the failover cluster instance.

Quorum failure is a more complicated situation that is generally caused by persistent communications failure or by the problematic configuration of cluster nodes. Quorum failure must be resolved manually by performing the following steps:

1. Start the Windows Server Failover Cluster by using forced quorum on a single node. You do this by choosing Force Cluster Start from the Actions pane of the Failover Cluster Manager.

2. Start the Windows Server Failover Cluster service on additional nodes that can communicate with the node you started by using forced quorum.

3. Configure a new quorum mode and node vote configuration that reflect the realities of the quorum topology. For example, if two nodes are frequently unavailable due to persistent communication failure, reconfigure the quorum mode and vote assignments to remediate this problem.

MORE INFO   **RESOLVING QUORUM FAILURE**

You can learn more about resolving quorum failure at *http://msdn.microsoft.com/en-us* */library/hh270277.aspx*.

PRACTICE   **Building a SQL Server 2012 Failover Cluster**

In this practice, you create a Windows Server failover cluster and then deploy a SQL Server failover cluster instance. After you have deployed the failover cluster instance, you perform failover.

EXERCISE 1   Configure iSCSI Volumes for Failover Clustering

In this exercise, you configure iSCSI volumes so they can be used as shared storage in a Windows Server failover cluster. You also configure firewall rules and a service account. To complete this exercise, perform the following steps:

1. Log on to server DC with the Kim_Akers user account.

2. Ensure that the SQL-C and SQL-D computer accounts are included in the SQL Server organizational unit (OU).

3. Download and install the iSCSI Software Target.

4. Create a folder named **C:\SAN**.

5. On DC, configure inbound rules for TCP ports 135 and 3260 and for the inbound rule for the following executables:

   - %systemroot%\System32\WinTarget.exe

   - %systemroot%\System32\WTStatusProxy.exe

6. On DC, create an iSCSI target named **DC-TARGET** and configure it to be accessible to sql-c.contoso.com and sql-d.contoso.com.

7. Create a virtual disk named **c:\SAN\disk-one.vhd**. Set the size to 2 GB. Allow access to the DC-TARGET iSCSI target.

8. Create a virtual disk named **c:\SAN\disk-two.vhd**. Set the size to 10 GB. Allow access to the DC-TARGET iSCSI target.

9. Use the iSCSI initiator to connect to the domain controller as a target on both SQL-C and SQL-D.

10. Using the Disk Management node of the Server Manager console on SQL-C to bring each of the two volumes online, initialize them and create new simple volumes formatted with the NTFS file system.

11. Use the DNS console to create a DNS A record for the address sql-cluster.contoso.com mapped to IP address 10.10.10.111.

12. Use Active Directory Users And Computers to create a user account named **SQL-Cluster** with the password **Pa$$w0rd**.

13. Edit the Computer Configuration\Windows Settings\Security Settings\Local Policies \User Rights Assignment\Log On As A Service policy in the SQL-POLICY Group Policy Object (GPO) and grant the SQL-Cluster user account the Log On As A Service right.

EXERCISE 2 Configure a Windows Server 2008 R2 Failover Cluster

In this exercise, you configure a Windows Server 2008 R2 failover cluster by using the shared storage device configured in the previous exercise. To complete this exercise, perform the following steps:

1. When logged on with the Kim_Akers user account, install the Failover Clustering and .NET Framework 3.5.1 features on SQL-C and SQL-D.

2. Run the Create Cluster Wizard from the Failover Cluster Manager console. Configure the failover cluster with the following properties:

   - Cluster Servers: SQL-C and SQL-D
   - Cluster Name: SQL-Cluster
   - Cluster IP Address: 10.10.10.111

EXERCISE 3 SQL Server Failover Cluster Advanced Cluster Preparation

In this exercise, you run the advanced cluster preparation process on the nodes that will participate in the failover cluster instance. To complete this exercise, perform the following steps:

1. Log on to servers SQL-C and SQL-D with the Kim_Akers user account.

2. From SQL Server Installation Center, run Advanced Cluster Preparation on SQL-C and SQL-D with the following options:

   - Install the Database Engine Services, SQL Server Replication, Management Tools - Basic, and Management Tools - Complete features.
   - Use the Default instance with the default settings.
   - Use the CONTOSO\SQL-Cluster account for the SQL Agent and Database Engine service accounts.

3. You might need to restart SQL-C and SQL-D to complete the advanced cluster preparation.

EXERCISE 4 SQL Server Failover Cluster Advanced Cluster Completion

In this exercise, you complete the failover cluster instance installation process. To complete this exercise, perform the following steps:

1. Log on to server SQL-C with the Kim_Akers user account.

2. Verify that SQL-C has control of the two SAN disks that will be used with the cluster.

3. On the Advanced page of SQL Server Installation Center, run Advanced Cluster Completion and provide the following settings:

   - SQL Server network name: SQL2012Cluster

   - Cluster resource group name: SQLCRG

   - Cluster Network Configuration IP address: 10.0.0.120 with subnet mask 255.255.255.0

   - Use Windows Authentication mode; set CONTOSO\Kim_Akers as SQL Server administrator

4. After installation is complete, open the Failover Cluster Manager and verify that the SQLCRG service is online, as shown in Figure 8-14.

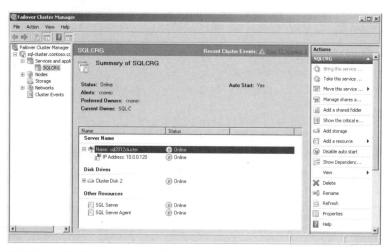

FIGURE 8-14 Verifying cluster configuration

EXERCISE 5   Perform Cluster Failover

In this exercise, you perform failover of the failover cluster instance. To complete this exercise, perform the following steps:

1. Log on to server SQL-C with the Kim_Akers user account.

2. Use Failover Cluster Manager to move the SQLCRG resource from SQL-C to SQL-D.

3. Verify that SQLCRG comes online on the other node and that the current owner is set to SQL-D.

4. Use the appropriate PowerShell cmdlet to move the SQLCRG resource back to SQL-C from SQL-D.

Lesson Summary

- A Windows Server Failover Cluster must be created prior to installing a failover cluster instance.

- Windows Server 2008 Enterprise and Datacenter editions and Windows Server 2008 R2 Enterprise and Datacenter editions can function as host operating systems for failover cluster instances.

- To install a failover cluster instance, first run advanced cluster preparation on all nodes and then run advanced cluster completion on the node that has control of the shared storage device.

- Multi-subnet failover clusters have nodes on separate TCP/IP subnets.

- Use the Failover Cluster Manager console or the Move-ClusterGroup PowerShell cmdlet to perform manual failover.

- In the event of hardware failure, evict the failed node from the cluster and then join it after it is repaired before reinstalling SQL Server.

Lesson Review

Answer the following questions to test your knowledge of the information in this lesson. You can find the answers to these questions and explanations of why each answer choice is correct or incorrect in the "Answers" section at the end of this chapter.

1. Which of the following operating systems can you use as the host operating system for a SQL Server 2012 multi-subnet failover cluster instance?

   A. Windows 7 Enterprise edition

   B. Windows Server 2008 Enterprise edition

   C. Windows Server 2008 R2 Enterprise edition

   D. Windows Vista Ultimate edition

2. Which of the following Windows PowerShell commands can you use to perform failover of a SQL Server failover cluster instance from one node to another?

   A. Move-ClusterGroup

   B. Move-ClusterResource

   C. Move-ClusteredSharedVolume

   D. Move-ClusterVirtualMachineRole

3. The primary node of a four-node SQL Server failover cluster instance fails due to a hardware failure. Replacement hardware will not arrive for 48 hours. Which of the following steps should you take first to remedy this situation?

   A. Evict the failed node.

   B. Evict the new primary node.

   C. Reinstall SQL Server on the failed node.

   D. Join the failed node to the cluster.

4. You have configured servers SYD-A and SYD-B to be members of a Windows Server failover cluster. Server SYD-B has control of the shared disk resources. You will deploy SQL Server 2012 as a failover cluster instance on these servers. Which of the following steps must you take to accomplish this goal? (Each correct answer forms part of a complete solution. Choose all that apply.)

   A. Run Advanced Cluster Preparation on SYD-A.

   B. Run Advanced Cluster Preparation on SYD-B.

   C. Run Advanced Cluster Completion on SYD-A.

   D. Run Advanced Cluster Completion on SYD-B.

Lesson 2: AlwaysOn Availability Groups

This lesson covers AlwaysOn Availability Groups, a high-availability feature that is new in SQL Server 2012. In this lesson, you learn about the infrastructure requirements for implementing AlwaysOn and what steps to take to enable AlwaysOn functionality.

> **After this lesson, you will be able to:**
> - Configure an instance to support AlwaysOn Availability Groups.
> - Create and configure availability groups.
> - Add and remove databases from availability groups.
> - Perform availability group failover.
>
> **Estimated lesson time: 60 minutes**

What Are AlwaysOn Availability Groups?

AlwaysOn Availability Groups are an alternative to database mirroring. An *availability group* is a collection of user databases, termed *availability databases*, that can fail over together. Unlike mirroring that is limited to a principal and a mirror database, availability groups support a set of read-write primary databases and up to four sets of secondary databases. Availability groups also enable you to configure one or more sets of secondary databases so that they are accessible for read-only operations.

Failover occurs on a per-replica basis, and all databases in the replica fail over. Database failover is not caused by issues related to individual databases, such as database file or transaction log corruption, but by factors at the instance level, as is the case with normal failover clusters. Availability groups support automatic failover.

Although you must deploy AlwaysOn Availability Groups on an instance that resides on a failover cluster, you usually do not deploy availability groups on a failover cluster instance. Put another way, even though you deploy AlwaysOn with a cluster, you install availability groups on an instance that was deployed by using the typical method outlined in Chapter 1 rather than by using the advanced cluster preparation and advanced cluster completion processes outlined in Lesson 1, "Clustering SQL Server 2012," of this chapter. You can deploy AlwaysOn Availability Groups on a Windows Server failover cluster that does not include a shared storage resource.

> *MORE INFO* **ALWAYSON AVAILABILITY GROUPS**
>
> You can learn more about availability groups at *http://msdn.microsoft.com/en-us/library /hh510230.aspx*.

Meeting Availability Group Prerequisites

For production environments, only SQL Server 2012 Enterprise edition supports AlwaysOn Availability Groups. When planning the deployment of AlwaysOn Availability Groups, the host server must meet the following conditions:

- Host servers cannot be domain controllers.

- Each host server must be a participant node in a Windows Server failover cluster. Failover clustering is supported only on Windows Server 2008 Enterprise and Datacenter editions and Windows Server 2008 R2.

- You must ensure that appropriate hotfixes are applied to the host server operating system.

Although not a requirement, best practice is to ensure all host systems that participate in an availability group can handle identical workloads and to provide host systems with separate network adapters dedicated for availability group traffic. You should also configure a Time To Live (TTL) of 60 seconds on the zone that hosts the DNS records related to the availability group.

If you must support Kerberos authentication with availability groups, you must perform the following extra steps:

- The SQL Server service on each participating instance must use the same domain account.

- You must manually register a Service Principal Name (SPN) for the virtual network name (VNN) of the availability group listener with the domain account used as each instance's SQL Server service account.

These steps are unnecessary if you are using the default NTLM authentication option.

> **MORE INFO**   **AVAILABILITY GROUP PREREQUISITES**
>
> You can learn more about availability group prerequisites at *http://msdn.microsoft.com /en-us/library/ff878487.aspx*.

Configuring Availability Modes

AlwaysOn Availability Groups support similar modes to database mirroring. The type of availability mode that is appropriate depends on data loss and transaction latency requirements. You configure availability modes on a per-availability replica basis. AlwaysOn Availability Groups support the following availability modes:

- **Asynchronous-commit mode**   This mode is suitable when you must place availability replicas at geographically dispersed locations. When you configure all secondary replicas to use asynchronous-commit mode, the primary will not wait for secondaries to harden the log (write log records to disk) and will run with minimum transaction latency. If you configure the primary to use asynchronous-commit mode, the transactions for all replicas will be committed asynchronously independently of which mode you've configured on each secondary replica.

- **Synchronous-commit mode**   This mode increases transaction latency but minimizes the chance of data loss in the event of automatic failover. When you use this mode, each transaction is applied to the secondary replica before being written to the local log file. The primary verifies that the transaction has been applied to the secondary before entering a SYNCHRONIZED state.

You can configure the availability mode on the Availability Group Properties page, as shown in Figure 8-15. You can also use the ALTER AVAILABILITY GROUP Transact-SQL statement with the AVAILABILITY_MODE option to change the availability mode. For example, to change the availability mode of the SQL-C\AlwaysOn replica to synchronous commit for the AG-Alpha availability group, execute the statement:

```
ALTER AVAILABILITY GROUP AG-ALPHA MODIFY REPLICA ON 'SQL-C\AlwaysOn' WITH
( AVAILABILITY_MODE = SYNCHRONOUS_COMMIT);
```

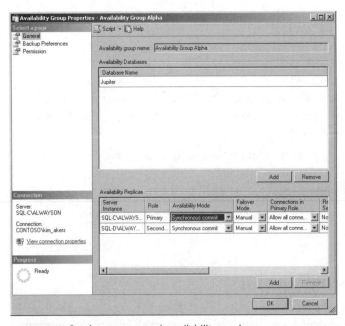

FIGURE 8-15 Synchronous-commit availability mode

> **MORE INFO   AVAILABILITY MODES**
>
> You can learn more about availability modes at *http://msdn.microsoft.com/en-us/library /ff877931.aspx*.

Selecting Failover Modes

Availability groups fail over at the availability-replica level. Failover involves another instance becoming the primary replica, with the original primary replica being demoted to become a secondary replica. AlwaysOn Availability Groups support three forms of failover:

- **Automatic failover** This form of failover occurs without administrator intervention. No data loss occurs during automatic failover. Automatic failover is supported only if the current primary and at least one secondary replica are configured with a failover mode set to AUTOMATIC, and at least one of the secondary replicas set to AUTOMATIC is also synchronized. Automatic failover can occur only if the primary and replica are in synchronous-commit mode, as shown in Figure 8-16.

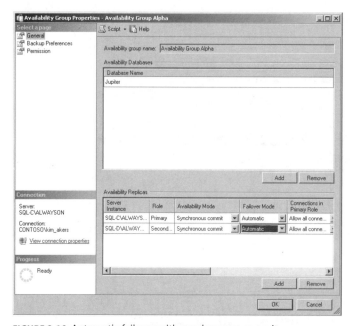

FIGURE 8-16 Automatic failover with synchronous commit

- **Planned manual failover** This form of failover is triggered by an administrator. No data loss occurs during planned manual failover. You perform this type of failover when you must perform a type of maintenance on a host instance that requires the instance or the host server to be taken offline or restarted. Planned manual failover can occur only if at least one of the secondary replicas is in a SYNCHRONIZED state. You can perform planned manual failover only if the primary and replica instances are in synchronous-commit mode.

- **Forced manual failover** This form of failover involves the possibility of data loss. Use forced manual failover when no secondary replica is in the SYNCHRONIZED state or when the primary replica is unavailable. This type of failover is the only type supported if asynchronous-commit mode is used on the primary, or if the only available replica uses asynchronous-commit mode.

To perform manual failover by using SQL Server Management Studio, perform the following steps:

1. Connect to the server instance that hosts the secondary replica of the availability group that you will make the primary replica.

2. Right-click the availability group and click Failover. This starts the Fail Over Availability Group Wizard.

3. On the Select New Primary Replica page, shown in Figure 8-17, select the instance on which to perform failover and then click Next.

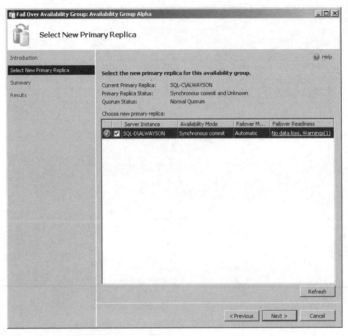

FIGURE 8-17 Manual failover

You can use the ALTER AVAILABILTY GROUP statement with the FAILOVER option on the replica instance that you will make the primary instance. For example, to perform manual failover of the AG-Alpha availability group, execute the following statement:

```
ALTER AVAILABILITY GROUP AG-Alpha FAILOVER;
```

You can use the Switch-SqlAvailabilityGroup PowerShell cmdlet to perform manual failover. For example, to perform manual failover of availability group AG-Alpha to the SQL-D\AlwaysOn instance, execute the command:

```
Switch-SqlAvailabilityGroup -Path SQLSERVER:\SQL\SQL-D\AlwaysOn\AvailabilityGroups\AG-Alpha
```

To perform forced failover by using SQL Server Management Studio, perform the following steps:

1. Connect to the server instance that hosts the secondary replica of the availability group you will make the primary replica.

2. Right-click the availability group and click Failover. This starts the Fail Over Availability Group Wizard.

3. On the Select New Primary Replica page, select the instance on which to perform failover.

4. On the Confirm Potential Data Loss page, shown in Figure 8-18, select Click Here To Confirm Failover With Potential Data Loss and click Next.

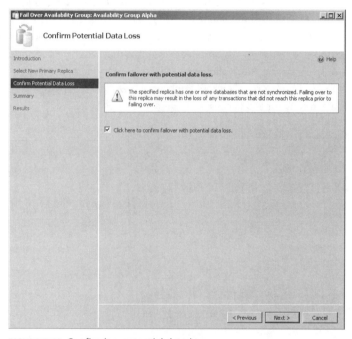

FIGURE 8-18 Confirming potential data loss

You can use the ALTER AVAILABILTY GROUP statement with the FORCE_FAILOVER _ALLOW_DATA_LOSS option on the replica instance that you will make the primary instance to force failover. For example, to force failover of the AG-Alpha availability group, execute the following statement:

```
ALTER AVAILABILITY GROUP AG-Alpha FORCE_FAILOVER_ALLOW_DATA_LOSS;
```

You can use the Switch-SQLAvailabilityGroup PowerShell cmdlet with the AllowDataLoss option to force failover. For example, to force failover of availability group AG-Alpha to the SQL-D\AlwaysOn instance, execute the command:

```
Switch-SqlAvailabilityGroup -Path SQLSERVER:\SQL\SQL-D\AlwaysOn\AvailabilityGroups\AG-Alpha -AllowDataLoss
```

You can also use the Force option with the preceding PowerShell command if you do not want to be prompted, such as when using the command in a script.

MORE INFO   **FAILOVER MODES**

You can learn more about failover modes at *http://msdn.microsoft.com/en-us/library /hh213151.aspx.*

Configuring Readable Secondary Replicas

Readable secondary replicas can service read-only requests for database access, which enables you to offload read-only workloads from the primary replica. You can configure a secondary replica to be readable from the Availability Group Properties dialog box, as shown in Figure 8-19. There are three options when configuring a readable secondary: No, Yes, and Read-intent only. The difference between Yes and Read-intent is that when you configure Read-intent, only read-only connections are allowed to the secondary databases on the secondary replica. When you configure Yes, all connections are allowed to secondary databases on the secondary replica but only for read access.

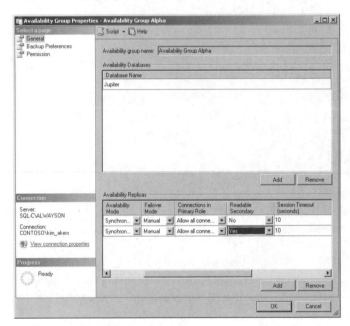

FIGURE 8-19 Readable secondary replicas

You can configure readable secondary properties for a replica by using the ALTER AVAILABILITY GROUP Transact-SQL statement with the SECONDARY_ROLE option.

MORE INFO **READABLE SECONDARY REPLICAS**

You can learn more about readable secondary replicas at *http://msdn.microsoft.com/en-us/library/ff878253.aspx*.

> ✔ **Quick Check**
>
> - Which availability mode is more suitable when replicas are located in geo-graphically dispersed sites?
>
> **Quick Check Answer**
>
> - Asynchronous-commit mode is more suitable for availability replicas distrib-uted over geographically dispersed topologies.

Deploying AlwaysOn Availability Groups

Even when you have the requisite instances deployed on a Windows Server failover cluster, deploying AlwaysOn Availability Groups involves performing several tasks in order. These tasks are as follows:

- Creating a mirroring endpoint
- Enabling AlwaysOn
- Creating an availability group
- Creating an availability group listener
- Adding a secondary replica

Creating an AlwaysOn Endpoint

Unless you are using a domain-based account for each SQL Server service, you must cre-ate a mirroring *endpoint* prior to creating an AlwaysOn Availability Group. If you are using a domain-based account for all SQL Server services that will participate in the availability group, the Database Engine can create the appropriate mirroring endpoint automatically as part of the availability group creation process.

Prior to creating the endpoint, check whether there is an existing endpoint on the instance because you can have only one mirroring endpoint on an instance. You can check whether there are any mirroring endpoints on an instance by querying the sys.database_mirroring _endpoints catalog view.

You can create an endpoint from the SQL Server PowerShell module by using the New-SqlHadrEndpoint cmdlet. For example, to create an endpoint named AlwaysOnEndpoint that uses TCP port 7028 on instance SQL-A\ALTERNATE, issue the command:

```
$endpoint = New-SqlHadrEndpoint AlwaysOnEndpoint -Port 7028 -Path SQLSERVER:\SQL\SQL-A\
ALTERNATE
```

After an endpoint has been created, you must start that endpoint. You can do so by using the Set-SqlHadrEndpoint cmdlet. For example, to start the endpoint created in the previous example, issue the command:

```
Set-SqlHadrEndpoint -InputObject $endpoint -State "Started"
```

Enabling AlwaysOn Availability Groups

Before you can create an AlwaysOn Availability Group, you must enable the AlwaysOn Availability Groups functionality at the instance level. To enable AlwaysOn Availability Groups on an instance, perform the following steps:

1. In SQL Server Configuration Manager, navigate to the SQL Server Services node.

2. Right-click the SQL Server service related to the instance on which you want to enable AlwaysOn Availability Groups and not select Properties.

3. On the AlwaysOn High Availability tab, select Enable AlwaysOn Availability Groups, as shown in Figure 8-20.

    This tab should also display the name of the failover cluster to which the node belongs.

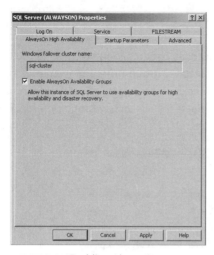

FIGURE 8-20 Enabling AlwaysOn

4. You must now restart the SQL Server service before AlwaysOn is enabled. When enabling AlwaysOn Availability Groups, you should enable only one instance at a time. You should then wait until the SQL Server service has restarted before enabling AlwaysOn on other instances that will participate in the availability group.

You can also enable AlwaysOn by using SQL Server PowerShell with the Enable-SQLAlwaysOn cmdlet. For example, to enable AlwaysOn on the ALTERNATE instance on server SQL-B, issue the following command:

```
Enable-SqlAlwaysOn -Path SQLSERVER:\SQL\SQL-B\ALTERNATE
```

If you choose to disable AlwaysOn on a Database Engine instance, either by using the Disable-SqlAlwaysOn PowerShell cmdlet or by using SQL Server Configuration Manager, you must restart the associated SQL Server service.

> **MORE INFO   ENABLING ALWAYSON**
>
> You can learn more about enabling AlwaysOn at *http://msdn.microsoft.com/en-us/library /ff878259.aspx.*

Creating an Availability Group

After AlwaysOn is enabled at the Database Engine instance level, you can create availability groups. To create an availability group by using SQL Server Management Studio, perform the following steps:

1. In SQL Server Management Studio, on the instance that hosts the primary replica, expand the AlwaysOn High Availability node.

2. Right-click Availability Groups and click New Availability Group Wizard.

3. On the Specify Availability Group Name page, provide a name for the availability group.

4. On the Select User Databases For The Availability Group page, shown in Figure 8-21, select the databases you will add to the availability group. You cannot create an availability group by using this wizard unless you can add at least one database. This page also informs you of whether the database meets the availability group's prerequisites or must be backed up before it can be added.

FIGURE 8-21 Adding a database to an availability group

5. On the Specify Replicas page, shown in Figure 8-22, click Add Replica. In the Connect To Server dialog box, specify the credentials you use to connect. Add the instances that will function as replicas. You can also use this page of the wizard to configure an availability group listener.

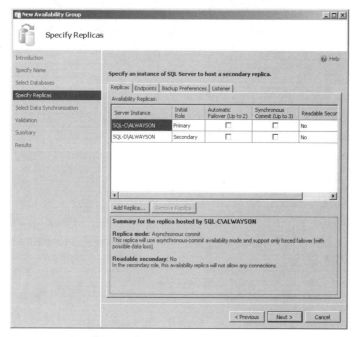

FIGURE 8-22 Specifying replicas

6. On the Select Initial Data Synchronization page, specify the location of a network share that allows read/write access to the SQL Server service account of all replicas.

7. On the Validation page, verify that all processes except Checking The Listener Configuration are competed successfully. You learn how to create an availability group listener in the "Creating or Adding an Availability Group Listener" section in this chapter.

8. Review the summary and complete the wizard.

You cannot use the New Availability Group Wizard or Add Database To Availability Group Wizard to add a database to an availability group if that database is encrypted or contains a Database Encryption Key. You also cannot use the New Availability Group Wizard to add replicas that use different paths for database and log files. You must add these replicas manually. You learn how to perform this task in the "Adding Secondary Replicas" section in this chapter.

MORE INFO   **NEW AVAILABILITY GROUP WIZARD**

You can learn more about the New Availability Group Wizard at *http://msdn.microsoft.com /en-us/library/hh403415.aspx*.

You can use the CREATE AVAILABILITY GROUP Transact-SQL statement to create an availability group. For example, to create an availability group with the following properties:

- Name: AG-BETA
- Database: Saturn
- Replica instances: SQL1.contoso.com\newinstance, SQL2.contoso.com\newinstance
- Endpoint TCP port: 7030
- Failover mode: Manual
- Availability mode: Asynchronous

execute the following Transact-SQL code:

```
CREATE AVAILABILITY GROUP AG-BETA
      FOR
                DATABASE Saturn
      REPLICA ON
      'SQL1\newinstance' WITH
              (
              ENDPOINT_URL = 'TCP://sql1.contoso.com:7030',
              AVAILABILITY_MODE = ASYNCHRONOUS_COMMIT,
              FAILOVER_MODE = MANUAL
      ),
      'SQL2\newinstance' WITH
              (
              ENDPOINT_URL = 'TCP://sql2.contoso.com:7030',
              AVAILABILITY_MODE = ASYNCHRONOUS_COMMIT,
              FAILOVER_MODE = MANUAL
      );
GO
```

> **MORE INFO**   **CREATING AN AVAILABILITY GROUP BY USING TRANSACT-SQL**
>
> You can learn more about creating an availability group by using Transact-SQL at *http://msdn.microsoft.com/en-us/library/ff878307.aspx*.

Creating or Adding an Availability Group Listener

 An *availability group listener* is a network connectivity endpoint for an availability group. Clients connect to the listener, which in turn connects them to the availability group's primary instance. You can create one listener per availability group by using SQL Server Management Studio. If you need more than one listener for an availability group, it is possible to create additional listeners by using Windows PowerShell or the Failover Cluster Manager console.

To create an availability group listener, you must be connected to the Database Engine instance that hosts the primary replica. To create an availability group listener for an existing availability group by using SQL Server Management Studio, perform the following steps:

1. In SQL Server Management Studio, navigate to the AlwaysOn High Availability node and then expand the Availability Groups node. Right-click the availability group for which you will create a listener and click Add Listener.

2. On the New Availability Group Listener page, shown in Figure 8-23, specify a Listener DNS Name and a TCP Port. In the Network Mode box, select either DHCP or Static IP. If using a static IP, specify the static IP address.

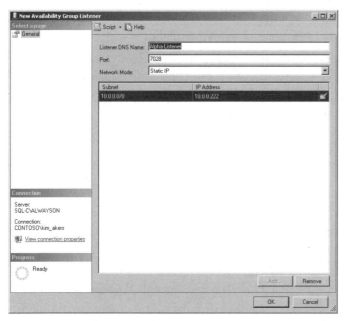

FIGURE 8-23 Availability group listener

You can add a listener to an existing availability group by using the ALTER AVAILABILITY GROUP Transact-SQL statement. For example, to add a listener named Beta-Listener to the AG-Alpha availability group that uses IP address 10.0.0.222, subnet mask 255.0.0.0, and port 7028, execute the statement:

```
ALTER AVAILABILITY GROUP [AG-Alpha]
     ADD LISTENER 'Beta-Listener' (with IP (('10.0.0.222','255.0.0.0')), PORT=7028);
GO
```

You can create an availability group listener by using the New-SqlAvailabilityGroupListener cmdlet. For example, to create a new availability group listener on instance SQL-C\AlwaysOn named Gamma-Listener to the AG-Gamma availability group that uses IP address 10.0.0.224, subnet mask 255.0.0.0, and port 7030, use the command:

```
New-SqlAvailabilityGroupListener -Name Gamma-Listener -StaticIP '10.0.0.224/255.0.0.0'
-Port 7030 -Path SQLSERVER:\SQL\SQL-C\ALWAYSON\AvailabilityGroups\AG-Gamma
```

> **MORE INFO   AVAILABILITY GROUP LISTENERS**
>
> You can learn more about availability group listeners at *http://msdn.microsoft.com/en-us /library/hh213080.aspx*.

Adding Secondary Replicas

You can add secondary replicas to an existing availability group under the following conditions:

- The availability group has fewer than four secondary replicas.
- The primary replica of the availability group is online.
- You are connected to the Database Engine instance that will host the secondary replica.
- The Database Engine instance that will host the secondary replica can connect to the mirroring endpoint on the primary replica.
- You have enabled AlwaysOn Availability Groups on the Database Engine instance that will host the secondary replica.

To join a secondary replica to an availability group by using SQL Server Management Studio, perform the following steps:

1. On the Database Engine instance that hosts the secondary replica, right-click the secondary replica under the AlwaysOn High Availability\Availability Groups node and click Join To Availability Group.
2. In the Join Replica To Availability Group dialog box, verify the details and click OK.

You can use the ALTER AVAILABILITY GROUP Transact-SQL statement to join a secondary replica to an availability group. For example, to join the AG-Delta availability group, execute the following Transact-SQL statement on the Database Engine instance that hosts the secondary replica:

```
ALTER AVAILABILITY GROUP AG-Delta JOIN;
```

You can also use the Join-SqlAvailabilityGroup cmdlet to join a secondary replica to an availability group. For example, to join the SQL-E\AlwaysOn instance to the AG-Delta availability group, execute the command:

```
Join-SqlAvailabilityGroup -Path SERVER:\SQL\SQL-E\AlwaysOn -Name 'AG-Delta'
```

> **MORE INFO** **SECONDARY REPLICAS**
>
> You can learn more about adding secondary replicas to availability groups at *http://msdn* *.microsoft.com/en-us/library/ff878473.aspx*.

Using Availability Groups on Failover Cluster Instances

Although you must deploy availability groups on a host server that is a member of a Windows Server failover cluster, the instance on which you deploy availability groups is not usually a failover cluster instance. You can use availability groups with SQL Server failover cluster instances, but you cannot use all availability group functionality. The following restrictions apply in this scenario:

- Only one failover cluster instance partner can host a replica. A failover partner cannot host a secondary replica for the same availability group.

- Failover cluster instances support only manual failover. You cannot configure AlwaysOn automatic failover to a replica on a failover cluster instance.

- Failover cluster instances do not support initial data synchronization by using the New Availability Group Wizard, Add Database To Availability Group Wizard, or Add Replica To Availability Group Wizard.

If you are using a failover cluster instance with AlwaysOn Availability Groups, you must prepare the secondary database on the instance by using a different method, such as backup and restore, and then join that secondary database to the availability group.

> **MORE INFO**   **FAILOVER CLUSTER INSTANCES AND ALWAYSON**
>
> You can learn more about failover cluster instances and AlwaysOn at *http://msdn.microsoft .com/en-us/library/ff929171.aspx.*

PRACTICE   Deploying AlwaysOn Availability Groups

In this practice, you deploy AlwaysOn Availability Groups.

EXERCISE 1   Prepare for AlwaysOn Availability Groups

In this exercise, you prepare the servers for the deployment of AlwaysOn Availability Groups. To complete this exercise, perform the following steps:

1. On the domain controller, edit the SQL-POLICY GPO.

    A. Add an Isolation connection security rule that requires authentication for inbound connections and requests authentication for outbound connections by using Computer (Kerberos V5) authentication for all profiles.

    B. Create an Inbound Port–based rule that allows TCP traffic on all local ports if the connection is secure and comes from computers DC, SQL-A, SQL-B, SQL-C, SQL-D, and SQL-CORE, as shown in Figure 8-24. Enable this rule in all profiles.

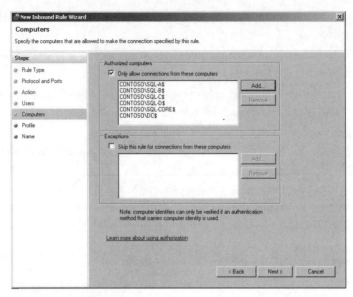

FIGURE 8-24 Isolation rule

   C. Create an Inbound Port–based rule that allows UDP traffic on all local ports if the connection is secure and comes from computers DC, SQL-A, SQL-B, SQL-C, SQL-D, and SQL-CORE. Enable this rule in all profiles.

2. Log on to servers SQL-C and SQL-D with the Kim_Akers user account.

3. Run **gpupdate /force** from an elevated command prompt to apply the new firewall rule to these computers.

4. Create a new shared folder named **Share** on SQL-C in the C:\Share directory. Configure the share so that the Contoso\SQL-CLUSTER user has read\write access.

5. Install a new Database Engine instance named **AlwaysOn** on SQL-C and SQL-D. Configure Contoso\SQL-Cluster as the SQL Server service account and configure Kim_Akers as the SQL Administrator on these instances by running the following command from an elevated command prompt on each server:

```
setup.exe /qs /ACTION=Install /FEATURES=SQLEngine /INSTANCENAME=AlwaysOn /
SQLSVCACCOUNT="CONTOSO\SQL-CLUSTER" /SQLSVCPASSWORD="Pa$$w0rd" /
SQLSYSADMINACCOUNTS="Contoso\Kim_Akers" /AGTSVCACCOUNT="CONTOSO\SQL-CLUSTER" /
AGTSVCPASSWORD="Pa$$w0rd" /IACCEPTSQLSERVERLICENSETERMS
```

6. On server SQL-C, use SQL Server Management Studio to connect to the SQL-C \AlwaysOn instance. Right-click the SQL-C\ALWAYSON node and click Start PowerShell. Create a mirroring endpoint on this instance by using the following commands:

```
$endpoint = New-SqlHadrEndpoint AlwaysOnEndpoint -Port 7026 -Path
    SQLSERVER:\SQL\SQL-C\ALWAYSON
Set-SqlHadrEndpoint -InputObject $endpoint -State "Started"
```

7. On server SQL-D, use SQL Server Management Studio to connect to the SQL-D \AlwaysOn instance. Right-click the SQL-C\ALWAYSON node and select Start PowerShell. Create a mirroring endpoint on this instance by using the following commands:

```
$endpoint = New-SqlHadrEndpoint AlwaysOnEndpoint -Port 7026 -Path
    SQLSERVER:\SQL\SQL-D\ALWAYSON
Set-SqlHadrEndpoint -InputObject $endpoint -State "Started"
```

8. Use SQL Server Configuration Manager to enable AlwaysOn Availability Groups on the SQL Server (ALWAYSON) service on SQL-C and SQL-D.

9. Use SQL Server Configuration Manager to restart the SQL Server (ALWAYSON) service on SQL-C and SQL-D.

EXERCISE 2 Create a Database and Add It to a New Availability Group

In this exercise, you create a database and add it to a newly created availability group. To complete this exercise, perform the following steps:

1. On the SQL-C\ALWAYSON instance, create a new database named **Jupiter** by using the default settings.

2. Perform a full backup of database Jupiter.

3. Use the New Availability Group Wizard to create a new availability group named **Availability Group Alpha**.

4. Add the Jupiter database to the new availability group.

5. Ensure that SQL-C\ALWAYSON and SQL-D\ALWAYSON are configured as replicas.

6. Choose Full as the data synchronization preference and use the \\SQL-C\Share share as the accessible network location.

EXERCISE 3 Create an Availability Group Listener

In this exercise, you create an availability group listener for the availability group you configured in the previous exercise. To complete this exercise, perform the following steps:

1. Use SQL Server Management Studio to create an availability group listener for the Availability Group Alpha availability group that uses the following properties:
   - Listener DNS Name: Alpha-Listener
   - Port: 7028
   - Static IP: 10.0.0.222

EXERCISE 4 Configure Availability and Failover Mode

In this exercise, you configure availability modes and failover modes and then perform manual failover. To complete this exercise, perform the following steps:

1. Configure Availability Group Alpha so that:
   - Both instances use the synchronous-commit availability mode.

- SQL-C\AlwaysOn uses the automatic failover mode.
- SQL-D\AlwaysOn is a Readable Secondary.

2. Perform manual failover from the primary to the replica instance.

Lesson Summary

- The AlwaysOn Availability Groups feature is an alternative to database mirroring.
- Availability groups are supported in production on SQL Server 2012 Enterprise edition only.
- An AlwaysOn availability group can have one primary and four secondary replicas.
- You must create mirroring endpoints either before or during the availability group creation process.
- An availability group replica can contain multiple databases.
- You can configure secondary replicas to be available to read-only queries.
- Failover occurs on a per-replica basis.
- Synchronous-commit mode involves higher transaction latency but allows manual and automatic failover.
- Asynchronous-commit mode minimizes transaction latency, is suitable for geographically dispersed clusters, but only supports forced failover.
- You can perform availability group failover by using SQL Server Management Studio, the ALTER AVAILABILITY GROUP Transact-SQL statement, or the Switch-SqlAvailabilityGroup PowerShell cmdlet.
- Each availability group listener must have a unique DNS name.

Lesson Review

Answer the following questions to test your knowledge of the information in this lesson. You can find the answers to these questions and explanations of why each answer choice is correct or incorrect in the "Answers" section at the end of this chapter.

1. Which tool can you use to enable AlwaysOn Availability Groups on a SQL Server 2012 instance?

   A. SQL Server Management Studio

   B. SQL Server Installation Center

   C. SQL Server Configuration Manager

   D. SQL Server Data Tools

2. Which Windows PowerShell cmdlet can you use to perform manual availability group failover?

   A. Switch-SqlAvailabilityGroup

   B. New-SqlHadrEndpoint

C. New-SqlAvailabilityGroupListener

   D. Enable-SqlAlwaysOn

3. Which Windows PowerShell cmdlet can you use to create a mirroring endpoint on an instance when preparing it for the deployment of AlwaysOn Availability Groups?

   A. New-SqlAvailabilityGroupListener

   B. Switch-SqlAvailabilityGroup

   C. Enable-SqlAlwaysOn

   D. New-SqlHadrEndpoint

4. You will configure an AlwaysOn Availability Group to support automatic failover from the primary replica to any available secondary replica. Which of the following availability modes should you configure for the replicas in this availability group? (Each correct answer forms part of a complete solution. Choose all that apply.)

   A. Configure the primary replica to use the asynchronous-commit availability mode.

   B. Configure the primary replica to use the synchronous-commit availability mode.

   C. Configure the secondary replica to use the asynchronous-commit availability mode.

   D. Configure the secondary replica to use the synchronous-commit availability mode.

Case Scenarios

In the following case scenarios, you apply what you have learned about SQL Server clustered instances and AlwaysOn. You can find answers to these questions in the "Answers" section at the end of this chapter.

Case Scenario 1: Failover Cluster Instances at Contoso

You are designing a failover cluster instance solution at Contoso. You will deploy a four-node failover cluster at the Melbourne site. You will also deploy a failover cluster instance that has nodes in the cities of Brisbane, Sydney, Adelaide, and Perth. Each of these cities resides on a different TCP/IP subnet.

With these facts in mind, answer the following questions:

1. Which edition of SQL Server 2012 should you deploy to support the proposed cluster configuration at the Melbourne site?

2. Which host operating systems can you use to support the proposed cluster configuration at the Brisbane, Sydney, Adelaide, and Perth sites?

3. Which tools can you use to perform manual failover when performing maintenance?

Case Scenario 2: AlwaysOn Availability Groups at Fabrikam

You are planning an AlwaysOn Availability Groups deployment at Fabrikam. Fabrikam wants to deploy replica instances in the cities of Sydney, Brisbane, Canberra, and Melbourne. Fabrikam security policy dictates that you must use local virtual accounts rather than domain security accounts for the SQL Server service accounts for each of the replica instances. The Chief Information Officer (CIO) at Fabrikam wants you to configure the AlwaysOn Availability Group so that automatic failover is possible.

With these facts in mind, answer the following questions:

1. Which editions of Windows Server 2008 R2 could you use to support the proposed configuration?

2. What factors influence the choice of authentication method for the mirroring endpoints?

3. Which availability mode should you configure on the primary and secondary replicas, given the project requirements?

Suggested Practices

To help you successfully master the exam objectives presented in this chapter, complete the following tasks.

Implement a SQL Server Clustered Instance

Prior to completing each task in the following practices, list the steps you would take to accomplish the task. After completing the task, assess how accurately you predicted the necessary steps.

- **Practice 1** Create a new database on the failover clustering instance you created during the exercises at the end of Lesson 1.

- **Practice 2** Shut down server SQL-C. Verify that the database you created on the cluster is still available on server SQL-D.

Implement AlwaysOn

Prior to completing each task in the following practices, list the steps you would take to accomplish the task. After completing the task, assess how accurately you predicted the necessary steps.

- **Practice 1** Create a new database and add it to availability group Alpha.

- **Practice 2** Delete the existing listener and create a new listener for availability group Alpha by using Transact-SQL.

Answers

This section contains the answers to the lesson review questions and solutions to the case scenarios in this chapter.

Lesson 1

1. **Correct Answer: C**

    A. **Incorrect:** Windows 7 Enterprise edition cannot be used as the host operating system for a multi-site failover cluster instance.

    B. **Incorrect:** Windows Server 2008 Enterprise edition does support failover clustering but does not support multi-site failover clusters.

    C. **Correct:** Windows Server 2008 R2 Enterprise edition supports multi-site failover clustering.

    D. **Incorrect:** Windows Vista Ultimate edition cannot be used as the host operating system for a multi-site failover cluster instance.

2. **Correct Answer: A**

    A. **Correct:** The Move-ClusterGroup cmdlet enables you to move a clustered service or application from one node to another in a failover cluster. You can use this cmdlet to perform manual failover of a SQL Server clustered instance from one node to another.

    B. **Incorrect:** The Move-ClusterResource cmdlet enables you to move a clustered resource from one clustered application to another but not to move a clustered service or application from one node to another.

    C. **Incorrect:** The Move-ClusteredSharedVolume cmdlet enables you to move the ownership of a clustered shared volume from one node to another. You cannot use this cmdlet to perform failover on a SQL Server clustered instance.

    D. **Incorrect:** The Move-ClusterVirtualMachineRole cmdlet enables you to move a clustered virtual machine to a different cluster node. You cannot use this cmdlet to perform failover on a SQL Server clustered instance.

3. **Correct Answer: A**

    A. **Correct:** You should evict the failed node. After this is done, you can repair the server, join it back to the cluster, and then reinstall SQL Server.

    B. **Incorrect:** You should not evict the new primary node; you should instead evict the failed node from the cluster.

    C. **Incorrect:** You should not reinstall SQL Server on the failed node until you have evicted the node, repaired the failure, and joined the node back to the cluster.

    D. **Incorrect:** You should not join the failed node back to the cluster until you have evicted and repaired the node.

4. **Correct Answers: A, B, and D**

   A. **Correct:** You must run advanced cluster preparation on all nodes that will partici-pate in the failover cluster instance.

   B. **Correct:** You must run advanced cluster preparation on all nodes that will partici-pate in the failover cluster instance.

   C. **Incorrect:** You run advanced cluster completion only on the node that has control of the shared disk resource. Because SQL-B has control of this resource, you should not run this process on SYD-A.

   D. **Correct:** You run advanced cluster completion only on the node that has control of the shared disk resource.

Lesson 2

1. **Correct Answer: C**

   A. **Incorrect:** You can enable AlwaysOn Availability Groups by using either SQL Server Configuration Manager or PowerShell. You cannot perform this task by using SQL Server Management Studio.

   B. **Incorrect:** You can enable AlwaysOn Availability Groups by using either SQL Server Configuration Manager or PowerShell. You cannot perform this task by using SQL Server Installation Center.

   C. **Correct:** You can enable AlwaysOn Availability Groups by using either SQL Server Configuration Manager or PowerShell.

   D. **Incorrect:** You can enable AlwaysOn Availability Groups by using either SQL Server Configuration Manager or PowerShell. You cannot perform this task by using SQL Server Data Tools.

2. **Correct Answer: A**

   A. **Correct:** You use the Switch-SqlAvailabilityGroup cmdlet to perform manual avail-ability group failover.

   B. **Incorrect:** You use the New-SqlHadrEndpoint cmdlet to create a mirroring end-point for AlwaysOn Availability Groups. You use the Switch-SqlAvailabilityGroup cmdlet to perform manual availability group failover.

   C. **Incorrect:** You use the New-SqlAvailabilityGroupListener cmdlet to create a new availability group listener. You use the Switch-SqlAvailabilityGroup cmdlet to per-form manual availability group failover.

   D. **Incorrect:** You use the Enable-SqlAlwaysOn cmdlet to enable AlwaysOn on an instance. You use the Switch-SqlAvailabilityGroup cmdlet to perform manual avail-ability group failover.

3. **Correct Answer: D**

   A. **Incorrect:** You use the New-SqlAvailabilityGroupListener cmdlet to create a new availability group listener.

   B. **Incorrect:** You use the Switch-SqlAvailabilityGroup cmdlet to perform manual availability group failover.

   C. **Incorrect:** You use the Enable-SqlAlwaysOn cmdlet to enable AlwaysOn on an instance.

   D. **Correct:** You use the New-SqlHadrEndpoint cmdlet to create a mirroring endpoint for AlwaysOn Availability Groups.

4. **Correct Answers: B and D**

   A. **Incorrect:** To support automatic failover to any available secondary replica, all replicas must use synchronous-commit mode. Automatic failover cannot occur if the primary replica uses asynchronous-commit mode.

   B. **Correct:** To support automatic failover to any available secondary replica, all replicas must use synchronous-commit mode. Automatic failover cannot occur if the primary replica uses asynchronous-commit mode.

   C. **Incorrect:** To support automatic failover to any available secondary replica, all replicas must use synchronous-commit mode. Automatic failover cannot occur if the primary replica uses asynchronous-commit mode.

   D. **Correct:** To support automatic failover to any available secondary replica, all replicas must use synchronous-commit mode. Automatic failover cannot occur if the primary replica uses asynchronous-commit mode.

Case Scenario 1

1. You must deploy SQL Server 2012 Enterprise edition to support the proposed cluster configuration because this is the only edition that supports four nodes.

2. You must support multi-subnet failover clustering, which requires either Windows Server 2008 R2 Enterprise or Datacenter editions. Windows Server 2008 does not support multi-subnet failover clustering.

3. You can use either the Failover Cluster manager or the Move-ClusterGroup PowerShell cmdlet to perform manual failover.

Case Scenario 2

1. You can use the Enterprise or Datacenter editions of Windows Server 2008 R2 to support the proposed configuration.

2. Because the SQL Server service uses local accounts, you must use certificate-based authentication for the endpoints.

3. You must configure the synchronous-commit availability mode, given the requirement for automatic failover.

CHAPTER 9

Troubleshooting SQL Server 2012

Exam objectives in this chapter:

- Collect and analyze troubleshooting data.

In a perfect world, you would be able to install Microsoft SQL Server and there would be nothing more to do. However, we do not live in a perfect world and, like any system, SQL Server needs ongoing administration and management. In this chapter, you learn how to monitor your SQL Server environment and diagnose problems that are identified.

Lessons in this chapter:

Before You Begin

To complete the lessons in this chapter, make sure that you have completed the setup tasks for installing computers DC, SQL-A, SQL-B, and SQL-CORE as outlined in the introduction to this book.

No additional configuration is required for this chapter.

Lesson 1: Working with Performance Monitor

 Performance Monitor, often referred to as *PerfMon*, is a Microsoft Windows utility that captures statistical information about the hardware environment, operating system, and any applications that expose properties and counters. It can collect and display real-time performance data in the form of counters for server resources such as processor and memory use and for many SQL Server–specific resources such as locks and transactions.

In this lesson, you learn how to use Performance Monitor to gather counters into counter logs, which can be used to troubleshoot system and performance issues.

> **After this lesson, you will be able to:**
> - Use Performance Monitor.
> - Select performance counters.
>
> **Estimated lesson time: 30 minutes**

Getting Started with Performance Monitor

Performance Monitor can be used to collect and view system metrics so administrators can gather information to aid in diagnosing performance issues. It provides real-time monitoring of health and performance counters. Performance Monitor also provides the ability to capture data from different data collectors either on demand or on a scheduled basis.

 Windows Server 2008 introduced the concept of data collector sets for Performance Monitor. A *data collector set* provides the ability to group data collectors into reusable elements for different performance-monitoring scenarios.

The following is the basic terminology for Windows Performance Monitor:

- An *object* is a resource that can be monitored.
- An object exposes one or more counters.
- A *counter* might have several instances if more than one resource of that type exists.

For example, an object called Processor consists of a number of counters. The Processor object provides metrics related to the processors that are available for the server. One of the most commonly used counters for the Processor object is the % Processor Time counter, which offers a set of instances that represent the individual processor cores that exist on the system. In addition, the _Total value represents all the instances combined.

Many applications expose application-related statistical data to Performance Monitor. SQL Server exposes a large number of objects and counters. The SQL Server objects have the naming convention shown in Table 9-1.

TABLE 9-1 Performance Monitor Object Name Format for SQL Server–Specific Objects

Object Name Format	Usage
SQLServer:<object name>	Used for default instances
MSSQL$<instance>:<object >	Used for named instances
SQLAgent$<instance >:<object >	Used for SQL Server Agent

Performance Monitor uses a polling architecture to capture and log data that is exposed by applications, including SQL Server. The applications are responsible for updating the counters that are exposed to Performance Monitor. An administrator chooses the counters to capture for analysis and the polling interval to gather ongoing data. Performance Monitor then uses the definition supplied for the counters and polling interval to gather only the counters desired on the interval defined.

> **NOTE MINIMIZE THE NUMBER OF COUNTERS**
>
> Because the only data Performance Monitor allows is numeric, and processes are not being executed to calculate the values as data is gathered, the overhead for Performance Monitor is very small. You will, however, want to minimize the number of counters being captured to avoid being overwhelmed with data.

Performance Monitor counters are organized into a three-level hierarchy: object, counter, and instance. An object is a component, application, or subsystem within an application. For example, Processor, Network Interface, and SQLServer:Databases are all objects.

Every object has at least one counter associated with it. For example, within the SQLServer:Databases object, you have counters for active transactions, data file size, transactions/sec, and the percentage of the transaction log space currently in use.

Every counter has zero or more instances associated with it. For example, the System object has a Processor Queue Length counter that does not have any instances, whereas the counter that captures the percentage of the log space used within the SQLServer:Databases object has an instance for each database and a cumulative instance named _Total.

When you define counters to capture, you can specify criteria at any level within the hierarchy. If you decide to capture an entire object, Performance Monitor gathers data for every counter within the object and for each instance available within the counter. If you do not want to capture everything, you can capture data for a subset of counters within an object and for a subset of instances within a counter.

As with all performance monitoring tools, expect some performance overhead when you use Performance Monitor to monitor SQL Server. The actual overhead in any specific instance depends on the hardware platform, the number of counters, and the selected polling interval. However, the integration of Performance Monitor with SQL Server is designed to minimize any reduction in performance.

EXAM TIP

You should be familiar with the basic performance objects and counters and be able to use that information to diagnose problems within a SQL Server instance. SQL Server is typically affected by the following bottlenecks:

- CPU
- Memory
- File I/O
- Locking, blocking, or deadlocking
- Networking

You can use Performance Monitor to identify how these potential bottlenecks might affect SQL Server. When SQL Server is not the only process using the resources on a server, you can also use performance counters to determine whether that application is negatively affecting the performance on your SQL Server instance. You learn more about bottlenecks in Lesson 5, "Identifying Bottlenecks," later in this chapter.

Capturing Performance Monitor Data

To start Performance Monitor, complete the following steps:

1. On the Start menu, point to Run, type **perfmon** in the Run dialog box, and then click OK. Performance Monitor opens, as shown in Figure 9-1.

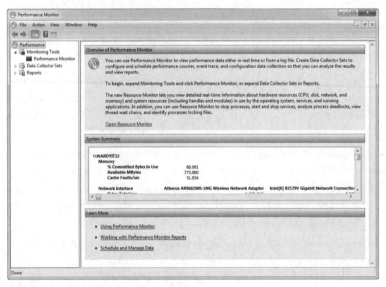

FIGURE 9-1 Performance Monitor

2. After Performance Monitor has opened in the navigation pane, expand Monitoring Tools and then click Performance Monitor.

Viewing counters in the graphical interface, as shown in Figure 9-2, is useful for looking at the immediate state of a system.

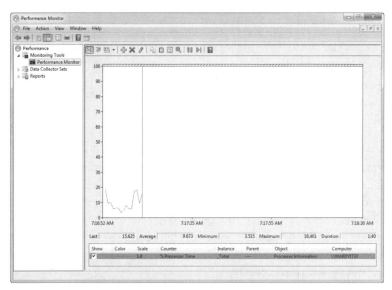

FIGURE 9-2 Performance Monitor graphical interface

Although you can capture thousands of counters and tens of thousands of counter instances, you can use a small set of common counters to troubleshoot a variety of problems.

An individual counter is generally used in conjunction with other counters and additional information about your environment to diagnose a problem. Individual counters and groups of counters can direct you to an area of the system that might need further investigation but does not directly indicate a problem on the system. However, three counters indicate a system problem on their own:

- System Processor Queue Length
- Network Interface Output Queue Length
- Physical Disk Avg. Disk Queue Length

When the processor, network interface, or disk becomes overwhelmed with activity, processes need to wait for resources to become available. Each thread that has to wait for a resource incrementally increases the corresponding queue-length counter. For example, a processor queue length of eight indicates that there is insufficient processor capacity on the machine and that eight requests are waiting in a queue for a processor core to become available. Although the queue length can be greater than zero for very short durations, having any queue length greater than zero on a routine or extended basis means that you might have a hardware bottleneck that affects application performance.

Performance counters that are included with the operating system or installed as part of an application can be added to a data collector set or to a Performance Monitor session. You can access the full list of available counters in the Add Counters dialog box. To open the Add Counters dialog box, you can:

- Create a custom data collector set and choose to include performance counters. (The wizard will open the Add Counters dialog box.)
- Click the Add (+) button in Performance Monitor to add a counter to the current Performance Monitor display.
- Right-click the Performance Monitor display and select Add Counters.

Creating Data Collector Sets

A data collector set is the building block of performance monitoring and reporting in Windows Performance Monitor. It organizes multiple data collection points into a single component that can be used to review or log performance. A data collector set can be created and then recorded individually; grouped with other data collector sets and incorporated into logs; viewed in Performance Monitor; configured to generate alerts when thresholds are reached; or used by non-Microsoft applications. Data collection sets can be scheduled to run at specific times. Windows Management Interface (WMI) tasks can be configured to run upon the completion of data collector set collection.

Data collector sets can contain the following types of data collectors:

- Performance counters
- Event trace data
- System configuration information (registry key values)

You can create a data collector set from a template, from an existing set of data collectors in a Performance Monitor view, or by selecting individual data collectors and setting each option in the data collector set properties.

PRACTICE **Using Performance Monitor**

In this practice, you create a data collector set from Performance Monitor.

EXERCISE 1   Create a Data Collector

To complete this exercise, perform the following steps:

1. Start Performance Monitor and the following counters to create a custom view you want to save as a data collector set:

Counter	Object	Description
SQLServer:Locks	Number of Deadlocks/sec (Total)	Number of lock requests per second that resulted in a deadlock
SQLServer:Buffer Manager	Page Life Expectancy	Number of seconds a page will stay in the buffer pool without references
SQLServer:General Statistics	User Connections	Number of users currently connected to SQL Server

2. Right-click anywhere in the Performance Monitor display pane, point to New, and click Data Collector Set.

   The Create New Data Collector Set Wizard starts. The data collector set created will contain all the data collectors selected in the current Performance Monitor view.

3. Enter a name for your data collector set and click Next.

4. The Root Directory will contain data collected by the data collector set. Change this setting if you want to store your data collector set data in a different location from the default. Browse to and select the directory or type the directory name.

5. Click Next to define a user for the data collector set to run as or click Finish to save the current settings and exit.

6. Click Next and configure the data collector set to run as a specific user. Click the Change button to enter the user name and password for a different user from the default listed.

7. Click Finish to return to Windows Performance Monitor.

   - To view the properties of the data collector set or make additional changes, right-click the data collector set and select Properties.

   - To start the data collector set immediately (and begin saving data to the location specified in Step 4), right-click the data collector set and select Start.

   - To save the data collector set as a template, right-click the data collector set and select Save Template.

Lesson Summary

- Performance Monitor captures numeric statistics about hardware and software components.

- Counters are organized into a three-level hierarchy: counter object, counter, and counter instance.

- A counter object must have at least one counter.

- A counter can have zero or more instances.

- You capture counter logs with Performance Monitor to perform analysis.

- Use Performance Monitor to capture metrics for Windows Server and SQL Server.

Lesson Review

Answer the following questions to test your knowledge of the information in this lesson. You can find the answers to these questions and explanations of why each answer choice is correct or incorrect in the "Answers" section at the end of this chapter.

1. What does the System Processor Queue Length counter measure?

   A. The number of system requests waiting for a processor

   B. The number of SQL Server requests waiting for a processor

   C. The number of processors actively performing work

   D. The amount of time that a processor is in use

2. What does the Buffer Manager performance object counter Page Life Expectancy counter measure?

   A. The total number of pages on all free lists

   B. The number of requests to find a page in the buffer pool

   C. The number of physical database page reads that are issued per second

   D. The number of seconds a page will stay in the buffer pool without references

3. What does the Physical Disk:Avg.Disk Queue Length counter measure?

   A. The number of system requests, on average, that are waiting for disk access

   B. The time that the disk is busy with read/write activity

   C. The number of physical database page reads that are issued per second

   D. The number of physical database page writes that are issued per second

Lesson 2: Working with SQL Server Profiler

When a performance issue with SQL Server is identified, the issue can often be improved through a process of tuning poor performing queries. However, with this continual improvement, you must be able to identify where you should focus the performance tuning efforts. SQL Server Profiler and Extended Events Profiler capture activity against SQL Server to assist in this process.

> **After this lesson, you will be able to:**
>
> - Capture activity by using SQL Server Profiler and Extended Events Profiler.
>
> **Estimated lesson time: 30 minutes**

Capturing Activity with SQL Server Profiler

SQL Server Profiler and Extended Events Profiler both provide the ability to trace the activity that is occurring in the SQL Server Database Engine. SQL Server Profiler can also trace SQL Server Analysis Services activity. The traces captured by the Profiler utilities can be used for diagnosing performance issues and for replaying workloads. SQL Server Profiler captures SQL Server events when they occur, as shown in Figure 9-3. Unlike Extended Events, when filtering is applied for SQL Server Profiler, the events are captured, examined for filtering, and then discarded based on the applied filters. This process uses additional overhead.

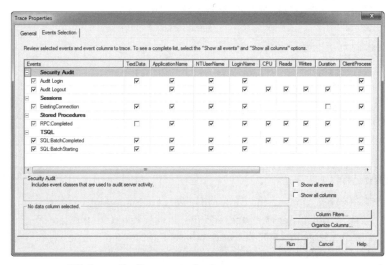

FIGURE 9-3   SQL Server Profiler event selection

SQL Server Profiler can filter events; filters limit the events collected in a trace. If a filter is not set, all events of the selected event classes are returned in the trace output. It is not mandatory to set a filter for a trace; however, a filter minimizes the overhead that is incurred during tracing.

SQL Server Profiler supports the use of templates, which are predefined sets of events, and the use of event data columns to simplify the creation of a SQL Profiler trace. Standard templates are provided with the tool, and the user can create and reuse custom templates. You can use captured traces when tuning the performance of an application or when specific performance issues are occurring. If you are using a trace to diagnose an issue, you can use it in conjunction with data from the Windows Performance Monitor to correlate the relationship between system resources and the execution of queries.

SQL Server Profiler is a graphical tool, and it is important to realize that it can have significant performance impact on the server being traced. SQL Trace is a library of system stored procedures that can minimize this impact. The SQL Trace stored procedures are described in more detail in the "Understanding SQL Trace" section later in this chapter.

Extended Events also provides capabilities for tracing SQL Server activity. Extended Events was first made available in SQL Server 2008, and in SQL Server 2012 the number of lightweight events has been increased. All the events and fields available in SQL Profiler are now available in Extended Events and in a graphical user interface (shown in Figure 9-4), covering more use cases and enabling new debugging opportunities. You learn more about Extended Events in the "Capturing Activity with Extended Events Profiler" section later in this chapter.

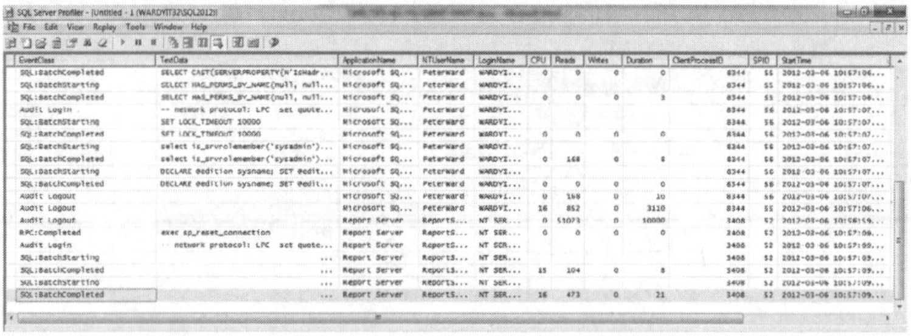

FIGURE 9-4 SQL Server Profiler graphical user interface

Tracing Output Options

When a SQL Server Profiler trace is running, the captured events are loaded into a graphical grid within the SQL Server Profiler user interface, and the profiler can store the captured event details to either a file or a table in a SQL Server database. Capturing a SQL Server Profiler trace to a file is the most efficient output option. When configuring the file output, use Trace Properties, as shown in Figure 9-5.

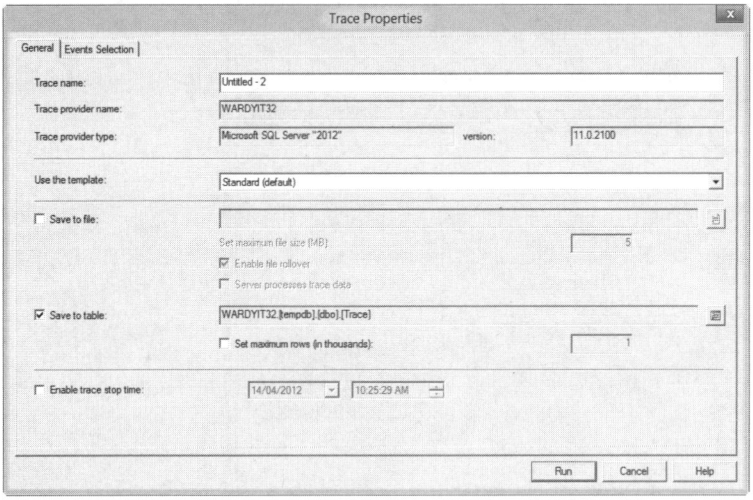

FIGURE 9-5 Saving a trace to a table

After you check Save To File, you enter the following information:

- A Trace Name, which is the filename for the trace, is required. The default file type for a trace file is .trc.

- Select the Save To File check box and then set the file size of the trace file. The default is 5 MB. The file size should be based on the amount of activity that is being captured. When the Enable File Rollover check box is selected and the maximum file size is reached, SQL Server Profiler creates a new trace file and incrementally increases the file number.

> **NOTE EFFICIENCIES WITH TRACE DATA**
>
> Creating trace files is an efficient way to quickly store trace data by using minimal system resources. You can store trace data into a trace table on another server, but this process is a heavy user of system resources.

- The Server Processes Trace Data description for the trace properties means that the SQL Server service, rather than SQL Server Profiler, will write the output file. SQL Server Profiler can also capture trace data to a database table.

To avoid any additional performance overhead, it is recommended that trace data not be written directly to the SQL Server system that is being monitored.

Trace Events

The information stored in a trace is divided into categories that contain events, each of which has attributes that are defined by columns on the Events Selection tab, as shown in Figure 9-6.

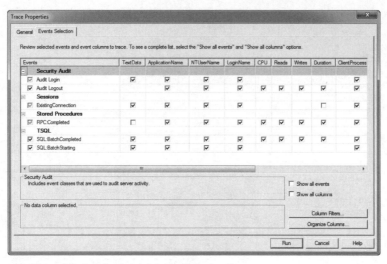

FIGURE 9-6 Events Selection tab in Trace Properties

 In SQL Server Profiler, a *category* is a group of related event classes. An *event class* contains all the data columns that can be reported by an event. An *event* is defined as the occurrence of an action within an instance of the SQL Server Database Engine and is further defined by its attributes, which are listed in data columns. Some commonly traced events are described in Table 9-2.

TABLE 9-2 Common Trace Events

Event	Description
SQL:BatchComplete	A SQL Server batch completed.
SQL:StmtCompleted	A T-SQL statement completed.
RPC:Completed	A remote procedure call (stored procedure) completed.
Audit Login / Audit Logout	A login or logout of SQL Server occurred.
Deadlock Graph	An XML description of a deadlock was captured.

The most commonly used event groups are Locks, Performance, Security Audit, StoredProcedures, and TSQL. The Stored Procedure and TSQL event groups are commonly captured along with events from the Performance group to baseline and troubleshoot query performance. The Security Audit event group defines auditing quickly across a variety of security events, although the new SQL audit specification feature provides more secure and more flexible auditing capabilities. Events from the Locks event group are commonly used to troubleshoot concurrency issues.

Trace Columns

Trace columns represent data that can be captured when an event occurs. Data columns contain the attributes of events. SQL Server Profiler uses the data columns in the trace output to describe events that are captured when the trace runs. SQL Server has a number of potential columns, but not every event writes values to all the possible columns. To see all the event classes available, select the Show All Events check box on the Events Selection tab (shown earlier in Figure 9-6). To see all traceable data columns, select the Show All Columns check box.

You should minimize the number of columns that you capture when events occur to help minimize the overall size of the captured trace.

Filtering Traces

As shown in Figure 9-7, filters can be set for each of the columns that are captured in a trace. It is important to ensure that you are capturing only events of interest by limiting the events with filters. Effective use of filters helps minimize the size of the trace file and therefore assists with the analysis by reducing the number of captured events.

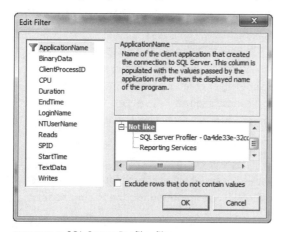

FIGURE 9-7 SQL Server Profiler filters

Trace Templates

Trace templates are sets of event classes and trace columns. SQL Server Profiler enables you to create templates that define the event classes and data columns to include in traces. After you have defined a template, you can run a trace that captures data based on those event classes.

SQL Server Profiler provides a number of predefined templates, which have common event classes and Event Data columns preselected for you. Templates can be generated in SQL Server Profiler by creating a trace, starting and stopping the trace, and then selecting File, Save As, as illustrated in Figure 9-8.

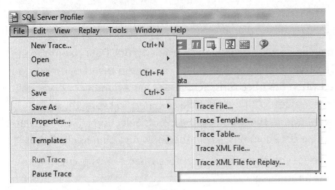

FIGURE 9-8 Creating a trace template

Understanding SQL Trace

SQL Server Profiler provides a graphical interface for capturing activity, although it can place a heavy load on the systems that are being profiled. It can create a trace and then script the trace for use with SQL Trace. The SQL Trace programming interface manages traces by using system stored procedures to create lightweight traces.

SQL Trace is a feature that runs within the SQL Server Database Engine to create and run traces, which are managed by using system stored procedures. SQL Server Profiler uses the SQL Trace facility in SQL Server when SQL Server Profiler creates a trace. Traces run in the process of the SQL Server Database Engine and can be used to write events to a file or to an application by using the SQL Server Management Objects (SMO) .NET Framework.

It is important to understand the differences between SQL Trace and SQL Server Profiler and to understand when each tool should be used.

- SQL Trace must be defined by using a series of system stored procedure calls, whereas SQL Server Profiler provides a graphical interface for configuring the tracing activity.
- SQL Trace runs directly inside the Database Engine, whereas SQL Server Profiler runs on a client machine or on the server and communicates to the Database Engine by using the SQL Trace procedures.

Traces do not automatically restart if the SQL Server instance is restarted. If a trace needs to run constantly, the trace should be scripted and launched from a startup procedure.

 SQL Server runs a default server-side trace that is started automatically whenever SQL Server starts. The trace is called *default trace* and has the trace ID of 1. The default trace is a lightweight trace that keeps up to 5 MB of data at any point in time. This trace captures key SQL Server events such as database growth and objects being created or dropped. It can be enabled or disabled by using sp_configure. The default trace cannot be modified, and its default file location cannot be changed. It provides troubleshooting assistance to database administrators by ensuring that they have the log data necessary to diagnose problems the first time they occur. This trace is also used by the Configuration Changes History report in SQL Server Management Studio.

> **MORE INFO   DEFAULT TRACE**
>
> You can learn more about the default trace at *http://msdn.microsoft.com/en-us/library /ms175513(v=sql.110).aspx.*

Reviewing Trace Output

Traces that are written to trace files are not easy to read directly. SQL Server provides the following two options to assist with analyzing the information captured in a trace file:

- Opening the trace in SQL Server Profiler
- Importing the trace into a SQL Server table

SQL Server Profiler can open trace files. Within SQL Server Profiler, the trace output can be filtered and grouped for analysis.

Trace files can also be imported into a SQL Server table by using the fn_trace_gettable function. After the table has been imported, Transact-SQL statements can query the trace data in the table.

Capturing Activity with Extended Events Profiler

As illustrated in Figure 9-9, the Extended Events profiler is a new tool introduced in SQL Server 2012 that captures activity for the SQL Server Database Engine based on Extended Events, a lightweight event-monitoring infrastructure that was introduced in SQL Server 2008.

The Extended Events profiler is integrated directly into SQL Server Management Studio and can capture Database Engine activity similar to the way SQL Server Profiler is used.

> **NOTE   PLANNING AHEAD**
>
> Because of the ability to capture activity by using Extended Events, SQL Server Profiler for Database Engine Trace Capture and Trace Replay have been announced as deprecated. The announcement indicates that these features will be supported in the next version of SQL Server (the specific version is not yet determined) but will be removed in a later version.

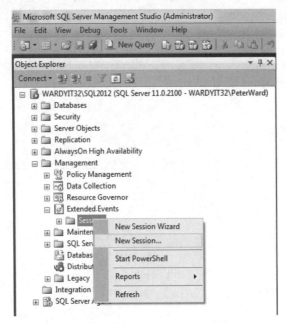

FIGURE 9-9 Starting an Extended Events profiler session

PRACTICE **Creating Traces**

In this practice, you establish a performance baseline and import a trace into a table.

EXERCISE 1 Establish a Performance Baseline

In this exercise, you configure a trace to establish a performance baseline for stored procedures and ad hoc SQL execution and import this trace file to a table for further analysis.

To complete this exercise, perform the following steps

1. Start Profiler. Select File, New Trace and connect to your instance.

2. Specify the trace name **70462.trc** and options to save to a file in c:\temp.

3. On the Events Selection tab, clear the Audit Login, Audit Logout, ExistingConnection, and SQL:BatchStarting event check boxes.

4. Review the selected columns.

5. Click Column Filters and specify a filter on the AdventureWorks2012 database.

6. Click Run.

7. Execute several queries and stored procedures against the AdventureWorks2012 database and observe the output in Profiler.

EXERCISE 2 Import a .trc File

In this exercise, you import a trace file into a table for further analysis. To complete this exercise, perform the following steps:

1. Open a query window and execute the following command:

```
SELECT * INTO ##baseline
FROM fn_trace_gettable('c:\temp\70462.trc', default);
GO
```

2. Execute the following query and inspect the results:

```
SELECT * FROM ##baseline
ORDER BY Duration DESC
```

Lesson Summary

- Profiler is the utility that enables you to interact graphically with the SQL Trace application programming interface (API).
- SQL Trace exposes events that can be captured to audit actions, monitor an instance, examine baseline queries, and troubleshoot performance issues.
- You can specify the columns of data you want to capture for a given event.
- Trace output can be limited by applying filters.
- Use SQL Trace for large and long-running traces.
- Use SQL Server Profiler to define traces and then script them for SQL Trace.

Lesson Review

Answer the following questions to test your knowledge of the information in this lesson. You can find the answers to these questions and explanations of why each answer choice is correct or incorrect in the "Answers" section at the end of this chapter.

1. You are troubleshooting a performance issue with a SQL Server instance. Query performance declines every Monday morning from 9 A.M. to 10 A.M. Which tools can you use to diagnose the cause of the performance problems? (Choose all that apply.)

    A. Extended Events Profiler

    B. Database Engine Tuning Advisor

    C. Resource Governor

    D. SQL Server Profiler

2. Which trace event would you use to determine when a T-SQL statement has completed?

    A. SQL:BatchComplete

    B. SQL:StmtStarting

    C. SQL:StmtCompleted

    D. RPC:Completed

3. Which SQL Server Profiler events can identify the users involved in a deadlock? (Each answer presents a complete solution. Choose two.)

    A. Lock:DeadLock

    B. Lock:DeadLock Chain

    C. Process:DeadLock

    D. Chain:DeadLock List

Lesson 3: Monitoring SQL Server

SQL Server is an enterprise database management system that can run for long periods of time with minimal administration. Despite this, it requires a process for ongoing monitoring of your SQL Server databases against a baseline so you can proactively identify any issues before they might arise. SQL Server 2012 provides a number of tools for monitoring. In this lesson, you become familiar with a number of the tools and how they can be used to monitor SQL Server.

> **After this lesson, you will be able to:**
>
> - Monitor current activity.
>
> **Estimated lesson time: 30 minutes**

Monitoring Activity

Several tools are available for monitoring SQL Server activity. Dynamic management views (DMVs) and dynamic management functions (DMFs) provide insight into current and historical SQL Server activity. These views and functions are useful for monitoring SQL Server, and it is important to be familiar with how to use them.

SQL Server Management Studio (SSMS) provides a graphical representation of monitoring information known as *Activity Monitor*, shown in Figure 9-10, which uses information from some of these DMVs and DMFs. Activity Monitor can identify current issues such as what processes are currently running or the last Transact-SQL command batch for a process.

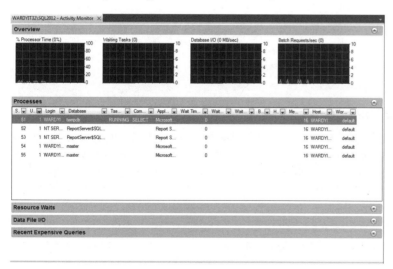

FIGURE 9-10   Activity Monitor

The SQL Server process also provides a number of performance objects and counters that can be accessed by using System Monitor.

Dynamic Management Views and Functions

Dynamic management views and functions return server state information that can be used to monitor the health of a server instance, diagnose problems, and tune performance.

There are two types of dynamic management views and functions:

- Server-scoped dynamic management views and functions. These require VIEW SERVER STATE permission on the server.

- Database-scoped dynamic management views and functions. These require VIEW DATABASE STATE permission on the database.

Table 9-3 lists some of the most commonly used categories of dynamic management objects.

TABLE 9-3 Commonly Used Categories of Dynamic Management Objects

Category	Description
sys.dm_exec_*	These objects provide information about connections, sessions, requests, and query execution.
sys.dm_os_*	These objects provide access to SQL Server operating system–related information.
sys.dm_tran_*	These objects provide access to transaction management.
sys.dm_io_*	These objects provide information on I/O processes.
sys.dm_db_*	These objects provide database-scoped information.

> **MORE INFO** **DYNAMIC MANAGEMENT OBJECTS**
>
> You can learn more about other categories of dynamic management objects at
> *http://msdn.microsoft.com/en-us/library/ms188754(v=sql.110).aspx.*

Querying Dynamic Management Views

Dynamic management views can be referenced in Transact-SQL statements by using two-part, three-part, or four-part names. *Dynamic management functions,* however, can be referenced in Transact-SQL statements by using either two-part or three-part names. Dynamic management views and functions cannot be referenced in Transact-SQL statements by using one-part names.

All dynamic management views and functions exist in the sys schema and follow this naming convention: dm_*. When you use a dynamic management view or function, you must prefix the name of the view or function by using the sys schema. For example, to query the dm_os_wait_stats dynamic management view, run the following query:

```
SELECT wait_type, wait_time_ms
FROM sys.dm_os_wait_stats;
```

The information exposed by DMVs and DMFs is not persisted in the databases. The views and functions expose in-memory structures, which will be cleared if the SQL Server instance is restarted.

You can see the list of available DMVs in Object Explorer on the System Views node for any databases. The DMFs are shown on the Table Valued Functions node under the System Functions node that is under the master database.

There are two types of dynamic management objects:

- Objects that provide real-time state information
- Objects that provide recent historical information

Most DMVs and DMFs are designed to provide information about the current state of the system. In the following example, two DMVs are being joined. The sys.dm_exec_sessions view returns one row for each current user session. The sys.dm_os_waiting_tasks view returns a row for each task that is currently waiting for a resource. By joining the two views and adding a filter, you can locate a list of user tasks that have been waiting for longer than 2,000 milliseconds (2 seconds).

```
SELECT s.original_login_name,  s.program_name, t.wait_type,  t.wait_duration_ms
FROM sys.dm_os_waiting_tasks t JOIN sys.dm_exec_sessions s
ON t.session_id = s.session_id
WHERE s.is_user_process = 1
AND t.wait_duration_ms > 2000
```

The second type of dynamic management object returns historical information. For example, you saw in the previous code sample that the sys.dm_os_waiting_tasks view returned details of tasks that are currently waiting on resources. By comparison, the sys.dm_os_wait_stats view returns information about how often and how long any task had to wait for a specific wait_type since the SQL Server instance started.

```
SELECT * FROM sys.dm_os_wait_stats
ORDER BY wait_time_ms DESC
```

Dynamic management objects can greatly assist with identifying performance issues. A common scenario causing poor performance is missing indexes on a table. The sys.dm_db _missing_index_* objects can be queried to identify missing indexes.

Working with Activity Monitor

Activity Monitor is a graphical tool in SSMS that provides an overview of the system performance and information about processes, waits, I/O resources, and expensive queries. To open Activity Monitor, right-click the server name and then click Activity Monitor, as shown in Figure 9-11.

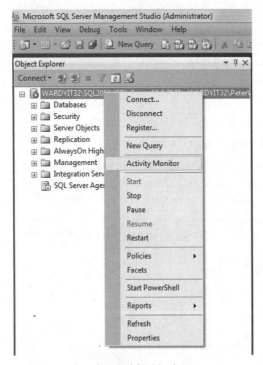

FIGURE 9-11 Opening Activity Monitor

Activity Monitor is broken into five sections:

- The Overview section provides graphical information about processor usage, waiting tasks, database I/O, and the number of batch requests per second.

- The Processes section includes information on processes, including the server process ID (SPID), login, database, and command. The Processes section also provides information on any blocking processes.

- The Resource Waits section shows categories of processes that are waiting for resources and shows wait times.

- The Data File I/O section provides information about the physical database files in use and their performance.

- The Recent Expensive Queries section shows information about the most expensive recent queries and the resources consumed by the queries. The query text and execution plan for each query can be viewed by right-clicking the query.

In this practice, you use dynamic management objects to identify performance issues.

EXERCISE 1   Identify Missing Indexes

In this exercise, you find and evaluate missing indexes. To complete this exercise, perform the following steps:

1.   Open a new query window and execute the following query:

```
SELECT City, PostalCode, AddressLine1
FROM AdventureWorks2012.Person.Address
WHERE City = 'Seattle'
GO
```

2.   Execute the following query to inspect the missing indexes suggested by the dynamic management objects:

```
SELECT *
FROM
(SELECT user_seeks * avg_total_user_cost * (avg_user_impact * 0.01) AS
index_advantage, migs.*
FROM sys.dm_db_missing_index_group_stats migs) AS migs_adv
JOIN sys.dm_db_missing_index_groups AS mig
ON migs_adv.group_handle = mig.index_group_handle
JOIN sys.dm_db_missing_index_details AS mid
ON mig.index_handle = mid.index_handle
ORDER BY migs_adv.index_advantage
```

Lesson Summary

- Use dynamic management objects for real-time monitoring and troubleshooting.
- Use Activity Monitor for easy access to performance information.
- The sys.dm_db_* DMVs provide general space and index usage information.
- The sys.dm_exec_* DMVs return information about currently executing queries and queries that are still in the query cache.

Lesson Review

Answer the following questions to test your knowledge of the information in this lesson. You can find the answers to these questions and explanations of why each answer choice is correct or incorrect in the "Answers" section at the end of this chapter.

1.   Which of the following are used to locate blocked processes?

   A.   sys.dm_os_wait_stats view

   B.   sys.dm_exec_sessions view

   C.   sys.dm_exec_requests view

   D.   sys.dm_os_waiting_tasks view

2. Which dynamic management object can be used to identify the names of any tables where the index is missing?

   A. sys.dm_db_missing_index_columns

   B. sys.dm_db_missing_index_groups

   C. sys.dm_db_missing_index_group_stats

   D. sys.dm_db_missing_index_details

Lesson 4: Using the Data Collector Tool

Dynamic management views (DMVs) and dynamic management functions (DMFs) expose information about the state of the system. The values that these dynamic management objects return are not persisted when the instance is restarted because the values reside in memory only while the server is running. One of the disadvantages of using dynamic management objects is that the majority of objects return real-time data, and those objects that return historical data return the data as an aggregation. To diagnose performance issues effectively, you must see high-level aggregated trends over time and see the detailed information to identify issues. The SQL Server data collector is designed to resolve this gap.

> **After this lesson, you will be able to:**
> - Capture and manage performance data.
> - Analyze collected performance data.
>
> **Estimated lesson time: 30 minutes**

Capturing and Managing Performance Data

To perform effective performance tuning and monitoring, you must be able to capture historical data and access detailed data when investigating issues. The data collector was introduced in SQL Server 2008 as a mechanism to collect this performance-based data. It contains a number of components, including a central warehouse for storing performance data, jobs for collecting and loading data to the warehouse, and a number of reports for analyzing the performance information.

Using the Data Collector

The *data collector* is a core component of the data collection platform for SQL Server 2012 and the tools that are provided in SQL Server. The data collector provides one central point for data collection across your database servers and applications. This collection point can obtain data from a variety of sources and is not limited to performance data, unlike SQL Trace (which was covered in the "Understanding SQL Trace" section in Lesson 2).

The data collector stores the collected data in a relational database known as the *management data warehouse (MDW)*. Data collection runs either constantly or on a user-defined schedule. You can adjust the scope of data collection to suit your test and production environments. For example, the data warehouse enables you to manage the data that you collect by setting different retention periods for your data. The data collector supports dynamic tuning for data collection and is extensible through its API.

Defining Data Collection Sets

When you configure the management data warehouse, a number of system data collection sets are created. These sets define the data that needs to be collected, including how often the data is uploaded to the central repository and how long the data is retained in that repository.

The data collector can collect information from several locations:

- It can query DMVs and DMFs to retrieve detailed information about the operation of the system.

- It can retrieve performance counters that provide metrics about the performance of both SQL Server and the entire server.

- It can capture SQL Trace events.

In addition to the system data collection sets, the SQL Server data collector can be extended by the creation of user-defined data collection sets. The ability to add user-defined data collection sets enables users to specify the data they wish to collect and to use the infra-structure provided by the SQL Server data collector to collect and centralize the data.

Designing a Data Collector Topology

Three components make up the data collection system in SQL Server:

- The data collector, which is a set of jobs that run on the local server that collect data from dynamic management objects, performance counters, and SQL Trace events and then upload that data to the management data warehouse.

- The management data warehouse, which can consolidate data from multiple SQL Server instances.

- Three standard reports and a rich set of subreports available to analyze the data in the management data warehouse. You can also write your own reports based on the data collected by the system data collection sets. The reports are accessed by using SQL Server Management Studio. You'll find more about these reports in the "Analyzing Collected Performance Data" section later in this chapter.

There are three goals for creating a centralized management data warehouse:

- You can access reports that combine information for all server instances in your enterprise.

- You can offload the need to hold collected data and to report on it from the produc-tion servers.

- You can use it to persist data that is stored in dynamic management objects.

The data collector has the following two methods for uploading captured performance data into the central warehouse:

- Lower-volume information is sent immediately to the warehouse.
- Higher-volume information is cached locally first and then uploaded to the warehouse by using SQL Server Integration Services (SSIS).

Configuring the Data Collector

Installing the data collection for SQL Server involves the following two steps:

- Configuring a central management data warehouse to store the collected data
- Configuring each server instance to collect and upload the required data

SQL Server provides a wizard that can be used for both these setup tasks. The wizard can be launched in SQL Server Management Studio by right-clicking Data Collection in the Management node, as shown in Figure 9-12.

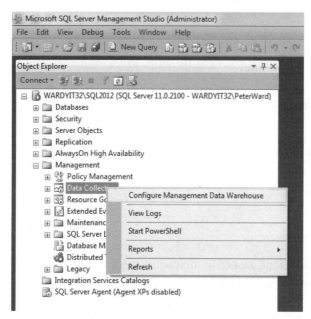

FIGURE 9-12 Configure the management data warehouse

The first step when running the wizard is to create a management data warehouse, which collects data from a number of SQL Server instances.

Sufficient disk space is required to support the management data warehouse. In a typical configuration, approximately 300 MB per day is required for each instance that is managed.

The only processes that are run on the local instances are the jobs that collect and upload the data to the management data warehouse. Some data is collected on a regular basis and is cached locally and later uploaded by using SSIS. Other data is captured infrequently and uploaded immediately.

System data collection sets are created automatically during setup. They can be enabled and disabled as needed, and both the frequency of the collection and the retention period for collected data can be customized for system data collection sets and for user-defined data collection sets.

Assigning Roles to Data Collector Security

The SQL Server data collector system has two security aspects:

- Who can access the management data warehouse
- Who can configure the data collection

Database roles exist for both these purposes, as outlined in Table 9-4 and Table 9-5.

TABLE 9-4 Roles for the Management Data Warehouse

Role	Description
mdw_admin	Full access to the management data warehouse
mdw_writer	Write and read access; required by data collectors
mdw_reader	Read access; required by users accessing reports

TABLE 9-5 Roles for Configuring the Data Collector

Role	Description
dc_admin	Full administrator access to the configuration
dc_operator	Read and update access to the configuration
dc_proxy	Read access to the configuration

Monitoring the Data Collector

The configuration and log information for the data collector is written to the msdb database and is implemented by stored procedures and the SSIS logging features. The retention for logging is based on the collection set retention. The log information for the data collector can be viewed by using Transact-SQL or the SQL Server Log File Viewer.

As with other SQL Server Agent jobs, the history of the jobs that are used by the SQL Server data collector to capture and upload performance data are held in the job history table and can be viewed by using the standard SQL Server Agent job history viewer.

The data that is logged into the msdb database is kept with the same retention period setting as the data collection sets to which it relates. The information that is retuned can be viewed through the log file viewer or by querying the following objects:

- fn_syscollector_get_execution_details()
- fn_syscollector_get_execution_stats()
- syscollector_execution_log
- syscollector_execution_log_full
- syscollector_execution_stats

Three levels of logging are available and can be set by calling the sp_syscollector_update _collection_set system stored procedure. The lowest level of logging records the starts and stops of collector activity. The next level of logging adds execution statistics and progress reports. The highest level of logging adds detailed SSIS packages logging.

Analyzing Collected Performance Data

After performance data has been collected from a number of server instances and has been consolidated into a management data warehouse, the data can be analyzed. You can write your own customized report by using SQL Server Reporting Services or the prebuilt reports.

The data collector provides a number of cross-linked reports on historical data. Its reports, shown in Table 9-6, are available from SQL Server Management Studio.

TABLE 9-6 Data Collector Reports

Report	Description
Server Activity History	CPU, memory, disk, and network I/O SQL Server waits and SQL Server activity
Disk Usage Summary	Trends and details of disk and file usage
Query Statistics History	Most expensive queries ranked by CPU, duration, reads, and writes

The SQL Server data collector reports are accessed by using SQL Server Management Studio by right-clicking the management data warehouse database or, alternatively, by right-clicking Data Collector in the Management node and selecting Reports, as illustrated in Figure 9-13.

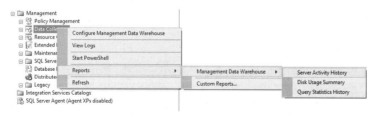

FIGURE 9-13 Opening the SQL Server data collector reports

Server Activity Report

The Server Activity Report is based on the Server Activity System Data Collection Set and is made up of the DMV snapshot and performance counter collector types. The collector runs every 60 seconds, and the data is uploaded every 15 minutes and retained for 14 days by default.

The Server Activity System Data Collection Set gathers information from a number of SQL Server–related statistics such as waits, locks, latches, and memory statistics from DMVs. In addition, the collection set gathers Windows Server and SQL Server performance counters to retrieve information such as CPU and memory usage from the system and from the processes that are running on the system.

Disk Usage Report

The Disk Usage Report is based on the Disk Usage System Data Collection Set. By default, the collection set gathers disk usage data every six hours and keeps the data for two years.

By default, the Disk Usage System Data Collection Set retains data for longer than other system data collection sets. The amount of data collected by the Disk Usage System Data Collection Set is minimal, and the longer retention enables tracking file space usage over time for capacity planning purposes.

Query Statistics Report

The Query Statistic Report is based on the Query Statics System Data Collection Set. This collection set runs every 10 seconds, and the data is uploaded every 15 minutes and retained for two weeks by default. This collection set is the most intensive. To avoid the constant overhead of uploading the data collected by this collection set, the data is cached on the local file system and uploaded by SSIS every 15 minutes.

SQL Server determines the most expensive queries to display in the Query Statistics Report based on the following factors:

- Elapsed time
- Worker time
- Logical reads
- Logical writes
- Physical reads
- Execution count

In this practice, you configure the Performance Data Warehouse, set up the built-in collection sets, and analyze the data collection results.

EXERCISE 1   Configure the Management Data Warehouse

In this exercise, you configure the management data warehouse and configure data collection for the newly created management data warehouse. You also explore reviewing the result for the collection.To complete this exercise, perform the following steps:

1. Start SQL Server Management Studio, connect to your instance, expand the Management node, right-click Data Collection, and select Configure Management Data Warehouse.

2. Click Next and select Create Or Upgrade A Management Data Warehouse.

3. Create a new database named **PerfData** with all the default settings. Click Next.

4. Select the login corresponding to your SQL Server service account and the mdw_admin role.

5. Click Finish to create the management data warehouse.

6. Review the objects that have been created in the PerfData database.

7. Right-click the Data Collection node, select Configure Management Data Warehouse, and click Next.

8. Select Set Up Data Collection and click Next.

9. Select the PerfData database for your management data warehouse and click Next.

10. Click Finish.

11. Right-click the Data Collection node, select Reports, Management Data Warehouse, and Disk Usage Summary.

12. Review the results.

Lesson Summary

- The data collector can query DMVs and DMFs to retrieve detailed information about the operation of the system.

- The data collector can retrieve performance counters that provide metrics about the performance of both SQL Server and the server.

- The data collector can capture SQL Trace events that have occurred.

- Use a central management data warehouse to capture historical performance information.

- Use a data collection to gather performance data for SQL Server instances.

Lesson Review

Answer the following questions to test your knowledge of the information in this lesson. You can find the answers to these questions and explanations of why each answer choice is correct or incorrect in the "Answers" section at the end of this chapter.

1. You must centralize your SQL Server capacity management tasks and evaluate the performance against a known baseline by implementing a solution that incurs minimal cost and requires the least effort to configure and maintain. Which solution should you implement?

    A. Install a SQL Server 2012 instance and collect data from the dynamic management objects.

    B. Install a SQL Server 2012 instance and implement a management data warehouse.

    C. Configure Windows Performance Monitor.

    D. Implement Microsoft System Center Operations Manager.

2. You need to grant a user access to the management data warehouse reports. To which role should you add the user?

    A. mdw_admin

    B. mdw_reader

    C. dc_operator

    D. dc_proxy

3. What does the Server Activity report include? (Each answer presents a complete solution. Choose two.)

    A. CPU, memory, disk, and network I/O

    B. Trends and details of disk and file usagedc_proxy

    C. Most expensive queries ranked by CPU, duration, reads, and writes

    D. SQL Server waits and SQL Server activity

Lesson 5: Identifying Bottlenecks

When a performance issue with SQL Server is identified, the issue often can be attributed to resource bottlenecks. In this lesson, you learn how to identify common bottlenecks and the impact they can have on the performance of SQL Server.

> **After this lesson, you will be able to:**
> - Identify I/O bottlenecks.
> - Identify memory bottlenecks.
> - Identify CPU bottlenecks.
>
> **Estimated lesson time: 30 minutes**

Monitoring Disk Usage

SQL Server uses the Microsoft Windows operating system I/O services to perform read and write operations on your disk. Although SQL Server makes the I/O requests, the operating system coordinates the actual disk I/O. The I/O subsystem includes the system bus, disk controller cards, disks, and other I/O devices. Disk I/O is frequently the cause of bottlenecks in a system.

Monitoring disk activity involves the following two areas of focus:

- Monitoring disk I/O and detecting excess paging
- Isolating disk activity that SQL Server creates

Monitoring Disk I/O and Detecting Excess Paging

Two counters that can be monitored to determine disk activity are:

- PhysicalDisk: % Disk Time
- PhysicalDisk: Avg. Disk Queue Length

In System Monitor, the PhysicalDisk: % Disk Time counter monitors the percentage of time that the disk is busy with read and write activity. If the PhysicalDisk: % Disk Time counter is high (more than 90 percent), check the PhysicalDisk: Current Disk Queue Length counter to see how many system requests are waiting for disk access. The number of waiting I/O requests should be sustained at no more than 1.5 to 2 times the number of spindles that make up the physical disk. Most disks have one spindle, although redundant array of independent disk (RAID) devices usually have more than one spindle. A hardware RAID device appears as one physical disk in System Monitor.

Use the values of the Current Disk Queue Length and % Disk Time counters to detect bottlenecks within the disk subsystem. If Current Disk Queue Length and % Disk Time counter values are consistently high, consider doing one of the following:

- Using faster disk drives
- Moving some files to an additional disk or server
- Adding disks to a RAID array if one is being used

If you are using a RAID device, the % Disk Time counter can indicate a value greater than 100 percent. If it does, use the PhysicalDisk: Avg. Disk Queue Length counter to determine how many system requests, on average, are waiting for disk access.

Applications and systems that are I/O bound might keep the disk constantly active.

Monitor the Memory: Page Faults/sec counter to make sure that the disk activity is not caused by paging. For a SQL Server instance, paging is not normally the cause of disk I/O bottlenecks; however, paging at the operating system level can impact the performance of the disk subsystem. In Windows-based operating systems, paging is caused by:

- Processes configured to use too much memory.
- File system activity.

If you have more than one logical partition on the same hard disk, use the Logical Disk counters rather than the Physical Disk counters. Look at the logical disk counters to help determine which files are frequently accessed. After you have found the disks with high levels of read/write activity, look at the read-specific and write-specific counters to learn the type of disk activity that causes the load on each logical volume, for example, Logical Disk: Disk Write Bytes/sec.

Isolating Disk Activity Created by SQL Server

Two counters that can be monitored to determine the amount of I/O generated by SQL Server components are:

- SQL Server:Buffer Manager: Page reads/sec.
- SQL Server:Buffer Manager: Page writes/sec.

In System Monitor, these counters monitor the amount of I/O generated by SQL Server components by examining the following performance areas:

- Writing pages to disk
- Reading pages from disk

If the values for these counters approach the capacity limit of the hardware I/O subsystem, try to reduce the values by tuning your application or database to reduce I/O operations (such as index coverage, better indexes, or normalization), increasing the I/O capacity of the hardware, or adding memory. For example, you can use Database Engine Tuning Advisor to analyze typical SQL Server workloads and produce recommendations for indexes, indexed views, and partitioning to improve server performance.

Monitoring Memory Usage

Monitor an instance of SQL Server periodically to confirm that memory usage is within typical ranges. To monitor for a low-memory condition, use the following object counters:

- Memory: Available Bytes
- Memory: Pages/sec

The Available Bytes counter indicates how many bytes of memory are currently available for use by processes. The Pages/sec counter indicates the number of pages that were either retrieved from disk due to hard page faults or written to disk to free space in the working set due to page faults.

Low values for the Available Bytes counter can indicate an overall shortage of memory on the computer or indicate that an application is not releasing memory. A high rate for the Pages/sec counter could indicate excessive paging. Monitor the Memory: Page Faults/sec counter to make sure that the disk activity is not caused by paging.

A low rate of paging (hence page faults) is typical, even if the computer has plenty of available memory. The Microsoft Windows Virtual Memory Manager (VMM) takes pages from SQL Server and other processes as it trims the working-set sizes of those processes. This VMM activity tends to cause page faults. To determine whether SQL Server or another process is the cause of excessive paging, monitor the Process: Page Faults/sec counter for the SQL Server process instance.

Isolating Memory Used by SQL Server

By default, SQL Server changes its memory requirements dynamically on the basis of available system resources. If SQL Server needs more memory, it queries the operating system to determine whether free physical memory is available and uses the available memory. If SQL Server does not need the memory currently allocated to it, it releases the memory to the operating system when requested. However, you can override the option to use memory dynamically by using the min server memory and max server memory server configuration options.

To monitor the amount of memory that SQL Server uses, examine the following performance counters:

- Process: Working Set
- SQL Server: Buffer Manager: Buffer Cache Hit Ratio
- SQL Server: Buffer Manager: Total Pages
- SQL Server: Memory Manager: Total Server Memory (KB)

The Working Set counter shows the amount of memory a process uses. If this number is consistently below the amount of memory that is set by the min server memory and max server memory server options, SQL Server is configured to use too much memory.

The Buffer Cache Hit Ratio counter is specific to an application. However, a rate of 90 percent or higher is desirable. Add more memory until the value is consistently greater than 90 percent. A value greater than 90 percent indicates that more than 90 percent of all requests for data were satisfied from the data cache.

If the Total Server Memory (KB) counter is consistently high compared to the amount of physical memory in the computer, it might indicate that more memory is required.

Monitoring CPU Usage

Monitor an instance of Microsoft SQL Server periodically to determine whether CPU usage rates are within normal ranges. A continually high rate of CPU usage can indicate the need to upgrade the CPU or add multiple processors. A high CPU usage rate might also indicate a poorly tuned or designed application. Optimizing the application can lower CPU usage.

An efficient way to determine CPU usage is to use the *Processor: % Processor Time counter* in System Monitor. This counter monitors the amount of time the CPU spends executing a thread that is not idle. A consistent state of 80 percent to 90 percent might indicate the need to upgrade your CPU or add more processors. For multiprocessor systems, monitor a separate instance of this counter for each processor. This value represents the sum of processor time on a specific processor. To determine the average for all processors, use the *System: % Total Processor Time counter* instead.

You can also monitor the following counters to monitor processor usage:

- **Processor: % Privileged Time**   Corresponds to the percentage of time the processor spends on execution of Microsoft Windows kernel commands such as processing SQL Server I/O requests. If this counter is consistently high when the Physical Disk counters are high, consider installing a faster or more efficient disk subsystem.

- **Processor: % User Time**   Corresponds to the percentage of time the processor spends on executing user processes such as SQL Server.

- **System: Processor Queue Length**   Corresponds to the number of threads waiting for processor time. A processor bottleneck develops when threads of a process require more processor cycles than are available. If more than a few processes attempt to use the processor's time, you might need to install a faster processor. Alternatively, if you have a multiprocessor system, you could add a processor.

When you examine processor usage, consider the type of work the instance of SQL Server performs. If SQL Server performs many calculations, such as queries involving aggregates or memory-bound queries that require no disk I/O, 100 percent of the processor's time can be used. If this causes the performance of other applications to suffer, try changing the work-load. For example, dedicate the computer to running the instance of SQL Server.

Usage rates around 100 percent when many client requests are being processed might indicate that processes are queuing up, waiting for processor time, and causing a bottleneck. Resolve the problem by adding faster processors.

PRACTICE Configuring Memory Options by Using SQL Server Management Studio

In this practice, you use SQL Server Management Studio to configure memory options for SQL Server.

EXERCISE 1   Configure a Fixed Amount of Memory

In this exercise, you set the memory options to use a fixed amount of memory. To complete this exercise, perform the following steps:

1. Start SQL Server Management Studio and connect to your instance.

2. In Object Explorer, right-click the server and select Properties.

3. Click the Memory node.

4. Under Server Memory Options, enter the amount you want for minimum server memory and maximum server memory.

Lesson Summary

- Monitor an instance of SQL Server periodically to confirm that memory usage is within typical ranges.

- Disk I/O is frequently the cause of bottlenecks in a system.

- Monitor an instance of Microsoft SQL Server periodically to determine whether CPU usage rates are within normal ranges. A continually high rate of CPU usage can indicate the need to upgrade the CPU or add multiple processors. A high CPU usage rate can also indicate a poorly tuned or designed application. Optimizing the application can lower CPU usage.

Lesson Review

Answer the following questions to test your knowledge of the information in this lesson. You can find the answers to these questions and explanations of why each answer choice is correct or incorrect in the "Answers" section at the end of this chapter.

1. Which counters would you use to determine whether CPU usage rates for SQL Server are within normal ranges? (Each correct answer presents a complete solution. Choose all that apply.)

   A. Processor: % Privileged Time

   B. Processor: % User Time

   C. SQL Server: Buffer Manager: Page reads/sec

   D. SQL Server: Buffer Manager: Page writes/sec

2. What does PhysicalDisk: % Disk Time measure?

   A. The percentage of time that the disk is busy with read/write activity

   B. The number of physical database page writes issued

   C. The number of pages used to store compiled queries

   D. The percentage of time that the disk system was not processing requests and no work was queued

3. By using Windows Performance Monitor, you have identified a large number of threads waiting for processor time. What should you do to resolve the performance issue?

   A. Add RAM.

   B. Add spindles to the storage subsystem.

   C. Disable Hyper-Threading.

   D. Install a faster processor.

Case Scenarios

In the following case scenarios, apply what you have learned about troubleshooting SQL Server 2012. You can find answers to these questions in the "Answers" section at the end of this chapter.

Case Scenario 1: Identifying Poor Query Performance

You have recently deployed SQL Server 2012 Enterprise edition to a new server with 128 GB of memory. The Sales application was also upgraded as part of this deployment. The sales team has identified that the performance of the end-of-month report is no longer satisfactory after the upgrade. With this information in mind, answer the following questions:

1. Which tool would you use to identify the query that this report is using?

2. How would you identify whether the unsatisfactory performance is caused by a missing index?

Case Scenario 2: Deploying Auditing

You have upgraded the SQL Server for the Payroll database from SQL Server 2008 to SQL Server 2012. Due to new regulatory requirements, you need to audit when any updates are made to the Employee table in the database. The regulation specifies that the audit information must be stored in the Application Event Log and that all events must be audited. With this information in mind, answer the following questions:

1. Which query would you use to create the server audit?

2. How would you enable the server audit?

3. Which query would you use to audit the Employee table?

Suggested Practices

To help you successfully master the exam objectives presented in this chapter, complete the following tasks.

Create a Trace by Using SQL Server Profiler

Prior to completing each task in the following practices, list the steps you would take to accomplish the task. After completing the task, assess how accurately you predicted the necessary steps.

- **Practice 1**   Create a trace to capture deadlock graphs and set the trace to start automatically when SQL Server starts.

- **Practice 2**   Create a trace to capture query performance statistics that can be used as a performance baseline for your instance.

Capture a Performance Baseline by Using Performance Monitor

Prior to completing each task in the following practices, list the steps you would take to accomplish the task. After completing the task, assess how accurately you predicted the necessary steps.

- **Practice 1**   Create a data collector set that captures operating system and SQL Server counters to produce a performance baseline.

Answers

This section contains the answers to the lesson review questions and solutions to the case scenarios in this chapter.

Lesson 1

1. **Correct Answer: A**

   A. **Correct:** The System: Processor Queue Length indicates the number of processes at a machine level that are waiting for a processor to be allocated.

   B. **Incorrect:** The System: Processor Queue Length includes any SQL Server requests that are waiting for processor resources to be allocated. The counter also includes requests from any other applications and the operating system that are waiting on processor resources.

   C. **Incorrect:** You can derive the number of processors actively performing work by using the Processor: % Processor Time counter with all associated instances.

   D. **Incorrect:** The amount of time a given processor is in use is retrieved from an instance of the Processor: % Processor Time counter.

2. **Correct Answer: D**

   A. **Incorrect:** Free pages is the total number of pages on all free lists.

   B. **Incorrect:** Page lookups/sec is the number of requests to find a page in the buffer pool.

   C. **Incorrect:** Page reads/sec is the number of physical database page reads that are issued per second.

   D. **Correct:** Page Life Expectancy is the number of seconds a page will stay in the buffer pool without references.

3. **Correct Answer: A**

   A. **Correct:** Physical Disk: Avg. Disk Queue Length counter determines how many system requests, on average, are waiting for disk access.

   B. **Incorrect:** PhysicalDisk: % Disk Time counter monitors the percentage of time that the disk is busy with read/write activity.

   C. **Incorrect:** SQL Server: Buffer Manager: Page reads/sec is the number of physical database page reads that are issued per second.

   D. **Correct:** SQL Server: Buffer Manager: Page writes/sec is the number of physical database page writes that are issued per second.

Lesson 2

1. **Correct Answers: A and D**

   A. **Correct:** Extended Events has a highly scalable and highly configurable architecture that enables users to collect as much or as little information as is necessary to troubleshoot or identify a performance problem.

   B. **Incorrect:** Database Engine Tuning Advisor suggests indexes and partitions that can optimize the performance of a query.

   C. **Incorrect:** Resource Governor enables you to limit the resources available to one or more connections.

   D. **Correct:** Profiler enables you to capture the query activity on the instance and then correlate the queries with performance counters captured by using System Monitor.

2. **Correct Answers: A and B**

   A. **Correct:** SQL:BatchComplete indicates a SQL Server batch completed.

   B. **Correct:** TSQL:StmtStarting indicates that a Transact-SQL statement has started.

   C. **Incorrect:** SQL:StmtCompleted indicates that a T-SQL statement completed.

   D. **Incorrect:** RPC:Completed indicates a remote procedure call (stored procedure) completed.

3. **Correct Answers: A and B**

   A. **Correct:** The Lock:Deadlock Chain event class is produced for each participant in a deadlock.

   B. **Correct:** The Lock:Deadlock event class is produced when an attempt to acquire a lock is canceled because the attempt was part of a deadlock and was chosen as the deadlock victim.

   C. **Incorrect:** There is no Process Event in SQL Server Profiler.

   D. **Incorrect:** There is no Chain Event in SQL Server Profiler.

Lesson 3

1. **Correct Answer: C**

   A. **Incorrect:** The view returns information about all the waits encountered by threads that executed. You can use this aggregated view to diagnose performance issues with SQL Server and with specific queries and batches.

   B. **Incorrect:** The sys.dm_exec_sessions view gives information about each connection to the instance but does not contain information about any actively running requests.

C. **Correct:** The blocking_session_id column lists the SPID that is blocking the connection.

D. **Incorrect:** Although the sys.dm_os_waiting_tasks view lists processes that are waiting on a resource to become available, you cannot locate blocked processes by using this view.

2. **Correct Answer: D**

A. **Incorrect:** sys.dm_db_missing_index_columns returns information about database table columns that are missing an index.

B. **Incorrect:** sys.dm_db_missing_index_groups returns information about what missing indexes are contained in a specific missing index group.

C. **Incorrect:** sys.dm_db_missing_index_group_stats returns summary information about groups of missing indexes,

D. **Correct:** sys.dm_db_missing_index_details returns detailed information about missing indexes, including the table name.

Lesson 4

1. **Correct Answer: B**

A. **Incorrect:** The policy-based management feature is used to check rules against instances, not to gather space and performance information.

B. **Correct:** The Performance Data Warehouse in SQL Server 2012 enables you to configure data collection quickly against SQL Server instances to consolidate all the capacity management and performance baseline analysis.

C. **Incorrect:** Although you could rewrite all the code by using SSIS packages, it requires more effort than using the built-in capabilities of the Performance Data Warehouse.

D. **Incorrect:** System Center Operations Manager 2007 cannot capture performance data to evaluate against a baseline.

2. **Correct Answer: B**

A. **Incorrect:** The mdw_admim role provides full access to the management data warehouse.

B. **Correct:** The mdw_reader role provides read access, which is required by users accessing reports.

C. **Incorrect:** The dc_operator data collector role provides read and update access to configurations.

D. **Incorrect:** The dc_proxy data collector role provides read access to configurations.

3. **Correct Answers: A and D**

A. **Correct:** The Server Activity History report includes CPU, memory, disk, and network I/O.

B. **Incorrect:** The Disk Usage Summary report includes trends and details of disk and file usage.

C. **Incorrect:** The Query Statistics History report includes the most expensive queries ranked by CPU, duration, reads, and writes.

D. **Correct:** The Server Activity History report includes SQL Server waits and SQL Server activity.

Lesson 5

1. **Correct Answers: A and B**

   A. **Correct:** Processor: % Privileged Time corresponds to the percentage of time the processor spends on execution of Microsoft Windows kernel commands, such as processing SQL Server I/O requests. If this counter is consistently high when the Physical Disk counters are high, consider installing a faster or more efficient disk subsystem.

   B. **Correct:** Processor: % User Time corresponds to the percentage of time that the processor spends on executing user processes such as SQL Server.

   C. **Incorrect:** The Buffer Manager object provides counters to monitor how SQL Server uses the buffer pool. Page Reads/sec measures the number of physical database page reads that are issued per second.

   D. **Incorrect:** The Buffer Manager object provides counters to monitor how SQL Server uses the buffer pool. Page Writes/sec measures the number of physical database page writes that are issued per second.

2. **Correct Answer: A**

   A. **Correct:** PhysicalDisk: % Disk Time counter monitors the percentage of time that the disk is busy with read/write activity.

   B. **Incorrect:** Page writes/sec indicates the number of physical database page writes that are issued per second.

   C. **Incorrect:** Procedure cache pages Number of pages used to store compiled queries.

   D. **Incorrect:** LogicalDisk|PhysicalDisk\% Idle Time reports the percentage of time that the disk system was not processing requests and no work was queued.

3. **Correct Answer: D**

   A. **Incorrect:** Increasing memory typically will not help reduce the number of threads waiting for processor time.

   B. **Incorrect:** Increasing IOPS or storage throughput typically will not help reduce the number of threads waiting for processor time.

   C. **Incorrect:** Disabling Hyper-Threading typically will not help reduce the number of threads waiting for processor time.

   D. **Correct:** Processor Queue Length corresponds to the number of threads waiting for processor time. A processor bottleneck develops when threads of a process require more processor cycles than are available. If more than a few processes attempt to use the processor's time, you might need to install a faster processor. Alternatively, if you have a multiprocessor system, you could add a processor.

Case Scenario 1

1. SQL Server Profiler can be used to help identify the slow query or queries executed by the report.

2. When SQL Server processes a query, the optimizer keeps a record of the indexes it attempts to use to satisfy the query. If these indexes are not found, SQL Server creates a record of the missing index. This information can be viewed by using the sys.dm_db_missing_index_details DMV.

Case Scenario 2

1. Use the following statement to create the server audit:

```
CREATE SERVER AUDIT PayrollAudit
TO APPLICATION_LOG
WITH (QUEUE_DELAY = 0, ON_FAILURE = SHUTDOWN);
    GO
```

2. Use the following statement to start the server audit:

```
ALTER SERVER AUDIT PayrollAudit
WITH
    (
            STATE = ON
    )
    GO
```

3. Use the following command to audit any updates to the employees table:

```
CREATE DATABASE AUDIT SPECIFICATION EmployeeUpdateAudit
FOR SERVER AUDIT PayrollAudit
ADD
    (
        UPDATE
        ON          HumanResources.Employees
```

```
        BY PUBLIC
   )
WITH

   (
        STATE = ON
   )
GO
```

CHAPTER 10

Indexes and Concurrency

Exam objectives in this chapter:

- Implement and maintain indexes.
- Identify and resolve concurrency problems.

As a database administrator, much of your day-to-day work involves making sure your database is performing well and can accommodate the desired number of concurrent users. In this chapter, you examine the concepts of indexes and how they can help solve performance issues. You also examine factors that affect concurrency.

Lessons in this chapter:

Before You Begin

To complete the practice exercises in this chapter, you must have:

- Microsoft SQL Server 2012 Enterprise edition installed.
- The AdventureWorks2012 database installed within the instance.
- The AdventureWorksDW2012 database installed within the instance.

Lesson 1: Implementing and Maintaining Indexes

This lesson introduces you to the various index types, their characteristics, and their suggested usage. By selecting appropriate indexes, you can have dramatic impact on the performance of a database. Although indexing is not the only method of solving performance issues, it is often one of the first approaches the database administrator considers.

> **After this lesson, you will be able to:**
> - Understand different index types and index structures.
> - Design indexes for efficient data retrieval.
> - Understand indexing internals to include statistics.
> - Create and modify indexes.
> - Determine appropriate strategies for removing fragmentation.
> - Create maintenance plans for indexes and statistics.
>
> **Estimated lesson time: 90 minutes**

Understanding the Anatomy of a Balanced Tree (B-Tree)

Prior to discussing the details of the various index types, you must understand the concept of a balanced tree data structure. The start of the tree is known as the root node. Beneath the root node are *1..n* intermediate-level pages. Each intermediate-level page can have additional intermediate-level pages. The last level comprises the leaf-level pages. You can see this structure in Figure 10-1.

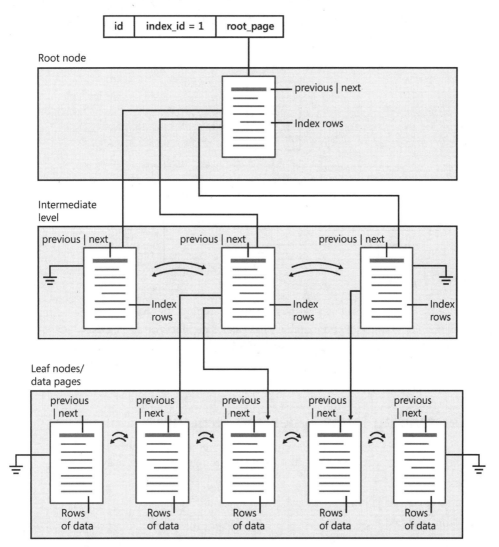

FIGURE 10-1 Balanced tree (B-Tree)

If the tree is not balanced, the storage engine might have to access six levels to reach one piece of data but only three to reach another piece of data. However, due to the structure of the B-Tree, the Query Optimizer knows at most how many page accesses are needed to reach a leaf page. When a page is full, it must be split to maintain this balanced condition.

A *heap* is an unorganized collection of data. As data is presented for storage, it is appended to the last data page, as shown in Figure 10-2. Because of this lack of organization, heaps perform poorly for data retrieval because every leaf page must be scanned to look for rows that satisfy the query predicates. However, heaps are very efficient for bulk loading data. Often when loading a table with millions of rows of data, all indexes are removed, data is loaded at maximum speed, and then indexes are reapplied.

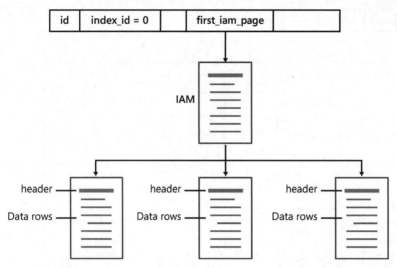

| id | index_id = 0 | | first_iam_page | |

FIGURE 10-2 Heap structure

Both *clustered* indexes and *non-clustered indexes* can be partitioned to provide better performance. For example, if your database has sales data that is organized by sales year, you can partition the index by sales year. For each partition, there is a separate B-Tree, so if you are interested in data only for 2010, you would have a considerably smaller B-Tree to navigate than you would if 15 years of data were all in one B-Tree.

Understanding Index Types and Structures

This section examines each of the different index types and discusses their primary characteristics, purposes, and restrictions. The following are the index types available in SQL Server 2012:

- Clustered
- Non-clustered
- Covering
- Filtered
- Primary XML
- Secondary XML {Path, Property, Value}
- Spatial
- Full-text
- Columnstore

Clustered Indexes

A clustered index is a structure in which the actual table data resides in the leaf-level pages of the index. The data is physically sorted in the order of the clustering key. To read the data for a row, the storage engine navigates the tree structure until it reaches the appropriate leaf-level page, and it can then retrieve the requested data.

The *clustered index key* (CIK) is the row identifier for the table data. This key is also added to any non-clustered indexes created on the table. It is therefore preferred and recommended to have a key with the following characteristics to reduce overhead:

- **Unique** Either naturally or by adding Uniqueifier for duplicates
- **Narrow** The smaller number of bytes, the better
- **Static** No updates on the CIK; updates to the clustered and non-clustered indexes because CIK is part of their non-clustered index structures

> **IMPORTANT** **UNIQUEIFIER**
>
> This term describes a clustered index that has duplicate rows based on the key column values. A clustered index must be unique. To make those rows unique, SQL Server adds a 4-byte internal integer to any duplicate values.

Non-Clustered Indexes

A non-clustered index contains only keys and no actual data. (You examine a variation of this later, in the "Covering Indexes" section of this chapter.) In addition to the key columns, SQL Server stores the clustering key for that row in the table. This enables the storage engine to use a non-clustered index to reduce the number of rows returned and then use the clustering key to go to the clustered index to retrieve the data requested.

> **NOTE** **INDEX LIMITATIONS**
>
> The definition of an index key (both clustered and non-clustered) can contain a maximum of 16 key columns and be a maximum of 900 bytes total in length.

Non-clustered indexes can be applied to either heaps or clustered tables. The only difference is in how rows are identified. For non-clustered indexes based on a clustered table, the non-clustered index contains the clustered index key to locate the rows in the base table. For heaps, the non-clustered index uses a row identifier (RID) in place of the clustered index key.

Covering Indexes

A non-clustered index that contains all the information needed to satisfy a query is known as a *covering index*. Covering indexes are a key strategy for improving query performance. The concept of included columns was introduced in SQL Server 2005. They enable the database administrator to add information to the non-clustered index data pages and avoid having to look up the row in the clustered index. Just as with any optimization, you must decide whether included columns are worth the additional maintenance that must occur when data in the table is modified.

Filtered Indexes

Introduced in SQL Server 2008, *filtered indexes* can be used to reduce the size of a B-Tree. Consider a case in which you have a table of statuses. At any time, less than 5 percent of the statuses are pending. To process pending requests, you often want to select only those rows in which the status is pending. By adding a filtered index (essentially an index with a WHERE clause), you can once again limit the amount of data in the B-Tree. Rather than scanning millions of rows to search for pending statuses, you have to navigate only the filtered index to find those rows.

Filtered indexes are also useful in conjunction with another feature, known as *sparse columns*. In the case of sparse columns, you might have a table with 1,500 columns, but for each row, only 5 percent of the columns contain data. By creating a filtered index and specifying that the WHERE column IS NOT NULL, you create a B-Tree with only those rows that contain data.

Primary XML and Secondary XML Indexes

The *XML data type* was introduced in SQL Server 2005 and enables the storage of XML documents or fragments in a table column. To provide reasonable performance when querying the XML data, you must create one or more XML indexes. If XML indexes are not created, the entire XML document must be loaded into an XML Document Object Model (DOM) and searched. By the proper application of XML indexes, you can avoid the overhead of creating an XML DOM for each row you examine. The four types of XML indexes and the data access patterns they support are discussed later in this lesson.

Spatial Indexes

The *GEOGRAPHY* data type and *GEOMETRY data type* were introduced in SQL Server 2005 and represent coordinate-type data. A specialized index type known as a *spatial index* is important for good performance when querying spatial data. The process of creating spatial indexes is examined later in this lesson.

Full-Text Indexes

Full-text indexes enable the efficient searching of text data, often by using words that occur near each other in the text, by specifying fuzzy search criteria, or even by requesting a word inflectionally generated from another word. For example, if you asked for "drive," you would be returned "drives," "drove," "driving," and "driven."

Columnstore Indexes

A new index type added in SQL Server 2012 is the *columnstore index*. This index does not use the B-Tree structure but rather uses a column-oriented storage that is very efficient for data warehouse operations.

Quick Check

- Which index type stores the actual table data at the leaf-level data page?

Quick Check Answer

- A clustered index stores the actual data at the leaf-level data page.

Designing Indexes for Efficient Retrieval

When you are designing your indexes, there are additional considerations for improving performance. These considerations apply to both clustered and non-clustered indexes.

When constructing multicolumn indexes, always list equality columns before you list inequality columns. *Equality columns* are those columns that are listed in a WHERE clause with an equals sign (=). *Inequality columns* might be listed as greater than (>) or BETWEEN.

When choosing the order of equality columns, always list the most selective column first. After listing all equality columns, continue by listing inequality columns, listing the most selective first.

If you are joining to another table, you should index the column that is used to join to the other table. This provides very efficient filtering.

Clustered Indexes

There are three cases in which a clustered index is the most efficient index for retrieving data:

- Queries that return a large percentage of the columns in the table
- Queries that return a single row based on the clustered index key
- Queries that return range-based data

When inserting data, if the clustered index key is a sequentially increasing value, inserts are appended to the last data page. This reduces page splits. Splitting pages is a resource-intensive operation that can degrade performance.

Non-Clustered Indexes

There are two cases in which a non-clustered index is the most efficient index for retrieving data:

- Queries that return few rows
- Queries that can be covered by the index

Covering Indexes

To create efficient covering indexes, consider using INCLUDE columns for columns in the SELECT list that are not already part of the key columns.

Filtered Indexes

There are two cases in which a filtered index is the most efficient index for retrieving data:

- When combined with sparse columns to locate specific non-null rows
- When queries that are a small subset of the rows are selected often

Primary XML and Secondary XML Indexes

When XML data is stored in a column with the XML data type, access to the individual nodes within an XML document can be slow. The XML data type columns can't be indexed by using the non-clustered index type. XML indexes are specifically designed for indexing this complex data type.

The first XML index must be a primary XML index type. The primary XML index builds a nodes table. For each element in the XML document, there will be one row in the nodes table. Therefore, if you have many rows, each of which contains an XML document with many nodes, the size of the XML index can be quite large. This can be seen in the definition of the XML index shown in Table 10-1.

TABLE 10-1 Primary XML Index Nodes Table

Column Name	Column Description	Data Type
Id	node identifier in ordpath format	varbinary(900)
Nid	node name (tokenized)	int
Tagname	tag name	nvarchar(4000)
Taguri	tag uri	nvarchar(4000)
Tid	node data type (tokenized)	Int
value	first portion of the node value	sql_variant
Lvalue	long node value (pointer)	nvarchar(max)

Hid	path (tokenized)	varchar(900)
Xsinil	is it NULL (xsi:nil)	Bit
xsitype	does it use xsi:type	Bit
pk1	primary key of the base table	int

In addition to the primary XML index, there are three secondary XML index types:

- The PATH secondary XML index consists of a regular non-clustered index on the hid and value columns. This index supports operations such as the .exist() method of the XML data type.

- The PROPERTY secondary XML index consists of a regular non-clustered index on the pk1, hid, and value columns. This index is useful for searching for nodes that have particular values.

- The VALUE secondary XML index consists of a regular non-clustered index on the value and hid columns. This is essentially the reverse of the PATH index and is most useful if you are searching for descendent nodes for a given PATH.

Full-Text Indexes and Semantic Searches

SQL Server provides the functionality to create special indexes on char, varchar, nchar, nvarchar, text, ntext, image, xml, varbinary, and varbinary(max) data types. These are not B-Tree style indexes; rather, they are token-based functional indexes that store information about significant words, where they exist within text within a column or table in the database.

Only one full-text index is allowed per table, and it contains all the tokens for all columns that were indexed for that table. This enables you to search for words in one column that have significant words in other columns in an efficient manner. Full-text search also enables you to perform inflectional searching. Searching for the word "Runtime" would also return rows that contained "run-time," "run-time's," "run-times," "run-times'," and so on. This can be a very powerful feature and one that would be impossible to implement by using traditional T-SQL constructs.

Full-text indexes use IFilters to perform the internal word breaking, stemmer, and other grammatical work. Some default IFilters are installed (XML, HTML, and Office 2007), and additional IFilters can be installed manually, such as those for Office 2010 and Adobe products.

MORE INFO **FULL-TEXT SEARCH VS. SEMANTIC SEARCH**

You can learn more about semantic search at *http://msdn.microsoft.com/en-us/library /gg492075.aspx*. System catalog views for full-text and semantic search can be found at *http://msdn.microsoft.com/en-us/library/cc280702.aspx*.

Columnstore Indexes

SQL Server 2012 introduces a non-B-Tree type index: columnstore. The columnstore index is based on the VertiPaq engine technology that is used by PowerPivot. The columnstore indexes have been added to provide performance improvements for the typical data warehouse–type queries that perform aggregations over large data sets. Those queries often take minutes or hours to process by using traditional indexes. Online analytical processing (OLAP) cubes are commonly used to provide the performance levels required by businesses.

Data warehouse–type queries often use only a few of a table's columns for each query. Performance can be improved by using column-based index structures instead of the row-based indexes in these scenarios.

Because columnstore indexes organize data by columns rather than by rows, SQL Server can optimize storage by compressing repeating data values. This higher level of compression, which is approximately double the compression rate of PAGE compression, makes this index type a very effective indexing tool.

The following T-SQL sample is a typical example of a data warehouse query that can benefit from the addition of a columnstore index on its fact table. Often, these data warehouse queries contain multiple aggregations (AVG and SUM), GROUP BY for multiple columns, and sorting by using the ORDER BY clause.

T-SQL

```
USE [AdventureWorksDW2012]
GO
SET STATISTICS TIME ON

SELECT Dp.EnglishProductName, Dd.WeekNumberOfYear, Dd.CalendarYear,
AVG(fpi.UnitCost), SUM(fpi.UnitsOut)
FROM    dbo.FactProductInventory as fpi
    INNER JOIN dbo.DimProduct as Dp  ON   fpi.ProductKey = dp.ProductKey
    INNER JOIN dbo.DimDate       as Dd ON    fpi.DateKey = Dd.DateKey
    WHERE Dd.CalendarYear >= 2000
    GROUP BY Dp.EnglishProductName, Dd.WeekNumberOfYear, Dd.CalendarYear
    ORDER BY Dp.EnglishProductName, Dd.CalendarYear, Dd.WeekNumberOfYear

SET STATISTICS TIME OFF
```

Take a note of the time taken (Messages tab); it will look something like this:

```
(93744 row(s) affected)
SQL Server Execution Times:
   CPU time = 5870 ms,  elapsed time = 4525 ms.
```

The following script adds to the sample database AdventureWorksDW2012 the following columnstore index. This further demonstrates the performance benefits the columnstore index can provide:

T-SQL

```
USE [AdventureWorksDW2012]
GO
```

```
CREATE NONCLUSTERED COLUMNSTORE INDEX [IX_CS_FactProductInventory]
ON dbo.FactProductInventory
(ProductKey, DateKey, UnitCost, UnitsIn, UnitsOut, UnitsBalance)
GO
```

After adding the columnstore index and rerunning the same query, the execution statistics are significantly faster:

```
(93744 row(s) affected)
SQL Server Execution Times:
  CPU time = 1015 ms,  elapsed time = 1730 ms.
```

By examining the query plan shown in Figure 10-3, you see that it used a columnstore index scan in batch mode. It can also run in row mode; however, this is slower and reduces many of the performance benefits the columnstore index brings.

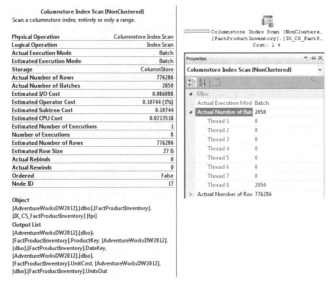

FIGURE 10-3 A columnstore index scan run in batch mode

Although this shows as a parallel operation, this example uses only one thread to execute 2,050 batches. Similar queries against a larger dataset would use multiple threads. A columnstore index is segmented into approximately 1 million rows, internal metadata exists to track the minimum and maximum value for the segments, and segment elimination is also used when necessary.

> **NOTE COLUMNSTORE INDEX LIMITATIONS**
>
> Columnstore indexes have limitations. Many of the initial limitations might be removed in subsequent releases. Currently:
>
> - The following data types are not permitted in a columnstore index:
>
>   text, ntext, image, varchar(max), nvarchar(max), rowversion, binary, varbinary, sql_variant, uniqueidentifier, spatial, xml,

```
timestamp, hierarchyid, datetimeoffset (scale > 2), decimal
(precision > 18), numeric (precision > 18)
```

- Updating the base table when a columnstore index is present is not permitted. If you must load data into a table with a columnstore index, you must design an appropriate data-loading strategy. There are three strategies to consider, but as the columnstore index is more widely used, newer strategies are likely to appear:

  - Disabling the columnstore index, performing the data load in the base table, and then rebuilding the columnstore index is one of the most common strategies in use today.

  - Loading new data into a table and then using partition switching to introduce the new data into the base table can be effective.

  - If the majority of the data is static, one interesting strategy is to write your query by using the UNION ALL statement to combine your static, columnstore-indexed data with an active data set. Although not as optimal as a full columnstore index, this can be useful when the active data is a small percentage of the overall data. Then, during a maintenance window, the columnstore index can be dropped and re-created across the entire dataset.

Understanding Statistics

 Statistics are objects in the database that contain statistical information about how the values in a column are distributed. The query optimizer uses this statistical information to determine the cardinality of the rows. *Cardinality* refers to the number of rows that exist for a given value.

For example, in a table that contains Sales Order Header information, the sales order number would have a cardinality of 1. This tells the optimizer that this column is highly selective and would limit the number of rows returned for the query. As a result, the query optimizer would choose an Index Seek operator instead of an Index Scan operator. When you create an index, SQL Server creates a histogram of the distribution of values in the leading column of the index. When the combination of the leading and second columns in an index makes that column very selective, manually creating multicolumn statistics can be useful. However, it is a best practice to allow SQL Server to autocreate and autoupdate these statistical objects. Only in rare cases should you consider turning off this feature and manually updating the statistics.

The following are automatic options that can be turned ON or OFF for each database:

- **AUTO_UPDATE_STATISTICS** Existing statistics that are out of date are updated automatically as the query optimization needs them when this setting is on. This can lead to compile locks being taken and recompilation of execution plans occurring.

- **AUTO_UPDATE_STATISTICS_ASYNC** Query execution will not be blocked by the updating of the statistics. The statistics will be updated by a background thread and will be available the next time the optimizer needs them.

- **AUTO_CREATE_STATISTICS** Missing statistics that are required during the query optimization phase are automatically created as needed when this setting is on. To determine whether SQL Server is automatically creating statistics on your behalf, run the following query:

T-SQL

```
-- Note set the context to your database as each database
-- Maintains its own sys.stats system table
USE [AdventureWorksDW2012]
GO

SELECT OBJECT_NAME(object_id),name, auto_created
FROM sys.stats
WHERE auto_created = 1
```

> *NOTE* **AN INTERESTING FACT**
>
> An interesting historical side note: When you run the preceding query, you will notice that all the AUTOCREATE statistics begin with the _WA_Sys_ prefix. This is a naming convention that dates back to the code base that was originally ported from Sybase. Contrary to common opinion, the WA does not refer to Washington (home of SQL Server) but rather to Waterloo, Canada, where the Sybase product was developed.

Statistics can be either a sampling of the rows or full (that is, all rows), based on how they were created or updated and the number of rows in the table. Automatic statistics updates occur when any of the following thresholds are reached:

- A table having zero rows has one or more rows added.
- A table having fewer than 500 rows has more than 500 rows added.
- A table having more than 500 rows has more than 500 rows added, and the accumulated row modification is more than 20 percent of the total number of rows in the table.

This can be problematic for temporary tables created in tempdb. By definition, these are always empty and can cause multiple statement recompilations because they have rows added, updated, and deleted.

SQL Server 2012 now allows statistics to be refreshed or updated on snapshots and readable secondaries through the creation of temporary statistic objects placed in tempdb on the secondary server.

Using Index Internals

There are several specific dynamic management views (DMVs) that can be used to retrieve information about indexes. One such DMV is sys.dm_db_index_physical_stats.

The type of information that is available includes:

- Record and page counts.
- Breakdowns for each of the three allocation unit types: IN_ROW_DATA, ROW_OVERFLOW_DATA, and LOB_DATA.

- Fragmentation levels for each allocation unit, index depths, and levels.
- Available free space.
- Compression levels.
- Forwarded records.

Different parameters ('SAMPLED'; 'LIMITED'; and 'DETAILED') can be supplied to sys.dm _db_index_physical_stats. The 'SAMPLED' parameter examines 1 percent of the data pages. If the index or heap has fewer than 10,000 pages, SQL Server automatically converts the 'SAMPLED' parameter to the 'DETAILED' option. The 'LIMITED' parameter is the fastest mode because it scans the non-leaf-level pages only. The 'DETAILED' parameter scans all pages and all statistics, which can be a resource-intensive operation.

The following example interrogates the index statistics and returns details on the index structures:

T-SQL

```
DECLARE @db_id SMALLINT, @object_id INT;
SET @db_id      = DB_ID(N'AdventureWorks2012');
SET @object_id  = OBJECT_ID(N'AdventureWorks2012.Person.Person');

SELECT
    index_id, index_type_desc, alloc_unit_type_desc,
    index_level, index_depth,
    record_count, forwarded_record_count,
    page_count, compressed_page_count,
    avg_page_space_used_in_percent, avg_fragmentation_in_percent
FROM sys.dm_db_index_physical_stats
    (@db_id, @object_id, NULL, NULL , 'Detailed');
```

Moving Row-Overflow Data

Variable-length data has a maximum limit of 8,060 bytes. If this limit is surpassed, some data must be moved off row. The data engine identifies the column with the largest width, moves that column in a ROW_OVERFLOW_DATA allocation unit, and then places a 24-byte pointer on the original page from which the data was moved. This is a dynamic process, and data can move off row and back on row as data is updated.

Creating and Modifying Indexes

In SQL Server Management Studio (SSMS), you create or modify indexes by using the following procedure:

1. Open the Object Explorer pane.
2. Expand the Databases node.
3. Select the database.
4. Select the table.

5. Expand and right-click the index folder for the New Index menu (see Figure 10-4) and then select the index type you want to create.

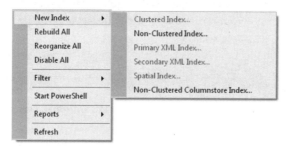

FIGURE 10-4 Index menu (Object Explorer)

The Index Wizard opens. The menu choices depend on what is available for the selected object and existing requirements; for example, Secondary XML Index is not available until a primary XML index exists.

Alternatively, by right-clicking the desired table and choosing Design, the Table Designer displays menu options for creating and modifying indexes, as shown in Figure 10-5.

FIGURE 10-5 Table Designer menu

You can also create and modify indexes by scripting T-SQL statements. T-SQL provides a richer set of options, some of which cannot be specified through the GUI versions. Several examples in the following T-SQL sample provide the general syntax of the CREATE INDEX statement:

T-SQL

```
USE AdventureWorks2012
GO
CREATE NONCLUSTERED INDEX IX_SalesPerson_SalesQuota_SalesYTD
    ON Sales.SalesPerson (SalesQuota, SalesYTD);
GO
CREATE CLUSTERED INDEX IX_PartTab2Col1
ON PartitionTable1 (Col1)
WITH (DATA_COMPRESSION = PAGE ON PARTITIONS(1),
    DATA_COMPRESSION = ROW ON PARTITIONS (2 TO 4 ) ) ;
GO
```

Choosing Fill Factors

When creating an index, one of the optional clauses for the CREATE statement is the FILLFACTOR. This determines how much free space will be left on the leaf data pages. By default, SQL Server completely fills leaf pages of an index. (This corresponds to the default FILLFACTOR of 0.)

When considering a non-default fill factor, it is crucial for the database administrator to understand the data access patterns of a given table. For example, if your clustered index key is an IDENTITY column (that is, always increasing), using a fill factor other than the default will leave unused space on the leaf-level pages of the index because new entries are always written to the last page. However, if your clustered index key is a random value, choosing a non-default fill factor might make sense to limit page splits (which will affect performance). This is further compounded by the frequency with which new rows are inserted. When you have chosen a non-default fill factor, if the frequency of INSERTs is low, the overhead of having partially filled pages (requiring more disk I/O) can have a more detrimental effect than the infrequent page splits.

To rebuild an index with a specified fill factor, use the ALTER INDEX REBUILD statement with argument FILLFACTOR = <Value>, as shown in the following example:

T-SQL

```
USE [AdventureWorks2012]
GO

ALTER INDEX ALL ON [Production].[Product] REBUILD
WITH (FILLFACTOR = 80);
GO
```

Determining Fragmentation

Fragmentation is defined as index pages in which the logical ordering, based on the key value, does not match the physical ordering within the data file. When an index is first created, it is free from fragmentation. Over time, as data is modified, the index can become fragmented.

It is relatively easy to determine which indexes have fragmentation. This information is available in the sys.dm_db_index_physical_stats DMV, which tracks the current levels of fragmentation for indexes. You can then take appropriate action to reduce fragmentation by reorganizing or rebuilding an index that meets your organization's standards for fragmentation.

The following script provides details of the fragmentation levels that exist in a database. Decisions about maintenance operations are often based on the results. Figure 10-6 shows a typical results page with fragmentation levels.

T-SQL

```
USE [AdventureWorks2012]
GO
SELECT  SCHEMA_NAME(so.schema_id)              AS [SchemaName],
        OBJECT_NAME(idx.OBJECT_ID)             AS [TableName],
        idx.name                               AS [IndexName],
        idxstats.index_type_desc               AS [Index_Type_Desc],
        CAST(idxstats.avg_fragmentation_in_percent
        AS decimal(5,2))                       AS [Frag_Pct],
        idxstats.fragment_count,
        idxstats.page_count,
        idx.fill_factor
FROM    sys.dm_db_index_physical_stats
        (DB_ID(), NULL, NULL, NULL, 'DETAILED') idxstats
INNER JOIN sys.indexes idx
        ON idx.OBJECT_ID = idxstats.OBJECT_ID
        AND  idx.index_id = idxstats.index_id
INNER JOIN  sys.objects so
        ON so.object_id = idx.object_id
WHERE idxstats.avg_fragmentation_in_percent > 20
ORDER BY idxstats.avg_fragmentation_in_percent DESC
```

	SchemaName	TableName	IndexName	Index_Type_Desc	Frag_Pct
1	Production	TransactionHistoryArchive	PK_TransactionHistoryArchive_TransactionID	CLUSTERED INDEX	100.00
2	Person	Person	PK_Person_BusinessEntityID	CLUSTERED INDEX	87.50
3	Sales	SalesOrderDetail	PK_SalesOrderDetail_SalesOrderID_SalesOrderDetailID	CLUSTERED INDEX	85.71
4	dbo	DatabaseLog	PK_DatabaseLog_DatabaseLogID	NONCLUSTERED INDEX	75.00
5	Production	Product	AK_Product_Name	NONCLUSTERED INDEX	75.00
6	Production	ProductCostHistory	PK_ProductCostHistory_ProductID_StartDate	CLUSTERED INDEX	66.67
7	Production	ProductDescription	AK_ProductDescription_rowguid	NONCLUSTERED INDEX	66.67
8	Production	ProductListPriceHistory	PK_ProductListPriceHistory_ProductID_StartDate	CLUSTERED INDEX	66.67
9	Sales	SpecialOfferProduct	PK_SpecialOfferProduct_SpecialOfferID_ProductID	CLUSTERED INDEX	66.67
10	Sales	Store	AK_Store_rowguid	NONCLUSTERED INDEX	66.67
11	Production	TransactionHistory	PK_TransactionHistory_TransactionID	CLUSTERED INDEX	66.67
12	Sales	SalesOrderDetail	AK_SalesOrderDetail_rowguid	NONCLUSTERED INDEX	66.67
13	HumanResources	Employee	AK_Employee_LoginID	NONCLUSTERED INDEX	66.67
14	Person	BusinessEntityContact	IX_BusinessEntityContact_PersonID	NONCLUSTERED INDEX	66.67
15	Person	BusinessEntityContact	IX_BusinessEntityContact_ContactTypeID	NONCLUSTERED INDEX	66.67
16	Production	ProductReview	IX_ProductReview_ProductID_Name	NONCLUSTERED INDEX	66.67
17	Production	WorkOrderRouting	PK_WorkOrderRouting_WorkOrderID_ProductID_Operat...	CLUSTERED INDEX	60.00
18	Person	Person	XMLVALUE_Person_Demographics	XML INDEX	57.14

FIGURE 10-6 Fragmentation levels

Some industry guidelines indicate that an index should be rebuilt when fragmentation levels are above 30 percent. For levels between 10 percent and 30 percent, the guidelines suggest running a less intensive reorganize process. For levels below 10 percent, you can ignore the index until it exceeds the 10 percent fragmented level. These types of recommendations are generic and should be viewed purely for what they are: guidelines. Establish the appropriate thresholds that make sense for your environments and data usage patterns.

Small indexes that have low page counts can easily return high fragmentation values due to their low page counts. These are often small enough not to be adversely affected by the fragmentation that might exist and can often be ignored in your index maintenance routines until they become larger.

Removing Index Fragmentation

Index fragmentation can be reduced by performing a rebuild or a reorganize operation. Each of these operations is an option of the ALTER INDEX statement. When deciding whether to use REBUILD or REORGANIZE, consider the following factors:

- **Fragmentation levels**
  - By using the T-SQL script shown in the preceding "Determining Fragmentation" section, determine the level of fragmentation within the object. Refer to the avg_fragmentation_in_percent column in the output from the sys.dm_db_index _physical_stats DMV.
  - REORGANIZE is suited to tackle light-to-moderate fragmentation levels; these are generally values below 20 percent to 30 percent. However, this threshold must be based on your data access patterns, and this operation should be performed only after determining that fragmentation is degrading performance. In some cases, it is appropriate not to defragment an index. REORGANIZE will not update the statistics histogram for the object. This operation is interruptible, and you can restart the process if it is interrupted.
  - REBUILD is more likely to be used when heavier fragmentation levels exist or when you have determined that out-of-order extents are limiting read-ahead operations. When rebuilding an index, sampled statistics are calculated. REBUILD is a fully transacted operation, and if you cancel the REBUILD, the transaction must be rolled back.

- **Online | Offline**
  - REORGANIZE is always online and doesn't hold any blocking locks.
  - REBUILD often requires long-term locks. This can affect concurrency levels and cause blocking during the process unless it is performed as an online rebuild. The next lesson discusses concurrency in detail.

- **Space available**
  - REORGANIZE requires 8 KB of free space in the database.
  - REBUILD builds a second copy of the index, so space is required to hold this copy. This might cause the database file to grow. If this is an online rebuild, the requirement applies to tempdb.

- **CPU usage**
  - REORGANIZE is single threaded only.
  - REBUILD can use parallel operations.

When SQL Server Enterprise edition is installed, you can perform online index rebuild operations. This is useful if your database is constantly in use by clients, and you need to rebuild indexes. Prior to SQL Server 2012, online index operations were not permitted if the indexes contained large object binary (LOB) data types such as image, text, ntext, varchar(max), nvarchar(max), and varbinary(max). In SQL Server 2012, the only two data types that are prohibited from online index rebuild operations are the XML and spatial data types.

> **NOTE PARALLEL INDEX REBUILD OPTIONS**
>
> Parallel index rebuild operations are available in SQL Server Enterprise, Developer, and Evaluation editions only.

Updating Statistics

If you have made the decision to not have SQL Server automatically update statistics for you, or you have special requirements for a specific table or index, you can update statistics manually. These statistics update operations can be scheduled by using maintenance plans or by executing T-SQL scripts.

To add a maintenance plan, complete the following steps:

1. In SSMS, expand the Instance node and then expand the Maintenance node.
2. Right-click the Maintenance Plan folder and select either New Maintenance Plan or, if you want to be guided through the process, Maintenance Plan Wizard.
3. Select New Maintenance Plan and then select Update Statistics Task, as shown in Figure 10-7.

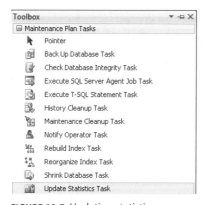

FIGURE 10-7 Updating statistics

4. Choose Databases, Objects, and select one of the following Update options, as shown in Figure 10-8:

- All Existing Statistics
- Column Statistics Only
- Index Statistics Only

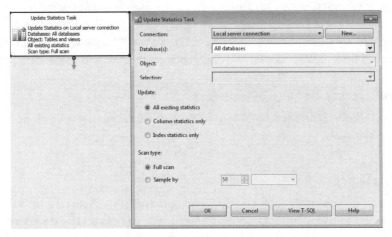

FIGURE 10-8 Maintenance plan Statistics Task dialog box

5. Select the Scan Type option: Full Scan or Sample By. If you select Sample By, enter a percentage amount or a number of rows.

> **NOTE VIEW T-SQL**
>
> Click the View T-SQL button (see Figure 10-8) to generate T-SQL commands quickly. These commands can be edited to suit your specific requirements.

These operations can also be run by using the relevant T-SQL command, as shown in the following sample. T-SQL allows more granular control of the operations to suit specific requirements.

T-SQL

```
/* Examples of the different options to run UPDATE STATISTICS with */

UPDATE STATISTICS schemaname.tablename WITH FULLSCAN
UPDATE STATISTICS schemaname.tablename WITH FULLSCAN, INDEX
UPDATE STATISTICS schemaname.tablename WITH FULLSCAN, COLUMNS
UPDATE STATISTICS schemaname.tablename WITH SAMPLE 10000 ROWS
UPDATE STATISTICS schemaname.tablename WITH SAMPLE 80 PERCENT
```

Tracking Missing Indexes

Each time the query optimizer compiles a T-SQL statement, SQL Server 2012 keeps track of the 500 latest indexes that the optimizer could have used to satisfy the query more efficiently, had they existed. This intelligence is found in three DMVs and one dynamic management function (DMF). Due to the nature of DMVs (that is, they are in-memory structures and are not persisted to disk), they are only accurate as of the last time the SQL Server service was restarted.

- **sys.dm_db_missing_index_columns** DMF (index_handle) lists the columns that would comprise the missing index, which can be used to build the CREATE INDEX statement.

- **sys.dm_db_missing_index_details** Lists details on the columns used for equality, inequality, and included columns.

- **sys.dm_db_missing_index_groups** An intermediate joining table (many-to-many relationship) for sys.dm_db_index_details and sys.dm_db_missing_group_stats tables.

- **sys.dm_db_missing_index_group_stats** Provides the metrics on a group of missing indexes.

The following example generates a listing of missing indexes that could be beneficial for T-SQL batches that have been submitted to the query optimizer since the last time the SQL Server service was restarted:

T-SQL

```
SELECT    user_seeks
      * avg_total_user_cost
      * (avg_user_impact * 0.01)    AS [Index_Useful]
      ,igs.last_user_seek
      ,id.statement                 AS [Statement]
      ,id.equality_columns
      ,id.inequality_columns
      ,id.included_columns
      ,igs.unique_compiles
      ,igs.user_seeks
      ,igs.avg_total_user_cost
      ,igs.avg_user_impact
FROM            sys.dm_db_missing_index_group_stats    AS igs
INNER JOIN      sys.dm_db_missing_index_groups         AS ig
    ON igs.group_handle = ig.index_group_handle
INNER JOIN      sys.dm_db_missing_index_details        AS id
    ON ig.index_handle = id.index_handle
ORDER BY [Index_Useful] DESC;
```

Reviewing Unused Indexes

Indexes on a table are beneficial only when used to speed up access to data. It is possible that indexes defined on a table will never be used to satisfy a request for data. Each time data is inserted, updated, or deleted, all indexes for that table must be maintained to reflect those changes. Having too many indexes that the query optimizer will not choose can lead to performance issues, which will show up during insert, update, and delete operations. Periodic reviews of indexes to find those indexes that have not been used can increase performance.

> **NOTE   DELETING VS. DISABLING INDEXES**
>
> Be careful about blindly removing indexes based on this technique. Because the DMVs store only information since the last time the SQL Server service was restarted, you might get false positives by using these DMVs. Rather than deleting the indexes, consider disabling them. When an index is disabled, its definition is still contained in the system tables, but the indexes themselves are not maintained. This enables you to reintroduce a disabled index easily, if you later determine it is required, by simply rebuilding that index.

You can query index-specific DMVs to find the indexes that are currently unused or have little usage in comparison to their overhead.

The following script provides a summary for the number of operations that have occurred on the index, indicating how useful the index is in comparison to the index overhead:

T-SQL

```
SELECT
        OBJECT_SCHEMA_NAME(i.OBJECT_ID)    AS [SchemaName],
        OBJECT_NAME(i.OBJECT_ID)           AS [ObjectName],
        i.name                             AS [IndexName],
        i.type_desc                        AS [IndexType],
        ius.user_updates                   AS [UserUpdates],
        ius.last_user_update               AS [LastUserUpdate]
        FROM sys.indexes i
INNER JOIN sys.dm_db_index_usage_stats ius
        ON ius.OBJECT_ID = i.OBJECT_ID AND ius.index_id = i.index_id
WHERE OBJECTPROPERTY(i.OBJECT_ID, 'IsUserTable') = 1 -- User Indexes
AND NOT(user_seeks > 0 OR user_scans > 0 or user_lookups > 0)
AND i.is_primary_key = 0
AND i.is_unique = 0
ORDER BY ius.user_updates DESC, SchemaName, ObjectName, IndexName
```

 Quick Check

- If an index contains a column with either a text or ntext data type, can you perform an online index rebuild?

Quick Check Answer

- Yes. In SQL Server 2012, only XML and spatial data types are excluded from online index rebuild operations.

In this practice, you create non-clustered indexes that can aid in improving the performance of queries.

EXERCISE 1   Create a Filtered Non-Clustered Index

In this exercise, execute the following code to create a new filtered non-clustered index with included columns to create a covering index in the AdventureWorks2012 database.

T-SQL

```
USE [AdventureWorks2012]
GO
SET ANSI_PADDING ON
GO
CREATE NONCLUSTERED INDEX [NC_Person_Address_City_spi_pc]
ON [Person].[Address] ([City] ASC)
INCLUDE ([StateProvinceID], [PostalCode])

WHERE [City] = 'Seattle'
ON [PRIMARY]
GO
```

EXERCISE 2   Examine Index Fragmentation

In this exercise, execute the following T-SQL code, examine the fragmentation reported, and defragment the indexes that show 100 percent fragmentation.

T-SQL

```
USE [AdventureWorks2012]
GO
SELECT  SCHEMA_NAME(so.schema_id)           AS [SchemaName],
        OBJECT_NAME(idx.OBJECT_ID)          AS [TableName],
        idx.name                            AS [IndexName],
        idxstats.index_type_desc            AS [Index_Type_Desc],
        CAST(idxstats.avg_fragmentation_in_percent
        AS decimal(5,2))                    AS [Frag_Pct],
        idxstats.fragment_count,
        idxstats.page_count,
        idx.fill_factor
FROM    sys.dm_db_index_physical_stats
        (DB_ID(), NULL, NULL, NULL, 'DETAILED') idxstats
INNER JOIN sys.indexes idx
        ON idx.OBJECT_ID = idxstats.OBJECT_ID
        AND  idx.index_id = idxstats.index_id
INNER JOIN  sys.objects so
        ON so.object_id = idx.object_id
WHERE idxstats.avg_fragmentation_in_percent > 20
ORDER BY idxstats.avg_fragmentation_in_percent DESC
```

EXERCISE 3 Update Statistics

In this exercise, update the statistics for the Person.Address table and sample all rows.

Lesson Summary

- Most SQL Server indexes are balanced tree (B-Tree) structures, with the exception of PRIMARY XML indexes and columnstore indexes.
- Clustered indexes organize the data in a table in the logical order of the clustering keys.
- A covering index can improve performance by containing all the data necessary to satisfy the query without requiring additional data access. Although clustered indexes are always covering indexes, they often are not the most efficient.
- The query optimizer requires indexes and statistics to create optimal execution plans.
- SQL Server automatically maintains statistics on your behalf; however, sometimes manually created or updated statistics can be beneficial.
- Although indexes can improve SELECT performance, having too many indexes to maintain can result in decreased performance of INSERT, UPDATE, and DELETE statements.

Lesson Review

Answer the following questions to test your knowledge of the information in this lesson. You can find the answers to these questions and explanations of why each answer choice is correct or incorrect in the "Answers" section at the end of this chapter.

1. Which index type organizes the data in the table in the logical order of the key?
   - **A.** XML index
   - **B.** Spatial index
   - **C.** Clustered index
   - **D.** Non-clustered index

2. What are the limitations for non-clustered indexes?
   - **A.** One index key and 900 bytes
   - **B.** 249 index keys and 8,060 bytes
   - **C.** 16 index keys and 900 bytes
   - **D.** No maximum on number of key columns and 900 bytes

3. What are two situations in which you should consider adding filtered indexes to a table?
   - **A.** When you want to support sparse columns
   - **B.** When a column contains many duplicate values
   - **C.** When you query often for a small subset of rows based on the value in a column
   - **D.** When you want to support XML queries

4. Which DMV should you examine to determine whether there is index fragmentation?

   A. sys.dm_db_index_physical_stats

   B. sys.dm_db_index_operational_stats

   C. sys.dm_db_missing_index_details

   D. sys.dm_db_index_usage_stats

5. When you examine a query execution plan, you notice that for a given operator the actual number of rows and estimated number of rows returned are very different. What should you do?

   A. Execute the sp_updatestats system stored procedure, specifying 20 for the value of the @resample parameter.

   B. Execute the UPDATE STATISTICS command on the table in question, specifying the WITH SAMPLE 20 PERCENT option.

   C. Execute the UPDATE STATISTICS command on the table in question, specifying the WITH FULLSCAN option.

   D. Execute the UPDATE STATISTICS command on the table in question, specifying the WITH NORECOMPUTE option.

Lesson 2: Identifying and Resolving Concurrency Problems

As a database administrator, one of your tasks is to ensure that your database is accessible by the required number of concurrent users. Many factors can affect the concurrency of a database application. In this lesson, you examine those factors and learn how to provide higher levels of concurrency in your database.

> **After this lesson, you will be able to:**
> - Understand transactions and transaction scope.
> - Understand how SQL Server manages locks.
> - Understand transaction isolation levels.
> - Diagnose deadlock and blocking resources.
> - Determine the causes of waits and perform other activity monitoring.
>
> **Estimated lesson time: 90 minutes**

Defining Transactions and Transaction Scope

 A *transaction* is a way to group, or batch, a series of updates to a data source so that either all updates succeed and are committed at once or (if any one of them fails) none are committed and the entire transaction is rolled back. To preserve the consistency of the data involved in the batch of updates, SQL Server holds locks on the rows that are being updated. The length of time that these locks are held is known as the *transaction scope*. One way to improve the concurrency of your database application is to ensure that transaction scopes are kept as short as possible, allowing SQL Server to release the locks it is holding and allowing other users to access the rows you were modifying. Transactions are one way to ensure the atomicity, consistency, isolation, and durability (ACID) properties of a database.

> **MORE INFO   ATOMICITY, CONSISTENCY, ISOLATION, DURABILITY (ACID)**
>
> You can learn more about atomicity, consistency, isolation, and durability (ACID) at *http://technet.microsoft.com/en-us/magazine/hh70281.aspx*.

Understanding SQL Server Lock Management

SQL Server uses a dynamic, cooperative locking mechanism to protect the consistency of the data in the database. The many objects that SQL Server can lock are listed in Table 10-2.

TABLE 10-2 Objects That SQL Server Can Lock

Lock	What is being locked
RID	The row identifier within a heap
KEY	A key or range of keys in an index
PAGE	A full 8-KB page
EXTENT	An extent that is a block of eight pages
HoBT	A heap or B-Tree. Either an entire index or, if a heap, all data pages
TABLE	The entire table, including all data and indexes
FILE	A database file
APPLICATION	Defined by the application by using sp_getapplock
METADATA	Any system metadata
ALLOCATION UNIT	Internal unit used for storage of data
DATABASE	The entire database, often just a shared lock

SQL Server will *lock* the minimum number of resources needed to accomplish its goal; this is known as *multi-granular locking*. Because of this scheme, SQL Server must not only take the locks that it requires (such as a lock on one row of one page), but it must also announce its intent to higher levels. An example should help make this clear. Two transactions, T1 and T2, are each trying to modify different rows. To modify a row, SQL Server must take exclusive locks on the row it intends to modify. (Lock modes are discussed later in the lesson.) If SQL Server took only the exclusive lock for T1 on R1, and then T2 asked for a lock on R2, SQL Server would have to examine the tree structure to determine whether that row could be locked. This would be very costly, so SQL Server announces its intent to higher levels in the tree by placing *intent locks* above the row and navigating up the tree to the root. As you can see in Figure 10-9, by examining the intent locks SQL Server can quickly determine that there is an intent-exclusive lock on the table, but T1's row is in a separate part of the tree, so SQL Server can now acquire the lock that T2 requires.

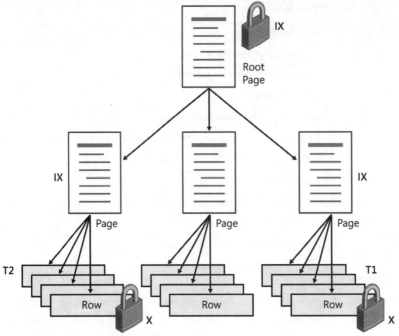

Exclusive lock (X); Intent exclusive (IX)

FIGURE 10-9 Intent locks

Lock Modes

In an effort to be efficient with locking, SQL Server supports different lock modes. The lock modes are listed in Table 10-3.

TABLE 10-3 Lock Modes

Lock mode	Description
Shared (S)	Used for read operations that do not change or update data, such as a SELECT statement.
Update (U)	Used on resources that might be updated.
Exclusive (X)	Used for data-modification operations such as INSERT, UPDATE, or DELETE. Ensures that multiple updates cannot be made to the same resource at the same time.
Intent	Used to establish a lock hierarchy. The types of intent locks are intent shared (IS), intent exclusive (IX), and shared with intent exclusive (SIX).
Schema	Used when an operation dependent on the schema of a table is executing. The types of schema locks are schema modification (Sch-M) and schema stability (Sch-S).
Bulk Update (BU)	Used when bulk copying data into a table and the TABLOCK hint is specified.
Key-range	Protects the range of rows read by a query when using the serializable transaction isolation level. Ensures that other transactions cannot insert rows that would qualify for the queries of the serializable transaction if the queries were run again.

The intent locks can be regarded as a modifier for the other lock modes, so you would place a shared lock (S) on a row to read it, and an intent shared lock (IS) would be placed along the navigation to the root of the B-Tree.

Explaining Lock Compatibility

Although some lock types prevent other transactions from acquiring locks on the same resource, many locks are compatible with each other. An abbreviated lock compatibility chart is shown in Table 10-4. Reading this chart can be confusing, so an example will help. Transaction T1 currently holds an update lock (U) on a row. Transaction T2 grants a shared lock on that row. By examining the matrix, you can see that T2 will be granted the shared lock. Based on the previous discussion about exclusive locks, you might wonder why a currently granted IX lock would be compatible with the request for another IX lock. This is because the intent locks are never held at the actual resource level (like a row); they are at least one level above in the tree.

TABLE 10-4 Lock Compatibility Matrix

Requested mode	Currently granted mode					
	IS	S	U	IX	SIX	X
Intent shared (IS)	Yes	Yes	Yes	Yes	Yes	No
Shared (S)	Yes	Yes	Yes	No	No	No
Update (U)	Yes	Yes	No	No	No	No
Intent exclusive (IX)	Yes	No	No	Yes	No	No
Shared with intent exclusive (SIX)	Yes	No	No	No	No	No
Exclusive (X)	No	No	No	No	No	No

> **MORE INFO**   **LOCK COMPATIBILITY MATRIX**
>
> You can learn more about the lock compatibility matrix at *http://msdn.microsoft.com /en-us/library/ms186396(v=sql.110).aspx.*

Understanding Dynamic Lock Management

SQL Server uses dynamic lock management to increase concurrency in the database. For example, if your transaction modifies one row in a table, SQL Server will take a row lock for the duration of the modification. However, in large tables in which many row locks would be required, SQL Server will instead take a page or table lock. This is dependent on all transactions that take locks on a table. If the query optimizer decides that a large number of rows will be affected, the higher-level locks can be taken at the beginning of the transaction.

However, SQL Server can also dynamically escalate the lock types during execution. If the total number of row locks taken by 100 user queries exceeds the threshold, SQL Server will take a table lock and then release all the row locks. This simplifies management of the locks but results in decreased concurrency.

Understanding Transaction Isolation Levels

The American Nations Standards Institute (ANSI) specifies four transaction isolation levels, each of which has very specific characteristics. The characteristics of the isolation levels are as follows:

- **Dirty read** A dirty read occurs when a transaction is allowed to read data from a row that has been modified by another running transaction that has not yet committed.
- **Non-repeatable read** A non-repeatable read occurs when, during the course of a transaction, a row is retrieved twice and the values within the row differ between reads.
- **Phantom read** A phantom read occurs when, in the course of a transaction, two identical queries are executed, and the collection of rows returned by the second query is different from that returned by the first.

Table 10-5 identifies which of these characteristics is associated with each isolation level.

TABLE 10-5 Isolation Levels and Concurrency Side Effects

Isolation Level	Dirty Read	Non-Repeatable Read	Phantom READ
SERIALIZABLE	No	No	No
REPEATABLE READ	No	No	Yes
READ COMMITED (default)	No	Yes	Yes
READ UNCOMMITED	Yes	Yes	Yes

MORE INFO   ISOLATION LEVELS

You can learn more about SQL isolation levels at *http://msdn.microsoft.com/en-us/library/ms378149(sql110).aspx*.

EXAM TIP

The read committed isolation level is the default isolation level in SQL Server.

In addition to the ANSI standard isolation levels, SQL Server provides a nonstandard isolation level that can improve concurrency and that has the same characteristics as the serializable isolation level. The isolation level specifies that the data read by any statement in a transaction will be the transactionally consistent version of the data that existed at the start of the transaction.

The transaction can recognize only data modifications that were committed before the start of the transaction. Data modifications made by other transactions after the start of the current transaction are not visible to statements running in the current transaction. The effect is that the statements in a transaction get a snapshot of the committed data as it existed at the start of the transaction.

To use this isolation level, a database option must be changed because this isolation level introduces additional resources in tempdb. Also, at the beginning of the transaction, you must specify the snapshot isolation level in your T-SQL code. This isolation level requires both steps for SQL Server to use this feature.

T-SQL

```
USE [AdventureWorks2012]
GO
ALTER DATABASE AdventureWorks2012 SET ALLOW_SNAPSHOT_ISOLATION ON
GO
SET TRANSACTION ISOLATION LEVEL SNAPSHOT;
GO
BEGIN TRANSACTION;
GO
SELECT *
    FROM HumanResources.EmployeePayHistory;
GO
SELECT *
    FROM HumanResources.Department;
GO
COMMIT TRANSACTION;
GO
```

> **NOTE SNAPSHOT ISOLATION LEVEL DATABASE OPTION**
>
> If you attempt to set the transaction isolation level to snapshot, but you have not enabled the database option to this transaction isolation level, you will receive the following error message:
>
> ```
> Msg 3952, Level 16, State 1, Line 1
> ```
>
> ```
> Snapshot isolation transaction failed accessing database 'AdventureWorks2012'
> because snapshot isolation is not allowed in this database. Use ALTER
> DATABASE to allow snapshot isolation.
> ```

DBCC USEROPTIONS can be used to determine the isolation level for the current connection:

T-SQL

```
USE [AdventureWorks2012];
GO
DBCC USEROPTIONS;
GO
```

Choosing the Read Committed Snapshot Isolation Database Option

The Read Committed Snapshot Isolation (RCSI) database option is similar to snapshot isolation level in that it enables readers to read data without being blocked by locks that have been acquired by writers. However, unlike snapshot isolation level, it does not require the user to ask for it explicitly by declaring a special isolation level. It is automatically applied whenever the transaction is at a read committed isolation level (which is the default transaction isolation level).

Lock Duration Based on Transaction Isolation Levels

Three factors affect the duration for which locks are held. The first factor is the lock owner, which can be at the transaction level; the second is a server-side cursor; and the third is a session. The duration of each lock type based on the isolation level is shown in Table 10-6.

TABLE 10-6 Lock Duration by Transaction Isolation Level

Mode	Read Committed	Repeatable Read	Snapshot	Serializable
Shared	Held until data read and processed	Held until end of transaction	N/A	Held until end of transaction
Update	Held until data read and processed unless promoted to Exclusive	Held until data read and processed unless promoted to Exclusive	Held until data read and processed unless promoted to Exclusive	Held until end of transaction unless promoted to Exclusive
Exclusive	Held until end of transaction	Held until end of transaction	Held until end of transaction	Held until end of transaction

Monitoring Locks

You now look at the dynamic management views that provide you with information about locks and transactions currently in effect. The sys.dm_tran_locks DMV can display a view of the locks currently being held by open transactions. The sys.dm_tran_database_transactions DMV displays the open transactions at the database level, whereas sys.dm_tran_session _transactions can be used to obtain correlation information for associated sessions and transactions.

Identifying Blocking

When one transaction is holding locks on a resource, other transactions that are waiting for that resource must queue up until the first transaction releases its locks. If the locks are being held for long periods, you see what is known as a *blocking chain*. Being able to determine that blocking is occurring and identify the transaction at the head of the blocking chain is an important skill. You can examine the request_status column of the sys.dm_tran_locks DMV for a value of Wait. Alternatively, if the blocking_session_id column of sys.dm_os_waiting_tasks or sys.dm_exec_requests has a value greater than zero, this indicates blocking and also indicates which session is blocking.

In addition to blocking caused by locks, compiling or recompiling query execution plans can cause blocking. You can identify this type of blocking by examining the wait_resource column of sys.dm_exec_requests DMV for a value of 'COMPILE' or by examining the resource _subtype column of the sys.dm_tran_locks DMV for a value of 'COMPILE'. If you are running a SQL Server Trace, you see SP:Recompile Events.

Avoiding Blocking

Be aware that design patterns can lead to blocking. Techniques that can help avoid blocking include:

- Keeping the transaction scope as short as possible and in the same batch.
- Not allowing user interaction during transactions. Don't display data to a user and wait for the user to perform an action before completing your transaction; the user might have just left for lunch!
- Practicing proper indexing to help limit locks acquired and reduce the chance of blocking.
- Elevating the transaction isolation level above the default only for a good reason.
- Examining the T-SQL code to see whether developers have added locking hints, index hints, or join hints.

Using AlwaysOn Replicas to Improve Concurrency

In many cases, queries that are used to support reporting can reduce concurrency in online transaction processing (OLTP) systems. Reporting must often read large amounts of data and perform aggregate operations on the results. When this happens in an OLTP system, the users trying to INSERT, UPDATE, or DELETE data are often blocked, waiting for the reporting process to complete. In SQL Server 2012, the capability now exists to offload this reporting load to a read-only replica. This is accomplished by adding a new clause to the connection string for the reporting application, indicating that it's ApplicationIntent=ReadOnly. AlwaysOn Availability Groups replicas are discussed fully in Chapter 8, "Clustering and AlwaysOn."

MORE INFO   **READABLE SECONDARY REPLICAS**

You can learn more about readable secondary replicas at *http://msdn.microsoft.com/en-us /library/ff878253.aspx.*

MORE INFO   **CONFIGURING READ-ONLY ACCESS ON AN AVAILABILITY REPLICA**

You can learn more about read-only routing at *http://msdn.microsoft.com/en-us/library /hh213002.aspx.*

Detecting and Correcting Deadlocks

A *deadlock* occurs when two or more tasks permanently block each other because each task has a lock on a resource that the other task(s) are trying to lock. Each user session might have one or more tasks running on its behalf, and each task might acquire or wait to acquire a variety of resources. The following types of resources can cause blocking that could result in a deadlock:

- Locks
- Worker threads
- Memory
- Parallel query execution-related resources
- Multiple active result sets (MARS) resources

The most common types of deadlocks are conversion, writer-writer, reader-writer, and cascading. *Conversion* deadlocks occur when two connections both own shared locks on a resource (which are compatible) and they both try to convert their locks to exclusive locks. *Writer-writer* deadlocks are caused by resource ordering, so ensuring that all code accesses resources in the same order will remove that specific type of deadlock. *Reader-writer* dead-locks are the most common. These occur when both connections hold exclusive locks on different resources, and each tries to request a shared lock on the other connection's resource.

One of the more difficult types of deadlocks is *cascading* deadlocks. These occur when there are more than two connections involved in the deadlock. Even after SQL Server chooses a deadlock victim, another deadlock still exists. SQL Server tries to choose deadlock victims until all the deadlocks in the chain have been resolved.

SQL Server has a thread dedicated solely to looking for deadlocks. By default, this thread executes every five seconds. If SQL Server encounters a deadlock, the deadlock monitor thread executes more frequently and, in systems with heavy deadlocking, it might execute as often as every 100 milliseconds. When no more deadlocks are detected, the default interval of five seconds is used.

Deadlocks raise a 1205 error. When a deadlock is encountered, one of the processes is selected by the deadlock monitor to be terminated and rolled back. The selected process is called the *deadlock victim*. The deadlock victim is usually the process that has generated the fewest transaction log records. You can override this default behavior by setting DEADLOCK _PRIORITY on the connection involved.

Capturing Deadlock Information

When you are notified that deadlocks are occurring (either by users of the application or by the developers of the application), you can take several steps to capture diagnostic information to help in troubleshooting the deadlock condition. You can enable two trace flags.

- Trace flag 1204 exists for backward compatibility and writes deadlock information into the SQL Server Activity log in a text-based format.
- Trace flag 1222 is the newer version of the information capture; it is an XML-based output and is often easier to read.

If you need more detailed information about deadlocks that are occurring, you can configure a SQL trace to capture the Lock:Deadlock Chain, the Deadlock Graph Event, and the Lock:Deadlock Event. In SQL Server 2012, SQL Trace has been marked as deprecated; you now have a lower-overhead method of capturing deadlock information by using a feature known as Extended Events. One of the standard Extended Events sessions that is always running is the system_health session. This session has the xml_deadlock_report event that you can view in the Extended Events viewer in SSMS. To view this session information:

1. Open SSMS and, in Object Explorer, expand the Management node.

2. Expand the Extended Events node and the Sessions node.

3. Right-click the system_health session and select Properties to view the events captured by the session. An example of this dialog box can be seen in Figure 10-10.

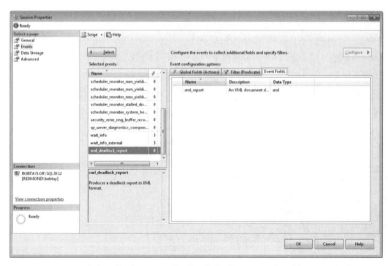

FIGURE 10-10 xml_deadlock_report in the default system_health extended events

Using Activity Monitor

One of your daily duties is to monitor the health of your SQL Server. By using proactive monitoring, you can often correct issues before they become database outages. The Activity Monitor (see Figure 10-11) is a tool in SSMS that you use to perform this monitoring. To display the Activity Monitor, either select the instance in Object Explorer and then select the Activity Monitor from the toolbar or right-click the instance and select Activity Monitor from the Context menu.

NOTE REQUIRED PERMISSION FOR ACTIVITY MONITOR

Use of Activity Monitor requires VIEW SERVER STATE permission.

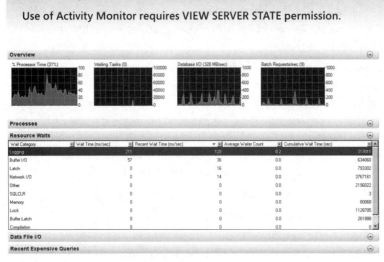

FIGURE 10-11 Activity Monitor – Resource Waits categories

The Activity Monitor has four graphical views that show key metrics in real time for the following: %Processor Time, Waiting Tasks, Database I/O, and Batch Requests per second.

Below the graphical views are four expandable panes:

- **Processes** This pane shows all current sessions. Select a server process id (SPID) and right-click Details to view the last T-SQL command batch for an active connection, as shown in Figure 10-12.

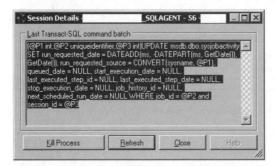

FIGURE 10-12 Details of the last T-SQL command batch

- **Waiting Tasks** This graph groups waiting resources into 11 wait categories, which include wait statistics.
- **Data File I/O** This graph lists files and their activity levels (MB/sec Read | Written).
- **Recent Expensive Queries** Expanding this pane shows queries that have high resource usage in the past 30 seconds. Information is gathered from the sys.dm_exec _requests and sys.dm_exec_query_stats DMVs.

Diagnosing Bottlenecks

If you are fortunate enough to have a single database on a single instance of SQL Server, determining where a bottleneck exists might not be difficult. However, in today's world of consolidation, many SQL Server servers host multiple instances, with each instance hosting many databases. Trying to diagnose the cause of a bottleneck can be challenging if you do not use a troubleshooting methodology. Microsoft recommends using the Waits and Queues methodology to troubleshoot bottlenecks.

> **MORE INFO** **WAITS AND QUEUES TROUBLESHOOTING METHODOLOGY**
>
> To download the complete whitepaper, see *http://technet.microsoft.com/library/Cc966413*.

The first step in diagnosing bottlenecks is to determine which resource is causing the bottleneck. By examining the sys.dm_os_wait_stats DMV, you can see the cumulative wait times for every possible wait type in SQL Server. This DMV, like many others, only reports totals since the last time the SQL Server service was restarted.

> **NOTE** **EXAMINING CURRENT WAIT STATISTICS**
>
> If you need to examine the current wait statistics rather than the cumulative totals since the last SQL Server service restart, you can execute the following command:
>
> DBCC SQLPERF ('sys.dm_os_wait_stats', CLEAR);

Note that as you examine the wait types on the system, there can be multiple wait types that all reflect a bottleneck on the same resource. For example, the PAGEIOLATCH_SH, PAGEIOLATCH_UP, PAGEIOLATCH_EX, and ASYNCH_IO_COMPLETION are all reflections of an I/O subsystem bottleneck.

> **MORE INFO** **COMMON WAIT TYPES**
>
> For a listing of the most common wait types and what they mean, see *http://msdn .microsoft.com/en-us/library/ms179984.aspx*.

A task in SQL Server is a unit of work that is scheduled for execution by SQL Server. Tasks in SQL Server can exist in only one of three states: running, runnable, and suspended.

- When a task is *running*, it is performing actual work.

- When a task is *runnable*, it has the resources it needs and is waiting for a scheduler to execute it.

> **NOTE IDENTIFYING CPU BOTTLENECKS WITH SIGNAL WAIT TIME**
>
> SQL Server keeps track of how long a task has been waiting for a CPU; this wait time is known as *signal wait time*. It is the amount of time a task waits to be signaled that a CPU is available to perform its work. If you see high values for signal wait time, this might be an indication of a CPU bottleneck.

- A task that is in the *suspended* state is waiting for a resource such as I/O, locks, and so on.

You can monitor the states of the active tasks by viewing the output of the sys.dm_os _waiting_tasks DMV. Examine the wait_duration_ms column for high values. The wait_type column will tell you what the wait type is for that session. The following T-SQL script lists each task that is waiting, the wait type, the status, and whether another session is blocking this session:

T-SQL

```
SELECT wt.session_id,wt.wait_duration_ms,wait_type, blocking_session_id, status
FROM sys.dm_os_waiting_tasks AS wt
        JOIN sys.dm_exec_sessions AS s ON wt.session_id = s.session_id
GO
```

Using Reports for Performance Analysis

Performance analysis of SQL Server is a wide topic that is well outside the scope of this chapter; however, one common approach can be covered here. This approach is to gather reporting information about the performance of the database by using the standard and custom reporting capabilities in SSMS.

Using Standard Reports

SQL Server 2012 has a standard set of reports that can be used effectively to gain insight into the usage patterns of the database server's resources. These reports can identify high-cost queries, identify transactions by locking and blocking, chronicle database health, list schema and configuration changes that have occurred, and generate other performance reports. Note that these reports consume many of the DMVs described in this chapter and provide an easy-to-use graphical representation of that information.

Figure 10-13 shows the Reports menu, which provides quick access to 23 standard reports and links to custom reports. To access this menu, in Object Explorer, right-click the instance and select Reports.

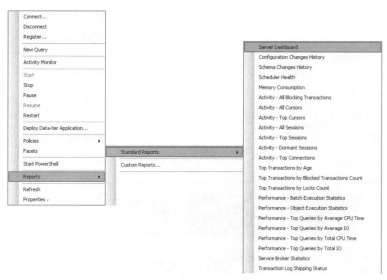

FIGURE 10-13 The Reports menu

Using Custom Reports

Custom reports can be downloaded, installed, and easily accessed from the Custom Reports menu. The SQL Server 2012 Performance Dashboard Reports page provides a quick and simple method to see current and historical reports for a database. It includes many links to other reports for additional information.

> **MORE INFO** **SQL SERVER 2012 PERFORMANCE DASHBOARD REPORT**
>
> You can download the Performance Dashboard Custom Reports installer from the Microsoft Download Center at *http://www.microsoft.com/download/en/details .aspx?id=29063*.

After you install the custom reports, you access them in Object Explorer by right-clicking the instance, selecting Reports, and then selecting Custom Reports. The first time you do this, you are prompted for a location of the report definition language file (.rdl). The default location for the Performance Dashboard files is C:\Program Files (x86)\Microsoft SQL Server\110 \Tools\Performance Dashboard. To create this file location, select the performance_dashboard _main.rdl file. Then, on subsequent selection of Reports, a new menu item named performance _dashboard_main appears. Select it to display the report.

Be sure to run the installer with elevated permissions. If you do not, and running the custom report tells you that the stored procedures are not installed, execute the setup.sql file, found in the Install directory, with elevated privileges.

Executing the KILL Process

There are times when, despite your proactive monitoring, performance tuning, and bottle-neck analysis, you have a session that is not responsive or is the head blocker in a long blocker chain. To restore your database to a functional state, you must end the execution of that session. You can end the session by performing the following steps:

1. Open Activity Monitor.

2. Locate the row for the session you need to stop, right-click that row, and select Kill Process from the Context menu, as shown in Figure 10-14.

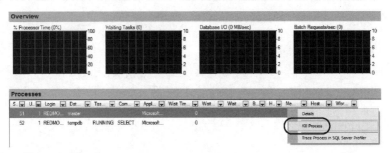

FIGURE 10-14 Activity Monitor - Kill Process

There are times when the server is not responsive enough to use the Activity Monitor to kill the process. In this case, you can use one of the following three KILL commands in T-SQL to end the session:

- KILL {Session id | UOW} [WITH STATUSONLY]

- KILL STATS JOB

- KILL QUERY NOTIFICATION

Executing the KILL User-Process as shown in Figure 10-14 requires the ALTER ANY CONNECTION permission. The KILL Stats Job requires the VIEW SERVER STATE permission. An example of killing the process with the SPID of 57 is demonstrated in the following T-SQL code:

T-SQL

```
/* KILL { session ID | UOW } [ WITH STATUSONLY ] */
KILL 57;
-- Determine the progress status of the KILL operation
KILL 57 WITH STATUSONLY;
--This is the progress report.
spid 57: Transaction rollback in progress.
Estimated rollback completion: 70% Estimated time left: 20 seconds.
```

When SQL Server kills a process, it must remain transactionally consistent and might have to roll back its transaction. This can be a lengthy process, so adding the WITH STATUSONLY clause to the KILL statement generates periodic reports to the console, indicating how much more work has to be rolled back.

> **NOTE LIMITATIONS OF KILL COMMANDS**
>
> You cannot use the KILL command to end your own user process session.

 Quick Check

- Which feature do snapshot isolation levels use?

Quick Check Answer

- Snapshot isolation levels use row versioning in tempdb to provide consistent rows for reads while writes are occurring.

PRACTICE **Examining Dynamic Management Views**

In this practice, you practice using the dynamic management views introduced in this lesson to locate bottlenecks.

EXERCISE 1 Find Resource Waits

In this exercise, you query the sys.dm_os_wait_stats and examine the wait_time_ms column to determine which wait types are a bottleneck on your SQL Server instance.

EXERCISE 2 Find Blocking Chains

In this exercise, you examine the sys.dm_exec_requests blocking_session_id column and the sys.dm_os_waiting_tasks DMV to determine whether there is blocking in your system.

Lesson Summary

- Transactions determine how long SQL Server will hold locks; this impacts concurrency.
- SQL Server uses dynamic lock management to improve concurrency.
- Read Committed is the default transaction isolation level.
- The Read Committed Snapshot Isolation database option can limit reader/writer blocking.
- SQL Server provides many tools to help identify and resolve blocking and deadlocking.

Lesson Review

Answer the following questions to test your knowledge of the information in this lesson. You can find the answers to these questions and explanations of why each answer choice is correct or incorrect in the "Answers" section at the end of this chapter.

1. What is the default transaction isolation level in SQL Server 2012?

   A. Serializable

   B. Read committed

   C. Repeatable read

   D. Snapshot

2. What is the dynamic management view that records the total time that tasks are waiting for resource types?

   A. sys.dm_tran_session_transactions

   B. sys.dm_tran_locks

   C. sys.dm_os_waiting_tasks

   D. sys.dm_os_wait_stats

3. You suspect that blocking is occurring. What can you examine to determine where the blocking is occurring?

   A. Examine the blocking_session_id of sys.dm_os_waiting_tasks.

   B. Examine the blocking_session_id of sys.dm_exec_requests.

   C. Examine the Procesess pane of Activity Monitor.

   D. Examine the blocked_process column of the system_health Extended Event Session.

4. You have determined that blocking is occurring due to an index rebuild operation. The server process id is SPID 57. You need to remove the blocking and must be able to give an estimate of the time remaining until the blocking is resolved. Which command should you execute?

   A. KILL 57 WITH STATUSONLY;

   B. KILL 57;

   C. ROLLBACK TRANSACTON

   D. KILL 'D5499C66-E398-45CA-BF7B-CD9CD104B48FD'

Case Scenarios

In the following case scenarios, apply what you have learned about indexes and concurrency. You can find answers to these questions in the "Answers" section at the end of this chapter.

Case Scenario 1: Fabrikam Year-Query Performance

You are a database administrator for Fabrikam. You are testing a query that will be used for the year-end report. This report performs many aggregate operations such as min, max, avg, sum, and standard deviation. The performance of this query is unacceptable. You will be deploying this query on SQL Server 2012. The table that is involved with the aggregate operations contains 3.5 million rows. It has a clustered index on its primary key column.

There are several queries for which you have captured execution plans due to poor performance. When you examine those plans, you notice that one large table is often causing a table scan, which is the cause of the poor performance. You also determine that a particular query, which is being supported by a non-clustered index, is not very selective. You know that the WHERE clause contains two columns, one of which is the leading column of the non-clustered index. That column by itself is not very selective, but is very selective when combined with the second column. A long-term reporting solution is required that will limit the impact on the OLTP system.

1. Without rewriting the query, which has been tested to ensure that the proper calculations are being made, how could you improve performance of the query?

2. How can you improve the multicolumn query performance?

3. How can you design a long-term reporting solution?

Case Scenario 2: Analyzing Concurrency at Tailspin Toys

You are a database administrator for Tailspin Toys. Users of your application are reporting that they are waiting significant amounts of time after they submit an order for it to process. During this time, you see that the Marketing team has been running its latest sales promotion reports. You examine sys.dm_os_waiting_tasks and sys.dm_exec_sessions and notice long blocking chains. Users are also reporting Error 1205 messages.

You cannot make source code changes at this time. What steps should you take to improve concurrency in the Tailspin Toys database?

1. The server is under heavy load, and you cannot run a SQL Profiler trace because of this. How can you capture the necessary information to diagnose and correct the deadlocks?

2. A maintenance job runs four times per day. Whenever this job runs, every process that needs access to the Status table is blocked until the maintenance job is complete. When the maintenance job is not executing, there are no issues. The maintenance job is reading data and copying it to a history table.

Suggested Practices

To help you successfully master the exam objectives presented in this chapter, complete the following tasks.

Implement and Maintain Indexes and Statistics

Prior to completing each task in the following practices, list the steps you would take to accomplish the task. After completing the task, assess how accurately you predicted the necessary steps.

- **Practice 1** Examine the detailed statistical information for the indexes defined on the Person.Person table in the AdventureWorks2012 database.

- **Practice 2** Examine the missing index DMVs to locate indexes that might be useful to support the queries you have issued.

Identify and Resolve Concurrency Problems

Prior to completing each task in the following practices, list the steps you would take to accomplish the task. After completing the task, assess how accurately you predicted the necessary steps.

- **Practice 1** While monitoring the AdventureWorks2012 database, you notice that there are many instances of reader/writer blocking. Change the AdventureWorks2012 database option to reduce the reader/writer blocking.

- **Practice 2** Application developers have reported receiving Error 1205 messages. You need to investigate the source of the deadlocks. First, enable the appropriate trace flags to capture the deadlock information in the SQL Server activity log and then start a Profiler Trace with the appropriate events to diagnose deadlocking.

Answers

This section contains the answers to the lesson review questions and solutions to the case scenarios in this chapter.

Lesson 1

1. **Correct Answer: C**

   A. **Incorrect:** An XML index is a specialized index that has one row for each node in the XML data.

   B. **Incorrect:** A spatial index is a geometric index that uses grids to improve spatial searching.

   C. **Correct:** A clustered index logically stores the rows in the table in the order of the key.

   D. **Incorrect:** A non-clustered index stores only keys and not the data from the table.

2. **Correct Answer: C**

   A. **Incorrect:** The maximum is not one index key and 900 bytes.

   B. **Incorrect:** The maximum is not 249 index keys and 8,060.bytes.

   C. **Correct:** The maximum is up to 16 index keys and/or 900 bytes.

   D. **Incorrect:** The maximum is not an unlimited number of keys and 900 bytes.

3. **Correct Answers: A and C**

   A. **Correct:** Filtered indexes were introduced to support sparse columns.

   B. **Incorrect:** Filtered indexes do not provide any benefit with a column with many duplicate values.

   C. **Correct:** When querying for a small subset of values in a column, filtered indexes can provide better performance.

   D. **Incorrect:** Filtered indexes will not support XML queries.

4. **Correct Answer: A**

   A. **Correct:** The sys.dm_db_index_physical_stats DMV will provide information about index fragmentation.

   B. **Incorrect:** The sys.dm_db_index_operational_stats will provide information about how SQL Server is using the indexes but will not provide information about index fragmentation.

   C. **Incorrect:** The sys.dm_db_missing_index_details will provide information about indexes that optimizer would like to have present but will not provide information about index fragmentation.

   D. **Incorrect:** The sys.dm_db_index_usage_stats will give high-level usage of indexes but will not provide information about index fragmentation.

5. **Correct Answer: C**

   A. **Incorrect:** Executing the sp_updatestats with the @resample parameter set to 20 will update the statistics of all tables and indexes at the default sampling rate.

   B. **Incorrect:** Executing the UPDATE STATISTICS command on the table specifying the WITH SAMPLE 20 PERCENT option will not fix the out-of-data statistics.

   C. **Correct:** Executing the UPDATE STATISTICS command on the table specifying the WITH FULLSCAN option will completely recalculate all statistics.

   D. **Incorrect:** Executing the UPDATE STATISTICS command on the table specifying the WITH NORECOMPUTE option will turn off automatic statistics updating and will not solve the problem.

Lesson 2

1. **Correct Answer: B**

   A. **Incorrect:** The default transaction isolation level is not serializable.

   B. **Correct:** The default transaction isolation level is read committed.

   C. **Incorrect:** The default transaction isolation level is not repeatable read.

   D. **Incorrect:** The default transaction isolation level is not snapshot.

2. **Correct Answer: D**

   A. **Incorrect:** sys.dm_tran_session_transactions displays the current executing transactions by session.

   B. **Incorrect:** sys.dm_tran_locks displays all locks currently held by transactions.

   C. **Incorrect:** sys.dm_os_waiting_tasks displays the tasks that are waiting and the time that session has been waiting.

   D. **Correct:** sys.dm_os_wait_stats displays the cumulative wait times for each SQL Server wait type.

3. **Correct Answers: A, B, C, and D**

   A. **Correct:** The blocking_session_id column of sys.dm_os_waiting_tasks enables you to determine where blocking is occurring.

   B. **Correct:** The blocking_session_id column of sys.dm_exec_requests enables you to determine where blocking is occurring.

   C. **Correct:** The Processess Pane of Activity Monitor enables you to determine where blocking is occurring.

   D. **Correct:** The blocked_process column of the system_health Extended Events Session enables you to determine where blocking is occurring.

4. **Correct Answer: A**

   A. **Correct:** The WITH STATUSONLY clause provides progress reports.

   B. **Incorrect:** The KILL 57; command kills the process but does not provide progress messages.

   C. **Incorrect:** The ROLLBACK TRANSACTION command does not kill the process, nor does it provide progress messages.

   D. **Incorrect:** KILL 'D5499C66-E398-45CA-BF7B-CD9CD104B48FD' is used to kill a unit of work, not a specific SPID, and it does not return progress messages.

Case Scenario 1

Because your application will be deployed on SQL Server 2012, you perform many aggregate operations, and the table contains a large number of rows, you can create a columnstore index on the table to improve query performance for the aggregate operations.

1. Examine the Missing Indexes DMVs to see whether an appropriate index exists that will remove the table scan from the execution plans.

2. Manually create statistics on the two columns. This will enable the optimizer to determine that the combination of the two columns is highly selective and choose a more optimum query plan.

3. Implement Readable Secondary Replicas and have the reporting application set its connection string to include the ApplicationIntent=ReadOnly clause.

Case Scenario 2

Because you are experiencing reader-writer blocking, you can set the Read Committed Snapshot Isolation database option to improve concurrency.

1. You can enable deadlock information capture to the SQL Server activity log by executing the DBCC TRACEON(1222,-1) command. This captures the information without the overhead of a SQL Server Profiler trace and does not require a service restart such as setting this trace flag as a start-up parameter.

2. The maintenance job might have its transaction set to SERIALIZABLE, effectively blocking all access to the Status table. Because only read access is required, you can remove the TRANSACTION ISOLATION LEVEL SERIALIZABLE statement. This will allow all connections access to the table while the maintenance job is being executed. Also, if correct, you can add a WITH NOLOCK hint to the maintenance job to improve concurrency as long as you are aware that you might get dirty reads.

CHAPTER 11

SQL Server Agent, Backup, and Restore

Exam objectives in this chapter:

- Manage SQL Server Agent.
- Configure and maintain a back up strategy.
- Restore databases.

Any task you must perform more than a few times is a task that you can automate. Automating tasks minimizes the amount of time you have to spend performing repetitive work and ensures that repetitive tasks are carried out in a consistent manner. SQL Server Agent is the key to automating Microsoft SQL Server administration tasks.

As a database administrator, it is your responsibility to ensure that the databases you are responsible for managing are properly backed up. When developing a data protection strategy, you must understand all the backup options that are available with SQL Server 2012, how to use each of those options, and what methods you use to restore that data.

Lessons in this chapter:

Before You Begin

To complete the practice exercises in this chapter, make sure that you have:

- Completed the setup tasks for installing computers DC, SQL-A, SQL-B, and SQL-CORE as outlined in the introduction of this book.
- Completed the setup tasks outlined in the end-of-lesson practice exercises in Chapter 1, "Planning and Installing SQL Server 2012," through to Chapter 10, "Indexes and Concurrency."

No additional configuration is required for this chapter.

Lesson 1: Managing SQL Server Agent

SQL Server Agent enables you to execute scheduled or event-driven administrative jobs, automating many processes you would otherwise have to execute manually. Each Database Engine instance has a separate SQL Server Agent. In this lesson, you learn how to create SQL Server Agent jobs, monitor job execution, manage alerts, and automate SQL Server Agent jobs across multiple databases and instances.

> **After this lesson, you will be able to:**
> - Create, maintain, and monitor jobs.
> - Manage jobs and alerts.
> - Automate setup, maintenance, and monitoring across multiple instances.
> - Manage operator and notification methods.
>
> **Estimated lesson time: 60 minutes**

Executing Jobs by Using SQL Server Agent

SQL Server Agent enables you to automate the execution of jobs. SQL Server Agent jobs are collections of tasks known as job steps. A step might be an activity such as taking a transaction log backup or copying data from one location to another. You can use SQL Server Agent to configure jobs to run according to a schedule. You can also configure SQL Server Agent so that specific events trigger the execution of jobs.

The SQL Server Agent service is disabled by default on SQL Server 2012 Database Engine instances. You can start SQL Server Agent by right-clicking SQL Server Agent in SQL Server Management Studio and then choosing Start. You are prompted to confirm this action by a User Account Control dialog box. You are then presented with an additional dialog box asking you whether you want to start the SQL Server Agent on this particular instance.

By editing the properties of SQL Server Agent within SQL Server Management Studio, as shown in Figure 11-1, you can configure the restart behavior if the SQL Server service fails or if the SQL Server Agent service fails. You configure the SQL Server Agent service startup type, rather than the restart on failure settings, by using SQL Server Configuration Manager.

> **MORE INFO**   **SQL SERVER AGENT**
>
> You can learn more about SQL Server Agent at *http://msdn.microsoft.com/en-us/library /ms189237(SQL.110).aspx.*

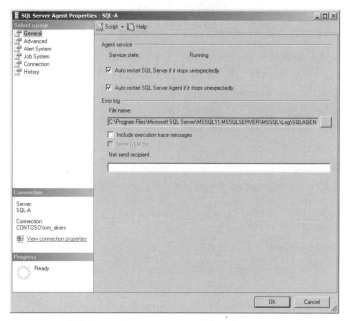

FIGURE 11-1 SQL Server Agent restart on fail settings

Configuring SQL Server Agent Account

You configure the account used by the SQL Server Agent service during setup or through SQL Server Configuration Manager. Although you can use the Local System or a local virtual account for the SQL Server Agent, this limits how the account can interact with resources external to the host server. The SQL Server Agent service account should not be a member of the local Administrators group on the host computer.

When choosing to use a domain-based security account, ensure that the account has the following permissions:

- The logon as a service right. You assign this right by using Group Policy.
- Membership of the Pre-Windows 2000 Compatible Access security group at the domain level. If you do not add the domain-based security account used for the SQL Server Agent service to this group, any jobs owned by domain users who are not members of the local Administrators group on the host computer will fail.

If you want to support SQL Server Agent proxies, you must assign the SQL Server Agent service account additional permissions. If these permissions are not assigned, only members of the sysadmin fixed server role will be able to create jobs. You can assign these permissions by using the following policies, found in the Computer Configuration\Policies\Windows Settings \Security Settings\Local Policies\User Rights Assignment node of a Group Policy Object:

- Bypass Traverse Checking
- Replace A Process-Level Token

- Adjust Memory Quotas For A Process
- Log On As A Batch Job

The account used for the SQL Server Agent service must be a member of the sysadmin fixed server role. The account you assign for the SQL Server Agent service during installation is added automatically to the sysadmin fixed server role during installation. If you modify the account used by the SQL Server Agent service at a later point, SQL Server Configuration Manager does not automatically add the account to this role.

If you need to support multi-server job processing, you must add the account used for the SQL Server Agent service to the TargetServersRole in the msdb database on the master server.

To configure the account used by the SQL Server Agent service, perform the following steps:

1. Open SQL Server Configuration Manager.
2. Expand the SQL Server Services node.
3. Right-click the SQL Server Agent service for the instance you want to configure and then choose Properties.
4. On the Log On tab, provide the details of the account, as shown in Figure 11-2.

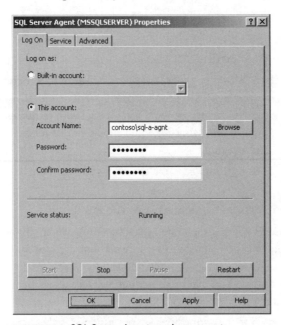

FIGURE 11-2 SQL Server Agent service account

5. You can configure the start mode for the agent by configuring the Start Mode item on the Service tab of the SQL Server Agent service account properties. The options are Manual, Automatic, and Disabled.
6. Restart the SQL Server Agent service to apply the changes.

Setting SQL Server Agent Security

If a user is not a member of the sysadmin fixed server role, he or she must be a member of
one or more of the following fixed database roles in the msdb database to use SQL Server
Agent:

- **SQLAgentUserRole**   This is the least privileged SQL Server Agent role. Role members
  have permissions only on the local jobs and job schedules they own. This role does not
  allow use of multi-server jobs.

- **SQLAgentReaderRole**   This role includes all the permissions assigned to the
  SQLAgentUserRole. In addition, members of this role can view the properties and
  history of all available jobs and job schedules, including multi-server jobs.

- **SQLAgentOperatorRole**   This role includes all the permissions assigned to the
  SQLAgentReaderRole. In addition, members of this role can execute, stop, or start all
  local jobs and delete job history for any local job. Members can also enable and disable all local jobs and schedules.

Quick Check

- Of which fixed server role must the SQL Server Agent service account be a
  member?

Quick Check Answer

- The SQL Server Agent service account must be a member of the sysadmin
  fixed server role.

EXAM TIP

Remember the fixed database role to which you add a principal to if the principal needs to
be able to stop, start, or execute any local job.

Configuring SQL Server Agent Mail Profile

SQL Server Agent uses Database Mail to transmit alerts as email messages. You learned about configuring Database Mail in Chapter 2, "Configuring and Managing SQL Server Instances." To configure SQL Server Agent to use Database Mail when there is an existing mail profile, perform the following steps:

1. In SQL Server Management Studio, right-click SQL Server Agent and then choose Properties.

2. Click Alert System in the left pane under Select A Page.

3. On the Alert System page, shown in Figure 11-3, select the Enable Mail Profile check box. In the Mail System drop-down list, select Database Mail and then select an existing Mail Profile.

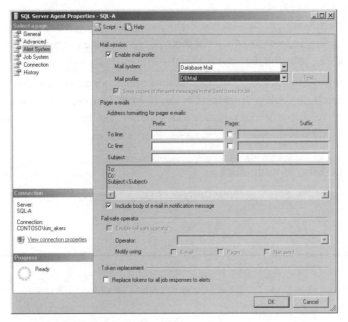

FIGURE 11-3 SQL Server Agent mail

4. Click OK and then restart the SQL Server Agent service.

> **MORE INFO**   **USING SQL SERVER AGENT WITH DATABASE MAIL**
>
> You can learn more about configuring Database Mail and SQL Server Agent at *http://msdn .microsoft.com/en-us/library/ms186358(SQL.110).aspx*.

Setting Up the SQL Server Agent Error Log

The *SQL Server Agent error log* stores warnings and error messages from SQL Server Agent, as shown in Figure 11-4. You can also configure the SQL Server Agent error log to store informational events by choosing Information in the Agent log–level category in the error log properties. Up to nine error logs are maintained. You can cycle the error log by right-clicking the Error Logs node under SQL Server Agent and then choosing Recycle. If you cycle the error log when there are nine logs, the oldest log will be deleted.

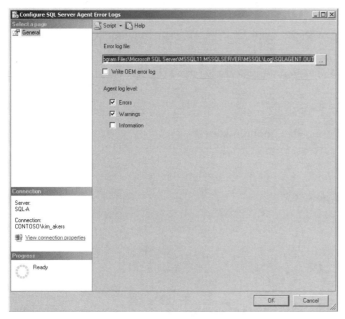

FIGURE 11-4 SQL Server Agent error log properties

MORE INFO   **SQL SERVER AGENT ERROR LOG**

You can learn more about the SQL Server Agent error log at *http://msdn.microsoft.com /en-us/library/ms175488.aspx.*

Managing Alerts

Alerts can be triggered by event log events, WMI events, or performance conditions. You configure SQL Server Agent to look for a specific event or performance condition; when SQL Server Agent detects that event or performance condition, it triggers an alert. When you configure replication, a series of replication-related alerts are automatically created to inform you about the progress of the process.

You can create an alert by right-clicking the Alerts node under SQL Server Agent in SQL Server Management Studio and choosing New Alert. You can also create alerts by executing the sp_add_alert stored procedure from the msdb database. Creating an alert involves the following steps:

1. Create an alert name.

2. Specify an alert trigger.

3. Specify an alert action.

For example, to create an alert that is triggered when the number of transactions per second on the AdventureWorks2012 database exceeds 10 and that runs an existing job, perform the following steps:

1. In SQL Server Management Studio, right-click the Alerts node under SQL Server Agent and select New Alert.

2. On the General page of the New Alert dialog box, shown in Figure 11-5, provide the following details:

   - Name: AdventureWorks-TransactionAlert

   - Type: SQL Server Performance Condition Alert

   - Object: Databases

   - Counter: Transactions/sec

   - Instance: AdventureWorks2012

   - Alert If Counter: Rises Above

   - Value: 10

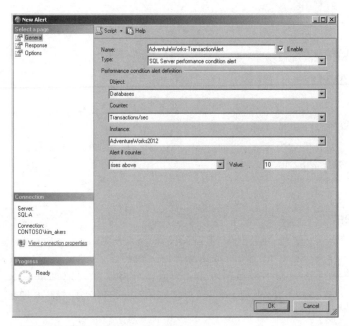

FIGURE 11-5 Alert properties, General page

3. On the Response page, choose Execute Job.

   You can choose an existing job or create a new job. You can also choose to notify an operator from this page.

4. On the Options page, you can choose to include the alert text in an email, pager, or net send message.

If you want to create an alert based on a SQL Server event, as shown in Figure 11-6, you must choose to generate an alert based on:

- **A specific error number**   You can view all possible error numbers by querying sys.messages view in the master database.

- **A specific error severity**   You can choose from 25 error severities.

- **Message text**   When choosing error number or severity, you can also configure an alert to be raised only if the event message contains a specific text string.

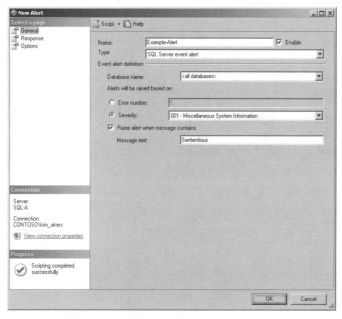

FIGURE 11-6 Alert generated by specific error message

MORE INFO   **ALERTS**

You can learn more about alerts at *http://msdn.microsoft.com/en-us/library /ms180982.aspx*.

Managing Jobs

Database administrators use *jobs* to automate routine tasks such as index maintenance or database backup. Jobs can involve a single Transact-SQL statement or a large number of tasks. When you configure a job, you build a collection of job steps, add a schedule, and choose appropriate alerts and notifications.

Each job step can include one of the following execution types:

- Operating system command
- PowerShell command or script
- Integration Services package
- Transact-SQL statement
- Replication Distributor, Merge, Queue Reader, Snapshot, or Transaction-Log Reader
- Analysis Services command or query
- ActiveX script

You can use only a single execution type in a job step, but each job step can use a different execution type. For example, the first job step might run a Microsoft Windows PowerShell script, the second a Transact-SQL statement (as shown in Figure 11-7), and the third an Integration Services package.

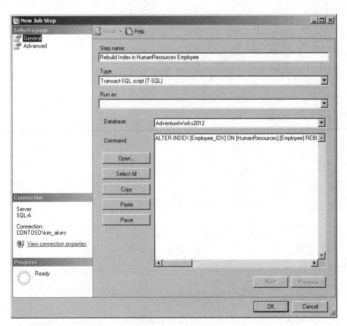

FIGURE 11-7 Transact-SQL job step

When configuring a job step, you define what happens if the step completes successfully and what happens if the step fails. You do this on the Advanced page of the Job Step

Properties dialog box, as shown in Figure 11-8. You can configure the following options for the On Success Action and On Failure Action:

- Go To The Next Step
- Quit The Job Reporting Success
- Quit The Job Reporting Failure

You can also configure the number of retry attempts for the step and the interval, in minutes, between retry attempts.

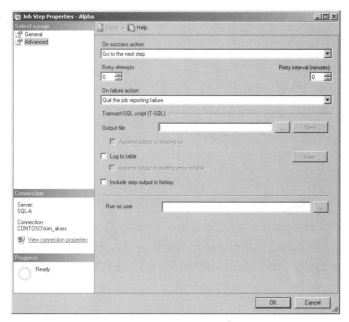

FIGURE 11-8 Configuring job step actions on success and failure

Schedules enable you to configure when a job executes. You configure the schedule for a job on the Schedules page of the job properties. You can create a new schedule or choose an existing schedule. When creating a new schedule, you can configure jobs to occur according to a recurring frequency, as shown in Figure 11-9; configure jobs to execute once; configure jobs to start automatically when SQL Server Agent starts; or configure jobs to start whenever the CPU falls below the idle threshold value.

MORE INFO **JOBS**

You can learn more about jobs at *http://msdn.microsoft.com/en-us/library/ms187880.aspx*.

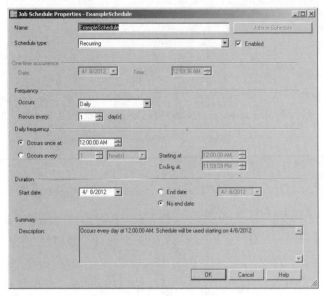

FIGURE 11-9 Example schedule

Creating a Job

To create a job in SQL Server Management Studio, perform the following general steps:

1. Using an account that has the appropriate permissions, expand SQL Server Agent in SQL Server Management Studio, right-click the Jobs folder, and then choose New Job.

2. On the General page, provide the following information:

   - **Job Name**   This is a meaningful name for the job that indicates its function to others.

   - **Job Owner**   By default, this is the job creator. The owner can execute the job. If you must change which security principal owns a job, change this setting.

   - **Category**   This is the type of job. This enables you to organize jobs into folders. You can create new categories and delete existing categories by using the Manage Job Categories dialog box.

   - **Description**   This is a description providing information about the job's function.

   - **Enabled**   This indicates whether the job is enabled.

3. On the Steps page, click New to add a step.

   You can add, remove, and adjust step order by using this page.

4. On the Schedules page, either create a new schedule or choose an existing execution schedule for the job.

5. On the Alerts page, specify the alerts associated with the job.

6. On the Notifications page, shown in Figure 11-10, choose which actions to perform when the job completes. Actions include sending notifications, writing an event to the Windows Application Event Log, and automatically deleting the job.

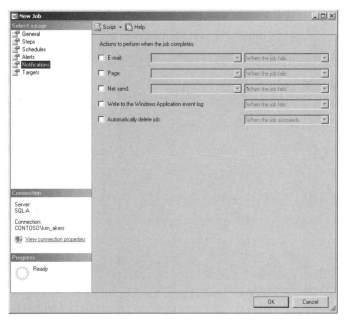

FIGURE 11-10 Notification options

7. On the Targets page, specify the database instances that are targets for the job. Remote instances must already be configured as target servers.

You can execute the following stored procedures from the msdb databases to create jobs:

- **sp_add_job**   Enables you to create jobs
- **sp_add_jobstep**   Adds a job step to an existing job
- **sp_add_schedule**   Creates a schedule that can be used by any job
- **sp_attach_schedule**   Attaches an existing schedule to an existing job
- **sp_add_jobserver**   Adds a job to a server

> **MORE INFO   CREATING JOBS**
>
> You can learn more about creating jobs at *http://msdn.microsoft.com/en-us/library /ms190268(SQL.110).aspx*.

Monitoring Jobs

You can use the *Job Activity Monitor*, shown in Figure 11-11, to start and stop jobs, view job properties, and view the history of particular jobs. You can use the Job Activity Monitor to determine which jobs are scheduled to run in the future and whether the job's last execution was successful.

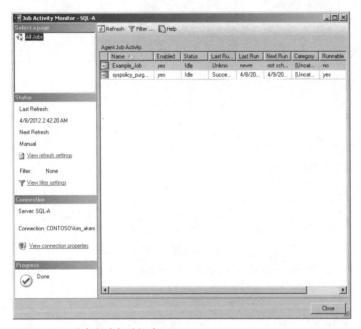

FIGURE 11-11 Job Activity Monitor

> **MORE INFO** **MONITORING JOBS**
>
> You can learn more about monitoring jobs at *http://msdn.microsoft.com/en-us/library /ms188272(SQL.110).aspx.*

Managing Operators

Operators represent groups or individuals who can receive notifications from SQL Server Agent. For example, SQL Server Agent can notify an administrator that a job has completed executing through an operator that includes the administrator's email address.

You can use the following methods to transmit notifications to operators:

- **Email** Sends an email message through Database Mail.
- **Pager notification** Sends a message to a pager by using a special email-to-pager gateway. The pager gateway is provided by the pager provider and is usually present on an external network. Support for pager notifications will be removed in a future version of SQL Server.

- **Net send**   Uses the net send command by using the Microsoft Windows Messenger service, which is different from the Windows Live Messenger Instant Messaging Client. Support for using net send for notifications will be removed in a future version of SQL Server.

A fail-safe operator is an operator that receives a notification if the designated operator is unavailable. You can configure the fail-safe operator on the Alert System page of the SQL Server Agent Properties dialog box, as shown in Figure 11-12.

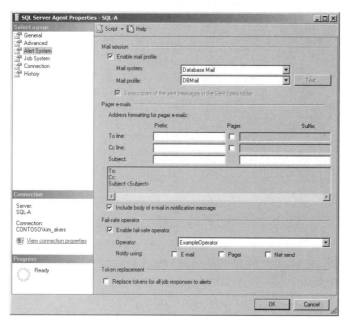

FIGURE 11-12 Fail-safe operator

You can create an operator by executing the sp_add_operator stored procedure from the msdb database. To create an operator by using SQL Server Management Studio, perform the following steps:

1. In SQL Server Management Studio, expand the SQL Server Agent node. Right-click the Operators node and then click New Operators.

2. In the New Operator dialog box, shown in Figure 11-13, specify the name and address details of the new operator.

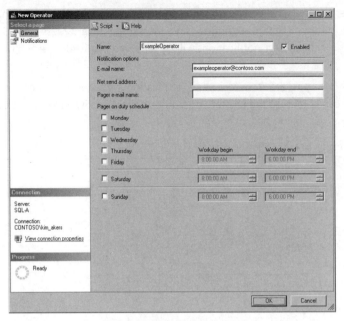

FIGURE 11-13 New Operator dialog box

You can use the Notifications page of the Operator Properties dialog box, shown in Figure 11-14, to view all alerts and jobs that are configured to send notifications to a specific operator. You can also use this page to change how notifications are sent to a particular operator.

FIGURE 11-14 Operator notifications

MORE INFO **OPERATORS**

You can learn more about operators at *http://msdn.microsoft.com/en-us/library /ms179336.aspx.*

Monitoring Multi-Server Environments

When properly configured, you can use SQL Server Agent to manage jobs across multiple servers. Multi-server environments use *master servers* and *target servers*. Target servers report to master servers, and a target server can report to only a single master server. You should use a domain-based account when choosing the SQL Server Agent service account for a multi-server environment. You can use local accounts for the SQL Server Agent service in multi-server configuration only if all instances are hosted on the same computer.

To configure an instance as a master server, perform the following steps:

1. In SQL Server Management Studio, right-click SQL Server Agent, choose Multi Server Administration, and then choose Make This A Master.

2. On the Master Server Operator page, provide the email address and, if necessary, pager and net send address of the Multi Server Operator.

3. On the Target Servers page, shown in Figure 11-15, click Add Connection. Use the Connect To Server dialog box to specify a server to function as a target server. You can configure a server to function as a target server only if Agent XPs is enabled and the SQL Server Agent service is running. If you are not using a Secure Sockets Layer (SSL) certificate, you can disable encryption by configuring the MsxEncryptChannelOptions registry key for the target instance. You can find this key at the following path: \HKEY_LOCAL_MACHINE\SOFTWARE\Microsoft\Microsoft SQL Server\< instance _name >\SQLServerAgent\.

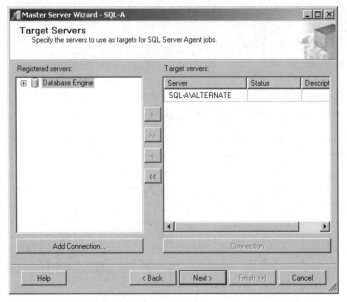

FIGURE 11-15 The Target Servers page

4. On the Master Server Login Credentials page, ensure that Create A New Login If Necessary And Assign It Rights To The MSX is selected.

You can use the sp_msx_enlist stored procedure on a target server to enlist the target server in a master server. If you must switch master servers for a specific target server, you must defect from the original master server before you can enlist in a new master server. If you must change the name of a target server, you must defect prior to performing the name change. You can reenlist the target server after you have changed the name. If you must remove an existing multi-server configuration, you must first defect all target servers. To defect a server, you can right-click SQL Server Agent, choose Multi Server Administration, and then click Defect, or you can use the sp_msx_defect stored procedure on the target server.

> **MORE INFO** **CONFIGURING MULTI-SERVER ENVIRONMENTS**
>
> You can learn more about configuring multi-server environments at *http://msdn.microsoft .com/en-us/library/ms191305(SQL.110).aspx*.

In this practice, you configure SQL Server Agent and create a job, an operator, and an alert.

EXERCISE 1   Configure SQL Server Agent

In this exercise, you prepare an account to be used with the SQL Server Agent service on SQL-A. You also configure the SQL Server Agent service. To complete this exercise, perform the following steps:

1. Log on to DC with the Kim_Akers user account.

2. Create a special domain account named **SQL-A-AGNT** that uses the password **Pa$$w0rd**.

3. Add this account to the appropriate domain group to ensure that users who are not members of the local administrators group can run jobs.

4. Configure SQL-POLICY GPO so that the SQL-A-AGNT account can log on as a service.

5. Log on to SQL-A with the Kim_Akers user account.

6. Run gpupdate /force on SQL-A.

7. Configure SQL Server Agent to use the SQL-A-AGNT account.

8. Configure SQL Server Agent to start automatically.

9. Configure SQL Server Agent to restart automatically if the agent service fails and if the SQL Server service fails.

10. Start SQL Server Agent on SQL-A.

EXERCISE 2   Create a Job

In this exercise, you create a job that runs several stored procedures on a weekly basis. To complete this exercise, perform the following steps:

1. Create a job that has the following properties:

   - Name: **Job_Alpha**

   - Owner: **Contoso\Kim_Akers**

   - Category: [Uncategorized (Local)]

   - Job Step 1: Execute the following stored procedure:

     ```
     exec sp_clean_db_free_space @dbname = [AdventureWorks2012];
     ```

   - Job Step 2: Execute the following stored procedure:

     ```
     exec sp_server_diagnostics;
     ```

   - Schedule: Recurring. Once A Week On Sunday At 1:00:00AM. No End Date.

   - Write to the Windows Application Event Log: When The Job Completes

   - Target: Local Server

2. Run the job. Check the Application Event Log to verify that the job has completed successfully.

EXERCISE 3 Create an Operator

In this exercise, you create an operator for SQL Server Agent and designate this operator as the fail-safe operator. To complete this exercise, perform the following steps:

1. Create an operator that has the following properties:
   - Name: **Hazem Abolrous**
   - Email Name: **hazem.abolrous@contoso.com**
2. Configure Hazem Abolrous as the fail-safe operator.

EXERCISE 4 Create an Alert

In this exercise, you create a performance condition alert that notifies an operator when a particular performance benchmark has been reached. To complete this exercise, perform the following steps:

1. Create an alert that has the following properties:
   - Name: **Transaction Alert**
   - Type: **SQL Server Performance Condition Alert**
   - Object: **Databases**
   - Counter: Transactions/sec
   - Instance: AdventureWorks2012
   - Alert If Counter: Rises Above
   - Value: 10
   - Response: Notify operator Hazem Abolrous through email.

Lesson Summary

- SQL Server Agent is disabled by default.
- Each Database Engine instance has a separate SQL Server Agent service.
- The account used for the SQL Server Agent service must be a member of the sysadmin fixed server role.
- SQLAgentUserRole enables members to have permissions on jobs they own; SQLAgentReaderRole enables members to view the properties and history of jobs; and SQLAgentOperatorRole enables members to execute and modify the schedule of all local jobs.
- Operators can be notified by email, net send, or pager; the fail-safe operator is contacted if the configured operator cannot be contacted.
- A job is a collection of job steps, which are independent tasks and can include command-line commands, Transact-SQL statements, and Windows PowerShell scripts.

- You can configure schedules for jobs.
- Jobs can be triggered by performance conditions.
- You can monitor job status and history by using the Job Activity Monitor.
- Multi-server environments enable you to run jobs across multiple servers.
- In multi-server environments, target servers report to master servers.

Lesson Review

Answer the following questions to test your knowledge of the information in this lesson. You can find the answers to these questions and explanations of why each answer choice is correct or incorrect in the "Answers" section at the end of this chapter.

1. Scheduled jobs owned by users who are not members of the local administrators group on server SYD-SQL-A fail. These users can create jobs. Jobs that are owned by administrators who are members of this group run normally. The SQL Server service on SQL-A uses a domain account named syd-sql-a-agnt. To which of the following domain groups should you add the syd-sql-a-agnt account to ensure that jobs owned by users who are not members of the local administrators group on server SYD-SQL-A do not fail?

    A. Backup Operators

    B. Cryptographic Operators

    C. Performance Monitor Users

    D. Pre-Windows 2000 Compatible Access

2. Rooslan needs to be able to create SQL Server Agent jobs and to manage the schedules of jobs that he has created. Rooslan should not have any permissions on the jobs of other users and should not be able to create or use multi-server jobs. To which of the following roles should you add Rooslan's account?

    A. SQLAgentUserRole

    B. SQLAgentReaderRole

    C. SQLAgentOperatorRole

    D. sysadmin

3. You want a specific job to run when the number of transactions per second on a particular database exceeds 20. You have created the job. Which of the following must you also create to accomplish this goal?

    A. Alert

    B. Operator

    C. Maintenance plan

    D. Proxy

4. You must automate the process of running a Windows PowerShell script followed by an Integration Services package and then a system stored procedure. These items should run every day at 2 A.M. Which of the following would you configure to accomplish this goal?

   A. Operator

   B. Alert

   C. Job

   D. Proxy

Lesson 2: Configuring and Maintaining a Backup Strategy

This lesson discusses backing up SQL Server 2012 databases. You can use several methods to accomplish this goal, and the one you choose often depends on the specifics of the situation.

> **After this lesson, you will be able to:**
> - Manage different backup models.
> - Know when to use full, differential, transaction log, and copy backups.
> - Enable backup compression.
> - Back up large databases.
> - View backup history.
>
> **Estimated lesson time: 60 minutes**

Understanding Backup Types

SQL Server 2012 supports several backup types, each of which is appropriate for certain circumstances. Several backup types can be used in conjunction with one another as part of a database backup strategy. SQL Server 2012 supports the following backup types:

- **Full database backups**   A *full database backup* includes all database objects, system tables, and data. Transactions that occur during the backup are also recorded. Full database backups allow you to perform a complete restoration of the database as it existed at the time the backup operation is performed.

- **Differential backups**   A *differential backup* backs up data that has altered since the last full backup. Differential backups require less time than full database backups. Differential backups record transactions that occur during the differential backup process. You use differential backups in conjunction with the last full backup.

EXAM TIP

Do not confuse differential backups with incremental backups. Incremental backups back up data that changed since the last full or incremental backup. Differential backups back up data that changed since the last full backup, even if there has been a subsequent differential backup.

- **Transaction log backups**   A *transaction log backup* records the changes that have occurred since the previous transaction log backup and then truncates the transaction log. A truncation removes transactions from the log that have been committed to the database or cancelled. Transaction log backups represent the state of the transaction log at the time the backup is initiated rather than at the time the backup completes. Transaction log backups function incrementally rather than differentially. When restoring transaction log backups, you must restore in sequence. You learn more about restoring transaction logs in the next lesson.

- **File and filegroup backups** File and filegroup backups back up individual database files and filegroups rather than performing a full database backup. This method backs up very large databases. You must back up the transaction log when performing a file and filegroup backup.

- **Copy-only backups** Copy-only backups are functionally the same as full database or transaction log backups but do not affect the backup sequence. For example, if you took a full backup, a copy backup, and then a transaction log backup, all the transaction logs since the full backup would be backed up, and the existence of the copy backup would be ignored. Copy backups cannot be used as the basis for a differential backup or transaction log backup.

You can use more than one backup type in a backup strategy. For example, you might perform full backups on a daily basis, differential backups every couple of hours, and transaction log backups every ten minutes to protect one or more user databases. To determine the most appropriate combination of backups for your situation, you must also consider the method you will use to restore data. You learn more about restoring data in Lesson 3, "Restoring SQL Server Databases."

SQL Server 2012 backup has the following restrictions:

- You cannot back up offline data, so if one filegroup of the database is offline when you perform a full backup, the backup will fail. If you perform a file and filegroup backup and one of the target files is offline, the backup will fail.

- File-management operations such as using the ALTER DATABASE statement with the ADD FILE or REMOVE FILE options initiated during a backup execute only after the backup completes. The same applies to database shrink operations.

MORE INFO **BACKUP OVERVIEW**

You can learn more about SQL Server backup at *http://msdn.microsoft.com/en-us/library /ms175477.aspx.*

EXAM TIP

Remember that a differential backup backs up data since the last full backup, even if there have been intervening differential backups.

Using Backup Compression

Backup compression reduces the amount of space required to store a backup at the cost of increased CPU load during the compression process. You can use Resource Governor to limit CPU usage, and it is possible to run compressed backups in a special session that minimizes the impact of CPU use on other processes running on the host server.

> **MORE INFO   RESOURCE GOVERNOR AND BACKUP COMPRESSION**
>
> You can learn more about using Resource Governor to reduce the impact of CPU usage on backup compression at *http://msdn.microsoft.com/en-us/library/cc280384.aspx*.

The space savings due to backup compression depend on the contents of the database being backed up and compressed. You can calculate the compression ratio of a compressed backup after you have performed the backup by querying, using the backup_size and compressed_backup_size columns of the backupset history table.

Backup compression is disabled by default. You can configure backup compression at the instance level by choosing the Compress Backup option on the Database Settings page of the Server Properties dialog box, as shown in Figure 11-16.

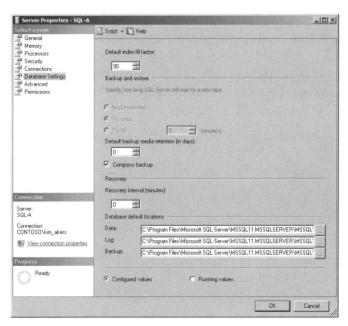

FIGURE 11-16 Instance compression setting

You can use the following Transact-SQL statement to enable backup compression on an instance:

```
EXEC sys.sp_configure [backup compression default], 1
GO
RECONFIGURE WITH OVERRIDE
GO
```

You can override the instance-level compression setting by using either the WITH NO_COMPRESSION or the WITH COMPRESSION option when using the BACKUP Transact-SQL statement. You can also choose to override the instance-level setting when performing backups by using SQL Server Management Studio.

You cannot store compressed and uncompressed backups in a media set.

> **MORE INFO** **BACKUP COMPRESSION**
>
> You can learn more about backup compression at *http://msdn.microsoft.com/en-us/library/bb964719.aspx.*

Understanding Recovery Models

Database *recovery models* determine how you back up a database and the strategy you implement to meet your Recovery Point Objective (RPO). RPO enables you to measure the amount of data that might be lost in the event of failure. For example, if your organization or department is subject to a Service Level Agreement (SLA) that specifies that no more than an hour's data can be lost from a database, the RPO is one hour. The Recovery Time Objective (RTO) is a separate measure used in SLAs to specify a maximum amount of time it can take to restore data to the RPO.

SQL Server 2012 databases support the following recovery models:

- **Simple** No transaction log backups are taken. It is possible to recover to the most recent database backup only; it does not allow point-in-time recovery.

- **Full** Full recovery requires you to take transaction log backups and full backups. Depending on the type of failure, you can recover either to the point of the last full backup or to the point of the last transaction log backup. If the active transaction log is still available, you might be able to recover to the most recent committed transaction. Full recovery enables point-in-time recovery.

- **Bulk-logged** Bulk-logged recovery is a special recovery model that minimizes transaction log activity during bulk operations. You cannot perform point-in-time recovery by using this model.

You can configure a recovery model for a database on the Options page of the Database Properties dialog box, as shown in Figure 11-17. You can change a database recovery model by using the ALTER DATABASE statement with the SET RECOVERY option. For example, to configure the AdventureWorks2012 database to use the full recovery model, execute the statement:

```
ALTER DATABASE [AdventureWorks2012] SET RECOVERY FULL;
```

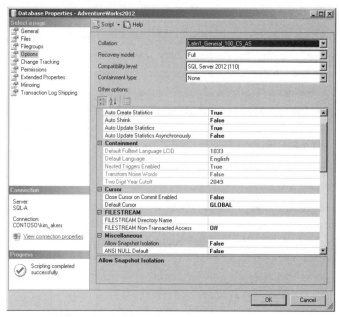

FIGURE 11-17 Database recovery model

MORE INFO **RECOVERY MODELS**

You can learn more about recovery models at *http://msdn.microsoft.com/en-us/library /ms189275.aspx*.

 Quick Check

- Which recovery models enable you to take transaction log backups?

Quick Check Answer

- The full and bulk-logged recovery models enable you to take transaction log backups.

Backing Up System Databases

Although backups of appropriate system databases should be performed on a regular basis, it is generally not necessary to back up these databases as frequently as you back up user databases. All system databases use the simple recovery model by default. This means that unless you make an alteration, you do not need to take transaction log backups.

Backup requirements for system databases are as follows:

- **master** This database hosts system-level information. Back up this database regularly.
- **model** You need to back up the template database only after you have made modifications. Because changes to the template database are usually infrequent, this database does not need to be backed up regularly.
- **msdb** This database hosts scheduling data for alerts and jobs and hosts operator information. It also stores the backup and restore history tables. You should back up this database whenever you make changes to jobs and alerts.
- **tempdb** This database is re-created each time the Database Engine starts. You can't back up the tempdb database.
- **Resource (RDB)** This read-only database holds copies of all system objects. You cannot back up this database by using the tools available in SQL Server 2012, but you can use a backup solution such as Windows Server Backup or System Center Data Protection Manager to perform a file-based backup. You should make a backup of this database, named mssqlsystemresource.mdf, after you apply updates and service packs to SQL Server 2012.
- **Configure Distribution** This system database is present only when the instance holds the distributor role in a replication topology. This database stores history information and metadata related to replication. It also stores transactions for transactional replication. This database should be backed up with the same frequency as the publication and subscription databases.

> **MORE INFO** **BACKING UP SYSTEM DATABASES**
>
> You can learn more about backing up system databases at *http://msdn.microsoft.com /en-us/library/ms190190.aspx*.

Backing Up Replicated Databases

When backing up replicated databases, you must also back up the system databases used by the replication process. You should include the following in your backup strategy:

- master, msdb, and publication databases at the publisher instance
- master, msdb, and distribution databases at the distributor instance
- master, msdb, and subscription databases at the subscriber instances

When backing up databases that use snapshot and transactional replication, you should set the sync with the Backup option on the publication and distribution databases. This ensures that transactions in the publication database transaction log are not truncated until they have been backed up at the distribution database.

Backing Up Mirrored Databases

When you have a mirroring session, you can back up only the principal database. You cannot back up the mirrored database in a mirroring session. When you perform a backup of the principal database, you cannot use the BACKUP LOG WITH NORECOVERY option.

Backing Up AlwaysOn Replicas

How you back up replicas in an AlwaysOn availability group depends on the automated backup preference setting applied at the availability group level. You can choose from the following options when configuring availability group backup preferences, as shown in Figure 11-18:

- **Prefer Secondary** This is the default. Backups should occur only on a secondary replica, which allows backups to be taken on the primary replica if that is the only replica online.
- **Secondary Only** All automatic backups occur on secondary replicas. Backups should not be taken if the primary replica is the only replica online.
- **Primary** Backups should always be taken on the primary replica. This allows differential backups to be taken.
- **Any Replica** Backups can occur on any replica in the availability group. Automated backups use the backup priority setting applied in the preference when choosing a replica as the target for a backup.

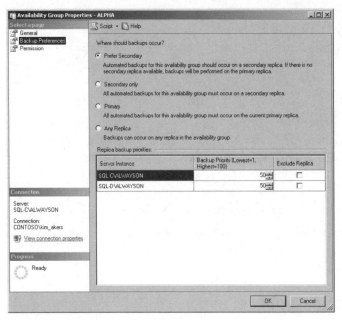

FIGURE 11-18 AlwaysOn backup preference

You can change the backup preference by using the ALTER AVAILABILITY GROUP statement with the AUTOMATED_BACKUP_PREFERENCE option. For example, to configure the AG_ALPHA availability group so that backups occur on secondary replicas only, execute the following statement:

```
ALTER AVAILABILITY GROUP [AG_ALPHA] SET ( AUTOMATED_BACKUP_PREFERENCE = SECONDARY_ONLY
);
```

Only BACKUP LOG operations are fully supported on secondary replicas. You can also perform copy-only full backups of the database, files, or filegroups. You cannot perform differential backups of active AlwaysOn secondary replicas. You can perform a backup on a secondary replica only if the secondary replica can communicate with the primary replica and is in either the SYNCHRONIZED or SYNCRHONIZING state.

> **MORE INFO** **BACKING UP ALWAYSON SECONDARY REPLICAS**
>
> You can learn more about backing up AlwaysOn secondary replicas at *http://msdn
> .microsoft.com/en-us/library/hh245119.aspx*.

Using Database Checkpoints

 A *database checkpoint* writes all modified pages held in memory to disk and then records that information in the transaction log. The Database Engine manages checkpoints automatically; usually, a checkpoint occurs every minute.

You can alter the frequency of database checkpoints at the instance level by configuring the recovery interval setting, as shown in Figure 11-19. You can also configure the recovery interval by using the sp_configure stored procedure and the recovery interval (min) option. You can alter the frequency of checkpoints at the database level by using the ALTER DATABASE statement with the SET TARGET_RECOVERY_TIME parameter.

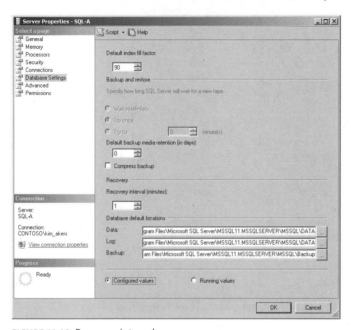

FIGURE 11-19 Recovery interval

> **MORE INFO** **DATABASE CHECKPOINTS**
>
> You can learn more about database checkpoints at *http://msdn.microsoft.com/en-us /library/ms189573.aspx.*

Using Backup Devices

SQL Server supports writing backups to local volumes, network shares, and compatible tape drives. You can create a *backup device* by performing the following steps:

1. In SQL Server Management Studio, expand the Server Objects folder.

2. Right-click the Backup Devices node and then choose New Backup Device.

3. On the Backup Device page, shown in Figure 11-20, provide a device name. If backing up to a file location, provide the filename and path.

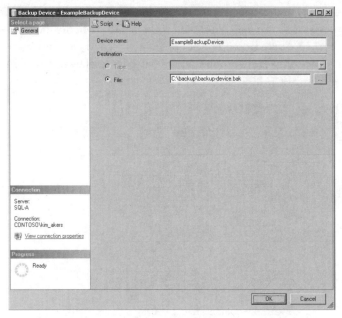

FIGURE 11-20 Example backup device

NOTE **TAPE DRIVE**

The tape drive option is available only if you have a tape drive connected.

You can create a backup device from Transact-SQL by using the sp_addumpdevice stored procedure. For example, to create a new backup device named Alpha-Backup that uses the file c:\backup\alpha-backup.bak location, execute the following statement:

```
EXEC sp_addumpdevice 'disk', 'Alpha-Backup', 'c:\backup\alpha-backup.bak'
```

When you create a backup device, you can back up to that device directly. For example, to back up the AdventureWorks2012 database to the backup device created in the previous code example, execute the statement:

```
BACKUP Database AdventureWorks2012 to [Alpha-Backup];
```

MORE INFO **BACKUP DEVICES**

You can learn more about backup devices at *http://msdn.microsoft.com/en-us/library /ms179313.aspx.*

Backing Up Media Sets

A *media set* can include a single file, multiple files, a tape, or multiple tapes. A single media set can include up to 32 backup devices. You create a media set by adding backup devices as destinations. A media set cannot be a combination of tape and files.

Mirrored backup media sets enable you to have multiple copies of a media set. A mirrored media set contains between two and four mirrors. Corresponding volumes in each mirror store identical contents. Mirrored media sets provide redundancy for the backup. If one backup device fails, data can still be restored from one of the mirrored backup devices.

> **MORE INFO   MIRRORED BACKUP MEDIA SETS**
>
> You can learn more about mirrored backup media sets at *http://msdn.microsoft.com/en-us /library/ms175053.aspx*.

Performing Backups

You can use SQL Server Management Studio to perform a one-off backup or to configure a backup job that runs according to a schedule.

Full and Differential Backups

To perform a one-off full backup of a database by using SQL Server Management Studio, execute the following steps:

1. Right-click the database you want to back up, choose Tasks, and then choose Back Up.

2. In the Back Up Database dialog box, shown in Figure 11-21, verify that Backup Type is set to Full. Specify a name for the Backup Set. Specify the destination by either using an existing backup device or creating a new backup device. Configuring a backup expiration enables SQL Server backup to overwrite the backup after the backup has expired.

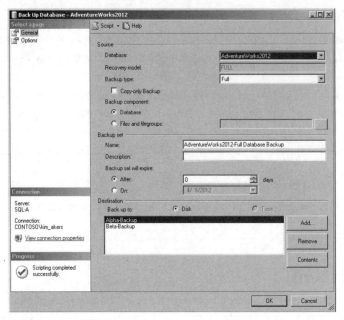

FIGURE 11-21 Full backup

3. On the Options page, shown in Figure 11-22, choose whether to append to the existing media set or overwrite the existing backup sets. You can choose to back up to a new media set, erasing all existing sets. You can also choose to verify backups or perform a checksum test on data before it is written to backup and whether to continue the backup operation if an error occurs. You can also set the backup compression setting here.

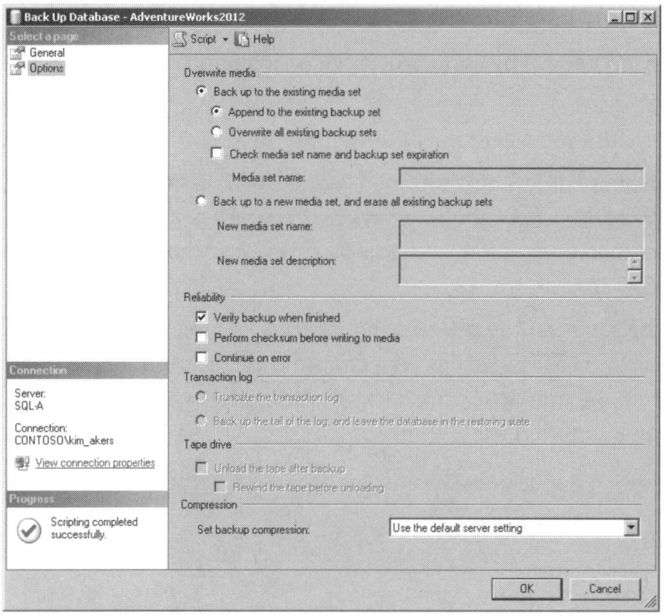

FIGURE 11-22 Full backup options

You can use the BACKUP DATABASE statement to perform both full and differential backups. For example, to perform a full backup of the AdventureWorks2012 database to the Alpha-Backup backup device, execute the following statement:

```
BACKUP DATABASE [AdventureWorks2012] to [Alpha-Backup];
```

The default option is not to overwrite existing media and to preserve the existing backup set. To perform a differential backup of the AdventureWorks2012 database to the Alpha-Backup backup device, execute the following statement:

```
BACKUP DATABASE [AdventureWorks2012] to [Alpha-Backup] WITH DIFFERENTIAL;
```

> *NOTE* **ENTERPRISE BACKUP**
>
> In real-world environments, when you are managing large numbers of instances, you are likely to use an enterprise backup solution, such as System Center Data Protection Manager or a third-party product, rather than the SQL Server native backup functionality. Enterprise products provide better notification and reporting functionality. They also provide optimized interfaces for performing backup and restore operations.

Performing Transaction Log Backups

To perform a transaction log backup by using SQL Server Management Studio, execute the following steps:

1. Right-click the database you want to back up, choose Tasks, and then choose Back Up.

2. In the Back Up Database dialog box, shown in Figure 11-23, verify that Backup Type is set to Transaction Log. You can choose to back up to a backup device that hosts existing full, differential, and transaction log backups, or you can choose to back up to a separate backup device.

3. If backing up to the same backup device as full backups, on the Options page, choose Append To The Existing Backup Set. You can choose either to truncate the transaction log after performing the transaction log backup or to perform a tail-log backup, leaving the database in a restoring state.

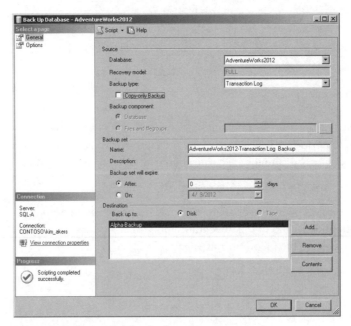

FIGURE 11-23 Transaction log backup

You perform a tail-log backup prior to performing a database restoration. The default option is to have the transaction log truncated. You can perform transaction log backups by using the BACKUP LOG Transact-SQL statement. For example, to perform a transaction log backup of the AdventureWorks2012 database to the Alpha-Backup backup device, execute the following statement:

```
BACKUP LOG [AdventureWorks2012] to [Alpha-Backup]
```

Viewing Backup History

Backup events are written to the SQL Server log from the backup source. These events are also written to the Application Event Log on the host computer. You can view backup events by using the log file viewer, as shown in Figure 11-24. To view only backup-related events, use the Filter option to view only events related to backup.

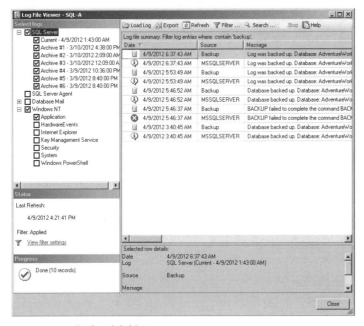

FIGURE 11-24 Backup job history

You can determine whether a backup was successful by querying the backupset table in the msdb database. For example, to get the backup name, backup finish time, and backup size, execute the following Transact-SQL statement:

```
SELECT database_name, backup_finish_date, backup_size, type FROM msdb.dbo.backupset;
```

> **MORE INFO** **BACKUP HISTORY**
>
> You can learn more about backup history at *http://msdn.microsoft.com/en-us/library /ms188653.aspx.*

In this practice, you perform backup operations on the AdventureWorks2012 database.

EXERCISE 1 Create a Backup Device and Prepare AdventureWorks2012

In this exercise, you prepare the AdventureWorks2012 database for backup operations. To complete this exercise, perform the following steps:

1. Log on to server SQL-A with the Kim Akers user account.
2. Open SQL Server Management Studio and connect to the default instance.
3. Verify that AdventureWorks2012 uses the full recovery model. If it does not, change the database so that it does.
4. Create a backup device named **adv2012back** that uses the c:\backup\adv2012back .bak file.

EXERCISE 2 Back Up AdventureWorks2012

In this exercise, you perform a full, a differential, and two transaction log backups of the AdventureWorks2012 database. To complete this exercise, perform the following steps:

1. Create a full backup of the AdventureWorks2012 database by using SQL Server Management Studio to the adv2012back backup device.
2. Use Transact-SQL to perform a differential backup of the AdventureWorks2012 database to the adv2012back backup device.
3. Create a transaction log backup of the AdventureWorks2012 database by using the Back Up Database dialog box. Have this backup written to the adv2012back backup device.
4. Create a second transaction log backup of the AdventureWorks2012 database by using Transact-SQL. Have this backup written to the adv2012back backup device.
5. Use the log file viewer to view only information about backups.
6. Use a Transact-SQL statement to query the msdb.dbo.backupset table for information on the database name, backup finish time, backup size, and backup type.

Lesson Summary

- Full database backups back up all database objects, system tables, and data.
- Differential backups back up all data that has changed since the last full backup.
- Transaction log backups back up all transaction log data that has been generated since the last transaction log backup.
- File and filegroup backups enable you to back up large databases.
- Copy backups enable you to perform backups without affecting the existing backup sequence.
- The system databases use the simple recovery model by default.

- You should back up the master and msdb databases regularly. You should back up the model database when you make changes to it.
- You can view backup history by using the log file viewer or by querying msdb.dbo .backupset.

Lesson Review

Answer the following questions to test your knowledge of the information in this lesson. You can find the answers to these questions and explanations of why each answer choice is correct or incorrect in the "Answers" section at the end of this chapter.

1. You perform a full backup daily at 1 A.M. and transaction log backups every half hour on a database. You want to perform a full backup of the database at 1 P.M. without affecting the existing restore sequence. Which of the following backup types should you perform to accomplish this goal?

   A. Full backup

   B. Transaction log backup

   C. Differential backup

   D. Copy backup

2. You perform a full backup daily at 1 A.M. You perform transaction log backups every 30 minutes. You want to back up all data that has changed since the last full backup. Which of the following backups should you perform?

   A. Full backup

   B. Transaction log backup

   C. Differential backup

   D. Copy backup

3. Which of the following system databases do you NOT need to back up because it is regenerated each time the Database Engine restarts?

   A. master

   B. msdb

   C. tempdb

   D. model

4. Which backup preference should you set for an AlwaysOn availability group if you want backups to occur on secondary replicas but which enables backups to occur on the primary replica if that replica is the only one online?

   A. Prefer Secondary

   B. Secondary Only

   C. Primary

   D. Any Replica

Lesson 3: Restoring SQL Server Databases

This lesson covers the techniques you can use to restore user and system databases, either completely or to a specific point in time.

> **After this lesson, you will be able to:**
> - Restore databases.
> - Perform page restore.
> - Restore system databases.
> - Perform file restore.
> - Restore databases protected by Transparent Data Encryption.
>
> **Estimated lesson time: 60 minutes**

Restoring Databases

Restore options depend on the backups that exist. If you have taken only full database backups, your options are going to be different than if you've taken full backups with transaction log backups. The following general rules apply to restoring databases for given existing backups:

- **Full backups only**   You can restore the database by using the last full backup to the point in time when the backup operation completed.
- **Full and differential backups**   You can restore the database to the point in time when the most recent differential backup operation completed. You do this by first restoring the most recent full backup by using the NORECOVERY option. You then restore the most recent differential backup by using the RECOVERY option.
- **Full and transaction log backups**   Depending on the state of the database, you might be able to restore to the most recent transaction. If possible, you first back up the current transaction log by using the NO_TRUNCATE option. You then recover the most recent full backup by using the NORECOVERY option. You then restore transaction logs in order from oldest, taken after the most recent full backup by using the NORECOVERY option, until you get to the most recent transaction log, which you restore by using the RECOVERY option. You learn about point-in-time recovery later in this lesson.
- **Full, differential, and transaction log backups**   Depending on the state of the database, you might be able to restore to the most recent transaction. If possible, you first back up the current transaction log by using the NO_TRUNCATE option. You then restore the most recent full backup by using the NORECOVERY option. After this is done, recover the most recent differential backup by using the NORECOVERY option.

You then restore transaction logs in order from oldest, taken after the most recent differential backup by using the NORECOVERY option, until you get to the most recent transaction log, which you restore by using the RECOVERY option. You learn about point-in-time recovery later in this lesson.

The following limitations apply to recovering databases:

- You can recover databases backed up on SQL Server 2000, SQL Server 2005, SQL Server 2008, and SQL Server 2008 R2 by using SQL Server 2012.

- You cannot recover databases backed up by using SQL Server 2012 backup on previous versions of SQL Server.

- You cannot restore system databases backed up on previous versions of SQL Server on SQL Server 2012.

MORE INFO **PLANNING RESTORE SEQUENCES**

You can learn more about planning restore sequences at *http://msdn.microsoft.com/en-us /library/ms189627.aspx*.

To perform a restore of a database that uses the full recovery model and for which there is an existing set of transaction log backups by using SQL Server Management Studio, perform the following steps:

1. In SQL Server Management Studio, determine whether the database is still running. If it is, perform a tail-log backup of the current transaction log, as shown in Figure 11-25.

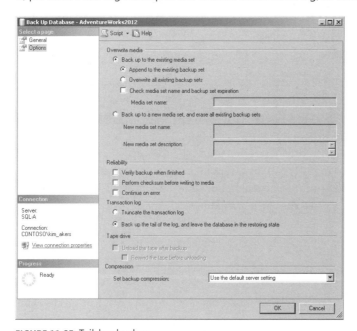

FIGURE 11-25 Tail-log backup

2. In SQL Server Management Studio, right-click the database you want to restore, choose Tasks, select Restore, and then choose Database.

If you have performed all backup operations by using SQL Server Management Studio, the Restore Database dialog box, shown in Figure 11-26, will list all full, differential, and transaction log backups that have been performed that are relevant to the restoration media. The dialog box shows the device that stores the most recent chain of backups. You can use the Device option to choose a different backup device and database from which to restore. You can use the Database drop-down list in the Destination section to specify an alternate database to which to restore. The default is to restore over the original database.

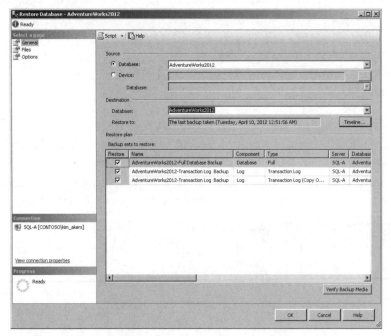

FIGURE 11-26 Restore database

3. If you do not want to restore to the last point in time, you can click the Timeline button to bring up the Backup Timeline dialog box shown in Figure 11-27, which enables you to perform a restore to a specific point in time.

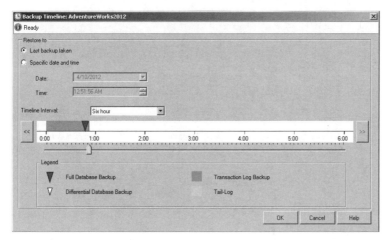

FIGURE 11-27 Restore timeline

4. On the options page, shown in Figure 11-28, you can choose whether to overwrite the existing database, to keep replication settings, and to set the restored database to RESTRICTED_USER mode. You can use the Recovery State drop-down menu to choose among the following options:

-   **RESTORE WITH RECOVERY**   This returns the database to normal operation.

-   **RESTORE WITH NORECOVERY**   The database is recovered but cannot be accessed. This mode is used when placing a database on a mirror in a mirroring set. When you choose the RESTORE WITH NORECOVERY option, further transaction log backups can be applied to the database.

-   **RESTORE WITH STANDBY**   The database is recovered but left in read-only mode. Additional transaction log backups can be applied, but it is possible for users with appropriate permissions to query the database to verify the integrity of the data.

If a tail-log backup of the database has not been taken, this option will also be available. You also have the option of closing existing connections to the database because you cannot perform a restore operation on a database if there are existing active connections.

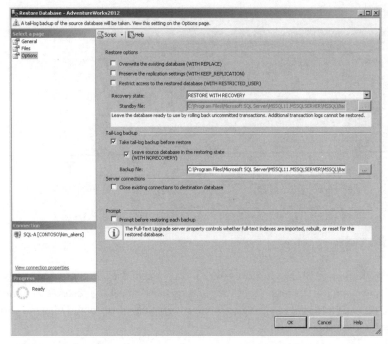

FIGURE 11-28 Restore options

> ✔ **Quick Check**
>
> ■ If the database that uses the full recovery model is currently running, what
>   step should you take prior to attempting a restore operation?
>
> **Quick Check Answer**
>
> ■ You should perform a tail-log backup prior to attempting a restore operation.

Performing File Restores

If a database contains multiple files or filegroups and uses the full or bulk-logged recovery model, you can perform a file restore rather than a full restore. You might perform a file restore if the volume that hosts a particular file fails or a file becomes corrupt, but the other files used by the database do not have any problems. All editions of SQL Server 2012 support offline file restores. You perform an offline file restore when the database is taken online.

SQL Server 2012 Enterprise edition supports online file restore. Online file restores enable you to restore files in secondary filegroups as long as the primary filegroup is online.

You can perform a file restore by taking the following steps:

1. If possible, take a tail-log backup of the database on which you want to perform the file restore. If it is not possible to take a tail-log backup, it will be necessary to perform a complete database restore.

2. Restore the corrupt file from the most recent backup that includes the file. You can perform file restores independently of whether you've taken full or file backups.

3. Restore any differential backups that were taken of the file.

4. Restore all transaction logs in sequence taken since the most recent differential, full, or file backup of the file.

Performing Page Restores

You can use *page restore* to repair a small number of damaged pages in an otherwise healthy database. Performing a page-level recovery can be quicker than performing other types of restores. If a database file constantly suffers from damaged pages, it is likely that the volume that hosts the file is faulty.

You can perform a page restore under the following conditions:

- It is possible to perform a page restore only on a database that uses the full or bulk-logged recovery model.

- You can perform page restores only on read/write filegroups.

- You can restore only database pages. You cannot restore pages in the transaction log, the full-text catalog, the database boot page, or the file boot page.

- SQL Server 2012 Enterprise edition supports online page restore. All editions of SQL Server 2012 support offline page restore.

To restore a page by using SQL Server Management Studio, perform the following steps:

1. Right-click the database on which you will perform the page restore. Click Tasks, Restore, and then Page.

2. In the Restore Page dialog box, shown in Figure 11-29, click Check Database Pages to locate all corrupt pages in the selected database. Click OK to restore those pages that were detected as corrupt.

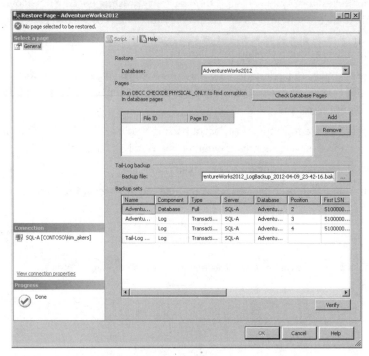

FIGURE 11-29 Restoring corrupted pages

You can use the RESTORE DATABASE statement to perform a page restore operation if you have the file ID of the file that hosts the page and the page ID of the page you want to restore. For example, pages 42, 81, and 1023 of file beta_file of the HOVERCRAFT database are corrupt. The ID of beta_file is 2, and you have taken a backup of beta_file named beta_file_backup. To recover the necessary pages, issue the statement:

```
RESTORE DATABASE HOVERCRAFT PAGE='2:42, 2:81, 2:1023' FROM beta_file_backup WITH
NORECOVERY;
```

After you have taken this step, restore any transaction logs taken after the file backup by using the NORECOVERY option. Then perform a new log backup. Complete the operation by restoring the newly created log backup by using the RECOVERY option.

> **MORE INFO** **RESTORING PAGES**
>
> You can learn more about restoring pages at *http://msdn.microsoft.com/en-us/library/ms175168.aspx.*

AlwaysOn Availability Groups and database mirrors support automatic page repair. In AlwaysOn Availability Groups, if the error occurs on the primary database, the primary broadcasts a request to all secondaries and retrieves the page from the first to respond. You can verify the status of automatic page repairs in the following manner:

- **AlwaysOn Availability Groups** Query the sys.dm_hadr_auto_page_repair dynamic management view.
- **Database mirroring** Query the sys.dm_db_mirroring_auto_page_repair dynamic management view.

> **MORE INFO** **AUTOMATIC PAGE REPAIR**
>
> You can learn more about automatic page repair at *http://msdn.microsoft.com/en-us/library/bb677167.aspx*.

Restoring a Database Protected with Transparent Data Encryption

You can restore a database that uses Transparent Data Encryption (TDE) as long as you have access to the certificate and private keys. When planning the backup of databases protected with TDE, include the certificate used to create the Database Encryption Key (DEK) and the Database Encryption Key in your backup scheme.

Prior to performing a restore, if the certificate used to create the DEK is not present, you must re-create this certificate by using the backup of the original certificate. You can do this by using the CREATE CERTIFICATE statement with the FROM FILE option. After the certificate is present on the server, you can restore the encrypted database.

> **MORE INFO** **RESTORING DATABASES PROTECTED WITH TDE**
>
> You can learn more about restoring databases protected with TDE at *http://msdn.microsoft.com/en-us/library/bb934049.aspx*.

Restoring System Databases

You can restore the model and msdb databases by using the same procedure you would use to restore a user database. Because these databases do not use the full recovery model by default, you do not need to worry about restoring transaction log backups with these databases. Because the tempdb system database is re-created each time the Database Engine starts, it is not necessary to restore this system database.

The master database is more complicated because it is possible that a corrupt master database might prevent the Database Engine from starting. If you can start the Database Engine in single-user mode, you can use the following statement to restore the master database from backup:

```
RESTORE DATABASE master from <backup_device> WITH REPLACE
```

> **MORE INFO**   **RESTORING SYSTEM DATABASES**
>
> You can learn more about restoring system databases at *http://msdn.microsoft.com/en-us /library/ms190190.aspx*.

If the Database Engine is unable to start, you can rebuild the master database and other system databases by using setup. Because the rebuild operation also rebuilds the msdb and model databases, it might be necessary to restore more recently backed-up versions of these databases after the Database Engine can start successfully.

To rebuild the system databases, run the following command, preferably from the setup. exe executable folder, stored by default in the following location: c:\Program Files\Microsoft SQL Server\110\Setup Bootstrap\SQLServer2012\setup.exe:

```
setup /Q /ACTION=REBUILDDATABASE /INSTANCENAME=MSSQLSERVER
```

> **MORE INFO**   **REBUILDING SYSTEM DATABASES**
>
> You can learn more about rebuilding system databases at *http://msdn.microsoft.com /en-us/library/dd207003.aspx*.

Restoring Replicated Databases

When you restore a publication, distribution, or subscription database, you must also restore the master and msdb databases on the instance. This ensures that all three databases are consistent with respect to replication configuration and settings.

> **MORE INFO**   **BACKING UP REPLICATED DATABASES**
>
> You can learn more about backing up replicated databases at *http://msdn.microsoft.com /en-us/library/ms151152.aspx*.

Checking Database Status

Whether you perform a restore operation depends on the current state of the database. You can check the status of a database by using the following statement:

```
SELECT databasepropertyex ('databasename', 'Status');
```

The output from this statement is as follows:

- **ONLINE**   The database is operating normally.
- **OFFLINE**   The database has been taken offline.
- **RESTORING**   The database is in the process of being restored.
- **RECOVERING**   The database is in the process of being recovered but will not respond to queries.
- **SUSPECT**   A recovery operation has failed, and the database might be corrupt.
- **EMERGENCY**   The database is in a read-only state accessible only to members of the sysadmin role.

You can check which users can access a database by using the following statement:

```
SELECT databasepropertyex ('databasename', 'UserAccess');
```

The output from this statement informs you of whether the access is set to:

- **SINGLE_USER**   Only a single user with the db_owner, dbcreator, or sysadmin roles can access the database.
- **RESTRICTED_USER**   Only members of the db_owner, dbcreator, and sysadmin roles can access the database.
- **MULTI_USER**   The database is accessible to multiple users.

You can check whether the database is read/write or read-only by executing the following statement:

```
SELECT databasepropertyex ('databasename', 'Updateability');
```

> **MORE INFO**   **DATABASEPROPERTYEX**
>
> You can learn more about the DATABASEPROPERTYEX function at *http://msdn.microsoft .com/en-us/library/ms186823.aspx*.

EXAM TIP

Remember to perform a tail-log backup when using the full recovery model prior to attempting a restore operation.

PRACTICE   Restoring the AdventureWorks2012 Database

In this practice, you perform restore operations on the AdventureWorks2012 database backed up in the practice in Lesson 2, "Configuring and Maintaining a Backup Strategy."

EXERCISE 1   Prepare the AdventureWorks2012 Database

In this exercise, you prepare the AdventureWorks2012 database for a restore operation by deleting a table that has no dependencies. To complete this exercise, perform the following steps:

1. Log on to SQL-A with the Kim_Akers user account and open SQL Server Management Studio.

2. Make a note of the system time.

3. After a minute has passed, drop the Sales.ShoppingCartItem table from the AdventureWorks2012 database.

EXERCISE 2   Perform a Restore of the AdventureWork2012 Database

In this exercise, you restore data from the backups taken at the end of Lesson 2 as a way of restoring the Sales.ShoppingCartItem table. To complete this exercise, perform the following steps:

1. Perform a restore of the AdventureWorks2012 database to the point of time you noted in Step 2 of Exercise 1. Ensure that the restore operation involves a tail-log backup automatically being performed. Also ensure that you choose Close Existing Connections To Destination Database.

2. When the restoration has occurred, verify that the Sales.ShoppingCartItem table that you deleted in Step 2 of Exercise 1 is now present in the database.

Lesson Summary

- A full backup–only strategy enables you to restore only to the point at which the full backup was taken.

- A full and differential backup strategy enables you to restore to the point at which the last differential backup was taken.

- A full and transaction log strategy, or a full, differential, and transaction log strategy enables you to restore to a specific transaction or point in time.

- You should perform a tail-log backup of the current database, if possible, prior to attempting a restore operation.

- The RESTORE WITH RECOVERY option returns a database to normal operation.

- The RESTORE WITH NORECOVERY option recovers the database, but the database cannot be accessed.

- The RESTORE WITH STANDBY option leaves the database in read-only mode.

- Only SQL Server 2012 Enterprise edition supports online file and page restores.

- When performing an online file restore, you must perform a backup after performing the file restore and transaction log restore to ensure that the database is consistent.

- You can rebuild the master, msdb, and model databases by using setup.exe.

Lesson Review

Answer the following questions to test your knowledge of the information in this lesson. You can find the answers to these questions and explanations of why each answer choice is correct or incorrect in the "Answers" section at the end of this chapter.

1. A database has become corrupted. You will restore the database, but you want to examine it prior to allowing client queries and updates. Which of the following restore options should you use?

   A. RESTORE WITH RECOVERY

   B. RESTORE WITH NORECOVERY

   C. RESTORE WITH STANDBY

   D. RESTORE WITH KEEP_REPLICATION

2. You are performing an online file restore. Which is the final step in this process?

   A. Take a transaction log backup.

   B. Restore the most recent transaction log WITH STANDBY.

   C. Restore the most recent transaction log WITH RECOVERY.

   D. Restore the most recent transaction log WITH NORECOVERY.

3. You take a full database backup every day at 6 A.M. Differential backups are taken at 10 A.M. and 3 P.M. Transaction log backups are taken on the half hour except when a full or differential backup is being taken. Database files and transaction log files are stored on the same volume. The volume hosting the database files fails at 10:15 A.M. You replace the disk. Which of the following backups will you use when performing a restore operation? (Each correct answer presents part of a complete solution. Choose all that apply.)

   A. 6 A.M. full backup

   B. 10 A.M. differential backup

   C. 9.30 A.M. transaction log backup

   D. 10.30 A.M. transaction log backup

4. Which of the following system databases can you rebuild by using the setup.exe command? (Each correct answer presents a complete solution. Choose all that apply.)

   A. msdb

   B. model

   C. tempdb

   D. master

Case Scenarios

In the following case scenarios, you apply what you have learned about SQL Server Agent and backup and restore options. You can find answers to these questions in the "Answers" section at the end of this chapter.

Case Scenario 1: SQL Server Agent at Contoso

You are configuring automation at Contoso. Over the next week, a developer will be performing maintenance on the Hovercraft database. You have a number of alerts configured that trigger specific jobs and don't want these jobs running while maintenance is being performed on the database. You've also been investigating running a Windows PowerShell script on a regular basis to perform system maintenance tasks. This Windows PowerShell script should run only if the results of a Transact-SQL query are successful. Finally, you want to ensure that your colleague, Kim, is contacted if other operators are unavailable. With these facts in mind, answer the following questions:

1. How can you ensure that the Windows PowerShell script runs only after the Transact-SQL statement executes successfully?

2. How can you ensure that alerts are not triggered for the next week but can be triggered after the maintenance is complete?

3. How can you ensure that Kim is contacted if other operators are not available?

Case Scenario 2: Fabrikam Backup Strategy

You are developing a backup strategy at Fabrikam, which uses AlwaysOn Availability Groups as a high-availability solution. A large number of user databases are hosted on servers that are not members of availability groups. You have the following requirements:

- Backups should be taken of secondary instances for the Victoria availability group only.

- You want to create a backup device named file_backup on each server that uses the local file e:\store\file_backup.bak.

- You should be able to perform a point-in-time recovery on any user database at Fabrikam.

With these facts in mind, answer the following questions:

1. Which command should you issue to configure the Victoria availability group so that backups are taken only on the appropriate replicas?

2. Which command should you issue to create the appropriate backup device on each server?

3. Which recovery model should all the databases at Fabrikam use?

Case Scenario 3: Recovery at Adatum

You are performing a recovery on several SQL Server 2012 servers that have suffered a severe malware infection, leading to database corruption. You are currently dealing with the following problems:

- The master database on server SQL-SYD-A is corrupt, and you are unable to start the Database Engine instance.

- You want to determine whether the HOVERCRAFT database on server SYD-SQL-D is in the emergency state.

- One of the four files used for the NEPTUNE database has become corrupt.

With these facts in mind, answer the following questions:

1. Which command would you use to rebuild the system databases on SYD-SQL-A?

2. Which Transact-SQL statement can you use to check the state of the HOVERCRAFT database?

3. Under what conditions would you be able to perform an online file restore of the corrupted file of the NEPTUNE database?

Suggested Practices

To help you successfully master the exam objectives presented in this chapter, complete the following tasks.

Manage SQL Server Agent

Prior to completing each task in the following practices, list the steps you would take to accomplish the task. After completing the task, assess how accurately you predicted the necessary steps.

- **Practice 1**   Configure SQL-A as a master and SQL-A\ALTERNATE as a target for multi-server administration.

- **Practice 2**   Configure the SQL Server Agent error log to record only error events. The error log should not record warnings or information events.

Configure and Maintain a Backup Strategy

Prior to completing each task in the following practices, list the steps you would take to accomplish the task. After completing the task, assess how accurately you predicted the necessary steps.

- **Practice 1**   Create a new backup device named **Backup_TDE** in the c:\backups folder.

- **Practice 2**   On the ALTERNATE instance of SQL-A, create a database named **HEXAGON** that uses Transparent Data Encryption. Perform a full backup of this database to the Backup_TDE device. Also, back up the certificate and keys related to this database.

Restore Databases

Prior to completing each task in the following practices, list the steps you would take to accomplish the task. After completing the task, assess how accurately you predicted the necessary steps.

- **Practice 1**   On the default instance on SQL-A, create a new certificate by using the backup of the certificate you created to support Transparent Data Encryption on the HEXAGON database. Restore the HEXAGON database on the default instance on SQL-A.

- **Practice 2**   Use setup.exe to restore the system databases on the ALTERNATE instance on server SQL-A.

Answers

This section contains the answers to the lesson review questions and solutions to the case scenarios in this chapter.

Lesson 1

1. **Correct Answer: D**

   A. **Incorrect:** Backup operators can back up and restore files. Membership in this group will not resolve the described problem.

   B. **Incorrect:** Cryptographic operators can perform special cryptographic operations. Membership in this group will not resolve the described problem.

   C. **Incorrect:** Members of this group can run Performance Monitor. Membership in this group will not resolve the described problem.

   D. **Correct:** You must add the agent account to the Pre-Windows 2000 Compatible Access group to ensure that jobs run by users who are not members of the local administrator group run correctly.

2. **Correct Answer: A**

   A. **Correct:** This role gives Rooslan the appropriate permissions without providing permissions on the jobs of other users.

   B. **Incorrect:** This role enables the holder to view information about other users' jobs.

   C. **Incorrect:** This role enables the holder to run other users' job.

   D. **Incorrect:** This role enables the holder to perform any SQL Server Agent job–related tasks.

3. **Correct Answer: A**

   A. **Correct:** An alert based on a performance condition can ensure that a job is triggered.

   B. **Incorrect:** An operator is a point of contact.

   C. **Incorrect:** A maintenance plan is a set of predefined maintenance tasks. You can schedule maintenance plans, but they are not directly triggered by performance conditions.

   D. **Incorrect:** A proxy is a set of credentials used to run a SQL Server Agent job.

4. **Correct Answer: C**

   A. **Incorrect:** An operator is a point of contact.

   B. **Incorrect:** An alert can trigger a job but cannot perform independent actions beyond triggering a job, notifying an operator, or writing an event to a log.

C. Correct: You can configure a job to perform a set of separate executable tasks according to a schedule.

D. Incorrect: A proxy is a set of credentials used to run a SQL Server Agent job.

Lesson 2

1. **Correct Answer: D**

   A. Incorrect: A full backup will capture the necessary data but will also affect the existing restore sequence.

   B. Incorrect: A transaction log backup will not capture all the necessary data, only the transaction log data since the last transaction log backup.

   C. Incorrect: A differential backup will capture only data that changed since the last backup.

   D. Correct: A copy backup will capture all the necessary data without affecting the existing restore sequence.

2. **Correct Answer: C**

   A. Incorrect: A full backup captures all data when you want to capture only data that changed since the last full backup.

   B. Incorrect: Transaction log backups capture only transaction log data that changed since the last transaction log backup.

   C. Correct: A differential backup captures all data that has changed since the last full backup.

   D. Incorrect: A copy backup can be either a transaction log or a full backup. It captures either a full copy of the database or a transaction log without affecting the existing backup sequence.

3. **Correct Answer: C**

   A. Incorrect: The master database is not regenerated each time you restart the Database Engine. You should back up the master database regularly.

   B. Incorrect: The msdb database is not regenerated each time you restart the Database Engine. You should back up the msdb database regularly.

   C. Correct: The tempdb database is re-created each time you restart the Database Engine.

   D. Incorrect: The model database is not regenerated each time you restart the Database Engine. You should back up this database whenever you make changes to it.

4. **Correct Answer: A**

   A. Correct: Backups are taken on secondary replicas but can be taken on the primary if the primary is the only available replica.

   B. Incorrect: Backups are taken on the secondary replica only.

C. **Incorrect:** Backups are taken on the primary replica only.

D. **Incorrect:** The Any Replica preference allows backups to occur on any replica.

Lesson 3

1. **Correct Answer: C**

   A. **Incorrect:** The RECOVERY option puts the database back into operation.

   B. **Incorrect:** When you use the NORECOVERY option, the database is restored but is not accessible.

   C. **Correct:** RESTORE WITH STANDBY puts the database into a read-only state, enabling members of the sysadmin role to check the integrity of the data.

   D. **Incorrect:** The KEEP_REPLICATION setting ensures that replication settings are kept. This does not ensure that the database is accessible only to members of the sysadmin role.

2. **Correct Answer: A**

   A. **Correct:** You must take a transaction log backup to complete an online file restore to bring the database into a consistent state.

   B. **Incorrect:** You do not need to restore the most recent transaction log by using the WITH STANDBY option. The final step in performing an online file recovery is to take a transaction log backup to bring the database into a consistent state.

   C. **Incorrect:** You do not need to restore the most recent transaction log by using the WITH RECOVERY option. The final step in performing an online file recovery is to take a transaction log backup to bring the database into a consistent state.

   D. **Incorrect:** You do not need to restore the most recent transaction log by using the WITH NORECOVERY option. The final step in performing an online file recovery is to take a transaction log backup to bring the database into a consistent state.

3. **Correct Answers: A and B**

   A. **Correct:** You will use the 6 A.M. full backup and the 10 A.M. differential backup in your restore sequence.

   B. **Correct:** You will use the 6 A.M. full backup and the 10 A.M. differential backup in your restore sequence.

   C. **Incorrect:** You will not use the 9:30 A.M. transaction log backup in your restore sequence. The existence of the 10 A.M. differential means that the 9:30 A.M. transaction log file is not required.

   D. **Incorrect:** You will not use the 10:30 A.M. transaction log backup in your restore sequence. The volume hosting the database files failed at 10:15 A.M., which means this log backup will not be available.

4. **Correct Answers: A, B, and D**

    A. **Correct:** You can rebuild the msdb database by using setup.exe.

    B. **Correct:** You can rebuild the model database by using setup.exe.

    C. **Incorrect:** The tempdb database is created when the Database Engine instance starts. You cannot rebuild this database by using setup.exe.

    D. **Correct:** You can rebuild the master database by using setup.exe.

Case Scenario 1

1. You can configure job steps so that the next step occurs only if the first step completes successfully.

2. Disable the alerts. You can re-enable them as necessary. While disabled, the jobs will not be triggered.

3. Configure Kim as a fail-safe operator.

Case Scenario 2

1. Issue the ALTER AVAILABILITY GROUP [Victoria] SET (AUTOMATED_BACKUP _PREFERENCE = SECONDARY_ONLY); command.

2. Execute the EXEC sp_addumpdevice 'disk', 'file_backup', 'e:\store\file_backup.bak' command to create the appropriate backup device.

3. All databases will need to use the full recovery model to ensure that point-in-time recovery is possible.

Case Scenario 3

1. Use the following command to rebuild the system databases on the default instance of SYD-SQL-A:

```
setup /Q /ACTION=REBUILDDATABASE /INSTANCENAME=MSSQLSERVER
```

2. Use the following command to check the current state of the HOVERCRAFT database:

```
SELECT databasepropertyex ('HOVERCRAFT', 'Status');
```

3. You can perform an online file restore of the corrupted file in the NEPTUNE database if you can perform a tail-log backup, the host instance is running SQL Server 2012 Enterprise edition, and the primary file group is online.

CHAPTER 12

Code Case Studies

Your real-world experience has given you opportunities to review and maintain code. The exam might also test your skills in this area. To help you prepare, this chapter presents multiple scenarios as code case studies. Review each case study and answer the questions.

Case Study 1

You are developing the necessary code to configure the Litware2012 database. This database will be hosted on a SQL Server 2012 instance. At present, the instance is configured in the following way:

- FILESTREAM is not currently enabled.
- No database master key exists.

```
01    USE [master]
02    GO
03    CREATE DATABASE [Litware2012]
04    GO
05    ALTER DATABASE [Litware2012] ADD FILEGROUP [Tertiary]
06    GO
07    ALTER DATABASE [Litware2012] ADD FILEGROUP [Quaternary]
08    GO
09    EXEC sp_configure filestream_access_level, 2
10    GO
11    RECONFIGURE
12    GO
13    ALTER DATABASE Litware2012 ADD FILEGROUP FileStreamFileGroup CONTAINS
FILESTREAM;
14    GO
15    ALTER DATABASE Litware2012 ADD FILE (
16         NAME = FileStrmFile,
17         FILENAME = 'C:\FSTRM')
18         TO FILEGROUP FileStreamFileGroup;
19    ALTER DATABASE Litware2012
20    SET FILESTREAM (NON_TRANSACTED_ACCESS = FULL, DIRECTORY_NAME = 'FTBLE');
21    USE [LitWare2012]
22    CREATE TABLE DocStore as FileTable;
23    GO
24    sp_configure 'contained database authentication', 1;
25    GO
```

```
26      RECONFIGURE;
27      GO
28              USE [master]
29      GO
30      ALTER DATABASE [Litware2012] SET CONTAINMENT = PARTIAL
31      GO
32      CREATE USER contained_user WITH PASSWORD = 'Pa$$w0rd';
33      USE master;
34      GO
35      CREATE MASTER KEY ENCRYPTION BY PASSWORD = 'P@ssw0rd';
36      GO
37      CREATE CERTIFICATE ServerCertificate WITH SUBJECT = 'Server Certificate';
38      GO
39      USE [LitWare2012];
40      GO
41      CREATE DATABASE ENCRYPTION KEY
42      WITH ALGORITHM = AES_128
43      ENCRYPTION BY SERVER CERTIFICATE ServerCertificate;
44      GO
45      ALTER DATABASE LitWare2012
46      SET ENCRYPTION ON;
47      GO
```

Questions

Answer the following questions to test your knowledge of the information in this case study. Refer to the code sample as necessary. You can find the answers to these questions and explanations of why each answer choice is correct or incorrect in the "Answers" section at the end of this chapter.

QUESTION 1

Prior to which line of code is it necessary to reconfigure and restart the Microsoft SQL Server service?

A. 01

B. 03

C. 13

D. 09

QUESTION 2

Which tool would you use to enable FILESTREAM on the SQL Server service?

A. SQL Server Management Studio

B. SQL Server Installation Center

C. SQL Server Configuration Manager

D. SQL Server Profiler

QUESTION 3

Which line configures the instance so that it supports use by database users who have no corresponding instance login?

A. 30

B. 24

C. 20

D. 32

QUESTION 4

Which Transact-SQL statement would you use to back up the database encryption key created on line 35?

A. BACKUP MASTER KEY

B. ALTER MASTER KEY

C. DROP MASTER KEY

D. CREATE MASTER KEY

QUESTION 5

Which line of code would you modify if you wanted to increase the database encryption key length to 256 bits?

A. 35

B. 37

C. 42

D. 46

QUESTION 6

Which of the following substitutions on line 42 would give you the strongest database encryption key?

A. WITH ALGORITHM = AES_128

B. WITH ALGORITHM = AES_192

C. WITH ALGORITHM = AES_256

D. WITH ALGORITHM = TRIPLE_DES_3KEY

QUESTION 7

This code creates a table mapped to a directory on the file system. You can add files to the database by copying them to this directory on the file system. What is the name of this table?

A. FILESTREAM

B. FTBLE

C. FSTRM

D. DocStore

QUESTION 8

Which line of code would you alter if you wanted to select a different directory to associate with file tables in the Litware2012 database?

- **A.** 20
- **B.** 22
- **C.** 30
- **D.** 17

QUESTION 9

After which line of code are you able to create contained users in the Litware2012 database?

- **A.** 24
- **B.** 09
- **C.** 30
- **D.** 35

QUESTION 10

Which of the following statements could you use to create a contained user mapped to the contoso\contained_user_b user in the Litware2012 database after all the code in the case study has been executed?

- **A.** CREATE USER contained_user_b WITH PASSWORD 'P@ssw0rd';
- **B.** CREATE LOGIN [contoso\contained_user_b];
- **C.** CREATE USER [contoso\contained_user_b] FOR LOGIN [contoso\contained_user_b];
- **D.** CREATE USER [contoso\contained_user_b];

QUESTION 11

After this statement has been executed, which of the following filegroups are associated with the Litware2012 database? (Choose all that apply.)

- **A.** Tertiary
- **B.** Secondary
- **C.** DocStore
- **D.** FileStreamFileGroup

QUESTION 12

Which of the following Transact-SQL statements would you use to remove the Tertiary filegroup?

- **A.** ALTER DATABASE
- **B.** ALTER SCHEMA
- **C.** DROP DATABASE
- **D.** DROP SCHEMA

QUESTION 13

After which line of code are you able to create databases that use contained authentication?

- **A.** 24
- **B.** 09
- **C.** 30
- **D.** 35

QUESTION 14

After you execute the code in the case study, you create a database named TailspinToys. Which of the following statements must you execute to apply transparent data encryption to this new database? (Choose all that apply.)

- **A.** CREATE MASTER KEY
- **B.** CREATE CERTIFICATE
- **C.** CREATE DATABASE ENCRYPTION KEY
- **D.** ALTER DATABASE

QUESTION 15

Which of the following Transact-SQL statements would you use to add a file named newfile.ndf in the c:\DBFILES to the Tertiary filegroup?

- **A.** ALTER DATABASE
- **B.** ALTER ENDPOINT
- **C.** ALTER SCHEMA
- **D.** ALTER TABLE

QUESTION 16

Which statement must be executed before it is possible to configure a database hosted on the instance to use FILESTREAM?

- **A.** 24
- **B.** 09
- **C.** 30
- **D.** 35

QUESTION 17

Which line of code would you modify if you wanted to alter the folder that hosts the FILESTREAM file?

- **A.** 22
- **B.** 30
- **C.** 17
- **D.** 20

QUESTION 18

Which of the following statements would you use to make the Tertiary filegroup read-only?

A. ALTER DATABASE

B. ALTER ENDPOINT

C. ALTER SCHEMA

D. ALTER TABLE

QUESTION 19

You have executed the code presented in the case scenario, but you want to change the database master key password. Which of the following statements would you use to accomplish this goal?

A. OPEN MASTER KEY

B. ALTER MASTER KEY

C. DROP MASTER KEY

D. CLOSE MASTER KEY

QUESTION 20

After which line of code is executed against the instance is it possible to create a server certificate?

A. 24

B. 09

C. 30

D. 35

Case Study 2

You are creating users, logins, and roles to secure the AdventureWorks2012 database. With this in mind, you have developed the following code:

```
01      USE [master]
02      GO
03      CREATE LOGIN "CONTOSO\Account_Two" FROM WINDOWS;
04      CREATE LOGIN "CONTOSO\Group_Two" FROM WINDOWS;
05      CREATE LOGIN sql_user_a WITH PASSWORD = 'Pa$$w0rd';
06      CREATE CERTIFICATE Dan_Bacon
07              WITH SUBJECT = 'Dan Bacon certificate in master database',
08                  EXPIRY_DATE = '01/01/2018';
09      CREATE LOGIN Dan_Bacon FROM CERTIFICATE Dan_Bacon;
10      CREATE ASYMMETRIC KEY sql_user_e WITH ALGORITHM = RSA_2048;
11      CREATE LOGIN sql_user_e FROM ASYMMETRIC KEY sql_user_e;
12      ALTER LOGIN sql_user_a DISABLE;
```

```
13    DENY CONNECT SQL TO [contoso\Account_Two];
14    ALTER SERVER ROLE serveradmin ADD MEMBER "contoso\Group_Two";
15    CREATE SERVER ROLE Modify_Databases;
16    GRANT ALTER ANY DATABASE TO Modify_Databases;
17    CREATE CREDENTIAL RemoteFTP with IDENTITY = 'FTP_Login', SECRET = 'Pa$$w0rd';
18    USE [AdventureWorks2012]
19    GO
20    CREATE USER "contoso\Group_Two" FOR LOGIN "contoso\Group_Two";
21    CREATE ROLE TableCreator AUTHORIZATION "contoso\administrator";
22    CREATE ROLE [Alpha-Role] AUTHORIZATION "contoso\administrator";
23    CREATE ROLE [Beta-Role] AUTHORIZATION "contoso\administrator";
24    GRANT CREATE TABLE TO TableCreator;
25    EXEC sp_addrolemember 'TableCreator', "contoso\Account_Two";
26    EXEC sp_addrolemember 'Alpha-Role', [Dan_Bacon]
27    GRANT INSERT ON [Person].[Address] TO [Alpha-Role]
28    DENY INSERT ON [Person].[Address] TO [Beta-Role]
```

Questions

Answer the following questions to test your knowledge of the information in this case study. Refer to the code sample as necessary. You can find the answers to these questions and explanations of why each answer choice is correct or incorrect in the "Answers" section at the end of this chapter.

QUESTION 1

Which step must you take prior to creating the Dan Bacon account?

- **A.** Enable contained database authentication.
- **B.** Execute the CREATE MASTER KEY statement.
- **C.** Execute the CREATE CERTIFICATE statement.
- **D.** Execute the CREATE DATABASE ENCRYPTION KEY statement.

QUESTION 2

What must you do before executing the CREATE ROLE TableCreator AUTHORIZATION "contoso\administrator" statement? (Choose all that apply.)

- **A.** You must create the "contoso\administrator" user by using the CREATE USER "contoso \administrator" for LOGIN "contoso\administrator" statement.
- **B.** You must create the "contoso\administrator" login by using the CREATE LOGIN "contoso\administrator" FROM WINDOWS statement.
- **C.** You must create the login Administrator by using the CREATE LOGIN [Administrator] WITH PASSWORD 'P@ssw0rd' statement.
- **D.** You must create the user Administrator by using the CREATE USER [Administrator] for LOGIN [Administrator] statement.

QUESTION 3

Which step must you take before adding Dan Bacon to the Alpha-Role role in line 26?

A. Create a user for Dan Bacon in the AdventureWorks2012 database.

B. Create a user for Dan Bacon in the msdb database.

C. Create a login for Dan Bacon in the msdb database.

D. Create a login for Dan Bacon in the AdventureWorks2012 database.

QUESTION 4

Which statement would you use to enable the sql_user_a login?

A. ALTER LOGIN

B. DROP LOGIN

C. ALTER USER

D. DROP USER

QUESTION 5

Which line of code would you change if you wanted to ensure that Dan Bacon could not authenticate after the first of January 2017?

A. 09

B. 10

C. 08

D. 11

QUESTION 6

Which login authenticates by using an asymmetric key?

A. contoso\Account_Two

B. sql_user_a

C. sql_user_e

D. Dan_Bacon

QUESTION 7

After the case study code has been executed, which of the following logins are members of the TableCreator role?

A. contoso\Account_Two

B. contoso\Group_Two

C. sql_user_a

D. Dan_Bacon

QUESTION 8

Which of the following logins is disabled after the case study code has been executed?

A. contoso\Account_Two

B. sql_user_a

C. sql_user_e

D. Dan_Bacon

QUESTION 9

After executing the code, you determine that one login was inadvertently added to the serveradmin role. Which of the following Transact-SQL statements would you execute to remedy this situation?

A. sp_addrolemember

B. DROP ROLE

C. ALTER ROLE

D. ALTER SERVER ROLE

QUESTION 10

Which of the following logins has not been disabled but has been denied the ability to connect to the instance?

A. contoso\Account_Two

B. sql_user_a

C. Dan_Bacon

D. sql_user_e

QUESTION 11

You have discovered that the password assigned to the FTP credential is incorrect. Which line of the case study code would you modify to correct this error?

A. 12

B. 21

C. 17

D. 28

QUESTION 12

After running the case study code, to which Active Directory group could you add an Active Directory user account to grant access to the instance?

A. Dan_Bacon

B. Alpha-Role

C. contoso\Group_Two

D. Beta-Role

QUESTION 13

After executing the case study code, you want to add two users to the Beta-Role role. Which of the following statements or stored procedures could you use to accomplish this goal? (Choose all that apply.)

A. ALTER ROLE

B. sp_addrolemember

C. CREATE ROLE

D. ALTER SERVER ROLE

QUESTION 14

Which statement would you use to modify the membership of the Modify_Databases role?

A. CREATE ROLE

B. ALTER ROLE

C. ALTER SERVER ROLE

D. CREATE SERVER ROLE

QUESTION 15

Which of the following principals could you add to the Beta-Role role? (Choose all that apply.)

A. TableCreator

B. Modify_Databases

C. contoso\Account_Two

D. sql_user_a

QUESTION 16

Which of the following principals could you add to the Modify_Databases role? (Choose all that apply.)

A. sql_user_a

B. TableCreator

C. sql_user_e

D. Beta-Role

QUESTION 17

Which of the following statements would you use to assign the ALTER ANY LOGIN statement to the Modify_Databases role?

A. ALTER SERVER ROLE

B. GRANT

C. DENY

D. REVOKE

QUESTION 18

You want to remove the DENY INSERT ON permission assigned to the Beta-Role role on line 28. Which statement would you use to accomplish this goal?

A. ALTER ROLE

B. GRANT

C. DENY

D. REVOKE

QUESTION 19

You have created a new role named Role_Beta by using the CREATE SERVER ROLE statement. Members of this role should be able to unlock locked SQL Server logins. Which of the following statements would you use to assign the appropriate permission?

A. GRANT ALTER ANY CREDENTIAL TO Role_Beta

B. GRANT ALTER ANY LOGIN TO Role_Beta

C. DENY ALTER ANY CREDENTIAL TO Role_Beta

D. REVOKE ALTER ANY CREDENTIAL TO Role_Beta

QUESTION 20

You want to create a database role that enables users to view data in a table but not to modify that data, remove that data, or insert new data. Which of the following database-level permissions should you assign to this database role on the table?

A. ALTER

B. SELECT

C. INSERT

D. DELETE

Case Study 3

You are planning the configuration of server-level and database-level audits. With this in mind, you have prepared the following code:

```
01    CREATE SERVER AUDIT [INSTANCE_AUDIT]
02    TO APPLICATION_LOG
03    WITH
04    ( QUEUE_DELAY = 1000
05      ,ON_FAILURE = SHUTDOWN
06    )
07    CREATE SERVER AUDIT SPECIFICATION [INSTANCE_SPEC]
08      FOR SERVER AUDIT [INSTANCE_AUDIT]
09      ADD (DATABASE_CHANGE_GROUP)
10    ALTER SERVER AUDIT SPECIFICATION [INSTANCE_SPEC]
11    ADD (DATABASE_LOGOUT_GROUP)
```

```
12      CREATE DATABASE AUDIT SPECIFICATION [DATABASE_SPEC]
13      FOR SERVER AUDIT [INSTANCE_AUDIT]
14      ADD (USER_CHANGE_PASSWORD_GROUP)
15      ALTER DATABASE AUDIT SPECIFICATION [DATABASE_SPEC]
16      ADD (SUCCESSFUL_DATABASE_AUTHENTICATION_GROUP)
```

Questions

Answer the following questions to test your knowledge of the information in this case study. Refer to the code sample as necessary. You can find the answers to these questions and explanations of why each answer choice is correct or incorrect in the "Answers" section at the end of this chapter.

QUESTION 1

Which line of code would you change if you wanted events to be written to the Security log?

A. 04

B. 02

C. 05

D. 01

QUESTION 2

If you are using a domain account for the SQL Server service account, which of the following must you ensure prior to configuring audit events to be written to the Security log? (Choose all that apply.)

A. Add the service account to the Generate Security Audits policy.

B. Configure the Audit Privilege Use policy for Success and Failure.

C. Configure the Audit Object Access policy for Success and Failure.

D. Add the service account to the Manage Auditing And Security Log policy.

QUESTION 3

After executing the case study code, you determine that you want to audit backup and restore operations at the instance level. Which of the following statements would you execute to accomplish this goal?

A. ALTER SERVER AUDIT SPECIFICATION [INSTANCE_SPEC] ADD (AUDIT_CHANGE_GROUP)

B. ALTER DATABASE AUDIT SPECIFICATION [DATABASE_SPEC] ADD (BACKUP_RESTORE_GROUP)

C. ALTER SERVER AUDIT SPECIFICATION [INSTANCE_SPEC] ADD (BACKUP_RESTORE_GROUP)

D. ALTER DATABASE AUDIT SPECIFICATION [DATABASE_SPEC] ADD (AUDIT_CHANGE_GROUP)

QUESTION 4

You execute the statements in the case study code. You then determine that you do not want to audit password change events on contained databases. Which of the following Transact-SQL statements should you execute to modify the appropriate audit specification so these events are no longer audited?

A. ALTER SERVER AUDIT SPECIFICATION [INSTANCE_SPEC] DROP (DATABASE_CHANGE_GROUP)

B. ALTER DATABASE AUDIT SPECIFICATION [DATABASE_SPEC] DROP (USER_CHANGE_PASSWORD_GROUP)

C. ALTER SERVER AUDIT SPECIFICATION [INSTANCE_SPEC] DROP (DATABASE_LOGOUT_GROUP)

D. ALTER DATABASE AUDIT SPECIFICATION [DATABASE_SPEC] DROP (SUCCESSFUL_DATABASE_AUTHENTICATION_GROUP)

QUESTION 5

Which line of code would you modify if you wanted to increase the amount of time that elapses before audit actions must be processed?

A. 04

B. 02

C. 05

D. 01

QUESTION 6

You start SQL Server Management Studio, connect to an instance, and run the case study code. In which database is the database audit specification created?

A. master

B. model

C. msdb

D. tempdb

QUESTION 7

After executing the statements in the case study code, you want to configure additional auditing at the database level. Specifically, you want to audit changes to auditing settings. Which of the following statements would you execute to accomplish this goal?

A. ALTER SERVER AUDIT SPECIFICATION [INSTANCE_SPEC] ADD (AUDIT_CHANGE_GROUP)

B. ALTER DATABASE AUDIT SPECIFICATION [DATABASE_SPEC] ADD (BACKUP_RESTORE_GROUP)

    C. ALTER SERVER AUDIT SPECIFICATION [INSTANCE_SPEC] ADD
        (BACKUP_RESTORE_GROUP)

    D. ALTER DATABASE AUDIT SPECIFICATION [DATABASE_SPEC] ADD
        (AUDIT_CHANGE_GROUP)

QUESTION 8

You want to audit the use of DBCC commands on a specific database. Which of the following audit action groups should you add to a database audit specification?

    A. FAILED_DATABASE_AUTHENTICATION_GROUP

    B. DATABASE_OBJECT_OWNERSHIP_CHANGE_GROUP

    C. DBCC_GROUP

    D. DATABASE_OWNERSHIP_CHANGE_GROUP

QUESTION 9

You run the statements in the case study code. After reviewing the audit logs, you determine that you no longer want to audit logout events for contained database users. Which of the following statements should you execute to accomplish this goal?

    A. ALTER SERVER AUDIT SPECIFICATION [INSTANCE_SPEC] DROP
        (DATABASE_CHANGE_GROUP)

    B. ALTER DATABASE AUDIT SPECIFICATION [DATABASE_SPEC] DROP
        (USER_CHANGE_PASSWORD_GROUP)

    C. ALTER SERVER AUDIT SPECIFICATION [INSTANCE_SPEC] DROP
        (DATABASE_LOGOUT_GROUP)

    D. ALTER DATABASE AUDIT SPECIFICATION [DATABASE_SPEC] DROP
        (SUCCESSFUL_DATABASE_AUTHENTICATION_GROUP)

QUESTION 10

The Database Engine instance is configured to shut down on audit failure. Recovery involves starting the Database Engine instance in a special mode. You want to allow the Database Engine instance to continue running if there is an auditing failure. Which line of code would you change in the case study code to accomplish this goal?

    A. 04

    B. 02

    C. 05

    D. 01

QUESTION 11

You want to audit changes to database ownership for a specific database. Which of the following audit action groups should you add to a database audit specification?

- **A.** FAILED_DATABASE_AUTHENTICATION_GROUP
- **B.** DATABASE_OBJECT_OWNERSHIP_CHANGE_GROUP
- **C.** DBCC_GROUP
- **D.** DATABASE_OWNERSHIP_CHANGE_GROUP

QUESTION 12

You configure a server audit specification to include the DATABASE_PRINCIPAL_CHANGE _GROUP audit action group. Which of the following events will be recorded due to the inclusion of this audit action group in a database audit specification? (Choose all that apply.)

- **A.** Use of the CREATE LOGIN statement
- **B.** Use of the CREATE USER statement
- **C.** Use of the CREATE SERVER ROLE statement
- **D.** Use of the CREATE ROLE statement

QUESTION 13

You execute the case study code. After reviewing the audit logs, you determine that you no longer want to audit database creation, modification, or deletion events. Which of the following statements would you execute to accomplish this goal?

- **A.** ALTER SERVER AUDIT SPECIFICATION [INSTANCE_SPEC] DROP (DATABASE_CHANGE_GROUP)
- **B.** ALTER DATABASE AUDIT SPECIFICATION [DATABASE_SPEC] DROP (USER_CHANGE_PASSWORD_GROUP)
- **C.** ALTER SERVER AUDIT SPECIFICATION [INSTANCE_SPEC] DROP (DATABASE_LOGOUT_GROUP)
- **D.** ALTER DATABASE AUDIT SPECIFICATION [DATABASE_SPEC] DROP (SUCCESSFUL_DATABASE_AUTHENTICATION_GROUP)

QUESTION 14

After executing the statements in the case study code, you want to configure additional auditing at the instance level. You want to track changes made to auditing settings. Which of the following statements would you execute to accomplish this goal?

- **A.** ALTER SERVER AUDIT SPECIFICATION [INSTANCE_SPEC] ADD (AUDIT_CHANGE_GROUP)
- **B.** ALTER DATABASE AUDIT SPECIFICATION [DATABASE_SPEC] ADD (BACKUP_RESTORE_GROUP)

C. ALTER SERVER AUDIT SPECIFICATION [INSTANCE_SPEC] ADD
(BACKUP_RESTORE_GROUP)

D. ALTER DATABASE AUDIT SPECIFICATION [DATABASE_SPEC] ADD
(AUDIT_CHANGE_GROUP)

QUESTION 15

You have enabled contained authentication on a database. You want to track failed logins
for database users. Which of the following audit action groups should you add to an existing
database audit specification to accomplish this goal?

A. FAILED_DATABASE_AUTHENTICATION_GROUP

B. DATABASE_OBJECT_OWNERSHIP_CHANGE_GROUP

C. DBCC_GROUP

D. DATABASE_OWNERSHIP_CHANGE_GROUP

QUESTION 16

You want to track changes to the membership of fixed server roles. Which of the following
audit action groups should you configure as part of a server audit specification?

A. DATABASE_ROLE_MEMBER_CHANGE_GROUP

B. SERVER_ROLE_MEMBER_CHANGE_GROUP

C. SERVER_PRINCIPAL_CHANGE_GROUP

D. DATABASE_PRINCIPAL_CHANGE_GROUP

QUESTION 17

You configure a server audit specification to include the SERVER_PRINCIPAL_CHANGE_GROUP
audit action group. Which of the following events will be recorded due to the inclusion of this
audit action group in the server audit specification? (Choose all that apply.)

A. Use of the CREATE LOGIN statement

B. Use of the CREATE USER statement

C. Use of the CREATE SERVER ROLE statement

D. Use of the CREATE ROLE statement

QUESTION 18

You execute the case study code. After reviewing the audit logs, you determine that you no
longer want to audit successful contained database user authentication. Which of the following statements should you execute to modify SQL Server auditing so these events are no
longer audited?

A. ALTER SERVER AUDIT SPECIFICATION [INSTANCE_SPEC] DROP
(DATABASE_CHANGE_GROUP)

B. ALTER DATABASE AUDIT SPECIFICATION [DATABASE_SPEC] DROP
(USER_CHANGE_PASSWORD_GROUP)

C. ALTER SERVER AUDIT SPECIFICATION [INSTANCE_SPEC] DROP
(DATABASE_LOGOUT_GROUP)

D. ALTER DATABASE AUDIT SPECIFICATION [DATABASE_SPEC] DROP
(SUCCESSFUL_DATABASE_AUTHENTICATION_GROUP)

QUESTION 19

You execute the statements in the case study code on an instance that hosts 200 databases.
You want to audit backup and restore operations on some but not all of these databases.
Which of the following Transact-SQL statements would you execute to accomplish this goal?

A. ALTER SERVER AUDIT SPECIFICATION [INSTANCE_SPEC] ADD (AUDIT_CHANGE_GROUP)

B. ALTER DATABASE AUDIT SPECIFICATION [DATABASE_SPEC] ADD
(BACKUP_RESTORE_GROUP)

C. ALTER SERVER AUDIT SPECIFICATION [INSTANCE_SPEC] ADD
(BACKUP_RESTORE_GROUP)

D. ALTER DATABASE AUDIT SPECIFICATION [DATABASE_SPEC] ADD
(AUDIT_CHANGE_GROUP)

QUESTION 20

You want to ensure that changes to database object ownership are recorded. Which of the
following audit action groups should you add to a database audit specification to accomplish
this goal?

A. FAILED_DATABASE_AUTHENTICATION_GROUP

B. DATABASE_OBJECT_OWNERSHIP_CHANGE_GROUP

C. DBCC_GROUP

D. DATABASE_OWNERSHIP_CHANGE_GROUP

Case Study 4

You are configuring Transact-SQL code that will configure options for your organization's
newly deployed database instances. The code is as follows:

```
01    EXEC sys.sp_configure 'show advanced options', 1;
02    GO
03    RECONFIGURE;
04    GO
05    EXEC sys.sp_configure 'min server memory', 1024;
06    GO
07    EXEC sys.sp_configure 'max server memory', 4096;
08    GO
09    sp_configure 'fill factor', 90;
10    GO
11    RECONFIGURE;
12    GO
```

```
13      USE [master]
14      GO
15      ALTER DATABASE [model] SET RECOVERY FULL WITH NO_WAIT
16      GO
17      sp_configure 'Database Mail XPs', 1;
18      GO
19      RECONFIGURE;
20      GO
21      EXECUTE msdb.dbo.sysmail_add_account_sp
22          @account_name = 'Litware2012 Administrator',
23          @email_address = 'litware2012@contoso.com',
24          @mailserver_name = 'smtp.contoso.com' ;
25      EXECUTE msdb.dbo.sysmail_add_profile_sp
26          @profile_name = 'Litware2012 Mail Profile',
27          @description = 'Profile used for administrative mail.' ;
28      EXECUTE msdb.dbo.sysmail_add_profileaccount_sp
29          @profile_name = 'LitWare2012 Mail Profile',
30          @account_name = 'Litware2012 Administrator',
31          @sequence_number = 1;
32      EXECUTE msdb.dbo.sysmail_add_principalprofile_sp
33          @profile_name = 'LitWare2012 Mail Profile',
34          @principal_id = 0,
35          @is_default = 1;
36      EXECUTE msdb.dbo.sp_set_sqlagent_properties @email_save_in_sent_folder=1,
37          @databasemail_profile='LitWare2012 Mail Profile',
38          @use_databasemail=1;
```

Questions

Answer the following questions to test your knowledge of the information in this case study. Refer to the code sample as necessary. You can find the answers to these questions and explanations of why each answer choice is correct or incorrect in the "Answers" section at the end of this chapter.

QUESTION 1

Which line of code would you change if you wanted to increase the maximum amount of memory available to the instance?

- **A.** 09
- **B.** 05
- **C.** 07
- **D.** 17

QUESTION 2

Which of the following steps must you perform before executing lines 36 through 38 of the case study code?

- **A.** Start the SQL Server Browser service.
- **B.** Stop the SQL Server Agent service.

C. Start the SQL Server Agent service.

D. Stop the SQL Server Browser service.

QUESTION 3

You want to modify the address of the SMTP mail server used by the Litware2012 Administrator database mail account. Which of the following lines of code would you modify to accomplish this goal?

A. 34

B. 23

C. 24

D. 37

QUESTION 4

Which line of code would you modify if you wanted to change the minimum amount of memory allocated to the instance?

A. 09

B. 05

C. 07

D. 17

QUESTION 5

Which configuration option would you use with the sp_configure stored procedure to set the processor cores that a Database Engine instance uses for processing tasks?

A. backup compression default

B. affinity I/O mask

C. affinity mask

D. recovery interval

QUESTION 6

Which line of code would you modify if you wanted to change the default recovery model for all future databases created on the instance?

A. 15

B. 17

C. 09

D. 38

QUESTION 7

Which line of code would you modify to change the principal database mail profile from public to private?

A. 34

B. 23

C. 24

D. 37

QUESTION 8

Which line of code would you modify if you wanted to change the default fill factor used with indexes on the instance?

A. 09

B. 05

C. 07

D. 17

QUESTION 9

Which configuration option would you use with the sp_configure stored procedure to set the maximum time between automatic checkpoints at the instance level?

A. backup compression default

B. affinity I/O mask

C. affinity mask

D. recovery interval

QUESTION 10

You want to ensure that specific standard options are present in each newly created database. Which of the system databases should you configure to accomplish this goal?

A. master

B. model

C. msdb

D. tempdb

QUESTION 11

Which line of code enables database mail?

A. 09

B. 05

C. 07

D. 17

QUESTION 12

Which line of code would you modify to alter the email address associated with the Litware2012 Administrator database mail account?

- **A.** 34
- **B.** 23
- **C.** 24
- **D.** 37

QUESTION 13

You want to disable backup compression by default on the instance configured through the case study code. Which of the following configuration options used with the sp_configure stored procedure would enable you to accomplish this goal?

- **A.** backup compression default
- **B.** affinity I/O mask
- **C.** affinity mask
- **D.** recovery interval

QUESTION 14

You are creating a large number of jobs and alerts. Which of the following system databases must you back up to ensure that the settings for these jobs and alerts are also backed up?

- **A.** master
- **B.** msdb
- **C.** tempdb
- **D.** model

QUESTION 15

A previous DBA configured an instance so that all new databases are configured to shrink automatically to reclaim space. You want to change this option. Which of the following options would you configure with the ALTER DATABASE statement applied to the model system database?

- **A.** ALLOW_SNAPSHOT_ISOLATION
- **B.** ENCRYPTION
- **C.** AUTO_SHRINK
- **D.** AUTO_CLOSE

QUESTION 16

You have created a large number of logins. Which system database should you immediately back up to ensure that the logins are also backed up?

- **A.** master
- **B.** model

C. msdb

D. tempdb

QUESTION 17

Which line of code would you alter to change the database mail profile used by SQL Server Agent?

A. 34

B. 23

C. 24

D. 37

QUESTION 18

You want to configure specific processor cores to handle disk input/output (I/O) operations. Which of the following configuration options of the sp_configure stored procedure would you set to accomplish this goal?

A. backup compression default

B. affinity I/O mask

C. affinity mask

D. recovery interval

QUESTION 19

You are configuring an instance that will host secure databases. You have enabled transparent data encryption on several databases already and want to ensure that all future databases have this option enabled. Which of the following statements would you issue to accomplish this goal?

A. ALTER DATABASE [tempdb] SET ENCRYPTION ON

B. ALTER DATABASE [master] SET ENCRYPTION ON

C. ALTER DATABASE [msdb] SET ENCRYPTION ON

D. ALTER DATABASE [model] SET ENCRYPTION ON

QUESTION 20

A previous database administrator configured databases on an instance to shut down cleanly when the last user closes his or her connection. This is causing performance problems when new users connect. Which of the following options would you use with the ALTER DATABASE statement to ensure that databases stay online even when no users are currently connected?

A. ALLOW_SNAPSHOT_ISOLATION

B. ENCRYPTION

C. AUTO_SHRINK

D. AUTO_CLOSE

Answers

This section contains the answers to the questions for each of the code case studies in this chapter.

Case Study 1

QUESTION 1   Correct Answer: C

   A. **Incorrect.** It is not necessary to reconfigure and restart the SQL Server service prior to line 01. The first line that cannot be executed without reconfiguring and restarting the SQL Server service is line 13.

   B. **Incorrect.** It is not necessary to reconfigure and restart the SQL Server service prior to issuing the CREATE DATABASE statement.

   C. **Correct.** FILESTREAM must be enabled on the service and the service must be restarted prior to line 13.

   D. **Incorrect.** It is not necessary to reconfigure and restart the service prior to configuring the FILESTREAM access level.

QUESTION 2   Correct Answer: C

   A. **Incorrect.** You cannot use SQL Server Management Studio to enable FILESTREAM on the SQL Server service. You can use SQL Server Management Studio to configure FILESTREAM on the instance, as you do on line 09, but you must also modify the service by using SQL Server Configuration Manager.

   B. **Incorrect.** You cannot use SQL Server Installation Center to enable FILESTREAM on the SQL Server service.

   C. **Correct.** You use SQL Server Configuration Manager to enable FILESTREAM on the SQL Server service.

   D. **Incorrect.** You cannot use SQL Server Profiler to enable FILESTREAM on the SQL Server service.

QUESTION 3   Correct Answer: B

   A. **Incorrect.** This line of code configures a database to use contained authentication but does not enable contained authentication at the instance level.

   B. **Correct.** The sp_configure 'contained database authentication', 1; statement allows the instance to support databases that use contained authentication.

   C. **Incorrect.** Line 20 allows the use of file tables in the Litware2012 database.

   D. **Incorrect.** Line 32 creates a user that uses contained authentication but doesn't enable this functionality at the instance level.

QUESTION 4   Correct Answer: A

  A.   Correct. You use the BACKUP MASTER KEY statement to back up a database master key.

  B.   Incorrect. You use the ALTER MASTER KEY statement to modify a database master key. You cannot use this statement to back up a database master key.

  C.   Incorrect. You use the DROP MASTER KEY statement to remove an existing database master key. You cannot use this statement to back up a database master key.

  D.   Incorrect. You use the CREATE MASTER KEY statement to create a database master key. You cannot use this statement to back up a database master key.

QUESTION 5   Correct Answer: C

  A.   Incorrect. Line 35 deals with the database master key rather than with the database encryption key.

  B.   Incorrect. Line 37 deals with the certificate rather than with the database encryption key.

  C.   Correct. You would modify line 42 to increase the database encryption key length by changing the algorithm from AES_128 to AES_256.

  D.   Incorrect. Line 46 enables encryption on the database but does not enable you to configure database key length.

QUESTION 6   Correct Answer: C

  A.   Incorrect. A 128-bit AES key is not as cryptographically strong as a 256-bit AES key.

  B.   Incorrect. A 192-bit AES key is not as cryptographically strong as a 256-bit AES key.

  C.   Correct. A 256-bit AES key will provide the strongest database encryption key.

  D.   Incorrect. A key generated by the TRIPLE_DES_3KEY algorithm is not as cryptographically strong as a key generated by AES_256.

QUESTION 7   Correct Answer: D

  A.   Incorrect. FILESTREAM must be enabled to use file tables.

  B.   Incorrect. Line 20 configures directory FTBLE to be used for file table operations.

  C.   Incorrect. Line 17 configures the FILESTREAM file to use the FSTRM directory.

  D.   Correct. Line 22 creates a file table named DocStore.

QUESTION 8   Correct Answer: A

  A.   Correct. Change this line of code to select a different directory to associate with file tables.

  B.   Incorrect. This line creates a new file table named DocStore.

C. Incorrect. This line configures the database as partially contained.

D. Incorrect. This line configures the directory used for FILESTREAM, not the directory associated with file tables.

QUESTION 9   Correct Answer: C

A. Incorrect. Line 24 allows databases to use contained database authentication, but it is not until line 30 that the Litware2012 database is configured to support contained authentication.

B. Incorrect. This line enables FILESTREAM at the instance level; it does not enable contained authentication.

C. Correct. Line 30 configures the Litware2012 database to support contained authentication.

D. Incorrect. Line 35 creates a database encryption key; it does not configure the database to support contained authentication.

QUESTION 10   Correct Answer: D

A. Incorrect. This statement creates a contained user that uses SQL Server authentication rather than database authentication.

B. Incorrect. This statement creates a login rather than a user.

C. Incorrect. This statement creates a normal, non-contained database user mapped to a login.

D. Correct. This statement creates a contained user mapped to the contoso\contained _user_b Active Directory account.

QUESTION 11   Correct Answers: A and D

A. Correct. The Tertiary filegroup is created on line 5 of the case study code.

B. Incorrect. No filegroup named Secondary is created in the case study code.

C. Incorrect. DocStore is the name of a table created by the code, not a filegroup created by the code.

D. Correct. The FileStreamFileGroup filegroup is created on line 13 of the case study code.

QUESTION 12   Correct Answer: A

A. Correct. You use the ALTER DATABASE statement with the REMOVE FILE option to remove any files in the filegroup and then the REMOVE FILEGROUP option to remove the filegroup.

B. Incorrect. You cannot use the ALTER SCHEMA statement to remove a filegroup.

C. Incorrect. You cannot use the DROP DATABASE statement to remove a filegroup.

D. Incorrect. You cannot use the DROP SCHEMA statement to remove a filegroup.

QUESTION 13   Correct Answer: A

A.   **Correct.** Line 24 allows the creation of databases that use contained authentication.

B.   **Incorrect.** Line 09 configures the instance to support FILESTREAM.

C.   **Incorrect.** Line 30 configures the Litware2012 database to support contained authentication. Line 24 enables this functionality at the instance level.

D.   **Incorrect.** Line 35 creates a database encryption key, which is not necessary for contained authentication.

QUESTION 14   Correct Answers: C and D

A.   **Incorrect.** It is not necessary to create a new database master key because one is already present on the instance.

B.   **Incorrect.** It is not necessary to create a new server certificate because one is already present after executing the case study code.

C.   **Correct.** You must create a database encryption key for the TailspinToys database before you can enable transparent data encryption.

D.   **Correct.** You must use the ALTER DATABASE ... SET ENCRYPTION ON statement to enable transparent data encryption for the TailspinToys database.

QUESTION 15   Correct Answer: A

A.   **Correct.** You use the ALTER DATABASE [Litware2012] ADD FILE (NAME=[newfile.ndf], FILENAME=[c:\DBFILES\newfile.ndf]) TO FILEGROUP [Tertiary] statement to add the file to the filegroup.

B.   **Incorrect.** The ALTER ENDPOINT statement enables you to modify the properties of an endpoint. You cannot use this statement to add a file to a filegroup.

C.   **Incorrect.** The ALTER SCHEMA statement enables you to change the properties of a schema. You cannot use this statement to add a file to a filegroup.

D.   **Incorrect.** The ALTER TABLE statement enables you to change the properties of a table. You cannot use this statement to add a file to a filegroup.

QUESTION 16   Correct Answer: B

A.   **Incorrect.** This statement is related to contained database authentication and is not related to FILESTREAM.

B.   **Correct.** You must enable FILESTREAM access at the instance level and at the SQL Server service level before it is possible to configure individual databases to use FILESTREAM.

C.   **Incorrect.** This statement configures a specific database for contained authentication and is not related to FILESTREAM.

D.   **Incorrect.** This statement creates a database encryption key and is not related to FILESTREAM.

QUESTION 17   Correct Answer: C

A. **Incorrect.** This line creates a new file table named DocStore.

B. **Incorrect.** This line configures the database as partially contained.

C. **Correct.** This line designates the folder that hosts the FILESTREAM file.

D. **Incorrect.** This line configures the directory used for file tables, not for FILESTREAM.

QUESTION 18   Correct Answer: A

A. **Correct.** You use the ALTER DATABASE statement with the MODIFY FILEGROUP parameter to make a filegroup read-only.

B. **Incorrect.** The ALTER ENDPOINT statement enables you to modify the properties of an endpoint. You cannot use this statement to make a filegroup read-only.

C. **Incorrect.** The ALTER SCHEMA statement enables you to modify the properties of a schema. You cannot use this statement to make a filegroup read-only.

D. **Incorrect.** The ALTER TABLE statement enables you to modify the properties of a table. You cannot use this statement to make a filegroup read-only.

QUESTION 19   Correct Answer: B

A. **Incorrect.** This statement is used when you attach an encrypted database to a new instance but cannot be used to change the master key password.

B. **Correct.** Use the ALTER MASTER KEY statement to change the password of the database master key.

C. **Incorrect.** This statement enables you to remove the database master key but cannot be used to change the master key password.

D. **Incorrect.** This statement enables you to close the master key in a session but cannot be used to change the master key password.

QUESTION 20   Correct Answer: D

A. **Incorrect.** Line 24 enables database authentication; it does not create a database master key.

B. **Incorrect.** Line 09 enables FILESTREAM at the instance level; it does not create a database master key.

C. **Incorrect.** Line 30 configures the Litware2012 database to use partial containment; it does not create a database master key.

D. **Correct.** You can create certificates only after you have created the database master key.

Case Study 2

QUESTION 1   Correct Answer: B

A. **Incorrect.** Contained database authentication allows user accounts without logins. You must create or open a database master key.

B. **Correct.** You cannot create a certificate for user authentication unless a master key is already present.

C. **Incorrect.** You cannot create a certificate for user authentication unless a master key is already present.

D. **Incorrect.** You cannot create a certificate for user authentication unless a master key is already present.

QUESTION 2   Correct Answers: A and B

A. **Correct.** A login and database user is not created for contoso\administrator. These principals must be created before it is possible to execute the CREATE ROLE TableCreator AUTHORIZATION "contoso\administrator" statement.

B. **Correct.** A login and database user is not created for contoso\administrator. These principals must be created before it is possible to execute the CREATE ROLE TableCreator AUTHORIZATION "contoso\administrator" statement.

C. **Incorrect.** This statement creates a SQL authenticated login rather than a login based on a Windows account.

D. **Incorrect.** This statement creates a database user that does not use the name of the security principal identified in the statement.

QUESTION 3   Correct Answer: A

A. **Correct.** You must create a user for the Dan_Bacon login in the AdventureWorks2012 database before you can add that user to a database role.

B. **Incorrect.** You must create a user for the Dan_Bacon login in the AdventureWorks2012 database.

C. **Incorrect.** Logins are created at the instance level. You must create a user in the AdventureWorks2012 database in which the role exists.

D. **Incorrect.** Logins are created at the instance level. You must create a user in the AdventureWorks2012 database in which the role exists.

QUESTION 4   Correct Answer: A

A. **Correct.** Use the ALTER LOGIN statement to lock, unlock, enable, or disable a login.

B. **Incorrect.** The DROP LOGIN statement enables you to delete a login. You can't use this statement to enable a disabled login.

C. **Incorrect.** The ALTER USER statement enables you to modify a user but not a login. You can't use this statement to enable a disabled login.

D. Incorrect. The DROP USER statement enables you to drop a user. You can't use this statement to enable a disabled login.

QUESTION 5   Correct Answer: C

A. Incorrect. The expiration of Dan Bacon's login is determined by the expiration date of the certificate that is configured on line 08.

B. Incorrect. The asymmetric key created in line 10 is not related to the expiration of Dan Bacon's login.

C. Correct. Altering line 08 enables you to alter the expiration date of the certificate associated with Dan Bacon's login.

D. Incorrect. The login created in line 11 is not related to the expiration of Dan Bacon's login.

QUESTION 6   Correct Answer: C

A. Incorrect. This account authenticates by using an Active Directory user account.

B. Incorrect. This account authenticates by using SQL Server authentication.

C. Correct. This account authenticates by using an asymmetric key.

D. Incorrect. This account authenticates by using a certificate.

QUESTION 7   Correct Answer: A

A. Correct. The contoso\Account_Two login is added to the TableCreator role in line 25.

B. Incorrect. The contoso\Group_Two login is not a member of the TableCreator role after the case study code has been executed.

C. Incorrect. The sql_user_a login is not a member of the TableCreator role after the case study code has been executed.

D. Incorrect. The Dan_Bacon login is not a member of the TableCreator role after the case study code has been executed.

QUESTION 8   Correct Answer: B

A. Incorrect. Login contoso\Account_Two is not disabled by the case study code.

B. Correct. Line 12 disables login sql_user_a.

C. Incorrect. Login sql_user_e is not disabled by the case study code.

D. Incorrect. Login Dan_Bacon is not disabled by the case study code.

QUESTION 9   Correct Answer: D

A. Incorrect. The sp_addrolemember stored procedure enables you to add users to roles. You cannot use this stored procedure to remove a login from a role.

B. Incorrect. The DROP ROLE statement enables you to drop a flexible database role. You cannot use this statement to remove a login from a role.

C. **Incorrect.** The ALTER ROLE statement enables you to modify the membership of a database role but does not allow you to remove a login from a server role.

D. **Correct.** You can use the ALTER ROLE statement with the DROP option to remove a login from a role.

QUESTION 10 **Correct Answer: A**

A. **Correct.** Line 13 applies the DENY CONNECT permission to the contoso\Account_Two login.

B. **Incorrect.** Although line 12 disables the sql_user_a account, the question asks which login has not been disabled but has been denied the ability to connect to the instance.

C. **Incorrect.** The Dan_Bacon login is not denied the ability to connect to the instance.

D. **Incorrect.** The sql_user_e login is not denied the ability to connect to the instance.

QUESTION 11 **Correct Answer: C**

A. **Incorrect.** Line 12 disables the sql_user_a login. Altering this line would not enable you to alter the password assigned to the FTP_LOGIN credential in the case study code.

B. **Incorrect.** Line 21 creates the TableCreator role. Altering this line would not enable you to alter the password assigned to the FTP_LOGIN credential in the case study code.

C. **Correct.** You would alter line 17 of the case study code to alter the password assigned to the FTP_LOGIN credential.

D. **Incorrect.** Line 28 applies the DENY INSERT permission on the Person.Address table. Altering this line would not enable you to alter the password assigned to the FTP_LOGIN credential in the case study code.

QUESTION 12 **Correct Answer: C**

A. **Incorrect.** The Dan_Bacon login authenticates by using a certificate. You cannot add an Active Directory user account to this login.

B. **Incorrect.** You cannot add an Active Directory user account directly to a database role.

C. **Correct.** After creating a login for contoso\Group_Two on line 04 of the case study code, you can grant access through this login to other Active Directory user accounts by adding those accounts to the Group_Two security group.

D. **Incorrect.** You cannot add an Active Directory user account directly to a database role.

QUESTION 13 **Correct Answers: A and B**

A. **Correct.** You can use the ALTER ROLE statement to add users to a database role.

B. **Correct.** You can use the sp_addrolemember stored procedure to add users to a database role.

C. **Incorrect.** The CREATE ROLE statement enables you to create a database role. You cannot use this statement to modify the membership of a database-level role.

D.   Incorrect. The ALTER SERVER ROLE statement enables you to modify membership of a server role. You cannot use this statement to modify the membership of a database-level role.

QUESTION 14   Correct Answer: C

A.   Incorrect. You use the CREATE ROLE statement to create new database roles. You cannot use this statement to modify the membership of an existing server-level role.

B.   Incorrect. You use the ALTER ROLE statement to modify the membership of a database role. You cannot use this statement to modify the membership of an existing server-level role.

C.   Correct. You use the ALTER SERVER ROLE statement to modify the membership of an existing server-level role.

D.   Incorrect. You use the CREATE SERVER ROLE statement to create new server-level roles. You cannot use this statement to modify the membership of an existing server-level role.

QUESTION 15   Correct Answer: A

A.   Correct. You can add a flexible database role to another flexible database role.

B.   Incorrect. You cannot add a server role to a flexible database role.

C.   Incorrect. There is no user in the AdventureWorks2012 database that maps to the contoso\Account_Two login.

D.   Incorrect. There is no user in the AdventureWorks2012 database that maps to the sql_user_a login.

QUESTION 16   Correct Answers: A and C

A.   Correct. You can add a server login to a database-level role.

B.   Incorrect. You cannot add a database-level role to a server-level role.

C.   Correct. You can add a server login to a database-level role.

D.   Incorrect. You cannot add a database-level role to a server-level role.

QUESTION 17   Correct Answer: B

A.   Incorrect. Use the ALTER SERVER ROLE statement to modify the membership of a server role.

B.   Correct. Use the GRANT ALTER ANY LOGIN TO Modify_Databases statement to grant this permission to this server-level role.

C.   Incorrect. The DENY statement blocks use of a particular permission. You must use the GRANT statement.

D.   Incorrect. The REVOKE statement revokes an existing permission. You must use the GRANT statement.

QUESTION 18 Correct Answer: D

A. **Incorrect.** You use the ALTER ROLE statement to modify the membership of a role. You cannot use this statement to revoke an assigned permission.

B. **Incorrect.** You cannot use the GRANT permission to revoke an assigned permission.

C. **Incorrect.** You cannot use the DENY statement to revoke an assigned permission.

D. **Correct.** You use the REVOKE statement to revoke an assigned permission.

QUESTION 19 Correct Answer: B

A. **Incorrect.** Executing the GRANT ALTER ANY CREDENTIAL statement enables you to alter credentials rather than logins.

B. **Correct.** Executing the GRANT ALTER ANY LOGIN statement enables members of this role to unlock locked SQL Server logins.

C. **Incorrect.** Executing the GRANT ALTER ANY LOGIN TO Role_Beta statement enables members of the role to unlock locked SQL Server logins. The DENY ALTER ANY CREDENTIAL statement blocks the modification of credentials.

D. **Incorrect.** Executing the GRANT ALTER ANY LOGIN TO Role_Beta statement enables members of the role to unlock locked SQL Server logins. The REVOKE ALTER ANY CREDENTIAL statement revokes the ability to modify credentials.

QUESTION 20 Correct Answer: B

A. **Incorrect.** The ALTER permission allows data to be modified in the securable.

B. **Correct.** The SELECT permission allows data to be read but not modified on the securable, in this case a table, on which the permission is applied.

C. **Incorrect.** The INSERT permission allows data to be inserted into the securable.

D. **Incorrect.** The DELETE permission allows the securable to be deleted.

Case Study 3

QUESTION 1 Correct Answer: B

A. **Incorrect.** Line 04 configures the queue delay. This is the maximum amount of time in milliseconds that can pass before audit actions must be processed.

B. **Correct.** Line 02 specifies where audit events are written. You would modify this line if you wanted events written to the Security log.

C. **Incorrect.** Line 05 determines what happens to the Database Engine instance if an audit event cannot be written.

D. **Incorrect.** Line 01 specifies the name of the server audit.

QUESTION 2 Correct Answers: A and C

A. **Correct.** The service account must be added to the Generate Security Audits policy if the Security log is used as a destination for SQL Server audit events.

B. Incorrect. You do not need to configure the audit privilege use policy when using SQL Server audit.

C. Correct. You must configure this policy when configuring SQL Server audit.

D. Incorrect. The service account does not need to manage this log; it needs only to be able to write events to this log. You do not need to add the service account to this policy.

QUESTION 3   Correct Answer: C

A. Incorrect. The ALTER SERVER AUDIT SPECIFICATION [INSTANCE_SPEC] statement configures auditing for changes to auditing at the instance level.

B. Incorrect. The ALTER DATABASE AUDIT SPECIFICATION [DATABASE_SPEC] statement configures auditing for backup and restore operations at the database level.

C. Correct. The ALTER SERVER AUDIT SPECIFICATION [INSTANCE_SPEC] statement configures auditing for backup and restore operations at the instance level.

D. Incorrect. The ALTER DATABASE AUDIT SPECIFICATION [DATABASE_SPEC] statement configures auditing for changes to auditing at the database level.

QUESTION 4   Correct Answer: B

A. Incorrect. This statement drops the database change group audit action type from the INSTANCE_SPEC server audit specification. This audit action group records the creation, modification, and deletion of databases.

B. Correct. This statement drops the user change password group audit action type from the DATABASE_SPEC audit specification. This audit action group records password change events on contained databases.

C. Incorrect. This statement drops the database logout group audit action type from the INSTANCE_SPEC server audit specification. This audit action group records the logouts of contained database users.

D. Incorrect. This statement drops the successful database authentication group audit action type from the DATABASE_SPEC audit specification. This audit action group records successful contained database user logins.

QUESTION 5   Correct Answer: A

A. Correct. Line 04 configures the queue delay. This is the maximum amount of time in milliseconds that can pass before audit actions must be processed. Modify this line to accomplish your goal.

B. Incorrect. Line 02 specifies where audit events are written. You would modify this line if you wanted events written to the Security log.

C. Incorrect. Line 05 determines what happens to the Database Engine instance if an audit event cannot be written.

D. Incorrect. Line 01 specifies the name of the server audit.

QUESTION 6   Correct Answer: A

A. **Correct.** The case study code does not specify a database in which to create the database audit specification. This means that the database audit specification will be created in the master database.

B. **Incorrect.** Because no database is specified, the database audit specification is created in the master database. This database audit specification is not created in the model database.

C. **Incorrect.** Because no database is specified, the database audit specification is created in the master database. This database audit specification is not created in the msdb database.

D. **Incorrect.** Because no database is specified, the database audit specification is created in the master database. This database audit specification is not created in the tempdb database.

QUESTION 7   Correct Answer: D

A. **Incorrect.** This statement configures auditing for changes to auditing at the instance level.

B. **Incorrect.** This statement configures auditing for backup and restore operations at the instance level.

C. **Incorrect.** This statement configures auditing for backup and restore operations at the database level.

D. **Correct.** This statement configures auditing for changes to auditing at the database level.

QUESTION 8   Correct Answer: C

A. **Incorrect.** Auditing the FAILED_DATABASE_AUTHENTICATION_GROUP action group means that failed contained database user logins are recorded.

B. **Incorrect.** Auditing the DATABASE_OBJECT_OWNERSHIP_CHANGE_GROUP action group means that changes to database object ownership are recorded.

C. **Correct.** Auditing the DBCC_GROUP action group means that the use of DBCC commands is recorded.

D. **Incorrect.** Auditing the DATABASE_OWNERSHIP_CHANGE_GROUP action group means that changes to database ownership are recorded.

QUESTION 9   Correct Answer: C

A. **Incorrect.** This statement drops the database change group audit action type from the INSTANCE_SPEC server audit specification. This audit action group records the creation, modification, and deletion of databases.

B. **Incorrect.** This statement drops the user change password group audit action type from the DATABASE_SPEC audit specification. This audit action group records password change events on contained databases.

C. Correct. This statement drops the database logout group audit action type from the INSTANCE_SPEC server audit specification. This audit action group records the logouts of contained database users.

D. Incorrect. This statement drops the successful database authentication group audit action type from the DATABASE_SPEC audit specification. This audit action group records successful contained database user logons.

QUESTION 10   Correct Answer: C

A. Incorrect. Line 04 configures the queue delay. This is the maximum amount of time in milliseconds that can pass before audit actions must be processed.

B. Incorrect. Line 02 specifies where audit events are written. You would modify this line if you wanted events written to the Security log or to a file.

C. Correct. Line 05 determines what happens to the Database Engine instance if an audit event cannot be written. Modify this line to ensure that the Database Engine instance does not shut down if there is an auditing failure.

D. Incorrect. Line 01 specifies the name of the server audit.

QUESTION 11   Correct Answer: D

A. Incorrect. Auditing the FAILED_DATABASE_AUTHENTICATION_GROUP action group means that failed contained database user logins are recorded.

B. Incorrect. Auditing the DATABASE_OBJECT_OWNERSHIP_CHANGE_GROUP action group means that database object ownership changes are recorded.

C. Incorrect. Auditing the DBCC_GROUP action group means that the use of DBCC commands is recorded.

D. Correct. Auditing the DATABASE_OWNERSHIP_CHANGE_GROUP action group means that changes to database ownership are recorded.

QUESTION 12   Correct Answers: B and D

A. Incorrect. The CREATE LOGIN statement creates a login. Logins are server principals.

B. Correct. The CREATE USER statement creates a database user, which is a database principal. Creation of database roles is tracked by including the DATABASE_PRINCIPAL _CHANGE_GROUP audit action group in a database audit specification.

C. Incorrect. The CREATE SERVER ROLE statement creates a server role. Server roles are server principals.

D. Correct. The CREATE ROLE statement creates a database role, which is a database principal. Creation of database roles is tracked by including the DATABASE_PRINCIPAL _CHANGE_GROUP audit action group in a database audit specification.

QUESTION 13 Correct Answer: A

A. Correct. This statement drops the database change group audit action type from the INSTANCE_SPEC server audit specification. This audit action group records the creation, modification, and deletion of databases.

B. Incorrect. This statement drops the user change password group audit action type from the DATABASE_SPEC audit specification. This audit action group records password change events on contained databases.

C. Incorrect. This statement drops the database logout group audit action type from the INSTANCE_SPEC server audit specification. This audit action group records the logouts of contained database users.

D. Incorrect. This statement drops the successful database authentication group audit action type from the DATABASE_SPEC audit specification. This audit action group records successful contained database user logons.

QUESTION 14 Correct Answer: A

A. Correct. This statement configures auditing for changes to auditing at the instance level.

B. Incorrect. This statement configures auditing for backup and restore operations at the instance level.

C. Incorrect. This statement configures auditing for backup and restore operations at the database level.

D. Incorrect. This statement configures auditing for changes to auditing at the database level.

QUESTION 15 Correct Answer: A

A. Correct. Auditing the FAILED_DATABASE_AUTHENTICATION_GROUP action group means that failed contained database user logins are recorded.

B. Incorrect. Auditing the DATABASE_OBJECT_OWNERSHIP_CHANGE_GROUP action group means that changes to database object ownership are recorded.

C. Incorrect. Auditing the DBCC_GROUP action group means that the use of DBCC commands is recorded.

D. Incorrect. Auditing the DATABASE_OWNERSHIP_CHANGE_GROUP action group means that changes to database ownership are recorded.

QUESTION 16 Correct Answer: B

A. Incorrect. The DATABASE_ROLE_MEMBER_CHANGE_GROUP audit action group enables you to track changes to database roles.

B. Correct. The SERVER_ROLE_MEMBER_CHANGE_GROUP audit action group enables you to track changes to fixed server roles.

C. Incorrect. The SERVER_PRINCIPAL_CHANGE_GROUP audit action group enables you to track the creation, modification, and deletion of server principals.

D. Incorrect. The DATABASE_PRINCIPAL_CHANGE_GROUP audit action group enables you to track the creation, deletion, and modification of database principals.

QUESTION 17   Correct Answers: A and C

A. Correct. The CREATE LOGIN statement creates a login. Logins are server principals and are tracked by including the SERVER_PRINCIPAL_CHANGE_GROUP audit action group in a server audit specification.

B. Incorrect. The CREATE ROLE statement creates a database user, which is a database principal rather than a server principal.

C. Correct. The CREATE SERVER ROLE statement creates a server role. Server roles are server principals and are tracked by including the SERVER_PRINCIPAL_CHANGE _GROUP audit action group in a server audit specification.

D. Incorrect. The CREATE ROLE statement creates a database role, which is a database principal rather than a server principal.

QUESTION 18   Correct Answer: D

A. Incorrect. This statement drops the database change group audit action type from the INSTANCE_SPEC server audit specification. This audit action group records the creation, modification, and deletion of databases.

B. Incorrect. This statement drops the user change password group audit action type from the DATABASE_SPEC audit specification. This audit action group records password change events on contained databases.

C. Incorrect. This statement drops the database logout group audit action type from the INSTANCE_SPEC server audit specification. This audit action group records the logouts of contained database users.

D. Correct. This statement drops the successful database authentication group audit action type from the DATABASE_SPEC audit specification. This audit action group records successful contained database user logons.

QUESTION 19   Correct Answer: B

A. Incorrect. This statement configures auditing for changes to auditing at the instance level.

B. Correct. This statement configures auditing for backup and restore operations at the database level.

C. Incorrect. This statement configures auditing for backup and restore operations at the instance level.

D. Incorrect. This statement configures auditing for changes to auditing at the database level.

QUESTION 20   Correct Answer: B

A. **Incorrect.** Auditing the FAILED_DATABASE_AUTHENTICATION_GROUP action group means that failed contained database user logins are recorded.

B. **Correct.** Auditing the DATABASE_OBJECT_OWNERSHIP_CHANGE_GROUP action group means that changes to database object ownership are recorded.

C. **Incorrect.** Auditing the DBCC_GROUP action group means that the use of DBCC commands is recorded.

D. **Incorrect.** Auditing the DATABASE_OWNERSHIP_CHANGE_GROUP action group means that changes to database ownership are recorded.

Case Study 4

QUESTION 1   Correct Answer: C

A. **Incorrect.** This statement configures the default index fill factor. You do not use this option to set a maximum memory limit.

B. **Incorrect.** This statement configures minimum server memory. You do not use this option to set a maximum memory limit.

C. **Correct.** You execute the sys.sp_configure stored procedure with the 'max server memory' option to set a maximum memory limit on the instance.

D. **Incorrect.** This statement enables database mail. You do not use this option to set a maximum memory limit.

QUESTION 2   Correct Answer: C

A. **Incorrect.** You do not need to have the SQL Server Browser service running to execute these lines of code. You must have the SQL Server Agent service running to execute lines 36 through 38.

B. **Incorrect.** You must have the SQL Server Agent service running to execute lines 36 through 38, so stopping SQL Server Agent would not accomplish this task.

C. **Correct.** You must have the SQL Server Agent service running to execute lines 36 through 38.

D. **Incorrect.** You do not need to have the SQL Server Browser service stopped to execute these lines of code. You must have the SQL Server Agent service running to execute lines 36 through 38.

QUESTION 3   Correct Answer: C

A. **Incorrect.** You modify line 34 to configure the principal profile as either public or private.

B. **Incorrect.** You modify line 23 to alter the email address of the Litware2012 Administrator database mail account.

C. Correct. You modify line 24 to alter the address of the SMTP mail server used by the Litware2012 Administrator database mail account.

D. Incorrect. You modify line 37 to alter which database mail profile is used by SQL Server Agent.

QUESTION 4   Correct Answer: B

A. Incorrect. This statement configures index fill factor.

B. Correct. This statement configures minimum instance memory.

C. Incorrect. This statement configures maximum instance memory.

D. Incorrect. This statement enables database mail.

QUESTION 5   Correct Answer: C

A. Incorrect. Use the backup compression default parameter to enable or disable default backup compression on an instance.

B. Incorrect. Setting the affinity I/O mask option enables you to configure which processor cores are used by the Database Engine instance for input/output operations.

C. Correct. Setting the affinity mask enables you to configure which processor cores are used by the Database Engine instance for processing tasks.

D. Incorrect. Setting the recovery interval parameter with the sp_configure stored procedure enables you to specify a maximum value of time between the creation of automatic checkpoints.

QUESTION 6   Correct Answer: A

A. Correct. You would change line 15 to alter the default recovery model of the model database, which is used as the template database for all newly created databases.

B. Incorrect. Line 17 enables database mail; it does not configure the default recovery model.

C. Incorrect. Line 09 configures the default index fill factor; it does not configure the default recovery model.

D. Incorrect. Line 38 configures SQL Server Agent to use database mail for sending notifications; it does not configure the default recovery model.

QUESTION 7   Correct Answer: A

A. Correct. You modify line 34 to configure the principal profile as either public or private.

B. Incorrect. You modify line 23 to alter the email address of the Litware2012 Administrator database mail account.

C. **Incorrect.** You modify line 24 to alter the address of the SMTP mail server used by the Litware2012 Administrator database mail account.

D. **Incorrect.** You modify line 37 to alter which database mail profile is used by SQL Server Agent.

QUESTION 8   Correct Answer: A

A. **Correct.** This statement configures the default index fill factor.

B. **Incorrect.** This statement configures the minimum instance memory.

C. **Incorrect.** This statement configures maximum instance memory.

D. **Incorrect.** This statement enables database mail.

QUESTION 9   Correct Answer: D

A. **Incorrect.** The backup compression default parameter enables you to enable or disable default backup compression on an instance.

B. **Incorrect.** Setting the affinity I/O mask option enables you to configure which processor cores are used by the Database Engine instance for input/output operations.

C. **Incorrect.** Setting the affinity mask enables you to configure which processor cores are used by the Database Engine instance for processing tasks.

D. **Correct.** Setting the recovery interval parameter by using the sp_configure stored procedure enables you to specify a maximum value of time between the creation of automatic checkpoints.

QUESTION 10   Correct Answer: B

A. **Incorrect.** The master database stores all system-level information for the instance.

B. **Correct.** The model database serves as the template database for all new databases.

C. **Incorrect.** SQL Server Agent uses the msdb system database for scheduling jobs and alerts.

D. **Incorrect.** The tempdb system database stores temporary objects; it is regenerated when the Database Engine restarts.

QUESTION 11   Correct Answer: D

A. **Incorrect.** This statement configures the default index fill factor.

B. **Incorrect.** This statement configures the minimum amount of memory available to the instance.

C. **Incorrect.** This statement configures the maximum amount of memory available to the instance.

D. **Correct.** The EXEC sys.sp_configure 'Database Mail XPs', 1; statement enables database mail, although lines 21 through 35 configure database mail with accounts and provide accounts and principal profiles.

QUESTION 12   Correct Answer: B

A.   **Incorrect.** You modify line 34 to configure the principal profile as either public or private.

B.   **Correct.** You modify line 23 to alter the email address of the Litware2012 Administrator database mail account.

C.   **Incorrect.** You modify line 24 to alter the address of the SMTP mail server used by the Litware2012 Administrator database mail account.

D.   **Incorrect.** You modify line 37 to alter which database mail profile is used by SQL Server Agent.

QUESTION 13   Correct Answer: A

A.   **Correct.** You use the backup compression default parameter to enable or disable default backup compression on an instance.

B.   **Incorrect.** Setting the affinity I/O mask option enables you to configure which processor cores are used by the Database Engine instance for input/output operations.

C.   **Incorrect.** Setting the affinity mask enables you to configure which processor cores are used by the Database Engine instance for processing tasks.

D.   **Incorrect.** Setting the recovery interval parameter by using the sp_configure stored procedure enables you to specify a maximum value of time between the creation of automatic checkpoints.

QUESTION 14   Correct Answer: B

A.   **Incorrect.** The master database stores all system-level information for the instance.

B.   **Correct.** This system database is used by SQL Server Agent for scheduling jobs and alerts.

C.   **Incorrect.** This system database stores temporary objects and is regenerated when the Database Engine restarts.

D.   **Incorrect.** This system database serves as the template database for all new databases.

QUESTION 15   Correct Answer: C

A.   **Incorrect.** The ALLOW_SNAPSHOT_ISOLATION option determines whether statements see a snapshot of data as it exists at the start of the transaction.

B.   **Incorrect.** The ENCRYPTION option determines whether new databases are created with transparent data encryption enabled.

C.   **Correct.** The AUTO_SHRINK option determines whether new databases are created with the automatic shrink option on. You would disable this option to accomplish your goal.

D.   **Incorrect.** The AUTO_CLOSE option determines whether the database is shut down cleanly when the last user exits.

QUESTION 16 Correct Answer: A

A. **Correct.** This system database stores all system-level information for the instance, including login information.

B. **Incorrect.** This system database serves as the template for all new databases.

C. **Incorrect.** This system database is used by SQL Server Agent for scheduling jobs and alerts.

D. **Incorrect.** This system database stores temporary objects.

QUESTION 17 Correct Answer: D

A. **Incorrect.** You modify line 34 to configure the principal profile as either public or private.

B. **Incorrect.** You modify line 23 to alter the email address of the Litware2012 Administrator database mail account.

C. **Incorrect.** You modify line 24 to alter the address of the SMTP mail server used by the Litware2012 Administrator database mail account.

D. **Correct.** You modify line 37 to alter which database mail profile is used by SQL Server Agent.

QUESTION 18 Correct Answer: B

A. **Incorrect.** You use the backup compression default parameter to enable or disable default backup compression on an instance.

B. **Correct.** Setting the affinity I/O mask option enables you to configure which processor cores are used by the Database Engine instance for input/output operations.

C. **Incorrect.** Setting the affinity mask enables you to configure which processor cores are used by the Database Engine instance for processing tasks.

D. **Incorrect.** Setting the recovery interval parameter by using the sp_configure stored procedure enables you to specify a maximum value of time between the creation of automatic checkpoints.

QUESTION 19 Correct Answer: D

A. **Incorrect.** You configure the model and not the tempdb database when you want to have all new databases on the instance use transparent data encryption.

B. **Incorrect.** You configure the model and not the master database when you want to have all new databases on the instance use transparent data encryption.

C. **Incorrect.** You configure the model and not the msdb database when you want to have all new databases on the instance use transparent data encryption.

D. **Correct.** You configure the model database with the SET ENCRYPTION ON option to have all new databases on the instance use transparent data encryption.

QUESTION 20   Correct Answer: D

A. **Incorrect.** The ALLOW_SNAPSHOT_ISOLATION option determines whether statements see a snapshot of data as it exists at the start of the transaction. Configuring this option would not enable you to accomplish your goal.

B. **Incorrect.** The ENCRYPTION option determines whether the database has transparent data encryption enabled.

C. **Incorrect.** The AUTO_SHRINK option determines whether the database attempts to shrink to reclaim space on an automatic basis.

D. **Correct.** The AUTO_CLOSE option determines whether the database is shut down cleanly when the last user exits. You would configure this option on each database to accomplish your goal.

Index

Numbers and Symbols

% Disk Time counter, 403–404
% Privileged Time counter, 406
% Processor Time counter, 372, 406, 452
% Total Processor Time counter, 406
% User Time counter, 406
32-bit processors, planning for installation, 4
64-bit processors
    Itanium architecture and, 154
    planning for installation, 4
    SQL Server Import and Export Wizard, 176
1205 error, 450
1204 trace flag, 451
1222 trace flag, 451

A

access control lists (ACLs), 27
Account Lockout Duration setting (Group Policy), 241
Account Lockout Threshold setting (Group Policy), 241
ACID properties (databases), 442
ACLs (access control lists), 27
Activity log, 451
Activity Monitor, 389, 392, 452–453
Add Counters dialog box, 376
Add Database To Availability Group Wizard, 357, 361
Add Publisher dialog box, 315
Add Replica To Availability Group Wizard, 361
Add-WindowsFeature Failover-Clustering cmdlet, 332
Adjust Memory Quotas For A Process policy, 468
ADMINISTER BULK OPERATIONS permission, 181
Administrators group
    Analysis Services and, 106–107
    SharePoint and, 114
    SQL Server Agent account and, 467, 482
    SQL Server Audit and, 250
    SSIS and, 114
    SSRS and, 110

Advanced Cluster Completion Wizard
    Cluster Disk Selection page, 337
    Cluster Network Configuration page, 338
    Cluster Node Configuration page, 336–337
    Cluster Resource Group page, 337
    Database Engine Configuration page, 338
    Ready To Install page, 338
    Server Configuration page, 338
Advanced Cluster Preparation Wizard
    about, 334–335
    Error Reporting page, 335
    Feature Selection page, 335
    Instance Configuration page, 335
    License Terms page, 335
    Product Key page, 335
    Ready To Install page, 335–336
    Server Configuration page, 335
Advanced Identifiers dialog box, 330
agents, defined, 300
Alert Properties dialog box, 316–317
alerts
    about, 471
    additional information, 473
    managing, 471–473
    practice exercises, 484
aligned index, 137
ALLOCATION UNIT object, 443
ALLOW_SNAPSHOT_ISOLATION database option, 68
ALTER ANY CONNECTION permission, 456
ALTER ANY DATABASE permission
    database audit specifications, 260
    partitioned tables and indexes, 138
    user-defined server roles and, 204
ALTER ANY DATASPACE permission, 138
ALTER ANY LOGIN permission, 194
ALTER ANY SERVER AUDIT permission, 258
ALTER ANY USER permission, 209
ALTER APPLICATION ROLE statement, 219
ALTER AUTHORIZATION statement, 246
ALTER AVAILABILITY GROUP statement
    ADD LISTENER option, 359

B

J

K

O

P

T

About the Authors

ORIN THOMAS, MCITP, MCT, MVP, is an author, trainer, and regular public speaker who has authored more than a dozen books for Microsoft Press. In addition to holding MCITP Server Administrator and Enterprise Administrator certifications, Orin is a Microsoft vTSP, and the convener of the Melbourne Security and Infrastructure Group. His most recent books are on Windows 7 and Exchange Server 2010. You can follow Orin on Twitter @orinthomas.

PETER WARD is the Chief Technical Architect of WARDY IT Solutions, a company he founded in 2005. WARDY IT Solutions has been awarded the Microsoft Data Platform Partner of the Year each year since 2009 and has been a member of the Deloitte Technology Fast 500 since 2012. Peter is a highly regarded speaker at SQL Server events, a sought-after SQL Server consultant, and a trainer who provides solutions for some of the largest SQL Server sites in Australia. He has been recognized as a Microsoft Most Valuable Professional since 2006 for his technical excellence and commitment to the SQL Server community.

BOB TAYLOR is the Principal Program Manager for the MCA/MCM program at Microsoft. He holds many industry certifications including Microsoft Certified Architect (2005/2008), Microsoft Certified Master (2005/2008), MCITP, MCSD.NET, MCT, and MCSE. boB's career in IT started over 39 years ago, when he programmed FORTRAN on punch cards (he has also written assembly language programs on a drum-based computer). He understands the entire development life cycle thanks to his experience as a line-of-business programmer, manager and Vice President of Software Engineering, and Director of Database Technologies. boB started working with SQL Server on version 4.2.1a in the early 1990s, and he has participated in the development of more than 10 Microsoft Certified Professional certification exams. You can find boB's blog at *http://blogs.msdn.com/boBTaylor*.

The unique spelling of boB's first name comes from the fact that he is a magician (*http://www.majikbybob.com*) and mentalist (*http://www.classicclairvoyant.com*)—the only things he has done longer than software development.

Contributor

NEIL HAMBLY is a database architect and SQL professional with more than 13 years' expertise in SQL Server, starting with Version 6.5 through to the very latest 2012 releases. Neil has held a number of database roles both with major organizations (BBC, ABN AMRO, ACCENTURE) and market-leading smaller companies. He is experienced in DBA, developer, and architect roles. Neil is now also a regular speaker at SQL Conferences, on webcasts, and for local user groups. The PASS chapter leader for UK SQL Server London, Neil often presents in the United Kingdom as well as at international events. He just loves learning and teaching SQL.

What do you think of this book?

We want to hear from you!

To participate in a brief online survey, please visit:

microsoft.com/learning/booksurvey

Tell us how well this book meets your needs—what works effectively, and what we can do better. Your feedback will help us continually improve our books and learning resources for you.

Thank you in advance for your input!